THE NEW ECONOMIC
SOCIOLOGY

THE NEW ECONOMIC SOCIOLOGY
DEVELOPMENTS IN AN EMERGING FIELD

EDITED BY
MAURO F. GUILLÉN, RANDALL COLLINS,
PAULA ENGLAND, AND MARSHALL MEYER

Russell Sage Foundation • New York

The Russell Sage Foundation

The Russell Sage Foundation, one of the oldest of America's general purpose foundations, was established in 1907 by Mrs. Margaret Olivia Sage for "the improvement of social and living conditions in the United States." The Foundation seeks to fulfill this mandate by fostering the development and dissemination of knowledge about the country's political, social, and economic problems. While the Foundation endeavors to assure the accuracy and objectivity of each book it publishes, the conclusions and interpretations in Russell Sage Foundation publications are those of the authors and not of the Foundation, its Trustees, or its staff. Publication by Russell Sage, therefore, does not imply Foundation endorsement.

Library of Congress Cataloging-in-Publication Data

Guillén, Mauro F.
  The new economic sociology : developments in an emerging field / Mauro F. Guillén . . . [et al.] editors.
    p. cm.
  Includes bibliographical references and index.
  ISBN 0-87154-343-5
  1. Economics—Sociological aspects.   I. Guillén, Mauro F.   II. Title.

  HM548 .G85 2003
  306.3—dc21

                                                                    2001057886

Text design by Suzanne Nichols

RUSSELL SAGE FOUNDATION
112 East 64th Street, New York, New York 10021
10 9 8 7 6 5 4 3 2 1

Contents

= Contributors =

Mauro F. Guillén is associate professor of management and sociology at the University of Pennsylvania.

Randall Collins is professor of sociology at the University of Pennsylvania.

Paula England is professor of sociology at Northwestern University.

Marshall Meyer is professor of management and sociology at the University of Pennsylvania.

James N. Baron is the Walter Kenneth Kilpatrick Professor of Organizational Behavior and Human Resources at the Stanford Graduate School of Business.

Denise D. Bielby is professor of sociology at the University of California, Santa Barbara.

William T. Bielby is president-elect of the Amercan Sociological Association and professor of sociology at the University of California, Santa Barbara.

Ronald S. Burt is the Hobart W. Williams Professor of Sociology and Strategy at the University of Chicago Graduate School of Business, professor of organizational behavior at the Institut Européen d'Administration d'Affaires (INSEAD) in Fontainebleau, France, and vice president at Raytheon Company.

Paul DiMaggio is professor of sociology at Princeton University.

Susan Eckstein is professor of sociology at Boston University.

Neil Fligstein is the Class of 1939 Chancellor's Professor in the Department of Sociology at the University of California, Berkeley.

Mark Granovetter is the Joan Butler Ford Professor in the Department of Sociology at Stanford University.

Michael T. Hannan is professor of sociology at Stanford University and the StrataCom Professor of Management in the University's Graduate School of Business.

Greta Hsu is a doctoral candidate in organizational behavior at the Stanford Graduate School of Business.

Ozgecan Kocak is a doctoral candidate in organizational behavior at the Stanford Graduate School of Business.

Margarita Mooney is a doctoral student in the Department of Sociology at Princeton University.

Alejandro Portes is the Howard Harrison and Gabrielle S. Beck Professor of Sociology at Princeton University.

Barbara F. Reskin is president of the American Sociological Association and professor of sociology at Harvard University.

Harrison C. White is the Giddings Professor of Sociology at Columbia University.

Viviana A. Zelizer is professor of sociology at Princeton University.

= Preface =

This edited volume, published under the auspices of the Russell Sage Foundation, seeks to contribute to the revival of economic sociology by bringing together the study of social stratification, culture, organizations, and economic development. The editors are all affiliated with the University of Pennsylvania. Our vision of economic sociology is in some ways a reflection of Penn's tradition and institutional peculiarities. Until the mid-1970s, social science departments at Penn were part of the Wharton School. At that time these departments were moved to the newly created School of Arts and Sciences. During the 1970s and early 1980s, Penn was the home of such first-rate social scientists as institutional economist Oliver Williamson, sociologist Erving Goffman, demographer James Easterlin, and economists Robert Pollak and Jere Behrman.

During the 1980s and 1990s the Wharton School and the Department of Sociology have added to their ranks a number of scholars in the fields of organizational sociology, economic demography, culture, and social stratification, including Bruce Kogut, Douglas Massey, Susan Watkins, Jerry Jacobs, John Kimberly, Marshall Meyer, Jitendra Singh, Michael Useem, and, more recently, Randall Collins, Paula England (now at Northwestern University), Lori Rosenkopf, Mauro Guillén, and Beth Bechky (now at U.C. Davis). This eclectic group of scholars has broken with the institutional boundaries of the past and launched a common effort to integrate various sociological approaches to the study of economic phenomena. The group is called Penn Economic Sociology & Organizational Studies (PESOS, website at *pesos.wharton.upenn.edu*).

In December 1998 and March 2000, PESOS organized the first and second Annual Conferences on Economic and Organizational Sociology at Penn. We brought together a group of scholars from around the country interested in pursuing the study of economic phenomena from a sociological perspective. This volume includes contributions from several of the scholars who presented their work at the Penn annual conferences. We would like to thank the people and institutions that have made it possible. The First Conference on Economic and Organizational Sociology at Penn was funded by the Reginald H. Jones Center, the Department of Management, and the Department of Sociology of the University of Pennsylvania. The Second Conference and the publication of this volume were funded by a generous grant from the Russell Sage Foundation. The editors are also grateful to Jonathon Mote for his organizational assistance, Lauren Tarantino for her editorial help, Rachel Barrett for providing logistical support, and John Rutter for copyediting the final version of the manuscript. Wharton doctoral student Linda Cohen went over the final version of the chapters and made many substantive suggestions for improvement. Three anonymous referees, and Suzanne Nichols of the Russell Sage Foundation provided excellent editorial feedback and suggestions.

= Chapter 1 =

The Revival of Economic Sociology

MAURO F. GUILLÉN, RANDALL COLLINS, PAULA ENGLAND,
AND MARSHALL MEYER

E CONOMIC sociology is staging a comeback after decades of relative obscurity. Many of the issues explored by scholars today
mirror the original concerns of the discipline: sociology
emerged in the first place as a science geared toward providing an
institutionally informed and culturally rich understanding of economic life. Confronted with the profound social transformations of
the late nineteenth and early twentieth centuries, the founders of sociological thought—Karl Marx, Emile Durkheim, Max Weber, Georg
Simmel—explored the relationship between the economy and the
larger society (Swedberg and Granovetter 1992). They examined the
production, distribution, and consumption of goods and services
through the lenses of domination and power, solidarity and inequality, structure and agency, and ideology and culture. The classics thus
planted the seeds for the systematic study of social classes, gender,
race, complex organizations, work and occupations, economic development, and culture as part of a unified sociological approach to economic life.

Subsequent theoretical developments led scholars away from this
originally unified approach. In the 1930s, Talcott Parsons rein-
terpreted the classical heritage of economic sociology, clearly distinguishing between economics (focused on the means of economic action, or what he called "the adaptive subsystem") and sociology
(focused on the value orientations underpinning economic action).
Thus, sociologists were theoretically discouraged from participating

1

in the economics-sociology dialogue—an exchange that, in any case, was not sought by economists. It was only when Parsons's theory was challenged by the reality of the contentious 1960s (specifically, its emphasis on value consensus and system equilibration; see Granovetter 1990, and Zelizer, ch. 5, this volume) that some of its inherent limitations were recognized and other theoretical models were seriously considered. Although in later work Parsons and Neil Smelser (1956) produced a more integrative sociological approach to the economy, many sociologists from the 1960s to the 1980s shifted to narrower research areas, devoting their attention to specific economic phenomena without making an attempt to arrive at a systematic sociological understanding of economic life. Throughout this period, different subfields within sociology—such as organizations, work and occupations, social stratification, professions, development, and culture—contributed important theoretical insights and empirical evidence related to the study of economic processes.

The sociological study of economic phenomena related to (market) production thrived during the 1960s in the subfields of organizations and of work and occupations. A series of key synthetic books developed a distinctively sociological approach to the study of production and administrative processes in organizations (Blau and Scott 1962; Etzioni 1964; Lawrence and Lorsch 1967; Perrow 1970; Thompson 1967). These new organizational sociologists embraced the study of organizations qua organizations (taking what might be called a Weberian approach, given Weber's interest in the emergence of highly rationalized bureaucracies) and relegated to the background the impact of organizations on group norms and solidarity. (This more Durkheimian approach had been adopted by earlier scholars such as Elton Mayo [1977 (1933), 1988 (1945)], Chester Barnard [1938], and F. J. Roethlisberger and William Dickson [1967 (1939)]). The new sociologists asked questions about the beneficiaries of organizations (Blau and Scott 1962), the dominant control system (Etzioni 1964), the impact of the environment on organizations (Lawrence and Lorsch 1967), and the impact of technology (Thompson 1967; Perrow 1970). Still other sociologists pursued the Weberian agenda by studying authority and stratification systems from a cross-national, comparative perspective (Bendix [2001 (1956)]).

Over the years, however, this organizational subfield drifted apart from sociology, in terms of both theoretical concerns and academic organization. While the Weberian scholars of the 1960s and early 1970s had something to say about society in general, the new organizational theorists of the 1970s and 1980s focused most of their research energies on for-profit organizations (on nonprofits, see Powell 1984). Their theories—resource dependence, transaction-cost economics, and population ecology—established few connections with other sociological areas (for surveys, see Perrow 1986; Scott 1998 [1981]). The new organizational sociology became known as organizational theory, and organizational sociologists increasingly moved from sociology departments to business schools (Gans 1990). More recently, however, efforts have been made to reintegrate organizational theory into other areas of sociological inquiry. For example, the new institutionalism in organizational sociology (see Powell and DiMaggio 1991) has built on, and contributed to, the sociology of culture. Also, some organizational sociologists have established a dialogue between organizational and social stratification research (see Baron 1984).

In addition to studying production inside organizations, sociologists have long studied work, labor, and occupations from the point of view of social stratification. This sociological subfield draws insights from Durkheimian, Weberian, functionalist, Marxist, feminist, and critical perspectives, and it has generated a wealth of empirical research on phenomena such as social mobility, occupational hierarchies, status attainment, and income and wage distribution (see Grusky 1994). Although of all the social sciences since the 1960s sociology has contributed the most extensive and systematic body of theory and evidence regarding gender and racial stratification, these are aspects of economic life that the new economic sociology of the 1990s and 2000s has thus far marginalized (see the contributions to part 3 of this volume). More recently, sociologists interested in social stratification have looked at household work, including the work of caring for children, as an area of production heretofore neglected by the social sciences. (Some argue that this neglect is due to the fact that household work is usually done by women and not paid for through formal market processes; see Zelizer, ch. 11, this volume; Milkman and Townsley 1994.) Some scholars have also sought to analyze stratification in the context of complex organization (Baron 1984; Baron et al., this volume).

The sociology of work and occupations developed fairly independently of organizational theory and social stratification, notwithstanding Reinhard Bendix's (2001 [1956]) early call for a more integrated approach. Much of the early research adopted a Durkheimian perspective, while later work was inspired by theories of monopoly capital (see, for example, Braverman 1974; Burawoy 1979; Edwards 1979). More recently, sociologists of work have returned to a comparative study of work and occupations, mostly from a multidimensional Weberian perspective (for example, Cole 1979; Lincoln and Kalleberg 1990). Meanwhile, the sociology of the professions has grown in importance and prominence, with scholars drawing from the functionalist (Wilensky 1964), Marxist (Larson 1977), knowledge-based (Freidson 1986), and ecological perspectives (Abbott 1988), among others.

Besides the sociology of organizations and social stratification, the sociology of development is another specialty that has devoted systematic attention to the study of economic processes, especially those having to do with industrialization and economic growth. Sociological studies of development have sought to understand the social and political bases of economic growth and development. Early students of development echoed the Parsonsian approach in their emphasis on the shift from traditional to modern values and on the gradual transformation of authority structures, and they offered fairly optimistic forecasts of the prospects for development around the world (see, for example, Kerr et al. 1964 [1960]). Others, by contrast, painted a bleaker view of development prospects in using Marxist theory to highlight the dependence of developing countries on the core industrialized and advanced countries (for example, Frank 1967; Cardoso and Faletto 1979 [1973]). These ideas were later elaborated by Immanuel Wallerstein (1974) in his highly influential "world-system" approach, which emphasizes states rather than social classes, and by Peter Evans (1979), whose "triple alliance" theory (of local, state, and foreign capital) combined both the class-based and state-centric approaches. Today's global economy has fueled the theoretical debates among modernization, dependency, and world-system scholars (Guillén 2001a, 2001b).

Culture is the fourth key subfield that has examined economic processes. During the 1960s and 1970s cultural anthropologists made major contributions to the sociological study of economic life. In fact, we find in this early work, particularly in studies that examine economic action in developing countries, concepts that have become central in economic sociology. For example, the term "embeddedness," introduced as a relational concept by Clifford Geertz in *Peddlers and Princes* (1963, 30, 89, 153), was later turned into economic sociology's most celebrated metaphor by Mark Granovetter (1985), who was also inspired by the work of Karl Polanyi. Furthermore, in his vivid description of the Javanese approach to credit, Geertz highlighted the fundamentally important interaction between economic and social relations and activities: he wrote, for example, that the "main function" of the Javanese approach to credit "is not simply to capitalize trade but to stabilize and regularize ties between traders, to give persistence and form to commercial relationships" (Geertz 1963, 39), and he noted that the Javanese peddler engages in "trading coalitions" and "alliances" (Geertz 1963, 40).

Thus far, we have examined the study of economic phenomena related to production and trade. Sociologists have traditionally devoted less systematic attention to consumption and leisure, although studies of consumption have appeared as far back as the early twentieth century—for example, Thorstein Veblen's (1994 [1899]) work on "conspicuous consumption" and Georg Simmel's (1957 [1904]) studies of fashion. During the 1950s Paul Lazarsfeld made major contributions to the study of public opinion, mass communication, and consumer behavior (see Frenzen, Hirsch, and Zerrillo 1994). Although no subfield in sociology specializes in the study of consumption, several have contributed insights to this important social process. For example, social history and Marxist approaches have long produced fascinating studies linking consumption patterns to social processes (see Frenzen et al. 1994). More recently, sociologists interested in culture and social networks have reawakened interest in the study of how consumption and tastes are socially embedded and consequently how they contribute to social reproduction. The work of Pierre Bourdieu (1988 [1984]) and Bourdieu and Jean Claude Passeron (1990) is perhaps among the most influential and novel in this respect (for a survey, see DiMaggio 1994). Sociologists have also enriched the study of consumption by paying attention to leisure as yet another manifestation of commercialized consumption (for a review, see Biggart 1994).

Renewed interest in economic sociology as a research area in its own right did not develop until the mid-1980s, despite attempts to stimulate interest in the field during the 1970s and early 1980s (see, for example, Smelser 1976; Stinchcombe 1983). In part, the revival of economic sociology was galvanized by the publication of several influential pieces, including Harrison White's paper on the sociology of markets (1981), Ronald Burt's *Toward a Structural Theory of Action* (1982; see also Burt 1992), and Mark Granovetter's paper on social embeddedness and economic action (1985). Other contributions followed quickly, such as Paula England and George Farkas's (1986) synthesis of economic and sociological approaches to the family and labor markets; Gary Hamilton and Nicole Biggart's (1988) paper on markets, culture, and authority; Viviana Zelizer's (1989a, 1989b) work on the meanings of money; Peter Evans's *Embedded Autonomy: States and Industrial Transformation* (1995); and Mary Brinton and Victor Nee's (1998) use of rational-choice theory to study institutions. Arguably, these pieces struck different notes, but the seeds were planted for the revival of economic sociology, this time built on theoretically sound and empirically useful foundations. The publication in 1994 of the *Handbook of Economic Sociology*, edited by Neil Smelser and Richard Swedberg and sponsored by the Russell Sage Foundation, consolidated the field of economic sociology.

Formal recognition of this renewed interest has also increased. For example, the Society for the Advancement of Socioeconomics was founded in 1989. (It is more narrowly focused on community-related issues than on economic sociology per se.) The American Sociological Association recognized a section on economic sociology in 2000. And there appears to be increasing acknowledgment of economic sociology within the popular press—for example, *U.S. News & World Report*'s yearly evaluation of graduate programs now includes a ranking of the best programs in economic sociology.

New Directions in Economic Sociology

Economic sociology is the study of the social organization of economic phenomena, including those related to production, trade, leisure, and consumption. These phenomena, which are not necessarily mediated by monetary payments, can be observed at various levels of analysis—namely, the individual, the group, the household, the organization, the network, the market, the industry, the country, and the world system. Although economic sociologists differ in their theoretical emphases and empirical techniques (see Fligstein, this volume), they share an interest in both processes and outcomes, and in inequality as well as efficiency.

In particular, economic sociology seeks to understand economic phenomena in their social and cultural contexts, without falling into the trap of three fallacies common to economic analysis. The first fallacy is that the social is a realm separate from the economic. (As mentioned earlier, this fallacy was perpetuated not only by economists but by Parsons within the field of sociology.) Economic sociologists argue that all economic activity is socially grounded and enabled (Swedberg and Granovetter 1992), and that no economic phenomenon can be assessed without the shared understandings (culture), institutional structures, symbols, and networks of inter-actor relationships that concretize it and give it form. The market is seen as a social and cultural product: market exchange is facilitated by social and cultural processes that provide market participants with shared understandings (in the forms of values, norms, and symbols) that help them to make sense of what goes on and how they should act. Economic sociologists also reject the notion that the social or cultural dimensions of society "interfere" with the smooth functioning of the economy (Zelizer 1989a, 1989b; see, in this volume, Granovetter; Fligstein; DiMaggio; Zelizer, both chapters).

Economists generally believe that individuals make conscious calculations about how to maximize utility, and that the preferences that determine their utility functions (that is, the sources and associated magnitude of their utilities) are exogenous to the models of interest. Economic sociologists consider this view, however, a fallacy. Drawing on a rich variety of anthropological, ethnographic, social-psychological, psychoanalytic, linguistic, and sociological research, economic sociologists see both preferences and actions as fundamentally connected to and affected by cognitive biases, limited powers of reasoning, nonconscious and ambivalent feelings, role expectations, norms, and cultural frames, schemata, classifications, and myths (see, in this volume, Granovetter; DiMaggio; Bielby and Bielby; Reskin). Hence, both utility maximization and the isolation of strictly "economic" variables are unacceptable to economic sociologists, since such reductionism necessarily hinders the understanding of economic phenomena. It is not just that these reductionist assumptions include the determination of preferences as part of what they seek to understand. Economic sociologists also recognize that social forces often affect reasoning in ways that defy a strict rationality assumption, and thus they dismiss economists' belief that knowing an individual's preferences (even if exogenous) and immediate constraints leads to unambiguous sequences of decisionmaking or action.

A final key theoretical difference is that economic sociologists reject the idea that the aggregation of individual-level behavior is straightforward and unproblematic. Drawing on previous research on social classes, social movements, social networks, power dynamics, and cultural blueprints (see, in this volume, DiMaggio; Burt; Portes and Mooney; Eckstein), economic sociologists seek to improve our understanding of economic behavior at levels of analysis higher than that of the individual or the group. To better explain aggregate processes and outcomes, they consider sociological concepts such as ideology, consciousness, collective action, neighborhood effects, trust, unintended consequences, decoupling, latent functions, and interaction rituals. Moreover, a sociological approach to economic phenomena pays attention to how social class, gender, and race mediate in the process of aggregation of individual decisions and actions generating patterns of inequality. The sociological contribution here is that all action— whether driven by interests, power, or trust—results in outcomes that are shaped not only by the individual actor's motives but also by larger social, cultural, and institutional structures (see Granovetter, this volume).

It is important to note that economic sociologists have produced theoretical insights about economic phenomena that represent either complementary or competing explanations to those proposed by the traditional rational-choice, utility-driven economic models. The following is an illustrative list of sociological contributions to key debates about economic action:

- *Culture:* Sociologists emphasize that economic action *cannot proceed* without shared understandings about appropriate behavior in a given social setting. Cultural understandings lie at the core of economic action because they provide stability and meaning; these shared understandings help actors make sense of the situation, develop strategies for action, and adjust their expectations and behavior as they interact with others (Hamilton and Biggart 1988; see also, in this volume, Granovetter; Zelizer, ch. 5). Economic sociologists invoke values and norms, network structures, the state, and ideologies as factors creating shared understandings among participants in the various arenas in which economic activity takes place, including markets, groups, organizations, and households (Evans 1995; Fligstein, this volume). It is argued that the resultant social structure helps participants search for a niche in which they develop an identity and adopt a certain set of roles (White 1981; White, this volume).

- *Networks and social capital:* Economic action can be facilitated or hindered by the actor's position in a network of relationships. Many economic sociologists invoke the concept of social capital to explain why some actors are more successful than others at mobilizing resources or attaining their goals (Burt 1982, 1992; Coleman 1990). Scholars have defined and assessed social capital at various levels of aggregation, including the individual, the group, the organization, and the country (see, in this volume, Burt; Portes and Mooney). Economic sociologists have also explored the interdependent mechanisms of this construct, pointing out that one actor's social capital may be another's social exclusion—an argument that brings power, interest, and discrimination into the analysis of economic action (see, in this volume, Baron et al.; Portes and Mooney).

- *Trust:* Empirical evidence has shown that economic action is often not based on a self-interested assessment of incentives, as argued by economists. Instead, it is often based on trust, which is historically developed and culturally specific, although not exclusive to any one culture (Dore 1983; Geertz 1963). Economic sociologists are keen to point out that trust helps to explain the observed order, stability, and continuity in social life that occurs because of genuine emotional caring or norms of obligation that bind actors in spite of their incentives (see Granovetter, this volume).

- *Effort and motivation:* Economic sociologists have pointed out several key factors that shape commitment and effort at work apart from the traditionally considered structure of material incentives. For instance, Bendix (2001 [1956]) demonstrated that blind obedience driven by economic incentives is not sufficient for organizations to accomplish their work. Good faith and initiative are required if complex organizations are to respond to unforeseen circumstances and opportunities—subordinates must "comply with general rules as well as specific orders in a manner which strikes some reasonable balance between the extremes of blind obedience and capricious unpredictability" (204)—and these qualities are guided by a culture, ideology, or ethic of work and effort. More recently, economic sociologists have revisited this important topic, and there has been renewed interest in social-psychological processes and group dynamics, as well as a better appreciation of the complexity of human motivations to work hard (see Bielby and Bielby, this volume).

These theoretical contributions have expanded the variables considered and led economic sociologists to recognize the complexity and interdependence of social and economic elements. They have also extended the type of economic activities studied. Scholars in this emerging field have called for more systematic attention to economic activity not done for money or in the market, including household work, gift giving, and volunteer work (see Wilson 2000; McPherson and Rotolo 1996; Biggart 1994; England and Farkas 1986; Zelizer, ch. 5, this volume), as well as collectivist types of organizations (Rothschild-Whitt 1979). This interest is in keeping with the main sociological contribution to the study of economic phenomena: showing that economic action is, after all, a form of social action.

The Plan of the Book

The contributions to this volume seek to define the field of economic sociology, take stock of its accomplishments to date, identify theoretical problems and opportunities, and formulate strategies for empirical research in each of the key topical areas of the field. There are many ways to group research in this field, and the goal is not to divide academic efforts; as we have seen, rigid boundaries are academically counterproductive. We have chosen to group the chapters into four topical parts. The first presents the main debates and conceptual approaches in economic sociology, with contributions by Mark Granovetter, Neil Fligstein, Paul DiMaggio, and Viviana Zelizer. Harrison White's and Ronald Burt's chapters in part 2 look at the study of economic phenomena from a network perspective. Part 3 considers the role of gender in economic sociology, with chapters by William Bielby and Denise Bielby; Barbara Reskin; James Baron, Michael Hannan, Greta Hsu, and Ozgecan Kocak; and Viviana Zelizer. The fourth part presents the study of economic development and change from a sociological perspective, with contributions by Alejandro Portes and Margarita Mooney, and Susan Eckstein. While this volume is not a comprehensive treatment of the field, it illustrates the various ways in which sociology can be used to understand and explain economic phenomena.

Major Debates and Conceptual Approaches in Economic Sociology

The first four chapters seek to define the boundaries of the field and to identify and develop opportunities for theoretical and empirical development. In his chapter, Mark Granovetter asks: What is distinctive about economic sociology? He submits the notion of "instrumental interests" to close analysis, pointing out that utilitarian theory decontextualizes actors and interests from the social relationships in which they typically exist. In ordinary social interaction, people act out of mixed motives, sometimes explicitly seeking gains, but also responding to social pressures, even those without obvious carrot-and-stick features. It is possible, of course, for individuals to make instrumental use of non-instrumental relations—for example, to cultivate social ties in order to exploit them for business purposes. But, as Granovetter notes, even in economic relations, social trust is most effective when it is not strategized and manipulated but instead operates autonomously. This observation undermines the utilitarian interpretation of social capital. At the same time, Granovetter argues, we should avoid going to the opposite extreme from the selfish rational actor and falling back into the oversocialized view of actors as completely dominated by norms.

These considerations show the limits of a micro focus on the problem; the issues of interests and agency vis-à-vis social obligations and ties are better understood if we view these "from the air"—that is, from a structural perspective. Both self-interested action and the character of culture are shaped by the type of network structure in which they operate. Thus, preexisting networks allow or prohibit various kinds of entrepreneurial action; one cannot engage in brokering across holes unless holes happen to exist.

Granovetter schematizes three kinds of networks: highly decoupled networks, in which each unit forms interests that conflict with those of the other units (for example, firms with strong barriers between them, like Boston's Route 128 high-tech firms); weakly coupled networks with enough weak ties to allow entrepreneurs to bridge holes and amass power; and strongly coupled networks (such as the fluidly bounded Silicon Valley firms) where personnel and information flow so rapidly that a cooperative shared culture overrides conflicting interests while allowing little opportunity for brokers to seize an advantage. This way of putting it makes it seem that the network structures are static background determining what can happen. But dynamics can be introduced into the model, especially by engaging in historical studies of the development of industries (such as Granovetter's current study of the electric power industry). Entrepreneurs do not just passively fall into situations where there are holes to be bridged; sometimes they pursue strategies to keep the holes from closing up behind them or to keep rivals from coming in and following in their paths. Such strategies may require that entrepreneurs operate on the level of several networks at once, bringing political and regulative networks to bear or constructing new kinds of financial ties.

Granovetter thus points us toward a new and more complex phase of network analysis: looking not merely at the immediate network and the presence or absence of structural holes within it, but at the relationships between several kinds of networks and at the special place of actors who can coordinate multiple ties. This is a way of translating into network terms the distinction, implicit elsewhere in economic sociology, between the institutions in which a market is embedded and the structure of the ties that constitute the market interaction itself.

Neil Fligstein's chapter ambitiously defines the scope of the field, lists our main accomplishments so far, and challenges us to move onward. Fligstein suggests that economic sociology has become prominent because of the way in which it brings together many sociological subdisciplines. If we define the field as the study not merely of markets but of all aspects of the organization of material production and consumption, then it provides a unifying perspective on households, labor markets, stratification, networks, and culture, as well as on product markets. Nevertheless, in keeping with the central interest of much of the field up to now, Fligstein narrows his focus to the sociology of markets as the most prominent mechanism of allocation. (For a wider perspective, see Zelizer's chapters in this volume.)

Fligstein adopts Harrison White's influential model of markets as a particular type of self-reproducing role structure, organized by firms that monitor one another to decide how much to produce and the quality level of their product, thereby finding profitable niches that enable them to stay in business. It should be added, in keeping with White's emphasis, that markets are variable and sometimes break down and fail to sustain an array of recognized producers; this variability in the reproducibility or sustainability of role structures in markets gives us empirical leverage for comparisons and thus for ferreting out the mechanisms by which markets are socially constructed. Fligstein goes on to note that we should explain action in markets as we do action in other spheres of social life, and hence our general theory of how society operates should apply here. In fact, we have a variety of such general theories; applied to markets, these theories give us five mechanisms: embeddedness in networks that generate trust; shared meanings or cultures in local or national arenas; institutional rules for property transactions; government power and conflicting political interests; and control by economic elites, as seen by class analysis.

Fligstein challenges economic sociologists to stop relying on conventional economic theory as a foil and to develop their own theoretical mechanisms. We have come through the first phase of economic sociology, having shown the kinds of phenomena that are exceptions to a neoclassical, utilitarian view of markets or the kind that are taken for granted as underpinnings if such markets are to operate. As we feel our way into a second phase, however, we are becoming dissatisfied with our existing arguments. Fligstein issues the challenge: If utilitarian economic theory follows the basic principle that markets operate to allocate resources most efficiently, are economic sociologists really saying anything different? In fact, many economic sociologists also hold that the social mechanisms underpinning markets promote efficiency; social relationships, for instance, in promoting trust, reduce the cost of doing business, and various forms of network structure break down boundaries between traditional firms, thereby making it less costly to enter and exit new markets. Far from challenging orthodox economics, many economic sociologists merely turn up new social patterns for economic theory to explain as Pareto-optimal.

Fligstein advocates focusing instead on the distinction between market "efficiency" and "effectiveness" in the sense of how organizations (and entire markets) manage to survive. This focus brings out a point implicit in some sociological analyses of what social relationships do for market transactions: they provide long-term legitimacy, resources, or other bases for social stability, as opposed to short-term profits. To put it another way, the utilitarian view of market efficiency fails to explain when there is selective pressure for long-term sustenance of market structures and when there is pressure for short-term profit. This is the challenge, and opportunity, for economic sociology—to develop just such a theory.

Fligstein further notes a key methodological problem in our research: we typically show the presence of social relationships in markets and then assert our interpretation that these are what generate legitimacy, social capital, and the like; we fail to show, however, what kinds of social relationships have what kinds of consequences. In other words, economic sociology needs to avoid falling into a contemporary version of functionalist comparative statics and instead to get beyond generalized categories of social capital or trust and become more focused on dynamics. Research on capitalist elites, interlocking directorates, and financial ties illustrates the problem: such analysis focuses on a static description of capitalist control, and misses what determines shifts in the way markets are structured. As emphasized classically by Schumpeter, and currently by Harrison White, markets as structures of niches are differentiated, both by type of product (which gives the entire market its social identity) and by quality niches within markets. It is this variety of markets and niches that we need to explain, not just market sustainability in general. And given the pressures of contemporary "postmodern" markets toward product turnover and niche proliferation, it is essential for us to show the mechanisms that create new product markets and niches, sustain them, control or monopolize them, and change them into new forms.

Granovetter and Fligstein recognize that in showing not only how various kinds of network structures shape and limit different kinds of economic action but also how new network patterns emerge from older ones, a key problem is network dynamics. Chapter 4 by Paul DiMaggio is concerned with just such dynamics. DiMaggio adopts Keynes's term "animal spirits" for the shared moods that propel economic swings—the emotions of business confidence, buoyancy, or indeed "irrational exuberance" and, in the other direction, pessimism, depression, or panic. Researchers measure these types of emotional confidence among consumers, executives, and investors; the theoretical problem is to show how these operate as collective phenomena over time.

The general principle is that animal spirits are not antirational per se but a response to situations in which information as to the behavior of others with whom one is interdependent is characterized by genuine uncertainty. Connecting this phenomenon with network configurations, we can say that decoupled networks increase variability in expectations and volatility in outcomes. DiMaggio then draws on several theoretical notions to explore how these collective moods rise and fall. Pluralistic ignorance, such as overestimating peers' propensities to certain kinds of behavior, reflects a particular kind of decoupled network, in conjunction with an official level of communication that defines reality in a misleading way. Somewhat opposite to pluralistic ignorance is the bandwagon effect: the propensity of participants to rush into conforming with whatever direction the group as a whole seems to be heading. Bandwagons occur quite differently depending on whether the distribution of propensities to join the bandwagon is a continuous normal distribution or is discontinuous or bimodal. The latter limits bandwagons to particular social regions. In our view, the source of these distributions of propensities remains a problem for which we must account. The answer might be found further down on the micro level of interpersonal encounters, conceived as interaction ritual chains that generate higher or lower emotional energy as actors interact with greater or lesser focus, equality, and deference.

An integrative view comes from seeing economic waves in markets as social movements. Both have qualities of emergent social constructions as participants come to redefine their identities and expand their roles. Both depend on recruitment through social networks. DiMaggio adds that the emotional aspects, the so-called animal spirits, are an additional feature making participants in commercial transactions feel a common identity, more generalized trust, and hence more willingness to purchase optional and expensive goods and services, which they would ordinarily acquire only through a close personal network.

In chapter 5, Viviana Zelizer makes an impassioned plea that economic sociology include a consideration of culture—that is, topics often seen as more cultural than economic. Revived in the 1980s, this subfield focuses on meanings, symbols, practices, and beliefs. Zelizer is anxious to see intellectual cooperation between economic and cultural sociologists and a sharing of turf. The economic is about all forms of production, distribution, and consumption, but economic sociologists often limit their subject to only what goes on in firms and markets. They exclude from their agenda production and distribution in the household and the economic transfers associated with intimate relationships, ethnic enclaves, and consumption.

This tacit delimitation of subject matter rests on several unexamined assumptions. In part, Zelizer thinks economic sociologists are imitating economists' typical focus on firms and markets. But there is also a gendered subtext to where the tacit boundaries are drawn by both sociologists and economists. Arenas of life seen as "women's sphere" (household, family, relationships, love, consumption, neighborhood) are off the map. It is disproportionately women scholars who have contributed to these "off-map" areas of study. Perhaps this is why, given these boundaries, so few of the leading scholars in economic sociology are women. These supposedly non-economic areas of life have been seen as appropriate topics for cultural sociologists and as part of the marginalizing of cultural sociology. Zelizer wants to break down these boundaries so as to look at the economic aspects of the household, intimate relationships, and consumption and examine the cultural aspects of what goes on in firms and markets. Here she joins feminist scholars across disciplines in arguing that seeing the world as divided into a commodified public realm and a private realm where love governs is a distortion of both realms that ignores their many interpenetrations.

The neoclassical economic paradigm focuses on rational individual choice within constraint. Zelizer itemizes three ways in which economic sociologists differentiate their approach from that of economists. First, they may use the same paradigm, but they extend it to subject areas that economists usually ignore, as in Gary Becker's work on the family and on addiction. Second, they talk about the social context in which individual decisions are made. Here they are adding a social element to constraints that economists are more likely to see as consisting in prices and laws. Third, they search for alternative descriptions and explanations of economic phenomena, challenging the focus on individual decisions within constraint.

Zelizer favors the third approach. She notes that economists can incorporate values into their paradigm by seeing values as the content of individual utility functions—the preferences that economists assume individuals use to decide what goals to pursue. Economic man or woman takes the goals determined by values or tastes, considers the constraints, and rationally calculates an optimal strategy. Zelizer emphatically rejects this limitation of the role of values. For her and other cultural sociologists, symbols, beliefs, and meanings also affect which strategies are taken for granted, which are seen as rational, the boundaries around arenas where people believe it is appropriate to use rational calculation, and the meanings that people give to constraints and strategies.

Zelizer believes that cultural sociology provides one set of tools that allow economic sociologists to challenge economists' paradigm. The major orienting concept she offers is that of differentiated ties.

Social ties are of different types, and the type of social tie involved in a transaction carries a host of meanings and beliefs about appropriate behavior and the kinds of movements of money that are appropriate. The concept of differentiated ties suggests a research agenda in which economic behavior is affected by gender, race, and other similarities between interactants that define the meaning of their ties. It also suggests research that connects with another prominent theme in economic sociology, that of social networks. Networks of informal ties can be classified according to the nature of the tie as it is conceptualized in cultural meanings.

Social Networks and Economic Sociology

The structural approach to economic sociology—and especially its social network variant—has made astonishing theoretical and empirical inroads over the last twenty years. Harrison White and Ronald Burt are among the most important contributors to the structural approach to economic sociology. In chapter 6, White summarizes his theory of markets, which he first set forth in his paper "Where Do Markets Come From?" (1981) and has elaborated in his book *Markets from Networks* (2001). White's theory has already been influential for economic sociology; using a network approach, it focuses not on the institutions and social relationships in which markets are embedded but on the inner network structure of the market itself. The theory is especially important for providing a predictive model of the parameters that determine the variety of different product markets that can exist. For our purposes, it is especially suggestive because it puts the dynamics of markets at the center of analysis; each region in the "state space" that he describes has its distinctive form of competition and distinctive stabilities or instabilities.

White's basic processes include niche-seeking identity construction by joint action and signaling, driven by producers' commitments rather than consumer demand. Seeking distinctive market niches is the key to economic action. Niches make it possible to avoid head-to-head competition and thus to make profit (similar to Schumpeterian entrepreneurs). Producers construct niches on two levels. On one level, they examine their competitors to find out not only what those competitors have been doing successfully (that is, where competitors have been finding customer demand) but where they can do something dissimilar enough to constitute a distinct niche. On yet another level, the entire industry or market molecule constitutes a product line, an identity amid other markets. Thus, producers depend on their peer rivals and must monitor them, and they rely on being monitored by others as part of such an array. The dynamics of markets are driven from the producers' side; producers do not respond to demand but attempt to anticipate it by judging their competitors. (Again, this may be seen as an extension of Schumpeter on entrepreneurs risking new combinations.) Producers commit to volumes of production into the future and thus have more of a stake in a given market than buyers.

The simplest version in White's model is a grid of the flexibility of supply (producers' cost) and demand (buyers' need or willingness to buy) for the two dimensions of volume and quality. Unlike conventional microeconomics, White's model emphasizes the flexibility of the adjustment of producers and buyers as volume or quality goes up. At the core of White's scheme is a fourfold space, that is, four quadrants that depend on two relationships (see figure 6.1): first, whether buyer demand for volume is greater or smaller than supplier cost per volume; and second, whether buyer demand for quality is greater or smaller than supplier cost by quality. In the first symmetrical region of figure 6.1 (lower left), increases in both volume and quality give the upper hand to buyers. In the upper right region (also symmetrical), the upper hand is held by producers for both volume and quality increases. The other two quadrants (lower right and upper left) are skewed or asymmetrical and present peculiar problems in sustaining markets. Each quadrant has its distinctive dynamics. Near the pure competition line, buyers pay no attention to differences in quality; they are still arrayed by volume cost, but all receive the same price, thereby eroding producer commitment. Thus, pure competition markets cannot sustain themselves and tend to shift to nonmarket forms, such as putting-out arrangements or hierarchy. This represents an alternative argument to Williamson's transaction-cost theory of the interplay between markets and hierarchies.

White's model also refers to upstream-downstream orientation. The state space is easiest to explain in a simple version that concentrates only on downstream market orientation. (Such an orientation was taken for granted in the earlier discussion, as it is in most microeconomics.) In reality, firms lie somewhere in a production chain of suppliers and customers, with some serving as the edge markets that deal with either the ultimate consumers or the raw material producers. Thus, a firm can choose a direction in which to be oriented, but bounded rationality tends to make it difficult to orient both ways at once.

Orientation is in the most problematic direction; the unproblematic direction is left to habitual ties (which become the most stable part of the network) or passive pricing. An upstream orientation may be produced by inflation or war shortages; in such a case, downstream prices are left as fixed or customary and firms focus on coaxing suppliers. Empirically, this orientation is indexed by the size and prestige of sales and advertising departments vis-à-vis procurement. Thus, there are dual-state spaces, for upstream and downstream orientations. The computational model shows where market regions in state space, favoring an upstream or downstream orientation, differ in their sustainability and profitability.

White's model also includes profits and prices as variables. Price is a by-product of market equilibrium: the stable array of niches in state space that constitutes a market. Price variations can be predicted from the four basic quality-volume and demand–producer cost parameters. Profitability is predicted by closeness to the diagonal through the symmetrical quadrants. (In other words, the maximal profit line is the diagonal in which the demand-cost of the production ratio goes up at exactly the same rate for both volume and quality.)

White's theory provides an entirely new method for analyzing the internal dynamics of markets and thus proposes an economic sociology alternative to mainstream economic theory, even proposing a new theory of prices and profits. It remains to be shown, of course, how the model may be worked out in detail, empirically tested, and implemented. The very existence of this kind of theoretical model, in however schematic a form, should make us optimistic, however, that the second phase of economic sociology is finding tools with which to decipher the varieties and dynamics of economic networks.

Like Harrison White, Ronald Burt (chapter 7) seeks to show how social relationships affect competitive dynamics. His chapter outlines the theory of structural holes, which makes an important contribution to economic sociology because it locates competitive advantage in social relationships rather than in attributes of firms such as capabilities, strategies, and market position. The theory is also important because it cuts across levels of analysis and can be applied to industries, firms, and individuals. Moreover, it allows quantification of the relative advantage (or disadvantage) of actors based on their network ties. And finally, Burt's theory is important because the core proposition—that advantage is found in sparse rather than in dense networks—is not obvious. In Burt's language, "structural holes . . . create a competitive advantage for an individual whose relationships span the holes" (this volume, 155). Information-hole spanners enjoy two kinds of advantages over people who inhabit smaller but denser networks: access to more information, and being better positioned to engage in brokerage and hence influence the outcome of transactions.

Burt's argument goes further by asserting that having the right connections—connections to people who are otherwise uncon- nected—constitutes a form of social capital. Social capital arising from social location is, in Burt's view, a "contextual complement" to more mundane forms of human capital such as education and skills. Social capital of this type is an asset that benefits individuals and groups. But whether social capital that benefits individuals is also a social asset that improves the efficiency of institutions and benefits society is less clear. Burt is mute on this point. His position is in sharp contrast to those of Robert Putnam (1993) and earlier political scientists like Edward Banfield (1958), for whom social capital lay principally in institutions and associations.

Burt presents evidence that advantages accrue to individuals and groups whose networks are rich in structural holes. To illustrate: structural holes promote career advancement and team performance, accelerate task completion, increase the probability that early-stage investments will advance to the initial public offering (IPO) stage, and foster organizational learning. Some of this evidence is drawn directly from network data, and other evidence is inferential because it is based on observed associations of contact diversity with the advan- tages accruing to individuals and groups. But evidence about the im- pact of structural holes on entrepreneurial behavior, which in some respects is at the core of the structural hole argument, remains lim- ited: "Although an obvious site for research on the network forms of social capital, quantitative research on networks in entrepreneurship has been limited to the most rudimentary of network data" (this vol- ume, 174). Network research on entrepreneurship will have to over- come the challenges of comparing successful entrepreneurs with failed entrepreneurs (or people who never attempted entrepreneurial careers) and, in particular, the challenge of comparing the holes sur- rounding people who subsequently succeed as entrepreneurs with the holes surrounding those who are less successful.

Burt's pioneering may lead to further theorizing about structural holes. The structural hole argument in its barest form is that position confers advantage. But position confers advantage only if two events mediate structural holes and advantage: people recognize that they occupy a potentially advantageous position, and they pursue this ad- vantage. The Burt formulation of structural holes thus becomes some- thing like: (1) occupy hole position; (2) recognize potential advantage of hole position; (3) pursue advantage; (4) realize advantage. Looking at structural holes this way raises the question of whether a different formulation is possible: (1) recognize advantage of hole position; (2) pursue hole position; (3) occupy hole position; (4) realize advantage of hole position. The Burt formulation, in other words, gives causal primacy to position (occupying a hole position), while the alternative gives primacy to cognition (recognizing that hole positions can be advantageous) and motivation (pursuing this advantage). This difference opens some questions not yet addressed by Burt. One question is closely tied to issues of entrepreneurship and innovation: How are structural holes discovered in the first place? The answer could lie in individual differences (in cognition, motivation, or capabilities), but a partial network explanation is also possible: people at the periphery of existing networks—for example, marginal individuals or sojourners—are more motivated to search for holes than people at the core. Another question not yet addressed is why holes persist given the standard microeconomic prediction that their advantages will be competed away. The answer could lie in the power of people occupying holes to protect their turf by building barriers to entry—think, for example, of Bill Gates.

Whether the advantages accruing to individuals and groups as a consequence of structural holes should be described as social capital depends largely on how one views social capital. Does one, following Burt, Portes and Mooney (this volume), Bourdieu (1977 [1972]), and Coleman (1990), think of social capital as accruing to individuals and groups, as human capital does? Or does one, following Putnam (1993) and others, think of social capital as above all social and accruing first to society and then to individuals? Research evidence will not settle these questions. We should point out, however, that fields like accounting and finance are paying greater attention to the intangible assets of firms, which are based in firms' knowledge and their customer relationships, as distinguished from the tangible assets reported on their balance sheets. It may be that new terms like "social capital" and "intangible assets" cut too broad a swath, and that, as research moves forward, more specific language will be utilized to describe the relationship-based and knowledge-based assets of individuals, groups, and firms.

Gender Inequality and Economic Sociology

What determines how hard people work? This question is fundamental to our understanding of the economy, and a rich area for integrating the research of sociologists, economists, and psychologists. William Bielby and Denise Bielby examine the literature on effort and commitment on the job and gender differences in this area. They criticize this literature for its sloppy conceptualizations of effort and commitment and its reliance on stereotypes about gender differences even in the absence of firm evidence of such differences.

We can delineate three broad approaches to thinking about determinants of effort on the job. Some approaches follow a narrow neoclassical model in which self-interested actors make rational decisions about how to allocate their effort. Here the assumption is that workers give less effort to their work except when material incentives make effort pay. Married women with children are presumed to be in a gender division of labor in the family that encourages this allocation of less energy to the job. Some evidence is supportive, such as the lower earnings of mothers. But other evidence subverts the view, such as the finding that on average women report slightly more effort and commitment than men.

The economic model also assumes that people prefer leisure to effort at work and will convert paid work time to leisure if such "shirking" is not penalized. Thus, economists have developed the efficiency wage theory, which argues that when surveillance of workers is especially expensive, employers decide that it is cheaper to pay an above-market-clearing wage than to pay for more supervisors or more surveillance equipment. Such "efficiency wages" motivate effort because, even with minimal surveillance, employees run some risk of getting fired for shirking, and the higher wage increases the cost of losing such a job. But economists have speculated that paying women workers efficiency wages would be less necessary (because of their alleged "docility" and the attendant ease of supervising them) or less effective (because more women than men plan to work intermittently and thus have less to gain in lifetime earnings from a given wage increment). This interpretation of the behavior of women workers has been offered as an explanation of the dearth of women in jobs that pay efficiency wages. Of course, sociologists also suggest the simpler hypothesis that garden-variety sex discrimination keeps women out of such jobs.

If economists' models have featured rational, selfish, lazy workers motivated only by money and inclined to be "free riders," a distinct psychological literature has seen organizational commitment and group effort as a collective orientation that involves other-regarding, altruistic behavior. The latter view of work effort and commitment easily incorporates the stereotype of women as socialized to be other-regarding to suggest that women would be better workers and citizens of organizations than men. This literature also sometimes finds women to be more public-spirited. However, Bielby and Bielby criticize these authors for being too quick to accept this conclusion because it corresponds with culturally held stereotypes, and they caution that often gender differences are tiny and explained by unexamined differences in the immediate structural constraints and incentives faced by men and women. Cecilia Ridgeway and Lynn Smith-Lovin (1999) and Elizabeth Aries (1996) have recently reached similar conclusions.

True to their structural bent as sociologists, Bielby and Bielby urge that future research on work effort and organizational commitment focus on the structural and situational features of the workplace that affect effort. They note that sociological research has found little effect of pay on effort or commitment; by contrast, the autonomy that a worker's job allows has been found to increase effort and commitment considerably. To be sure, these inferences, coming as they do from non-experimental, cross-sectional survey data, are subject to many possible selectivity biases, so it is hard to know whether causal effects are being accurately tapped. They suggest that we study how effort is affected by the characteristics of jobs and supervisors, the gender and race composition of work groups and the worker-supervisor match, and the gender meanings associated with tasks, as well as the material incentives examined in more conventional research.

In her chapter, Barbara Reskin rethinks conventional notions about discrimination. Her discussion ranges across the sociological, economic, legal, and psychological literatures. She argues that the conceptualization that lawmakers had in mind when they passed the Civil Rights Act of 1964—and that many judges still have in mind—is of discrimination as deliberate and based on animosity toward a group. Social scientists, she argues, have recognized two other types of discrimination.

Economists introduced the notion of statistical discrimination to refer to the practice of reducing information costs by using statistical generalizations about a race or sex group to infer an individual's probable characteristics. Although economists usually think of statistical discrimination in terms of using correct estimates of the direction and magnitude of group differences, some writers use the term more broadly to include perceived differences that do not exist at all or are not as large as believed, even at the group level. Like discrimination based on animosity, statistical discrimination is deliberate, but it is motivated by the desire to find qualified workers while minimizing information costs rather than by emotional aversion for a group.

Sociologists have also recognized structural discrimination, which Reskin defines as using a criterion other than race or sex that effectively screens out more members of one group than of another. For example, requiring twenty years of experience for a management job will screen out more women than men. With the *Griggs* decision, U.S. law encoded the doctrine of disparate impact, saying that if a screening device can be shown to have a disparate impact, employers can be prosecuted for discrimination if they cannot show that using it is job-relevant (*Griggs v. Duke Power Co.*, 401 U.S. 424, 1971). This type of discrimination, too, is deliberate, although it may not be based on animosity.

Reskin draws our attention to a fourth kind of discrimination, which is unconscious and unintentional. She reviews the social-psychological literature that documents the tendency of human cognition to be systematically distorted in a way that creates favoritism toward ingroup members. This tendency can come into play over and over in the decisions that affect employment outcomes, hiring, performance evaluation, promotion, mentoring, and termination. In Reskin's view, these pervasive, unconscious biases make discrimination the default option. The law, she argues, is not well tailored to redress this type of discrimination. Thus, we will eliminate it only if organizations explicitly tailor policies to minimize it. The impact of such discrimination could be decreased by laws that hold employers accountable for any correlation between race or sex and an organizational outcome that is not justified by qualification-relevant criteria. Among the organizational strategies that could discourage these biases are requiring that decisionmakers have individual information on the people on whom they are making decisions, and holding them accountable for using this information consistently.

In chapter 10, James Baron, Michael Hannan, Greta Hsu, and Ozgecan Kocak advance the institutionalist thesis that the cultural blueprints in the minds of the founders of a firm affect many aspects of how the firm is set up, with lasting effects that exemplify path dependence in organizational evolution. They examine how these cultural models affected the gender composition of the core technical and scientific workforce in 170 high-tech firms in Silicon Valley.

In-depth interviews with the founders of these firms led to a rich qualitative database on cultural blueprints. Their content analysis of these data led to five models. The "star" model, much like academic science, selects individuals based on their potential, assumes motivation from their intrinsic interest in the scientific work, and relies on internalized professional norms for social control. The "engineering" model selects individuals for their specific technical skills, assumes that these "techies" find the work inherently interesting, and relies on peer norms of excellence for social control. "Bureaucratic" and "autocratic" models also select for technical skills but rely on rules and monitoring for control. The "commitment" model (associated with firms like Hewlett-Packard) features a strong and motivating corporate culture in which individuals are selected on the basis of whether they are perceived to fit the culture.

The type of blueprint selected by the founders of these firms had no effect on women's share of the core technical, scientific, and engineering jobs at the start-up. However, net of women's initial representation, firms following the commitment model showed the worst record for increasing women's share of jobs over time. The authors explain this long-term effect in terms of what Rosabeth Kanter (1977) called "homosocial reproduction"—the tendency of leaders in an organization to trust others like themselves in terms of racial, sexual, and other sociodemographic markers, and thus to fill key positions with such people. Baron and his colleagues think it is the premium placed on fit and peer culture in the commitment model that makes homosocial reproduction more extreme in firms run on this model. We could speculate that a controlling culture with homogeneous leaders makes for more tightly linked social networks and social capital in "high-commitment" firms, and that this may be what makes it harder for women or other outsiders to penetrate such a culture. (As Alejandro Portes and Margarita Mooney note in their chapter, one individual's social capital can be another individual's exclusion.)

This analysis has broad implications for the study of organizations in economic sociology. Baron and his colleagues make a plea for recognition of the importance of the blueprints in place at an organization's founding. They call for research that incorporates measures of such founding conditions, noting that they have been absent from most data sets. Their chapter illustrates one area of convergence of the neo-institutional and population ecology perspectives in the study of organizations. Neo-institutional views stress cultural templates; population ecology assumes considerable inertia in organizational routines (in juxtaposition with the neoclassical view in which firms change strategies as market conditions and incentives in the regulatory environment change). The cultural blueprints of founders constitute a kind of organizational birthmark that is consistent with both ecological and neo-institutional views.

In chapter 11, Viviana Zelizer provides an example of what she calls for in chapter 5: extending economic sociology into spheres traditionally considered beyond its boundaries, and using a key idea from cultural sociology—that the type of social tie involved in an "intimate transaction" often determines the meanings that are invoked. By intimate transaction, Zelizer is referring to interactions that often involve both love and money, such as those in relationships between a husband and wife, a man and his mistress, or a parent and child. She criticizes the tendency to see this personal sphere as operating according to principles completely different from those of the public world of the economy and the polity. This private-public dualism (roundly criticized by feminists) sees the personal as the sphere of love and particularism, and the public sphere as the realm of self-interest and commodification. Underlying the notion that different principles explain behavior in the two realms is the often moral exhortation that the personal sphere be protected from contamination by commodification and self-interest. Such objections are often raised when feminists suggest that marriage should be more contractually based, or that economically dependent wives are owed some payment for their reproductive labor. Some feminists have pointed out that women's key problem is often too little commodification of what they do, not too much. Zelizer notes that money transfers coexist with intimacy all the time and in fact represent significant capital flows in the economy. Examples include support of an economically dependent spouse, payment of nannies, children's allowances, bequests to adult children, and wedding gifts of money to friends or relatives. These are large flows in the economy!

Zelizer proposes that we should not expect fundamentally different theories to explain the more and less personal spheres. Thus, she rejects the "Hostile-Worlds" view that different theories apply. But she also rejects what she calls the "Nothing-But" view, the main example of which is the imperialistic version of rational choice that sees all human behavior as explained by optimizing behavior. She rejects the idea that Nothing-But political processes, or "nothing but" some reductionist view of cultural beliefs, can explain both spheres. She proposes that we understand all spheres of action instead in terms of differentiated social ties. The type of social tie dictates which cultural meanings or rules or values are invoked, and which types of money flows and other exchanges or gifts for love are seen as appropriate. In this view, a major form that culture takes is defining what behavior and feeling is appropriate for what type of social tie.

A major lesson of her analysis for economic sociology reiterates the message of her other chapter in this volume—that we should not bound economic sociology too narrowly, and that boundaries should not be set using unexamined and incoherent criteria. She wants economic sociology defined broadly to include much that has usually been left out, such as household production and consumption and even sexual transactions. But such a definition raises the interesting question of what part of sociology *is not* economic sociology. She does not address this question, but her discussion suggests that it makes sense to define economic sociology as involving market and non-market production, distribution, and consumption.

The Economic Sociology of Development

The fourth part of this book focuses on economic development, which has been on the sociological research agenda for a long time. The chapters by Alejandro Portes and Margarita Mooney and by Susan Eckstein use concepts drawn directly from economic sociology. In chapter 12, Portes and Mooney elaborate on one of the key emerging concepts in economic sociology. They argue that social capital—as an attribute of communities and regions—can contribute to economic and social well-being by fostering collaboration and entrepreneurship. They warn, however, that the causal relationship is complex, contingent on a number of factors, and subject to a considerable degree of historical path dependence—and thus difficult to reproduce in a different context. Portes and Mooney begin by critically examining the concept of social capital, that is, the "ability to secure resources by virtue of membership in social networks." In this view, actors embedded in a dense network of relationships can benefit from altruistic norms of moral obligation or bounded solidarity to obtain desired resources. In addition to altruism, resource access can be facilitated by instrumental factors, including simple reciprocity and enforceable trust.

Portes and Mooney believe that entrepreneurship at the community and regional levels benefits from dense networks of relationships between actors. They are critical of the previous research linking social capital to development that confuses the ability to secure resources through networks with the resources themselves and neglects the tendency of excessive levels of social embeddedness to stultify entrepreneurial initiatives and reinforce patterns of inequality.

Portes and Mooney use three case studies to illustrate the usefulness of the concept of social capital to understand development outcomes: flexible manufacturing in the Italian region of Emilia-Romagna; handicraft production and trade among the Otavalan Indians of Ecuador; and community infrastructure projects funded by Salvadoran exiles in the United States. These cases suggest three general points. First, social capital is hard to "engineer" because it tends to originate from fairly unique historical processes, frequently unrelated to economic variables. Thus, fascism in Italy, colonialism in Ecuador, and the Salvadoran civil war of 1980 to 1992 prompted the development of ingroup identities. These identities led to altruistic and instrumental behaviors conducive to economic innovation and dynamism. Second, social capital does not necessarily reduce competitive behavior but rather infuses it with meaning, sets normative limits to its scope and intensity, and helps channel it toward the welfare of the community. And third, one possible path to successful economic transformation is to build on existing social structures and relationships to foster entrepreneurial collaboration between individual and organized actors in the community. Although persuasive, these arguments invite further research to explore exactly what contingencies may render the presence of social capital insufficient for development success.

While Portes and Mooney explore how social capital may contribute to development, Susan Eckstein seeks to understand forms of resistance to economic adversity. In chapter 13, she argues that responses to trade and price liberalization in Latin America and to state downsizing during the 1990s have not been primarily class-based. Rather, responses have ranged from individual exit strategies (emigration and migration) to popular resistance by groups defined according to their functional status, such as farmers, consumers, students, debtors, neighbors, or squatters. To expand her careful analysis of differences across Latin American countries, Eckstein draws on several key concepts in comparative political sociology as she assesses the likelihood of individual versus collective responses. She argues that the chances of collective responses are greater when the state is weak, state-society relations are not institutionalized, the level of politicization of the society is high, and few options other than exit are perceived.

The concepts of repertoires and interpretive frames also figure prominently in Eckstein's analysis. She documents how disgruntled individuals and groups throughout Latin America have drawn from modernist, premodernist, and postmodernist strategies of action to "address and redress the deprivations and injustices they experience" in their daily lives. Thus, protesters have embraced symbolic responses, emphasized custom and tradition over rights, and turned to new channels of communication, such as the Internet, to express their grievances. As Eckstein observes, the rise in nonmodern ways of protest runs counter to the fact that purely modernist and class-based ways of articulating demands and exercising protest have been made ostensibly easier by Latin America's recent turn to democratic rule after decades of more or less explicit authoritarianism.

Eckstein's analysis and conclusions contribute to an economic sociology that strikes a delicate balance between the macropolitical structure and culturally rooted action. This chapter invites more research on economic action and social mobilization aimed at exploring the limits of either approach in isolation when it comes to examining economic change.

The Revival of Economic Sociology

In our view, the independent evolution of organizational sociology, social stratification, the sociology of development, and the sociology of culture precludes the growth of a more integrated economic sociology focused on making sense of economic structures, changes, and trends in the contemporary world. As Bruce Carruthers and Brian Uzzi (2000) point out, actors' identities, relations, and roles are changing rapidly as the boundaries of social groups, occupations, professions, firms, industries, and even countries are becoming blurred. For example, the study of internal organizational processes is becoming difficult without attending to social stratification and culture, and the relationship between the organization and its environment is rooted in political, cultural, and developmental processes. Similarly, social stratification takes place in an organizational, cultural, and political context, and contemporary cultures and subcultures are shaped not only by social stratification but also by organizations such as firms and the state. Finally, cross-national patterns of economic development are intricately related to social, organizational, and cultural changes.

Like the social tumult of the 1960s, which challenged prevailing sociological theory and cleared the way for major theoretical developments, the dynamic complexity and globally connected nature of today's economic phenomena are driving economic sociology toward an even more integrative and sophisticated theoretical approach. The study of economic sociology is well positioned to rise to the challenge of addressing these loose ends and integrating organizational, stratification, cultural, and development processes into explanations of economic phenomena.

It is our conviction that at this moment of reemergence economic sociologists need to embrace multiple theoretical and methodological approaches. We see room for comparative-historical, cultural, evolutionary, and structural approaches to the study of economic phenomena, among others, and a need to collect both quantitative and qualitative data at different levels of analysis. Inductive and deductive reasoning remain powerful and complementary tools. We envision economic sociology as an opportunity for dialogue among all sociologists and as a way to reclaim the rich classic heritage of studying the economy and the society as a whole.

The revival of economic sociology promises to place the study of economic phenomena at the center of the sociological arena, where it will attract the participation of researchers who were previously focused on social stratification (including class, gender, and race), culture, organizations, or economic development. This integrative effort is an opportunity to reaffirm sociology's historical roots as a social science. Economic sociology will succeed to the extent that it can move beyond compartmentalized specialties and identify common concepts and postulates. Each of the chapters in this volume represents an attempt to reorient the sociological study of the economy and break free from the boundaries of the past.

References

Abbott, Andrew. 1988. *The System of Professions: An Essay on the Division of Expert Labor.* Chicago: University of Chicago Press.

Aries, Elizabeth. 1996. *Men and Women in Interaction: Reconsidering the Differences.* New York: Oxford University Press.

Banfield, Edward C. 1958. *The Moral Basis of a Backward Society.* Glencoe, Ill.: Free Press.

Barnard, Chester I. 1938. *The Functions of the Executive.* Cambridge, Mass.: Harvard University Press.

Baron, James N. 1984. "Organizational Perspectives on Stratification." *Annual Review of Sociology* 10: 37–69.

Bendix, Reinhard. 2001 [1956]. *Work and Authority in Industry.* New Brunswick, N.J.: Transaction Press.

Biggart, Nicole W. 1994. "Labor and Leisure." In *Handbook of Economic Sociology,* edited by Neil J. Smelser and Richard Swedberg. Princeton, N.J.: Princeton University Press.

Blau, Peter M., and W. Richard Scott. 1962. *Formal Organizations: A Comparative Approach.* Scranton, Penn.: Chandler Publishing.

Bourdieu, Pierre. 1977 [1972]. *Outline of a Theory of Practice.* New York: Cambridge University Press.

———. 1988 [1984]. *Homo Academicus.* Stanford, Calif.: Stanford University Press.

Bourdieu, Pierre, and Jean-Claude Passeron. 1990. *Reproduction in Education, Society, and Culture.* Newbury Park, Calif.: Sage Publications.

Braverman, Harry. 1974. *Labor and Monopoly Capital: The Degradation of Work in the Twentieth Century.* New York: Monthly Review Press.

Brinton, Mary C., and Victor Nee, eds. 1998. *New Institutionalism in Sociology.* New York: Russell Sage Foundation.

Burawoy, Michael. 1979. *Manufacturing Consent: Changes in the Labor Process Under Monopoly Capitalism.* Chicago: University of Chicago Press.

Burt, Ronald S. 1982. *Toward a Structural Theory of Action: Network Models of Social Structure.* New York: Academic Press.

————. 1992. *Structural Holes: The Social Structure of Competition.* Cambridge, Mass.: Harvard University Press.

Cardoso, Fernando Henrique, and Enzo Faletto. 1979 [1973]. *Dependency and Development in Latin America.* Berkeley: University of California Press.

Carruthers, Bruce G., and Brian Uzzi. 2000. "Economic Sociology in the New Millennium." *Contemporary Sociology* 29: 486–94.

Cole, Robert E. 1979. *Work, Mobility, and Participation: A Comparative Study of American and Japanese Industry.* Berkeley: University of California Press.

Coleman, James S. 1990. *Foundations of Social Theory.* Cambridge, Mass.: Belknap Press of Harvard University Press.

DiMaggio, Paul J. 1994. "Culture and Economy." In *Handbook of Economic Sociology*, edited by Neil J. Smelser and Richard Swedberg. Princeton, N.J.: Princeton University Press.

Dore, Ronald. 1983. "Goodwill and the Spirit of Market Capitalism." *British Journal of Sociology* 34: 459–82.

Edwards, Richard. 1979. *Contested Terrain: The Transformation of Work in the Twentieth Century.* New York: Basic Books.

England, Paula, and George Farkas. 1986. *Households, Employment, and Gender: A Social, Economic, and Demographic View.* New York: Aldine.

Etzioni, Amitai. 1964. *Modern Organizations.* Englewood Cliffs, N.J.: Prentice-Hall.

Evans, Peter. 1979. *Dependent Development.* Princeton, N.J.: Princeton University Press.

————. 1995. *Embedded Autonomy: States and Industrial Transformation.* Princeton, N.J.: Princeton University Press.

Frank, André G. 1967. *Capitalism and Underdevelopment in Latin America.* New York: Monthly Review Press.

Freidson, Eliot. 1986. *Professional Powers: A Study of the Institutionalization of Formal Knowledge.* Chicago: University of Chicago Press.

Frenzen, Jonathan, Paul M. Hirsch, and Philip C. Zerrillo. 1994. "Consumption, Preferences, and Changing Lifestyles." In *Handbook of Economic Sociology*, edited by Neil J. Smelser and Richard Swedberg. Princeton, N.J.: Princeton University Press.

Gans, Herbert J., ed. 1990. *Sociology in America.* Newbury Park, Calif.: Sage Publications.

Geertz, Clifford. 1963. *Peddlers and Princes: Social Development and Economic Change in Two Indonesian Towns.* Chicago: University of Chicago Press.

Granovetter, Mark. 1985. "Economic Action and Social Structure: The Problem of *Embeddedness.*" *American Journal of Sociology* 91(3): 481–510.

————. 1990. "The Old and the New Economic Sociology: A History and an Agenda." In *Beyond the Marketplace: Rethinking Economy and Society*, edited by Roger Friedland and A. F. Robertson. New York: Aldine.

Grusky, David B., ed. 1994. *Social Stratification: Class, Race, and Gender in Sociological Perspective.* Boulder, Colo.: Westview.

Guillén, Mauro F. 2001a. *The Limits of Convergence: Globalization and Organizational Change in Argentina, South Korea, and Spain.* Princeton, N.J.: Princeton University Press.

———. 2001b. "Is Globalization Civilizing, Destructive, or Feeble?: A Critique of Five Key Debates in the Social-Science Literature." *Annual Review of Sociology* 27: 235–60.

Hamilton, Gary G., and Nicole W. Biggart. 1988. "Market, Culture, and Authority: A Comparative Analysis of Management and Organization in the Far East." *American Journal of Sociology* 94: S52–94.

Kanter, Rosabeth Moss. 1977. *Men and Women of the Corporation*. New York: Basic Books.

Kerr, Clark, John T. Dunlop, Frederick Harbison, and Charles A. Myers. 1964 [1960]. *Industrialism and Industrial Man*. New York: Oxford University Press.

Larson, M. S. 1977. *The Rise of Professionalism*. Berkeley: University of California Press.

Lawrence, Paul R., and Jay W. Lorsch. 1967. *Organization and Environment: Managing Differentiation and Integration*. Boston: Graduate School of Business Administration, Harvard University.

Lincoln, James R., and Arne L. Kalleberg. 1990. *Culture, Control, and Commitment: A Study of Work Organization and Work Attitudes in the United States and Japan*. New York: Cambridge University Press.

Mayo, Elton. 1977 [1933]. *The Human Problems of an Industrial Civilization*. Salem, N.H.: Ayer.

———. 1988 [1945]. *The Social Problems of an Industrial Civilization*. Salem, N.H.: Ayer.

McPherson, J. Miller, and Thomas Rotolo. 1996. "Testing a Dynamic Model of Social Composition: Diversity and Change in Voluntary Groups." *American Sociological Review* 61(2): 179–202.

Milkman, Ruth, and Eleanor Townsley. 1994. "Gender and the Economy." In *Handbook of Economic Sociology*, edited by Neil J. Smelser and Richard Swedberg. Princeton, N.J.: Princeton University Press.

Parsons, Talcott, and Neil J. Smelser. 1956. *Economy and Society: A Study in the Integration of Economic and Social Theory*. Glencoe, Ill.: Free Press.

Perrow, Charles. 1970. *Organizational Analysis: A Sociological View*. Belmont, Calif.: Wadsworth.

———. 1986. *Complex Organizations*. New York: Random House.

Powell, Walter W., ed. 1984. *The Nonprofit Sector: A Research Handbook*. New Haven, Conn.: Yale University Press.

Powell, Walter W., and Paul J. DiMaggio, eds. 1991. *The New Institutionalism in Organizational Analysis*. Chicago: The University of Chicago Press.

Putnam, Robert D. 1993. *Making Democracy Work: Civic Traditions in Modern Italy*. Princeton, N.J.: Princeton University Press.

Ridgeway, Cecilia, and Lynn Smith-Lovin. 1999. "Interaction in the Gender System: Theory and Research." *Annual Review of Sociology* 25: 191–216.

Roethlisberger, F. J., and William J. Dickson. 1967 [1939]. *Management and the Worker: An Account of a Research Program Conducted by the Western Electric Company, Hawthorne Works, Chicago*. Cambridge, Mass.: Harvard University Press.

Rothschild-Whitt, Joyce. 1979. "The Collectivist Organization: An Alternative to Rational-Bureaucratic Models." *American Sociological Review* 44(4): 509–27.

32   The New Economic Sociology

Scott, W. Richard. 1998 [1981]. *Organizations: Rational, Natural, and Open Systems.* Englewood Cliffs, N.J.: Prentice-Hall.

Simmel, Georg. 1957 [1904]. "Fashion." *American Journal of Sociology* 62(6): 541–58.

Smelser, Neil J. 1976. *The Sociology of Economic Life.* Englewood Cliffs, N.J.: Prentice-Hall.

Smelser, Neil J., and Richard Swedberg, eds. 1994. *Handbook of Economic Sociology.* Princeton, N.J.: Princeton University Press.

Stinchcombe, Arthur L. 1983. *Economic Sociology.* New York: Academic Press.

Swedberg, Richard, and Mark Granovetter. 1992. "Introduction." In *The Sociology of Economic Life,* edited by Mark Granovetter and Richard Swedberg. Boulder, Colo.: Westview.

Thompson, James D. 1967. *Organizations in Action: Social Science Bases of Administrative Theory.* New York: McGraw-Hill.

Veblen, Thorstein. 1994. *The Theory of the Leisure Class.* New York: Penguin. (Originally published in 1899)

Wallerstein, Immanuel. 1974. *The Modern World-System: Capitalist Agriculture and the Origins of the European World-Economy in the Sixteenth Century.* New York: Academic Press.

White, Harrison C. 1981. "Where Do Markets Come From?" *American Journal of Sociology* 87: 514–47.

———. 2001. *Markets from Networks.* Princeton, N.J.: Princeton University Press.

Wilensky, Harold L. 1964. "The Professionalization of Everyone?" *American Journal of Sociology* 70(2): 137–58.

Wilson, John. 2000. "Volunteering." *Annual Review of Sociology* 26: 215–40.

Zelizer, Viviana A. 1989a. "Beyond the Polemics of the Market: Establishing a Theoretical and Empirical Agenda." *Social Forces* 3: 614–34.

———. 1989b. "The Social Meaning of Money." *American Journal of Sociology* 95: 342–77.

= Part I =

Major Debates and Conceptual Approaches in Economic Sociology

= Chapter 2 =

A Theoretical Agenda for Economic Sociology

MARK GRANOVETTER

ECONOMIC sociology is no longer a novelty. Born in the late nineteenth century and reborn in the 1970s, it has produced a long run of exciting studies and promising leads. (For a more detailed historical account, see Granovetter 1990.) As the century turns, it is timely to look beyond our accumulation of important empirical studies and reassess the theoretical agenda that a structural economic sociology might pursue, and where this agenda fits within the main concerns of sociology and economics.

In doing so, we should keep in mind that the production and distribution of goods and services is just one institutional complex of activities, and that the arguments appropriate to these activities should have some generic similarity to the arguments we might develop to explain political action, science and knowledge, family and kinship, and other persistent social patterns. Thinking about how the sociology of the economy is similar to and different from that of other institutions helps us see what kinds of arguments will work best.

Incentives, Individuals, Context, and History

We may begin by asking what is distinctive about economic sociology as a way to explain the economy. In part, this depends on one's concept of "distinctive." One way in which analysis of the economy is different from that of some other institutions is that it is largely dominated by one academic discipline, economics, which is focused theo-

35

retically on concepts of rational or instrumental action and where "methodological individualism" roots all explanation in the activity of concrete persons. Though sociology should develop its own agenda and argument rather than react to neoclassical economic analysis, concepts can be sharpened by clarifying where they stand in relation to those developed by economists. A unified theory should build on what both have accomplished.

I argue that the two very general ways in which the instrumental-reductionist vision is theoretically incomplete suggest the distinctive explanatory improvements that economic sociology can offer. The first is that any account of human interaction that limits explanation to individual interests abstracts away from fundamental aspects of *relationships,* which characterize economic action, as well as any other kind of action. In particular, horizontal relationships may involve trust and cooperation, and vertical relationships power and compliance, well beyond what individuals' incentives can explain. Trust and power drive a wedge between interests and action. And this happens in part because norms and identities result from and structure interaction in cognitive and emotional ways that escape reduction to self-interest and indeed are key in actors' definitions of what their interests are.

The second problem for reductionist accounts is that even though we see some spaces where we may adequately explain outcomes by a purely interest-driven model, there is rarely any simple reduction to individual action that can explain how such spaces evolved as they did, with the constraints and incentives that individuals find themselves acting out.[1] In fact, this is a corollary to a more general argument that both action driven by interests and action driven by trust or power occur and have outcomes in ways determined by larger contexts than those in which they are located. I mention the situation of interest-driven behavior first only because it is more typically analyzed as context-free.

This second point does not privilege structure over agency: individuals who find themselves in situations determined by forces beyond their control, and often far beyond their own life span, may nevertheless turn these situations to advantage and make a deep imprint on future actions and institutions. For example, although it was quite late in the game before Cosimo de Medici could "suddenly apprehend the political capacity of the social network machine that lay at his fingertips" (Padgett and Ansell 1993, 1264), a machine he had done little to create, once he did, he dramatically changed the course of Florentine history for many generations.

In practice, these two problems typically occur in the same cases, and though we should separate them analytically, it is hard and somewhat artificial to do so for any particular instance, and I do not succeed very well at it in what follows. I focus first on the mixed sources of action within confined social spaces of the sort that Harrison White (1992) refers to as "molecules," and then move in the following section to how such molecules are constituted.

Mixed Sources of Action in Social Spaces

To illustrate the first point, the inadequacy of a purely interest-based argument, I begin with information flow. Economic sociology has made major contributions to understanding this flow through social networks in labor markets, and within and between organizations (see, for example, Granovetter 1973, 1995; Burt 1992). One way to apply this understanding is to adapt it for instrumental argument about how best to manage one's networks. Not only economists but also sociologists such as Scott Boorman (1975, on investing in weak ties) and Ronald Burt (1992, on the use of "structural holes") have done so. These models follow a rational-choice approach to understand information flow through social networks, and they make contributions that are valuable but not wholly distinctive from those of economics.

However, even for this apparently tractable case, it is difficult to stay within a simple framework of instrumental rationality. My study of job information flow (Granovetter 1995), for example, made clear that it is often profoundly misleading to think of the acquisition of such information as the result of "investment" in contacts. One reason for this is well stated in Peter Blau's (1963, 62) discussion of "social exchange": he points out that positive responses from another are rewarding only insofar as the recipient does not think they are meant to be. People want sociability and hope to be liked, approved of, and admired by others. Insincere approval is better than none (as those who encourage sycophants well know) but pales in comparison to approval without ulterior motive. Though some "investors" in social relations may achieve great skill in simulating sincerity, as shown by the success of "confidence rackets," the desire of recipients for true approval, and the vigilance of most in ferreting out its opposite, sharply bound the role of calculated instrumentality in social life.

So economic sociology can make a first contribution to understanding the economy by calling attention to the mixture of economic and social purposes that motivate people while they are engaged in production, consumption, or distribution.[2] But there is more to say here about the contexts of social interaction and how they arise. People typically pursue multiple purposes simultaneously in intersecting social formations. For example, it seems implausible to consider the person going to a party with nothing more in mind than having a good time to be engaged in economically instrumental behavior, since the component of expected economic gain from loud and intense socializing is small to vanishing and thus unlikely to be anyone's main reason for attending.[3] And yet information about jobs does pass among partygoers (Granovetter 1995). The point is that the separate institutions of labor markets and expressive socialization routines intersect in ways that *cannot be accounted for by the incentives of individuals.* This point is related to the second problem for instrumental theory that I mentioned earlier, the problem of how the contexts of action arise. I will take up that question more generally later in the chapter when discussing the intersection of spheres and institutions.

We may summarize the argument so far by saying that in social interaction, people have mixtures of motives and consequently act in ways difficult to describe in terms of pure self-interest. Sociology has expanded on this point by considering how particular *kinds* of social relations make behavior diverge from the narrowly instrumental. To cut through a vast theoretical underbrush, I simply distinguish here between horizontal and vertical relations, and their respective effects on this divergence.

Analysis of horizontal (nonhierarchical) relations leads to discussions of trust or solidarity—states of relationships or groups that lead to cooperation beyond that to be expected from decision dilemmas such as the "free-rider problem" or the "prisoners' dilemma." Vertical (hierarchical) ties are defined by a quality of these relations that we refer to as power, to be distinguished from solidarity or trust. The behavioral consequences of power are domination and compliance; these are parallel to cooperation, the behavioral consequence of trust or solidarity.

Trust and power open a wedge between behavior and incentives that instrumental theorists try hard to close. Their efforts are strenuous because problems of trust and cooperation, and of power and compliance, pose difficult challenges for any theory based wholly on rational choice and self-interest. In this chapter, I challenge attempts to bring these problems within the orbit of such theory, but will note here simply that these attempts, even if successful, would still leave much of social life and economic action unexplained. They do not look at how the larger social setting determines the parameters within which self-interest is defined, a matter that I take up later.

Perhaps the most ink has been spilled on problems of trust and the cooperation that flows from it. The issue became especially pertinent

to arguments about rational choice when theorists pointed out para-
doxes of rationality: that interacting individuals, rationally pursuing
their own goals, achieve results worse than if each had adopted a
suboptimal strategy, as in the famous prisoners' dilemma. Mancur
Olson's *The Logic of Collective Action* (1965) applied this argument to
political theory by pointing out that cooperation to achieve mutually
shared goals would be derailed by genuinely rational actors, since
each would try to "free-ride." This chilling discovery parallels that
ten years later by Oliver Williamson (1975) of the likelihood in market
relations of "opportunism"—the alloying of simple self-interest with
"guile." These discoveries ended the long era in instrumental theory
dominated by what Albert Hirschman (1982) has called the idea of
doux commerce, stemming from the time of Montesquieu: that rational
action and exchange transform people into gentlemen who automatically follow the rules of the game and are trustworthy despite incentives to the contrary. This oversocialized conception gave way rather
suddenly to a neo-Hobbesian conception of market relations as nasty,
brutish, and short—an accurate characterization only in the unlikely
event that people are anonymous atoms in relation to one another,
and highly undersocialized (Granovetter 1985).

For in practice, decision dilemmas and opportunism are overcome
if the participants, to use the language of everyday life, "trust" one
another. Two separated prisoners both deny the crime despite the
dominant solution, because each trusts the other to do the same. Trust
thus leads to an outcome better for the collectivity. But no rational
account explains why prisoners would do such a thing; trust means
precisely that each expects the other to act against her own interest, as
defined by the payoff matrix.

Most instrumentalist literature on trust consists of elaborate efforts
to deny the data of everyday life and rescue trust from its usual
meaning by explaining that actors trust each other only when incentives are aligned in such a way as to make the trust reasonable. It is
said that we "trust" a company's promise to repay a debt if a rating
company has assigned a AAA to its debt obligation, or that we can
trust the other prisoner if the game is repeated ad infinitum. Companies keep good faith and avoid default because the loss of a high
rating is expensive, and prisoners deny because in the long run they
would be wiped out by their own malfeasance if they did not. Robert
Axelrod's (1984) well-known contribution takes this point into an
evolutionary framework.

Although all these phenomena are undeniable, they are hardly
conclusive. People often act with confidence because they expect
others' incentives to point them in the right direction, but the com-

monsense meaning of trust is that we expect good behavior of others *in spite* of their incentives. Moreover, such trust is vital for the conduct of social and economic life. If everyone assumed that others merely "did the right thing" because of incentives, economic life would be poisoned by incessant attempts to conceal the true incentive situation for one's own advantage. In fact, the well is not invariably poisoned. In most situations, economic actors drink freely despite incentives for their counterparts to act worse than they actually do. Thus, one central task of economic sociology is to lay bare the circumstances under which people may safely set aside the suspicions that rational action would require them to have.[4] By definition, such a task cannot be conceived or implemented from within a theory of behavior that admits only of rational action.[5]

Though I emphasize the divergence from self-interest resulting from trust in horizontal relations, dislike and corresponding *distrust* and failure to cooperate are equally important and are just the flip side of this argument, even though negative relations are rarely integrated into social theory. One nice example is provided by John Padgett and Christopher Ansell (1993), who describe how the Medicis sat astride the structural holes (Burt 1992) among their followers. These divergent networks resulted from low intermarriage rates among different groups of supporters; Padgett and Ansell comment that there is "no particular mystery" about this, since "patrician and new men supporters despised each other. Status-conscious patricians . . . usually would not dream of sullying their own honor by marrying into new men families" (1281). Yet it was just this separation that gave the Medicis so much leverage in relation to supporters who could not unite.

The concepts of trust and distrust refer to horizontal relations in which neither party can dictate to the other what she must do. If we transpose the issues from horizontal and symmetrical to vertical and asymmetrical relations, we see that much of the discussion of trust and the cooperation that flows from it has a parallel in discussions of power and the compliance that flows from it. At all scales in economic action and institutions, people comply at times with what they understand others want them to do. Unlike the language of trust, however, we have no clear-cut usage to demarcate compliance based on incentives from that rooted in other elements of relationships and institutions.

Yet this issue is commonly understood to be important. Blau (1963, 91), trying to carve out a distinctive niche for the concept of social exchange, rules out situations where compliance is not plausibly construed as voluntary—as when a thief offers the choice, "Your money or your life." Max Weber (1968 [1921], ch. 10) classifies types of power in similar ways. For him, the least interesting case, which he discusses only briefly, is power based on a "constellation of interests," such as a monopoly position in the economy, though it obviously is important in its own right. Correspondingly, he notes almost in passing that to run a civil administration on the basis of incessant coercion is too expensive and unwieldy for any but the most unimaginative to pursue. Instead, most of his analysis of distinct historical formations dissects the different circumstances under which people consider it *appropriate* to follow instructions given by someone in an authority position over them—the "types of legitimate authority."

This distinctively sociological argument about compliance and legitimacy, which can be made in relation to industrial organizations as well as states (Burawoy 1979; Granovetter and Tilly 1988; Freeland 1996), leads us to observe that one reason it is artificial to consider either cooperation or subordination as always reflecting the pursuit of self-interest is that actors usually have definite conceptions of what action is *appropriate* and do not explicitly construe these shared norms or conventions of action—constructed, learned, and absorbed within social groups—as matters of self-interest. This is a core part of the meaning of such norms.[6]

Most sociologists have veered away from theoretical arguments based on actors' shared value commitments because of the excesses of mid-twentieth-century sociology. This view, which has been called "oversocialized" (Wrong 1961; Granovetter 1985), leaped from observing that such commitments are a significant force in social life to the conclusion that all social action flows from them. The opposite extreme is to imagine that moral sense about the economy is entirely subordinated to and derived from some teleological quest for efficiency pursued by social systems, so that observed norms, though admitted to be important, can be assumed to have been selected out for their economic efficiency. The time has come to find a balanced account that is, to acknowledge the importance of such norms and conventions while fitting them into a broader frame of social theory.

For the economy, a beginning of this more balanced account is offered by the historian E. P. Thompson (1971) in his landmark essay on eighteenth-century English crowds and the meaning of the collective action they frequently took to protest and prevent the movement of essential foods such as bread. Thompson's point was twofold. One was that what appeared to be mass hysteria and highly nonrational crowd action could, upon closer observation, be seen as part of an organized and sensible campaign with goals easily understood in instrumental terms. But Thompson did not stop at this point, which fits well into a rational-choice framework; he also insisted that quite aside from their sensible goals, people in these crowds were also heavily animated by outrage at the way economic actors pursued their activities. They had definite beliefs about what were legitimate and non-legitimate actions, based on some sense of what individuals owe to the collectivities in which they are embedded—what he called their sense of "moral economy."

Note that in this formulation, Thompson, dealing as he was with hungry people, was not likely to fall into the expansionist reductionism of normative hegemony—to claim that norms and values alone motivated his actors. The purely instrumental aspect of food riots was tough to miss—crowds overturned and looted carts of bread headed for distant markets—and this led him implicitly to a formulation in which norms, identities, and instrumental rationality jointly motivate and shape action. To discover the process by which these perhaps incommensurable motivations act together was not part of his analysis, but it would have to be part of any general explanatory scheme in economic sociology.

Institutions and the Economy: Cooperation, Compliance, and Strategic Action as By-Products of Interactions and Intersections

Though my comments thus far have only scratched the surface of the question of how actors are motivated in confined social spaces, I move here to the second main issue I have raised: that such spaces rarely stand on their own, independent of larger network, institutional, cultural or historical trends. For example, while cooperation and compliance depend strongly on individual interpersonal relations and their history, they also depend on the overall configuration of social networks in which individuals are situated. Thus, two actors' previous relations only partly determine whether they will cheat one another; also important is whether the overall network that contains both is dense (news of malfeasance spreads quickly) or sparse (such news can be concealed for a long time).

But network structure is itself problematic, and can be seen as an outcome of larger social processes, if we rise to higher altitudes and observe "from the air" how networks have been constructed over time. In this regard, considerations of social boundaries—or as White (1992) has described it, coupling and decoupling—are central and have entered social theory in many different guises. The general and most overarching commonality in arguments about coupling and decoupling is the need to understand how resources, information, and influence do or do not move among well-defined and self-reproducing spheres of social structure. The concept of blocked movement is just as important as that of flow, as in White's emphasis on how problematic it is to "get action" and overcome the usual blockage in social affairs (1992). This emphasis is often conceived in terms of individual rational action—that is, how individuals can coordinate spheres or move across them to benefit themselves—but we can also use it in more macrostructural perspective to explain why societies function as they do by understanding the underlying boundaries and linkages.

These two emphases illustrate a duality between structure and agency. One example is my work (Granovetter 1973) on the "strength" of "weak ties," which concerns well-defined, cohesive groups that are connected to one another, if at all, by weak ties between members of different groups. From the strategic point of view, the individual with many such ties to other groups can turn diverse and nonredundant information to his own advantage, as in competition with others for desirable jobs. But note also that having a presence in multiple networks can mute and muddle one's sense of identity and interests as first one network and then another becomes more salient. The resulting ambiguity can be confusing for an actor, but it may also confer advantage in the form of inscrutability to others, as in Padgett and Ansell's (1993) analysis of the "multivocality" and resulting "robust action" on the part of Cosimo de Medici.

One larger-scale implication is that because social structures deficient in weak ties are fragmented and find collective action difficult, they may fail to mobilize politically (as in my 1973 argument about the West End of Boston, discussed in the following section). Conversely, the fact that weak ties channel novel information to new groups links the number of such ties to overall community outcomes such as scientific progress (Friedkin 1980; Collins 1974). Burt (1992) points out that the relevant units could just as well be collectivities like firms, and that one should pay attention to the "structural holes" formed in the network by the *absence* of certain connections. He emphasizes the advantage to individual actors or firms from exploiting such holes and bridging across actors who could not otherwise be in contact with one another. Burt focuses more sharply than I do in my work on weak ties on how this advantage relies on manipulating the structural features of the network rather than merely collecting resources (such as information) for one's own use. In this regard, Burt's argument lends itself better to understanding power and compliance, based on the control of uncertainty (as first proposed by Crozier 1963;

see Burt 1992, 26, 30). Sustaining this control over time depends, however, on preventing structural holes from being closed up.[7]

Economic anthropology has broached similar topics in different language, noting that in many societies not all goods are commensurable with one another; they can be divided up into mutually exclusive sets of those that are. Such a set is called a "sphere of exchange" (Bohannan and Dalton 1962; see also Espeland and Stevens 1998). Goods or services that are not commensurable cannot be exchanged in part because people do not understand how to think about such an exchange, or consider it highly inappropriate. All societies, however technically advanced, retain such distinctions; most of us, for example, could not conceive the appropriate price at which to sell our children (Radin 1996).

Looking at one sure source of profit in exchange—exploiting one's counterparts' ignorance of the usual exchange ratios—the Norwegian anthropologist Fredrik Barth (1967) highlighted the ability to breach previously separated spheres of exchange as a crucial element of economic success. He gives the example of the Fur, a Sudanese tribal group that considered wage labor shameful (that is, labor and money were incommensurable). Certain products, like millet and the beer that could be made from it, were produced mainly to be exchanged for communal labor, such as mutual help in house building. In a separate sphere of exchange, food, tools, and other commodities were exchanged for money. Arab merchants, outsiders to this social system, arrived and hired local workers to grow tomatoes, a cash crop, and paid them with beer. The value of the tomatoes far exceeded the cost of the beer, but this was unclear to the workers since in this setting neither beer nor labor were exchanged for cash. Because the traders were not bound by the group's moral injunctions to keep the spheres separate, they could exploit the "structural hole" formed by their connections into two separated spheres. Barth defined "entrepreneurship" precisely as the ability to create such new transactions.

A nearly identical conception of entrepreneurship has come independently from the Austrian School economist Israel Kirzner (1973). In some ways, Kirzner borrowed from his fellow Austrian Joseph Schumpeter, who had previously (1979 [1926]) defined entrepreneurship as the ability to create new opportunities by pulling together previously unconnected resources for a new economic purpose. Kirzner's formulation is closer to Barth's, however, in that he defines the entrepreneur as someone who connects previously isolated markets by arbitrage. Although the arbitrageur needs the Schumpeterian trait of alertness, he plays a different role from Schumpeter's swashbuckling entrepreneur who disrupts the existing equilibrium and shakes up the economic landscape with innovation, opening new opportunities. Kirzner's entrepreneur is, by contrast, a gray figure who spots price discrepancies across markets, which are a disequilibrium in the general picture, and profits by linking the markets and reestablishing—not disrupting—a general equilibrium characterized by price uniformity. Having made obvious to everyone the failure of linkage that has led to his profits, he cannot then further profit from this opportunity and instead must find some new discrepancy to exploit.

Barth and Kirzner both, then, see the entrepreneur through the lens of optimistic, midcentury modernization theory. He spots inefficiencies and simultaneously profits from and remediates them. In the end, the drag on economic progress imposed by differential prices or the inability to exchange certain commodities against one another is cleared away, and the economy can move full speed ahead. Uniform prices are established, and previously disconnected elements of markets are brought together so that factors of production can find their optimum use through the unhampered mobility and perfect information that this optimum requires.

But this view diverges from the empirical reality of entrepreneurs, who, if they in fact recognize that their advantage lies in sitting astride disconnected chunks of social structure and monopolizing the ability to coordinate whatever flows between them, could hardly be expected to step aside cheerfully and invite any and all to join in this coordination. Here the Schumpeterian image of the entrepreneur as larger-than-life seems more suitable—such as the Rockefellers and the Carnegies, who had to be legally restrained from their favorite activity, the "restraint of trade" (a special case of what White [1992] calls "blocking action"). Correspondingly, we should not expect the Arab traders of Barth's Sudanese case to go quietly into the good night of arbitrage, but instead to try to parlay their advantage into prominence and local power, depriving others of the same opportunity.[8]

This is a case where power in the economy does not rest on legitimacy but rather flows from what Weber thought of as the rather boring source of a "constellation of interests"—a position of monopoly. What makes it seem boring, however, is the tacit assumption that this position results from some previously given situation—a "natural monopoly," so to speak—whereas in fact, for the cases I have described, it results from the existing structure and from active agency. The entrepreneur has no chance without a fragmented structure, so that flows between chunks would be a source of profit. But it is not a trivial matter to prime the pump of these flows: the effort requires not only the cognitive brilliance highlighted by the tradition of Austrian economics but also the ability to mobilize social resources through networks of solidarity and obligation. Monopoly positions are actively created in situations where other outcomes are technically plausible. Yet, especially in situations where legitimacy is important, the mobilizer who sits at the center of disconnected networks may need to act behind the scenes so as not to appear excessively self-interested; this is part of what Padgett and Ansell, in their analysis of the rise of the Medici, call "robust action" (1993). The combination of mobilization strategy and structural conditions that make centralization and expansion possible is what cries out for theoretical analysis from economic sociology.

Note that the feat of bridging differentiated spheres depends on the spheres first being separate. In analyzing the evolution of societies over time, a typical theme of comparative sociology, from Durkheim (1984 [1893]) to Parsons (1966), has been the movement from homogeneous structures to those with a high level of functional and structural differentiation. In political sociology, this differentiation has occupied a place in theory that is related to our problem of explaining the success of economic entrepreneurs. Always central has been the question of how political leaders manage to assemble the resources required to organize a system of power, coordinating large numbers of people into what they all recognize as a single political unit. Shmuel Eisenstadt's (1963) analysis of the rise of what he called "centralized bureaucratic empires" is instructive. His argument was that for such empires to be sustainable, two conditions are necessary: leaders must have purely political goals that are autonomous from other social formations or institutions; and the society must have developed "limited but pervasive differentiation" (378) in its various institutional spheres. That is, economic, political, legal, religious, educational, and cultural activities must have become relatively detached from families and households and taken on a life of their own, typically measured by the extent of specialized roles and professional identities.

Differentiation is prerequisite in this argument because without it the resources that would-be rulers need to draw on to build and sustain their power are locked up or embedded in undifferentiated kinship or other socially defined groups and cannot be mobilized. Historically, economic thought has taken liquid resources as the normal situation, but in fact, analysis of how this liquidity arises is one of the most difficult and important tasks for social theory. To the extent that land, labor, or other items construable as commodities cannot be alienated freely but are part and parcel of complexes of obligation and symbolic meaning, rulers are stymied. Differentiation creates what Eisenstadt referred to as "free resources," which can be appropriated and moved from one sphere to another by those with the will and wit to do so. This is because specialized sectors could not have evolved in the first place without detaching resources from their primordial social sources; once so detached, even though now in the service of specialized role-occupants, the resources are understood to be alienable. The first rulers who could appropriate food or other goods in kind from putative "subjects" moved these goods out of their normal subsistence circuit for purposes of their own and turned this newly profitable transaction to the purpose of expanding their political enterprises. All successful taxation has this quality, and it is no accident that systematic analysis of the rise of modern states focuses on this in detail (for the case of Western Europe, see Tilly 1975).

Thus, the argument that there is something to be gained by those who can bridge discrete social units can be posed at different levels of generality. In the discussions of weak ties, or "structural holes," the units are concrete networks of individuals or organizations. With "spheres of exchange," the units are defined as the boundaries around certain types of exchange defined by the set of items commensurable with one another. In Eisenstadt's formulation, the units are the institutional spheres of a society. Any of these might be analyzed in a discussion of mobilizing for either economic or political advantage. Successful economic entrepreneurs most likely engage in bridging at multiple levels.

For example, Samuel Insull, whom I and collaborators have studied in detail in our analysis of the early American electricity industry (Granovetter and McGuire 1998), was one of the few early leaders of the industry to have extensive social contacts in the separated networks of tinkerer-inventors, financiers, and politicians, at both the local and national levels. The way he moved resources back and forth between these networks can also be described at a more abstract institutional level: he was the first to mobilize political resources successfully in the interest of economic formations in his particular industry. He also applied innovative financial instruments and accounting techniques, such as balloon depreciation, in such a way as to support his particular favored path of technical development. Although Insull shared these innovations within a relatively closed and elite circle, he actively combated the efforts of those outside that circle, such as sponsors of isolated generation, municipal ownership, or decentralized provision. His legacy was one of highly monopolized generation of power, consistent with the argument that successful entrepreneurs do all they can to prevent others from following in their footsteps. Many of the characteristics of the huge holding companies that Insull and his collaborators controlled by the late 1920s were similar to those described by Eisenstadt as "centralized bureaucratic empires."

More recently, one could argue that the spectacular success of Silicon Valley's information technology industry would not have occurred without the development of a new type of financing. In the older model, financiers were largely decoupled from the industries they supported: they knew little of the technical detail and stood apart from the industry's social and professional circles. In such a model, the only information required was the likelihood of loan repayment, which could be gauged from a general perusal of balance sheets with an assumption of stable markets over the relevant time horizon. This model did not lend itself, however, to rapid technical change, which could not be adequately evaluated with the usual financial tools. Instead, from the 1960s onward in Silicon Valley, a new model emerged that facilitated innovation: engineers and other industry members themselves took their windfall profits and became financiers. In alliance with traditional and new sources of wealth, they created the concept and practice of "venture capital," in which financiers are members of or closely linked to technical networks, take substantial equity positions in newly financed firms, sit on boards of directors, and sometimes play active management roles (see Kaplan 1999, chs. 6 and 7).

The original breach of spheres—moving large profits out of the industry itself, or the families of its members, and into financial circles and institutions—made the financial innovators fabulously wealthy, because they could now deploy these funds not simply in the firms that had produced them but in promising innovations originating elsewhere. Moreover, initial successes attracted huge new inflows of funds from limited partners such as pension funds and wealthy individuals, themselves with no obvious connection to technical circles, just as nineteenth-century American banks funded economic expansion by drawing in funds from beyond the kinship groups that had set them up on behalf of industries whose advance could no longer be sustained by family funds alone (Lamoreaux 1994).

Those who executed this strategy had no grand plan; they were simply clearheaded enough to take advantage of unique structural opportunities that were presented to them. The "traitorous eight" who left William Shockley's transistor lab in the 1950s to form Fairchild Semiconductor went on to set the pattern that would dominate much of Silicon Valley's economy—and to take a central role in their own right. But as with Cosimo de Medici, the structure that permitted them to do so resulted from a conjuncture of more or less unrelated historical events (Padgett and Ansell 1993), such as Shockley's atrocious management style, and the peculiar equity-vesting arrangements of Fairchild, which presented strong incentives for them to cash out and start new enterprises such as Intel and other now well-known "Fairchildren" (Cringely 1996).

The Social Construction of Economic Institutions

The first part of this chapter deals mainly with the first problem I identified: that incentives alone are a fragile base on which to erect explanatory structures. Even this relatively microlevel point moves the initial analytic focus away from individuals, since the crucial explanatory complements to incentives—trust, power, norms, and identity—are enacted in horizontal and vertical relations. Only by confining analysis to individuals can we easily sustain a narrow instrumentalist view. I then moved to the second problem, identifying the social spaces and institutions or institutional sectors within which people act and sketching arguments about how such spaces arise, how they are coupled or decoupled, and how resources flow between them.

Now I want to sketch how we might draw together these micro and macro strands. How do individual actions, conditioned by incentives, trust and cooperation, power and compliance, and norms and identities that affect these states and actions, come to be shaped by and themselves reshape larger institutional configurations? As before, the issues in economic action have a family resemblance to those in theories of political action. For example, in "The Strength of Weak Ties" (Granovetter 1973) I discussed Herbert Gans's (1963) paradox that residents of Boston's West End were devoted to their neighborhood and horrified at the prospect of its demolition for "urban renewal" but nevertheless failed to resist by uniting and mobilizing behind local leaders. Gans argued that working-class culture, with its distrust of self-seeking leaders, sharply discouraged membership in political groups. The instrumental theorist might instead see garden-variety free-riding—every individual hoping that others would bear the cost of mobilization. My riposte to Gans applies also to the free-rider argument: much might be explained by social structural constraints. I proposed that the neighborhood consisted of cohesive network clusters that were, however, highly decoupled from one another, and that this fragmentation made mobilization difficult, whatever the intentions of individuals.[9]

In more current terms, I suspected a deficit of individuals who could sit astride the West End's structural holes and send out weak ties into various cliques to mobilize resources and claim a leadership role. Gans's account suggests that mobilization did occur within cliques but could not spread beyond them. Distrust of leaders beyond an individual's network may have stemmed from the lack of a short chain of social relations between ego and such leaders. Where such chains exist, reassurance about a leader's intentions flows along them and is plausible in part because the individual can exert influence through the chain in ways that restrain self-seeking.[10] Here, in fact, we see issues of trust and power combined as they may often be—through the overall configurations of horizontal and vertical ties.

Economic formations should follow similar principles. AnnaLee Saxenian's (1994) account of Silicon Valley success puts special emphasis on the openness of networks and the free flow of people, ideas, and capital across the porous boundaries of firms. Her argument highlights several reasons for an extraordinary amount of trust among companies and individuals who are nominally in competition: loyalties lie more with occupational groups than with firms; because of rapid mobility, people in separate firms have often worked together before; and the culture of engineers encourages individuals to exhibit their technical prowess to one another, a macho goal that is often more important to self-esteem than high salary or job security.[11] In contrast, the Route 128 complex in the Boston metropolitan area shows an uncomfortable resemblance to Gans's West End. A collection of what Gernot Grabher (1991) has called (in a German context) "cathedrals in the desert," these firms have tried to be self-sufficient, avoided the sharing of ideas or personnel, and ultimately found this strategy to be self-defeating in a fast-moving technical environment.[12] The successful model resulted from complex intersections of firms, occupational groups, and social networks, and from a mobilization of goals that were a mixture of personal pride, social standing, and financial gain, harnessed to one another in ways that led to achievements no single goal alone could have sustained.

Given the extensive network connections, there are few structural holes in such a setting. There is correspondingly little in the way of power centers among Silicon Valley industrial firms, even though some have grown large and important in revenues. But in the supporting infrastructure, such as finance and law, there is a much more striking stratification and hierarchy of power. Though the systematic research remains to be done on structures of status and influence, informal accounts suggest that having the right venture capitalist (for example, Kleiner, Perkins, Caulfield and Byers, or KP in local parlance) or the right law firm (for example, Wilson, Sonsini, Goodrich and Rosati) is a great advantage; such firms therefore have the power to dictate terms favorable to themselves. Historical accounts suggest that this dominance traces back to earlier periods when these leading firms faced a fragmented resource base and were unusually successful in mobilizing across separate networks and sources, as I briefly discussed earlier in the context of the relative coupling and decoupling of finance and industry.

Another example illustrates and further develops these themes. Richard Locke's *Remaking the Italian Economy* (1995) analyzes contrasting outcomes from the 1970s and 1980s restructuring of the two major Italian automakers, Fiat and Alfa-Romeo. When Fiat restructured by vigorously repressing labor unions, so much industrial conflict arose that the entire region suffered. Alfa-Romeo had a more complex negotiated process with a happier regional economic ending. Locke attributes this difference to how networks of political actors and associations were structured in Turin and Milan. In Turin, Fiat's base, political actors and associations mainly clustered in two opposing camps, one associated with business and the other with labor. Each camp had strong internal links, but there were few connections between them—a pattern that Locke refers to as "polarized networks." By contrast, Milan's pattern was "polycentric": associations and interest groups formed a dense network and were linked to one another through many horizontal ties. In polycentric regions, he argues, frequent communication and the larger number of intermediaries mute conflict and keep lines of communications open. Trust is facilitated in such a structure, whereas the absence of intermediaries in Turin stymied the attempts by moderates on both sides to reach compromise. Being familiar with the other side, intermediaries humanize its members and provide a line of communication for tentative discussions. In the absence of such familiarity, as in Turin, to express a sentiment of compromise toward the other side looks implausible and even treasonous. Such overtures would falter in any case, since there would be no obvious, known, and trusted interlocutors to receive them. So the structural situation creates cognitive and normative pressures that reinforce the separation and make conflict more likely.

In his analysis of the textile industry, Locke (1995) uses these distinctions to understand why the widely heralded success of small-firm networks in Italy in fact seems subject to sharp regional variations: these networks fail in some areas while flying high in others. He suggests that whether such a form works is not an abstract matter but depends on its compatibility with the local social and political networks. In particular, the rather polarized and hierarchical networks of Prato turned out to be much less fertile ground in the long run for this form than those of polycentric areas such as Biella. (For similar arguments on the auto industry, but at a national level, see Biggart and Guillén 1999.)

Here we veer into the territory of "social capital," but the puzzle from the point of view of Putnam's (1993) argument is that all these cities had a rich associational life, supposedly the progenitor of the norms, networks, and trust that compose this capital. The difference was that Turin's and Prato's associations were structured vertically, with few ties across to other types of association but with further vertical ties reaching out of the region to national parties or other organizations; Milan and Biella, by contrast, were richer in horizontal ties, of the sort that mute conflict in the one case and facilitate the myriad details of interfirm cooperation in the other. So it is not just the density of associational life that matters for economic (or political) outcomes but the structure of its ties (as also emphasized in, for example, Nan Lin's [2000] theory of social capital and in Portes and Mooney, this volume.)

These points link to an older tradition of thought, which might be called "neo-Tocquevillian,"[13] that emphasizes the importance for community, democracy, and other political and economic outcomes of associations and "cross-cutting ties." In Seymour Martin Lipset's classic formulation (1963, 77):

> Multiple and politically inconsistent affiliations, loyalties and stimuli reduce the emotion and aggressiveness involved in political choice. For example, in contemporary Germany, a working-class Catholic, pulled in two directions [that is, toward his class and toward his religion], will most probably vote Christian-Democratic, but is much more tolerant of the Social Democrats than the average middle-class Catholic. The chances for stable democracy are enhanced to the extent that groups and individuals have a number of cross-cutting, politically relevant affiliations.

More should be said in comparison of these older and newer theoretical traditions, but for now a couple of points seem interesting. First, the midcentury literature on "cross-cutting ties," emerging as it did from a structural-functional view, stressed the role of these ties in conflict reduction (see, for example, the anthropological tradition represented by Gluckman 1965). The very existence, however, of cross-cutting ties, which I would characterize as some level of coupling between discrete networks or institutions, also provides channels through which a strategic actor may leverage weak attachments across segments so as to assemble resources into a larger social entity. If that entity is a political structure, we might challenge the idea that such a pattern enhances democracy, since political entrepreneurs might find this the most fertile ground on which to assemble empires or other autocratic systems. If the larger entity is an economic organization, such as a business group, conglomerate, or strategic alliance, then we are talking about the organization of economic influence, such as that possessed by the Schumpeterian entrepreneur. Here we might think of Alfred Sloan pulling together the bits and pieces assembled earlier, but only lightly coupled by William Durant, into General Motors.

Thus, we may distinguish three kinds of structures and corresponding potentials. The highly decoupled structure, without cross-cutting ties, might be more prone to conflict when interests collide, but less likely to ever be pulled together into a social phenomenon of larger scale. The weakly coupled structure might lead to more consensual outcomes when conflict arises, but in the presence of an active entrepreneur, it might lend itself best to the amassing of power or influence over a large social entity. The highly coupled structure has, in effect, less structure. Though perhaps the most amenable to a high level of cooperation, it might also be even less likely than the first type to ever be highly coordinated from a center.

This rough typology has the advantage of stressing structure yet leaving an important role for agency. I take the structures and their connectedness as given, but this is only for convenience of exposition. Certainly one of the most interesting challenges is determining where these patterns originate. One of the most problematic aspects of early social capital formulations was the idea that current political outcomes are determined by the communal patterns of eight hundred years earlier. Overcoming this problem requires some focused historical argument about what determines network structures and about the extent to which they may be altered by strategic actors who understand how to assemble resources.

Summary and Discussion

In this chapter, I have emphasized the need for theory in economic sociology that moves away from reductionist conceptions and purely instrumental formulations. Much that is distinctive in sociological thought lends itself to this movement: the stress on multiple motives, on mixtures of instrumental and non-instrumental action, and on the importance of trust, power, and norms at a small-scale level of interaction. Larger-scale sociology, with its emphasis on the intersection of social networks and institutional arrangements and on the intricate interplay of structure and agency through coupling and decoupling, presents additional reasons to be suspicious of reductionist accounts, as well as a positive argument about how economic outcomes arise.

I have purposely *not* argued that what is distinctive about structural economic sociology is its emphasis on the embeddedness of action in social networks. Although I naturally believe that many of the important contributions of economic sociology stem from its interest in network analysis (Granovetter 1985), a focus on the mechanics of networks alone is not sufficiently distinctive theoretically from instrumentalist theories to lead us toward the more complex synthesis that we seek for understanding the economy. Instead, we need to work harder at connecting social network analysis to the central theoretical problems of sociology. In this regard, this chapter should be seen as a continuation and elaboration of the research program proposed in my 1985 paper on embeddedness.[14] The crucial point is that fundamental concepts like solidarity, power, norms, and identity cannot be understood except in relational terms; their very definition relies on social relationships, and they are produced in social networks, as is well understood in the classic works of Durkheim, Weber, Simmel, and Marx. In 1959 Kingsley Davis labeled as a myth the idea that "functional analysis" was a separate method in sociology and anthropology; structural sociologists must similarly move away from a sectarian view of network analysis as a separate theory or method. Its power is that it is coterminous with the central concerns of any institutional analysis, of which the economy is a special case.

If the comparative advantage of relational analysis is its indispensability for understanding trust, solidarity, cooperation, power, domination, compliance, norms, and identity, it does not follow that we should abandon the sophisticated analysis of how individuals pursue incentives in well-defined social spaces. This set of arguments, pursued for generations by cadres of many of the best and brightest social scientists, has reached a high level of refinement. The most daunting agenda for a unified social science is to integrate such analyses with the more contextually complex arguments of structural sociology. It is a rather special case where context stands still and is decoupled from rational action in a clearly identified social space, yet this special case has commanded the vast majority of intellectual resources poured into understanding the economy. The challenge for the new century is to build theory for the more general case where contexts, structures, and individual actions interact and change together. The world has not stood still, and theory has a lot of catching up to do.

For their valuable comments on an earlier draft, I am indebted to Randall Collins, my discussant at the Second Annual Economic Sociology Conference at the University of Pennsylvania, March 4, 2000, the other conference participants, and Richard Swedberg, Kiyoteru Tsutsui, and Valery Yakubovich.

Notes

1. See my exchange with Gibbons in Granovetter (1999) or such accounts as Padgett and Ansell (1993).

2. But this contribution remains unrealized, by and large, because we have so far paid surprisingly little attention to the details of interaction or even to why people pursue attachments, leaving these issues to psychological social psychology. The mixture of motives I cite may appear amenable to a purely instrumental argument of the sort made in rational-choice theories, if one "merely" conceives of actors as having not only economic but also social needs in their "objective functions." Proper consideration of this point would require a full discussion of whether in their social interaction people are what might be called "consequentialists" (see Sen and Williams 1982, 4). In other words, to what extent is their social action undertaken as a means to an end, where the end might be social approval as well as economic gain? Such a discussion is beyond my scope here, but I doubt whether it is possible to capture much of the texture of social life in such a formulation.

3. Such socializing behavior, in Weber's fourfold classification of types of social action, has stronger elements of "affectual" or "habitual" than of purposive (*zweckrational*) action (Weber 1968 [1921], ch. 1). Although he meant it in a somewhat different way, it is hard to resist mentioning Keynes's notion of "animal spirits" as a motive for partygoing; see the illuminating analysis of Keynes's usage in DiMaggio (this volume).

4. I claim no originality for this formulation of the problem of trust; it runs, for example, through most of the essays in Gambetta (1988). But despite this general agreement in the more or less philosophical literature, analyses of the economy continue to be dominated by attempts to reduce trust to incentive alignment.

   In practice, economic actors often find themselves in situations where trust in the sense I have proposed is supplemented by a clear assessment of incentives; this is what Alejandro Portes and Julia Sensenbrenner (1993, 1325) has called "enforceable trust." A sophisticated analysis of trust would have to move in the direction of understanding more fully such combinations of driving forces, since neither incentives nor pure trust would suffice in such situations.

5. Although, as pointed out by Neil Fligstein (this volume), some economic sociology that builds on network analysis assumes rational actors, I be-

lieve that my discussion of trust and my subsequent analysis of power and compliance show that network arguments lead directly to doubts about this assumption.

6. In discussions of behavior activated by norms and values, Weber's conception of "value-rational" action as action pursued for its own sake rather than as a means to an end—as in the pursuit of truth, beauty, or religious enlightenment—reflects the most radical departure from a consequentialist epistemology. But in his obsessively cautious way, Weber tempers this radicalism by the observation that pure value-rational behavior is rare (1968 [1921], ch. 1). A broader swath through the field of self-interest theories is cut by Amartya Sen (1977), who observes that many actions in the economy may be propelled by what he calls "commitments" to certain goals. Thus, even though Sen remains within a broadly instrumental conception of action, his main point is that the consequences that actors seek may be contrary to their economic or other self-interest if they are propelled to this goal by value commitments.

7. More sustained analysis of such efforts is needed. For an excellent account of recent theory and research on structural holes, see Burt (this volume).

8. Unfortunately, Barth's (1967, 172) account breaks off without following the later activity of these innovators; he does note, however, that resistance to their activity was beginning to emerge.

9. This seemed the more plausible since studies of other Boston neighborhoods that were facing urban renewal in the same period but had less fragmented social structures showed effective mobilization against this same threat, even though residents were also working-class and presumably equally rational.

10. See the classic account in William Whyte's *Street Corner Society* (1943) of how Boston's North End residents used their local networks to get a playing field erected.

11. What we might call "nerd culture" deserves more extensive theoretical and historical attention. Life inside Thomas Edison's laboratory sounds in some accounts (for example, Josephson 1959) strikingly similar to the supposedly unique atmosphere of hackers writing code all day and night, sustained by no more than gallons of cola and indulging only occasionally in the luxury of sleep, and then on the spot rather than in a separate location. Gavin Wright's (1998) account of American industrial growth in the nineteenth century suggests a long history of networks of male tinkerers, early "nerd" prototypes busily impressing one another, as an integral part of the progress of mechanical invention and innovation. Their propensity to travel around, showing off their achievements, may have been a crucial factor in accelerating technical developments.

One identifying characteristic of the nerd is awkwardness in social relationships, compared to facility with equations and mechanical devices. A common observation is that this technical facility becomes a way for people who are otherwise awkward to communicate with one another and achieve status and community. This observation is not time-bound but can be linked to very general themes in the history and sociology of science and technology. The French tradition in the sociology of science, for example, stresses that the networks that matter are not merely social but "socio-technical," that is, machines or techniques can be nodes that connect individuals to one another (Callon 1989). In his sociology of philosophy, Randall Collins (1998, 536) observes that technologies "evolve by tinkering. Earlier machines are modified, adapted . . . combined with other lineages of technology. Hence they may be conceived of as networks—indeed as genealogies—in their own right; there is a crucial connection *from machine to machine*, and not merely from person to person." Thus, if tinkerers are not communicating with one another through the medium of machines, technical development will slow or stop. "Boyle's vacuum pump could not be successfully imitated by anyone who had not physically used an earlier exemplar" (Collins 1998, 993, n. 10), and in general the "tacit knowledge" required to improve equipment requires face-to-face contact transmitted by a personal network (Collins 1974). Thus, the details of nerd networks and their coupling and decoupling may have a substantial impact on technical development. For Silicon Valley, see especially accounts of the central role of the "Homebrew Computer Club" in the development of the personal computer (Cringely 1996).

12. This argument seems strongly supported by the 1998 demise of the once-legendary Digital Equipment Corporation, which was bought out by up-start Compaq Computer.

13. I am indebted to Carlos Forment for this usage.

14. I ruminate further on the progression of my research program over time in my "Introduction for the French Reader" in Granovetter (2000). The unpublished English version is available on request.

References

Axelrod, Robert. 1984. *The Evolution of Cooperation.* New York: Basic Books.

Barth, Fredrik. 1967. "Economic Spheres in Darfur." In *Themes in Economic Anthropology,* edited by Raymond Firth. London: Tavistock.

Biggart, Nicole, and Mauro Guillén. 1999. "Developing Difference: Social Organization and the Rise of the Auto Industries of South Korea, Taiwan, Spain, and Argentina." *American Sociological Review* 64(October): 722–47.

Blau, Peter. 1963. *Exchange and Power in Social Life.* New York: Wiley.

Bohannan, Paul, and George Dalton, eds. 1962. *Markets in Africa.* Evanston, Ill.: Northwestern University Press.

Boorman, Scott. 1975. "A Combinatorial Optimization Model for the Transmission of Job Information Through Contact Networks." *Bell Journal of Economics* 6(1): 216–49.

Burawoy, Michael. 1979. *Manufacturing Consent: Changes in the Labor Process Under Monopoly Capitalism.* Chicago: University of Chicago Press.

Burt, Ronald. 1992. *Structural Holes.* Cambridge, Mass.: Harvard University Press.

Callon, Michel. 1989. "Society in the Making: The Study of Technology as a Tool for Sociological Analysis." In *The Social Construction of Technological Systems,* edited by Wiebe E. Bijker, Thomas P. Hughes, and Trevor J. Pinch. Cambridge, Mass.: MIT Press.

Collins, Harry. 1974. "The TEA Set: Tacit Knowledge and Scientific Networks." *Science Studies* 4: 165–86.

Collins, Randall. 1998. *The Sociology of Philosophies.* Cambridge, Mass.: Harvard University Press.

Cringely, Robert X. 1996. *Accidental Empires.* New York: HarperCollins.

Crozier, Michel. 1963. *The Bureaucratic Phenomenon.* Chicago: University of Chicago Press.

Davis, Kingsley. 1959. "The Myth of Functional Analysis as a Special Method in Sociology and Anthropology." *American Sociological Review* 24(December): 757–72.

Durkheim, Emile. 1984 [1893]. *The Division of Labor in Society.* New York: Free Press.

Eisenstadt, Shmuel N. 1963. *The Political Systems of Empires.* New York: Free Press.

Espeland, Wendy, and Mitchell Stevens. 1998. "Commensuration as a Social Process." *Annual Review of Sociology* 24: 313–43.

Freeland, Robert. 1996. "The Myth of the M-Form: Governance, Consent, and Organizational Change." *American Journal of Sociology* 102(September): 483–526.

Friedkin, Noah. 1980. "A Test of the Structural Features of Granovetter's 'Strength of Weak Ties' Theory." *Social Networks* 2: 411–22.

Gambetta, Diego. 1988. *Trust.* Oxford: Blackwell.

Gans, Herbert. 1963. *The Urban Villagers.* Glencoe, Ill.: Free Press.

Gluckman, Max. 1965. *Politics, Law, and Ritual in Tribal Society.* Chicago: Aldine.

Grabher, Gernot. 1991. "Rebuilding Cathedrals in the Desert." In *Regions Reconsidered,* edited by E. Bergman, G. Maier, and F. Tödtling. London: Mansell.

Granovetter, Mark. 1973. "The Strength of Weak Ties." *American Journal of Sociology* 78(May): 1360–80.

———. 1985. "Economic Action and Social Structure: The Problem of Embeddedness." *American Journal of Sociology* 91(November): 481–510.

———. 1990. "The Old and the New Economic Sociology: A History and an Agenda." In *Beyond the Marketplace: Rethinking Economy and Society,* edited by Roger Friedland and A. F. Robertson. New York: Aldine.

———. 1995. *Getting a Job: A Study of Contacts and Careers.* 2nd ed. Chicago: University of Chicago Press.

———. 1999. "Coase Encounters and Formal Models: Taking Gibbons Seriously." *Administrative Science Quarterly* 44: 158–62.

———. 2000. *Le marché autrement: Les réseaux dans l'économie.* Edited and translated by Isabelle This-Saint-Jean and Jean-Louis Laville. Paris: Desclée de Brouwer.

Granovetter, Mark, and Patrick McGuire. 1998. "The Making of an Industry: Electricity in the United States." In *The Laws of the Markets,* edited by Michel Callon. Oxford: Blackwell.

Granovetter, Mark, and Charles Tilly. 1988. "Inequality and Labor Processes." In *The Handbook of Sociology,* edited by Neil Smelser. Beverly Hills, Calif.: Sage Publications.

Hirschman, Albert. 1982. "Rival Interpretations of Market Society: Civilizing, Destructive, or Feeble?" *Journal of Economic Literature* 20(4): 1463–84.

Josephson, Matthew. 1959. *Edison: A Biography.* New York: McGraw-Hill.

Kaplan, David. 1999. *The Silicon Boys.* New York: Morrow.

Kirzner, Israel. 1973. *Competition and Entrepreneurship.* Chicago: University of Chicago Press.

Lamoreaux, Naomi. 1994. *Insider Lending: Banks, Personal Connections, and Economic Development in Industrial New England.* New York: Cambridge University Press.

Lin, Nan. 2000. *Social Capital: A Theory of Social Structure and Action.* New York: Cambridge University Press.

Lipset, Seymour M. 1963. *Political Man.* Garden City, N.Y.: Doubleday/Anchor.

Locke, Richard. 1995. *Remaking the Italian Economy.* Ithaca, N.Y.: Cornell University Press.

Olson, Mancur. 1965. *The Logic of Collective Action.* Cambridge, Mass.: Harvard University Press.

Padgett, John, and Christopher Ansell. 1993. "Robust Action and the Rise of the Medici, 1400–1434." *American Journal of Sociology* 98(6): 1259–1319.

Parsons, Talcott. 1966. *Societies: Comparative and Evolutionary Perspectives.* Englewood Cliffs, N.J.: Prentice-Hall.

Portes, Alejandro, and Julia Sensenbrenner. 1993. "Embeddedness and Immigration: Notes on the Social Determinants of Economic Action." *American Journal of Sociology* 98(6): 1320–50.

Putnam, Robert. 1993. *Making Democracy Work.* Princeton, N.J.: Princeton University Press.

Radin, Margaret. 1996. *Contested Commodities.* Cambridge, Mass.: Harvard University Press.

Saxenian, AnnaLee. 1994. *Regional Advantage: Culture and Competition in Silicon Valley and Route 128.* Cambridge, Mass.: Harvard University Press.

Schumpeter, Joseph. 1979 [1926]. *The Theory of Economic Development.* New Brunswick, N.J.: Transaction Press.

Sen, Amartya. 1977. "Rational Fools." *Philosophy and Public Affairs* 6(4): 317–44.

Sen, Amartya, and Bernard Williams. 1982. *Utilitarianism and Beyond.* New York: Cambridge University Press.

Thompson, E. P. 1971. "The Moral Economy of the English Crowd in the Eighteenth Century." *Past and Present* 50(February): 76–136.

Tilly, Charles. 1975. *The Formation of National States in Western Europe.* Princeton, N.J.: Princeton University Press.

Weber, Max. 1968 [1921]. *Economy and Society.* New York: Bedminster Press.

White, Harrison. 1992. *Identity and Control: A Structural Theory of Social Action.* Princeton, N.J.: Princeton University Press.

Whyte, William F. 1943. *Street Corner Society.* Chicago: University of Chicago Press.

Williamson, Oliver. 1975. *Markets and Hierarchies.* New York: Free Press.

Wright, Gavin. 1998. "Can a Nation Learn?: American Technology as a Network Phenomenon." In *Learning by Doing,* edited by Naomi Lamoreaux, Daniel Raff, and Peter Temin. Chicago: University of Chicago Press.

Wrong, Dennis. 1961. "The Oversocialized Conception of Man in Modern Sociology." *American Sociological Review* 26(2): 183–96.

= Chapter 3 =

Agreements, Disagreements, and Opportunities in the "New Sociology of Markets"

NEIL FLIGSTEIN

T HERE ARE signs everywhere that economic sociology is being constituted as a field. In 1994 Neil Smelser and Richard Swedberg edited the *Handbook of Economic Sociology*. It is nearly impossible to pick up a copy of one of the main sociology journals without finding a paper that claims to be a contribution to the new economic sociology. Conferences are being held in the United States and around the world on the topic. In the spring of 2000, the American Sociological Association officially formed a section called "Economic Sociology."

There are three purposes for this chapter. First, I want to consider some of the hard-won agreements that have been forged by scholars in this field to date. Second, in spite of some impressive achievements, I want to consider what I think are some of the major disagreements that exist. I want to appeal to scholars who are interested in doing this kind of work to think hard about our many disagreements in order to make progress on these issues. I am particularly interested in reaching out to younger scholars who are thinking about entering the field; it is up to them to resolve some of the dilemmas and debates through their own research practice. Finally, I conclude by briefly considering the problem of how economic sociology might become relevant to students, managers, policymakers, and activists.

There are three kinds of agreements that have been reached in the field of economic sociology; they have mostly to do with boundary questions about the types of phenomena under the purview of the field. I would argue that scholars share a common definition of the phenomena covered by the field of economic sociology, a sociological definition of what a market is, and some agreement over some of the main mechanisms by which market processes are embedded in society.

But in spite of these loose boundary conditions, there are deep disagreements as well. This chapter is mostly concerned with the sociology of markets as opposed to the more general problems of economic sociology, although some of my comments obviously apply there. I identify three interrelated problems about which there is a great deal of disagreement: the problem of efficiency, the problem of which social institutions constitute markets, and the problem of scholars paying greater attention to a more theoretically elaborated view of market processes in their work.

These problems have greatly affected what we have studied so far and caused us to miss opportunities to make more progress. To do so, our field must finally come into its own: it is time to stop focusing on what economists think and to figure out what we think. Scholars need to orient themselves to one another's concerns and try to be clearer about where they stand. Without doing this, it is difficult to see how economic sociology offers an alternative vision from economics.

I have an ambitious goal in mind for the field. I expect us to find a way to contribute to societal debates about welfare states, globalization, the role of financial integration in the world economy, and important questions like the causes of economic growth in the developed and developing world. I would like us to find a way to attach a normative set of concerns to our theoretical ones. I know that my goal is not shared by everyone, but I think that if we have a good sociological analysis of how society and the economy work, then we will have insight into how society and the economy should work.

Agreements

What is economic sociology? I offer a very simple definition of a field in sociology: a group of scholars who define one another as their relevant audience. They pay attention to the work of others doing what they consider similar work, and they address the questions raised by that work. The scholars who are defining the field of economic sociology have a broad, Polanyian view of its subject matter (Polanyi 1957, 1977). Karl Polanyi thought that the substantive meaning of the term "economic" was the entire social organization of material life.

Economic sociology should be concerned with all aspects of material production, including the organization of production and the organization of consumption. Thus, households, labor markets, firms, and product markets are all legitimate objects of study. (For an elaboration of this argument, see Zelizer, ch. 5, this volume.) Obviously, production and consumption have cultural components. Actors in different settings organize production according to local meanings and their common history. Economic sociology is not concerned with markets only as mechanisms of allocation. Like Polanyi, economic sociology views markets as one mechanism of allocation in society, and other factors, like reciprocity (people engaged in social relations helping one another) and redistribution (governments acting to equalize opportunities and outcomes), as equally important in capitalist societies. Economic sociology has brought together what were the fields of political economy, development, organizational theory, stratification, network theory, and the sociology of culture and pushed scholars in these fields to begin paying attention to one another's insights.

Most of my comments in this chapter pertain more narrowly to what I call the sociology of markets, which is mostly focused on the problem of the organization of production. This focus diminishes neither the importance of the rest of economic sociology nor its obvious relations to production, but we have to delimit the topic in order to move beyond broad generalizations. Markets can be thought of as social arenas where producers and consumers of goods meet. The main sociological problem in making sense of markets is to think about how producer and consumer social relationships are structured. The main goal of a sociology of markets should be to view what goes on in markets between producers and consumers as an example of the social processes that occur in all social arenas. The general theoretical tools of sociology can be applied to market situations, albeit adjusted to the specific conditions of market interactions. (Mark Granovetter makes a similar point in his contribution to this volume.)

A widely accepted sociological definition of markets derives from Harrison White's definition (1981): markets represent the "self-reproducing role structures of producers." The idea of a market as a "self-reproducing role structure" causes us to focus on the social relations between market participants. Although this definition does not tell us explicitly what the mechanisms are that could produce self-reproducing role structures, it does raise this question as the explicit object of study. It forces us to think about the social relations in particular markets and their ability to become self-reproducing. (White develops his more recent position on these issues in his contribution to this volume.)

It is this definition that creates a unique space for the sociology of markets, different from the space occupied by economics. In White's model, it is the firms that are the producers who watch one another on a period-to-period basis and decide how much to produce and of what quality. It is the ability of actors to do this that sometimes produces market stability (that is, self-reproduction of those actors). White's definition pushes us to understand what actors are paying attention to (raising the question of local culture), who they are paying attention to (social relations between competitors), and how stable markets emerge (how firms come to reproduce themselves by choosing a niche to occupy vis-à-vis one another).

As I suggested earlier, a sociological theory of economic sociology and markets should depend on a more general sociological theory of institutions. If we take seriously the idea that action in markets is just like action in any other sphere of social life, then our general theory of society ought to inform our theory of markets. Market institutions are social institutions, and to the degree that we as sociologists can contribute to discussions about social institutions, those same theoretical elements ought to inform our theory of markets. Unfortunately, sociologists lack a theory of society or institutions to which we all subscribe. It is useful, however, to review the relatively small set of social institutions structuring markets that the literature in the field has identified.

The most general view is provided by Granovetter's (1985) notion of "embeddedness." For Granovetter, networks or social relationships exist in all market interactions. These define who the actors are and the nature of their social relations. Networks indicate reciprocity in social relations and operate to generate trust between actors. Much empirical work invokes embeddedness or networks. For most studies, "trust" is not the only reason that social relationships exist. Scholars frequently invoke networks as sources of information, resource dependence, and power. This is an issue to which I return.

A second mechanism sees a reciprocal relation between social relationships and shared meanings. Actors interpret the actions of others with whom they have social relationships. These interpretations come to frame their subsequent actions. Wayne Baker, Robert Faulkner, and Gary Fisher (1998) and Joel Podolny (1993) show that producers and consumers in particular markets share understandings about the status hierarchy of producers and about the meanings that produce and sustain that hierarchy. Baker and his colleagues are interested in how that hierarchy becomes undermined over time. This is a kind of situation—a power structure of producers operating under a given set of understandings—that I have called a "conception of control" (Fligstein 1990, 1996).

Scholars have been concerned with the effect on the organization of markets of sets of rules that define broader institutions, such as property rights, laws, and means to enforce contracts. Douglass North (1990) presents this view from a more economic perspective. Other work (Fligstein 1990; Campbell and Lindberg 1990) has shown how the struggle over these issues greatly affected the emergence of stable markets. The problem of defining legal and illegal forms of competition is at the core of making markets work. Similarly, the division of property rights determines the nature of the relationships between firms, banks, owners, and workers (Roe 1994).

Governments fulfill a variety of roles to make markets possible (Block 1996). Governments can successfully aid development in a wide variety of ways—some interventionist, and some more regulatory. Governments can also produce more negative results for economic development, particularly when they lack the organizational capacity to intervene effectively or are captured by rent-seeking interests (Evans 1995). In addition, governments operate to set the rules of the game and legal frameworks and act as mediators (Fligstein 2001).

Finally, there has been a great deal of interest in sorting out the relationships between various economic elites. This interest has been stimulated mostly from a Marxist perspective that seeks to understand how the owners of capital are organized (Zeitlin 1974). Much of this debate began as an attempt to prove that capitalist firms in the United States were not controlled by managers but remained firmly in the grasp of owners, particularly families. The debate moved on to consider more closely who the owners were—families or banks and financial institutions (Kotz 1978; Mintz and Schwartz 1985). Others have been interested in considering how these relations define a "ruling class" (Useem 1984). Finally, there is a new literature that tries to use board-of-director interlocks as the mechanism of class coordination (Palmer et al. 1987, 1995). This literature has also become less strident in its view of these linkages as being about the representatives of capital; it has come to see them less as mechanisms of control and more as the way in which firms learn about what is going on in the population of other large firms (Mizruchi and Stearns 1988; Davis and Stout 1992).

Disagreements

Most of the disagreements stem from differences in opinion about the mechanisms that go into making markets "self-reproducing role structures." The observant reader can easily conclude that the mechanisms I have described imply very different social theories. They also seem quite orthogonal in their views of what is to be studied about firms in markets and the hypotheses for which such research provides evidence. I would like to show the deeper disagreements that these different mechanisms raise by considering how they play out across critical issues.

The Problem of Efficiency

In economics, what unites all of the different theories is the idea that social structures, be they firms, networks, or long-term contracts, are set up to attain efficient outcomes (defined as the optimal allocation of resources).[1] The sociology of markets may be able to carve out for itself the problem of the social structuring of markets and their reproducibility. But doing so immediately raises questions about how this happens, and to what end. We need to ask whether sociologists are simply saying something with which economists already agree: that social structures should aid the efficient allocation of resources, and that if they do not, they should be removed as impediments to that allocation. There is a deep difference of opinion here in sociology. Delineating three possible positions in the sociology of markets may help us answer this question.

Some scholars clearly think that the social structuring of markets is about efficiency (Burt 1983; Hannan and Freeman 1989; Uzzi 1996; Powell, Koput, and Smith-Doerr 1996). Social relationships in markets promote efficiency because they make the costs of doing business lower in a number of different ways. For example, some think that actors engage in long-term relationships that produce trust and lower costs (Uzzi 1997). Others see the social structure of relationships as being about the invention of new forms of contracting, such that firms organized as networks can not only be lean and mean but quick to enter new markets and ease the costs of exiting because they do not make long-term commitments (Powell 1990). Still others focus on particular relationships, like the links between banks and firms in Germany and Japan (Lincoln, Gerlach, and Takahashi 1992; Albert 1991). These views imply that patient investors are willing to invest in "market" share and are not so worried about short-term profits (Gerlach 1992). Finally, some see relationships as co-opting resource dependencies, so that firms secure capital and legitimacy to aid their survival (Burt 1983; Stuart 1998; Stuart, Huo Huang, and Hybels 1999).

A second position derives from the versions of political economy that stress the role of elites in market processes. In this view, economic elites, centered on families, and common social institutions, like banks and financial investors, reproduce their power and privilege by controlling the assets of firms and the lending practices of banks. In the United States, these elites maintain their position in society by contributing to both Democrats and Republicans in political processes. In this model, the question of the efficiency of social relations is somewhat orthogonal to what is going on. Instead, the reproduction of the power of elites through the social structures of ownership and interlocking directorates preserves a particular system of capitalism.

The third approach is one that I have written on extensively (Fligstein 1990, 1996, 2001). There is a long history in organizational theory of using the idea of "effectiveness," as opposed to "efficiency," as the criterion by which to evaluate how well the social structuring of markets works (Meyer and Rowan 1977). Organizations are effective when they find ways to survive. Attaining allocative efficiency is not the only way they survive (although it is one possible strategy if actors can figure out how to do it). Instead, actors who control firms basically do anything they can to survive. Their main effort is directed at finding ways to stabilize their relations with competitors, suppliers, customers, and governments.

The "self-reproducing role structure" that characterizes production markets is, in my perspective, a social structure with a status hierarchy of producers. In this hierarchy, large and dominant firms control the market by engaging in forms of competition that preserve their position and allow smaller firms to find niches. The hierarchy is based on a set of understandings held by all market actors about what their possible moves "mean" and about the purpose of these moves: to reproduce the positions of firms. This perspective immediately raises the issue of how such arrangements come into existence and what undermines them. Social relations index the system of power in the sense that they are mechanisms by which actors produce stability in the face of the competition engendered by capitalism. The "effectiveness" alternative rethinks the problem of market reproducibility as one not just about finding efficiency, but also about finding stable relations between producers to promote organizational survival (Fligstein 1996, 2001).

There are difficult problems for all three positions. The view of social relationships as efficiency has two main problems. First, it is never entirely clear which social relationships are necessary to generate efficiency. Acting on trust, co-opting resource dependence, or using networks to gain information or for learning are different kinds of social relations that may lead to the efficient allocation of resources. It is never clear in most analyses how we know that the particular market social relation chosen by the scholar for discussion is the one pivotal to market efficiency in that market.

Moreover, the exact meaning of the relationships is often open to interpretation. So, for example, Toby Stuart and his colleagues (1999) show that small firms in the computer industry that link up with important large firms and venture capitalists are more likely to survive than firms that do not. In these authors' view, these linkages could signify "legitimacy" (a signal to others that these firms are in it for the long haul and therefore safe to buy from), access to important resources (such as sufficient capital to survive), or better technology, which enables them to get larger firms interested in underwriting them. Although these authors interpret such linkage as mostly about legitimacy, alternative interpretations seem equally plausible.

Second, if many of these arguments are true, then most sociological analyses can be easily subsumed under existing economic analyses. Social relationships have already been extensively theorized in the current literature in economics (Alchian and Demetz 1972; Milgrom and Roberts 1982; Williamson 1985; Fama 1980). They are thought to contribute to allocative efficiency, to solving the problem of incomplete contracting, to the reduction of transaction costs, to the reduction of agency costs, and to turning noncooperative one-shot games into cooperative repeated games. (Nash equilibrium essentially can be reduced to economic analyses of social relationships.) Such theorizing is worrisome to me, however, because we seem to be merely in the business of giving economics some social relationships to explain. If scholars think this is the main contribution they have to make, they should be explicit about it.

The elite approach makes it difficult to study the most interesting thing about capitalism: its dynamism. Since elites always have to be reproducing their power, elite theory can never see as interesting the substantial reorganization of capitalism that is constantly going on. Elite theorists have a hard time understanding why merger movements happen, why markets turn over, and why the dynamics of competition can wipe out the most entrenched elites. Some scholars interested in elites have begun to realize this (Davis and Thompson 1994).

Do elites get wiped out by other elites who have found a more efficient way to organize production, or is their downfall merely about power? If this dynamic is about efficiency, then elite theories give way to economics again because they are unable to think about the dynamics of market formation. If it is about power, then we are left wondering how and why things change. Is change simply the result of power struggles between various groups of capitalists who randomly fight it out? This is not a very satisfying notion. It is hard to argue that markets have not been dynamic in producing new "things" and that over time many of these things have become cheaper. A sociological theory of markets with little to say about this process is not very interesting.

Finally, the "effectiveness" hypothesis is good at seeing that social relationships are about stabilizing worlds but suffers from the problem of explaining capitalism's dynamism. Economists are sympathetic to the view that firms do try to create social structures to control competition. But they believe that those structures cannot hold out in the long run unless they are really about the most efficient way to organize a certain type of production.

The deep problem is that we do not talk about this problem. At the core of doing a sociology of markets is the assumption that we are analyzing markets differently than economists. But without a sense of what is different theoretically, we are not going to get very far.

A related issue concerns the significance of a sociological theory of action in markets as opposed to a rational actor model. I think that many perspectives—including, as I read it, Mark Granovetter's (1985)—are satisfied with a rational actor view of action in markets. That is, actors are rational (albeit boundedly so), and they are profit maximizers. But many of our best sociological studies undermine this view by showing that the organization of markets seems to be subject to multiple motives and forms of collective governance across local and national cultures. Very different logics of action are reflected in the Rheinish model in Germany (Albert 1991), the Japanese model (Gerlach 1992), and the Taiwanese and Korean models (Hamilton and Biggart 1988). Actors change their conception of interest and the functioning of their organization over time. This brings into focus the role of uncertainty, reflexivity, and culture in making sense of action.

This is an important sociological problem. Cultural differences (and by this I mean differences in practices, beliefs, and understandings) could cause actors to have different understandings of the same environment. The persistence of national styles of capitalism implies that even when firms from different societies meet to compete in a particular market, they do not necessarily converge to the same practices. How can this be? First, it may be that there is more than one way to organize a production process to produce goods and services reliably and still guarantee the owners of capital a profit. This interpretation suggests that it is hard to figure out what "best practices" are or should be for a particular product, a difficulty that is compounded by the possibility that some practices are better suited to particular national contexts. A second interpretation is that the social differences we observe are not really consequential to the efficient functioning of markets. Thus, issues of corporate governance may be only loosely related to economies of scale and scope. This interpretation suggests that it is less important for firms to converge on a single set of organizing principles and more important for them to make good products at reasonable prices. Sociologists are well positioned to make progress in understanding these differences because, unlike economists, we are not theoretically committed to viewing actors as rational or bounded rational profit maximizers.

The Problem of Institutions

Disagreements over efficiency and rationality naturally spill over into the problem of institutions. Although markets can be conceived of as self-reproducing role structures, it is less clear that we all agree on the mechanisms and the conditions under which these different mechanisms come into play. This raises the problem of defining market institutions. It is one thing to agree that markets are social structures, but it is quite another to agree on which social structures are necessary, the conditions that are necessary for markets to exist, and which of these issues are important to study.

Here there are clear differences of opinion. Many people interested in network analysis believe that networks are the main social structures necessary to characterize markets. Actors are assumed to be rational, but their actions depend entirely on their position in networks. The problem is that even among these scholars there is disagreement about which networks to study. As I have already pointed out, many scholars are studying the network represented by interlocking directorates, and others are looking at buyers and sellers within particular markets. Still others are studying firm ownership links (such as the keiretsu structures in Japan), supply chains, and resource dependence. These are not all the same thing, nor do they all index the same market relations. Indeed, I am struck that people who study networks quickly shift from talking about networks in general to talking about what the networks mean as social structures. No one ever explicitly specifies which social relations are necessary for markets to exist or why the particular network they study plays that role.

I have frequently heard complaints from scholars with political economy and "new" institutionalist perspectives (in both political science and sociology) that the focus on networks is incredibly myopic. To consider networks alone is to ignore states, firms, capitalists, and the rules, laws, and practices that make it possible for actors to have networks in the first place. Those of us who think that rules and meanings are important to interaction in any particular situation are unhappy about the way these general rules or logics of action are treated. If nothing matters except network relations within markets, why are there so many lawyers, rules, laws, international agreements, and business consultants, and why are they proliferating so rapidly? Moreover, firms are constantly appealing to governments to help them, in many different ways, including tax breaks, money for research and development, protection from foreign competition, and favorable regulatory regimes.

This brief discussion shows the deep differences of opinion among scholars of widely different perspectives. One could be a "pluralist" and argue that how one puts social institutions into play depends on what one is trying to explain. Thus, one could say that the role of networks between firms in the biotechnology industry (as a means of sharing information and spreading risk) has little to do with the writing of international laws like the North America Free Trade Agreement.

My feeling is that this approach is fine as a research strategy if scholars are clearer that this is what they are doing and more thoughtful about the generality of their conclusions. But I think that this approach is also dangerous: it tends to underestimate the causal power of other mechanisms by essentially ignoring the possibility that they are at work. Thus, whatever the effects of networks in the biotechnology industry, international laws about patenting and ensuring the safety and efficacy of products play a pivotal role in that industry as well. My main criticism is that by focusing relentlessly on some feature of markets we do not even entertain the possibility that what we are observing, in fact, has very different causes. Put simply, it is risky to ignore other people's variables.

Progress can be made only by directly integrating the insights of these various alternative mechanisms into our work. Scholars should make sure they consider how different mechanisms may contribute to an explanation of what they observe. For instance, to make sense of merger movements (which are about reorganizing the market for corporate control), we need to think about the link between current understandings of firms' practices, the role of government, the "crisis" that a merger movement seeks to solve, the set of understandings that actors construct about the problems and the solution, and how actors mobilize to exploit the situation.

One explanation of merger movements might go something like this. Some of the merger impetus no doubt travels through networks of people who are directly linked. But a lot of it starts in nearby fields, like business schools and consulting firms, and through the work of inspired individuals who propagate a new view and make lots of money imposing it on others. The business press, investment banks, and consultants then whip it up to make sure actors are confronted by it. Governments have always played some role in merger movements, mostly by their use of antitrust law (Fligstein 1990). Once merger movements get going, at least in the United States, firms often have little more than two choices: they can be predators or prey.

Taking the Mechanisms of Others More Seriously

My example of one way to make sense of events like merger movements does not privilege any set of actors, institutions, or networks. Instead, it situates the events in many of the likely series of relevant institutional settings. It considers motives, actors, rules and governments, and new conceptions of action. In essence, if we go back to the various mechanisms I described earlier, it is possible that all of them are pivotal to market organization at some point in the emergence, stabilization, or transformation of markets.

Such an account can be tested by considering how significant a role each of these mechanisms plays in a particular situation. Sometimes governments may direct merger movements—as was the case in France during the 1960s (Dyas and Thanheiser 1976)—and sometimes governments may be totally insignificant. It could also be that all of these factors, in a particular situation, contribute to a particular outcome. Understanding a mechanism and why it is likely to be important under certain conditions (and unimportant under others) is what scholarship is about.

Unfortunately, as the literature has developed, this has not been the main approach. Scholars tend to want their theory to be very general and to apply across time, space, and social interaction. So, for example, transaction-cost analysis in economics has been presented as a general theory of market interactions even for sociology (Williamson 1985). A Weberian approach to economic sociology would focus on a set of possible causal mechanisms by which markets could be socially structured. The common elements of actors, firms, social relationships, rules, and governments would help make sense of how markets as self-reproducing role structures get going. Such a theory would also be sensitive to how history and culture produce different outcomes.

If we accept the idea that "markets are self-reproducing role structures," then we should begin to think hard about what kind of role structures they are, how they become stable or attain self-reproduction, and the societal arrangements needed to allow actors in firms to produce such markets. Hard thinking on this question could yield big gains by causing us to focus on a smaller set of relationships that might be pivotal to the construction and maintenance of markets. But such thinking will also have to deal carefully with the question of efficiency, rationality, and stability.

Making the Sociology of Markets Relevant

Making the sociology of markets more theoretically sound is only the first step. It would be very heartening if such an analysis could also begin to inform the world of managers, policymakers, and our students. One of the most interesting things we now know is that national capitalisms are organized very differently around the world. These differences suggest that there may be many ways to attain positive economic outcomes from markets.

This idea has two obvious policy implications. These structures may be equally efficient, or they may provide actors with opportunities for rent seeking. Sociological analysts can be helpful in trying to determine whether the social embeddedness of particular markets produces rent seeking for powerful actors or, alternatively, provides a good allocation of societal resources. A sociological analysis in a policy setting begins with this question: Has the stable market division by firms led to efficient outcomes?

For example, the American health care system is not very efficient, even though it provides large income-making opportunities to private actors. Here is a clear case where the introduction of market forces has produced a miserable outcome. Yet sociologists who lack the intellectual tools to analyze this sector of the economy have not focused on the problem this way. The entire health care crisis is about sets of organized actors taking advantage of multiple markets to put in place institutions that benefit themselves.

That we were once "patients" and are now "consumers" reflects how far market logic has gone in redefining the situation. Part of the criticism of the market approach has to be that it has not produced efficient outcomes in the health care sector. The market model fails because patients cannot be informed consumers. When people are sick, they go to doctors to help them. When you are in a hospital, you do not shop around and you do not ask prices. We must ask whether society has pushed forward the allocation of scarce resources by marketizing the health care sector. I think the answer is a clear and resounding no. Many obvious policy implications follow from this perspective.

In my own work, I have tried to emphasize how political and economic organizations rely on one another to attain societal stability. In much of the current rhetoric about firms, their success or failure seems to be seen as independent of society more generally. Agency theory in economics argues that the only people who should matter to firms are shareholders. But the ability of shareholders to invest in the first place is heavily dependent on a large number of societal features. Society provides an educated labor force, a transportation and utilities system, a stable rule of law, and, in the United States, a relatively non-rent-seeking state. We underwrite research, maintain a tax system that favors investment, and produce regulation that protects shareholder rights. Put simply, in the United States it is easy to show that the influence of corporations over society is far greater than what they give back. Thus, society can make all sorts of moral claims on firms because it does not charge firms the real cost of what they consume.

The people over whom scholars have the greatest influence are students. In an average year, we see hundreds of thousands of them. It is imperative that we do a better job of giving them intellectual tools to evaluate what they hear and see in the media. We need to teach courses in how real markets work. Students are naive about the simplest matters—trade, competition, technology, and of course, American history. They have little or no understanding of the positive role that the government plays in making the production of wealth possible. Having grown up with the idea that politics is a venal circus, they do not understand the role of the government in making the Internet or underwriting the entire biotechnology revolution. And many are clueless about the ways in which law and regulation shape social policy and economic policy.

It is equally important how we train our graduate students. We have not done a good job of preparing our students for positions in policy-oriented organizations. There are a few sociologists working at the United Nations, the World Bank, the Organization for Economic Cooperation and Development, and the Brookings Institution, but not enough. We need to convince these organizations that our students can help them look at new kinds of facts and that with these new ways of looking at things they can make important contributions to policymaking. We should support our graduate students who want to do work that has more obvious policy implications by helping them make their projects more attractive to these potential employers. This can be done person by person and department by department.

The game here for economic sociology is to survive and help create a social space for alternative policy ideas. We need to continue to be opportunistic as individuals whenever we can. In our own work, we need to build bridges, produce theories, and be inclusive. The tendency to balkanize our fields and demonize our opponents is now too strong. We need analytic constructs that help us in many contexts. We need to develop new theories that can be used by social movements, politicians, and policymakers. But we also need to be acutely aware that without collective, cooperative organization, we as individuals will continue to be peripheral to these discussions.

Conclusions

If I were a student reading this chapter, I might walk away pretty depressed about the state of economic sociology in general and the sociology of markets in particular. But I would like to leave you with some hopeful thoughts. For the first time in twenty-five years, scholars are trying to create a more synthetic field of study, not one based on fragmenting already small communities of scholars. The constitution of economic sociology as a field and the advances in the sociology of markets are real. These are hard-won victories, and getting any agreements in a field as fragmented as sociology is a difficult and important process. There is an ongoing discussion; scholars who were not orienting themselves to one another as recently as five years ago are now talking. It seems to me that only something good can come out of this.

Also, the deep disagreements of which I speak are the kind of growth pains we would expect in a field that is so new and still being constituted. We have begun this work, and we have not been able to talk much about our deep differences. Part of the lack of communication was due to the hard work it took to get the field this far as we struggled with our critiques of economics. But the time is now ripe to push forward and put the sociology of markets on a firmer theoretical footing. The next task is to take the mechanisms that we think structure markets and try to produce a more integrated theoretical approach.

I would like to say that economics shares these same difficulties. In the past few years, I have realized that economists have differences of opinion on these questions as well. Most of the discipline remains faithful to the core assumptions of economics, but when you get economists offstage, they express grave doubts about the adequacy of their models to make sense of many of today's most vexing economic problems.

There is an amazing opportunity before us. We must get on with our discussions about efficiency, institutions, and what accounts for persistent differences between modes of social organization across societies. It is only by being more explicit about our differences of opin-

76 The New Economic Sociology

ion that we will advance the work that might have something to say about these questions.

Notes

1. Economists have become more interested in the problem of how institutions and social relationships may produce suboptimal outcomes, under certain conditions. Such outcomes can create stable social structures that last for a long time (North 1990; Stiglitz 2000). But the ultimate aim of economics is to understand how to remove impediments to inefficiency in the allocation of scarce resources. My point here is to consider whether or not that should be the aim of a sociology of markets.

References

Albert, Maurice. 1991. *Capitalism Versus Capitalism*. Paris: Éditions du Seuil.

Alchian, Armen, and Harold Demetz. 1972. "Production, Information Costs, and Economic Organization." *American Economic Review* 62: 777–95.

Baker, Wayne, Robert Faulkner, and Gary Fisher. 1998. "Continuity and Dissolution of Interorganizational Relationships." *American Sociological Review* 63: 147–77.

Block, Fred. 1996. *The Vampire State and Other Stories*. New York: New Press.

Burt, Ronald S. 1983. *Corporate Profits and Co-optation*. New York: Academic Press.

Campbell, John, and Leon Lindberg. 1990. "Property Rights and the Organization of Economic Activity by the State." *American Sociological Review* 55: 3–14.

Davis, Gerald, and Susan Stout. 1992. "Organization Theory and the Market for Corporate Control: A Dynamic Analysis of the Characteristics of Large Takeover Targets, 1980–1990." *Administrative Science Quarterly* 37: 605–33.

Davis, Gerald, and Tracy Thompson. 1994. "A Social Movement Perspective on Corporate Control." *Administrative Science Quarterly* 39: 141–73.

Dyas, Gareth P., and Herman Thanheiser. 1976. *The Emerging European Enterprise*. London: Unwin.

Evans, Peter. 1995. *Embedded Autonomy: States and Industrial Transformation*. Princeton, N.J.: Princeton University Press.

Fama, Eugene. 1980. "Agency Problems and the Theory of the Firm." *Journal of Political Economy* 88: 288–307.

Fligstein, Neil. 1990. *The Transformation of Corporate Control*. Cambridge, Mass.: Harvard University Press.

———. 1996. "Markets as Politics: A Political-Cultural Approach to Market Institutions." *American Sociological Review* 61: 656–73.

———. 2001. *The Architecture of Markets: An Economic Sociology of Twenty-first-Century Capitalist Societies*. Princeton, N.J.: Princeton University Press.

Gerlach, Michael. 1992. *Alliance Capitalism*. Los Angeles: University of California Press.

Granovetter, Mark. 1985. "Economic Action, Social Structure, and Embeddedness." *American Journal of Sociology* 91: 481–510.

Hamilton, Gary, and Nicole Biggart. 1988. "Market Culture and Authority: A Comparative Analysis of Management and Organization in the Far East." *American Journal of Sociology* 94: S52–94.

Hannan, Michael, and John Freeman. 1989. *Organizational Ecology*. Cambridge, Mass.: Harvard University Press.

Kotz, David. 1978. *Bank Control of Large Corporations in the United States*. Berkeley: University of California Press.

Lincoln, Jim, Michael Gerlach, and Patricia Takahashi. 1992. "Keiretsu Networks in Japan." *American Sociological Review* 57(5): 561–85.

Meyer, John, and Brian Rowan. 1977. "Institutionalized Organizations: Formal Structure as Myth and Ceremony." *American Journal of Sociology* 85: 340–63.

Milgrom, Paul, and John Roberts. 1982. "Limit Pricing and Entry Under Complete Information: An Equilibrium Analysis." *Econometrica* 104: 347–69.

Mintz, Beth, and Michael Schwartz. 1985. *Power Structure of American Business*. Chicago: University of Chicago Press.

Mizruchi, Mark, and Linda Stearns. 1988. "A Longitudinal Study of the Formation of Interlocking Directorates." *Administrative Science Quarterly* 33: 194–210.

North, Douglass. 1990. *Institutions, Institutional Change, and Economic Performance*. Chicago: University of Chicago Press.

Palmer, Donald, Brad M. Barber, Xueguang Zhou, and Yasemin Soysal. 1995. "The Other Contested Terrain: The Friendly and Predatory Acquisition of Large American Corporations in the 1960s." *American Sociological Review* 60(4): 469–99.

Palmer, Don, Roger Friedland, P. Deveraux Jennings, and Michael Powers. 1987. "The Economics and Politics of Structure: The Multidivisional Form and the Large U.S. Corporation." *Administrative Science Quarterly* 32: 25–48.

Podolny, Joel. 1993. "A Status-Based Model of Market Competition." *American Journal of Sociology* 98: 829–72.

Polanyi, Karl. 1957. *The Great Transformation*. Boston: Beacon Books.

———. 1977. *The Livelihood of Man*. New York: Academic Press.

Powell, Walter. 1990. "Neither Market nor Hierarchy: Network Forms of Organizations." In *Research in Organizational Behavior*, vol. 12, edited by Larry L. Cummings and Barry M. Staw. Greenwich, Conn.: JAI Press.

Powell, Walter, Kenneth W. Koput, and Laurie Smith-Doerr. 1996. "Interorganizational Collaboration and the Locus of Innovation." *Administrative Science Quarterly* 41: 116–45.

Roe, Mark. 1994. *Strong Owners, Weak Managers*. Princeton, N.J.: Princeton University Press.

Smelser, Neil, and Richard Swedberg, eds. 1994. *Handbook of Economic Sociology*. Princeton, N.J.: Princeton University Press.

Stiglitz, Joseph. 2000. "The Contribution of the Economics of Information to Twentieth-century Economics." *Quarterly Journal of Economics* 48: 1471–78.

Stuart, Toby. 1998. "Network Positions and the Propensities to Collaborate:

Strategic Alliance in a High-technology Network." *Administrative Science Quarterly* 43: 668–98.

Stuart, Toby, Huo Huang, and Richard Hybels. 1999. "Interorganizational Endorsements and the Performance of Entrepreneurial Firms." *Administrative Science Quarterly* 44: 315–49.

Useem, Michael. 1984. *The Inner Circle.* New York: Oxford University Press.

Uzzi, Brian. 1996. "Embeddedness and Economic Performance: The Network Effect." *American Sociological Review* 61(4): 674–98.

———. 1997. "Social Structure and Consequences of Embeddedness for the Economic Performance of Organizations." *Administrative Science Quarterly* 42: 35–67.

White, Harrison. 1981. "Where Do Markets Come From?" *American Journal of Sociology* 87: 517–47.

Williamson, Oliver. 1985. *The Economic Institutions of Capitalism.* New York: Free Press.

Zeitlin, Maurice. 1974. "Corporate Control and Ownership: The Large Corporation and the Capitalist Class." *American Journal of Sociology* 79: 1073–1119.

= Chapter 4 =

Endogenizing "Animal Spirits": Toward a Sociology of Collective Response to Uncertainty and Risk

PAUL DiMAGGIO

I N HIS *General Theory of Employment, Interest, and Money,* John Maynard Keynes (1936) described "animal spirits" as the emotional feeling-states that shape economic behavior above and beyond what a purely cognitive, rational model might lead one to expect. When consumers borrow more than they should to buy more than they need, animal spirits are working their magic. When investors display "irrational exuberance" (Shiller 2000) and push price-earning ratios to historic highs, animal spirits render them confident. And when corporations borrow, and banks lend, more money than is wise, animal spirits make them reckless.

Keynes believed that the role of animal spirits must be understood in order to make sound economic policy. Taking Keynes as my text, my sermon shall be that:

1. Most economists have neglected Keynes's words at their peril. Sociologists should take them to heart. Sociologists may be better equipped to understand the causes and effects of animal spirits than economists because they are experienced in the study of collective behavior.

2. Understanding animal spirits can help us explain the dynamics of a large class of phenomena of which the stock market is perhaps the

paradigmatic example; this class also includes patterns of educational attainment by group and the relative success or failure of social movements, community development ventures, and efforts at organizational change. Just as Keynes may help us understand collective behavior, students of social movements may help us understand the stock market and assist us in designing macroeconomic policy.

3. Specifically, animal spirits matter most under conditions of Knightian uncertainty, when economic actors with rational intentions have little basis for estimating risk. Affective states influence how actors cope with such informational vacuums; high levels of affect and emotional energy, for instance, induce more positive expectations than do lower levels. Models of collective behavior that explicate the consequences of interdependence in judgment formation are required to understand how animal spirits rise and fall, under what conditions, and with what results.[1]

In a sense, this chapter complements Viviana Zelizer's on "intimate transactions" (ch. 11, this volume). She calls attention to the role of emotion in transactions between spouses, lovers, and family members. I suggest that emotions, albeit of different kinds, affect impersonal as well as intimate exchange, albeit in different ways. I also reinforce Mark Granovetter's call (this volume) to identify the relational bases of central concepts in economic sociology—in this case, the diffusion of economic confidence and willingness to assume risk.

John Maynard Keynes, Animal Spirits, and Economics

Keynes's remarks about animal spirits entered into his *General Theory* because he recognized that uncertainty about the future state of the economy creates an irreducibly emotional component to economic cycles and crises.[2] He mentions animal spirits and related factors at two points in the book: once in chapter 9, where he discusses "subjective factors" in the "propensity to consume," and again in chapter 12 when he discusses "long-term expectations." There is little doubt that he would have been pleased to dispense with such matters and base predictions instead on such measurable quantities as liquidity and employment. But in the wake of the boom of the 1920s and the world depression of the 1930s, so perceptive a scholar could not ignore the influence of subjectivity, especially in the face of genuine uncertainty.[3]

Keynes was not the first to recognize the influence of subjective factors on consumption and investment. A dozen years before, in *Ab-*

sentee Ownership, his study of corporate America, Thorstein Veblen (1967 [1923], 91) discussed what we now call "the monetary illusion," arguing that price inflation tends, at first, to stimulate the economy by arousing the spirits of capitalists:

> Inasmuch as in any community that is given to business enterprise men habitually rate their wealth and their gains in money-values, any inflation of money-values will bring on what is called "buoyancy" throughout the business community and lead to heightened business activity and a spirit of confident adventure.

These factors, "buoyancy" and the "spirit of confident adventure," are precisely what Keynes had in mind twelve years later when he wrote his *General Theory.*

Since then, research by social psychologists on mood generalization has revealed that Keynes's hunch that overall buoyancy shapes economic judgments was right on target (Lane 1991). More broadly, research by psychologists (reviewed in Aspinwall 1998) indicates that positive affect leads people to make more favorable judgments about persons and objects, to process information at a slower rate, to underestimate risk, and to overestimate the chances of positive outcomes.

Notwithstanding this cross-disciplinary affirmation, economists long ignored Keynes's insight. My search of ECONLIT, a wide-ranging bibliographic database of economics publications, found no item with "animal spirits" in the title before 1980. The eighteen prominent economics and finance journals in the JSTOR electronic-journal database likewise contain not one article with the phrase in its title or abstract before 1983.[4] As one economist puts it, "When John Maynard Keynes appealed to 'animal spirits' to explain irrational action, few followed. Animal spirits seemed a diabolus ex machina—an artificial element introduced to make the story come out wrong" (Koppl 1991, 203–4; see also Marchionatti 1999).

Economists began to acknowledge Keynes's views on animal spirits in the 1980s, when the term appeared in the titles of five papers listed in ECONLIT. During the 1990s interest in the topic experienced a minor revival: an ECONLIT title search yields twenty-seven entries. Revived attention to animal spirits was in part a reaction to the rise of "rational-expectations" models of investor behavior. It also reflected the rise of the stock market and the resemblance between the market's precipitous ascent and the expansion that preceded the Great Depression. Much of this attention, however, emanated from the discipline's margins, especially from economists critical of strong forms of rational-expectations models (see, for example, Farmer and

Guo 1994; Levin 1995). In the more elite JSTOR journals, only five papers alluding to animal spirits in title *or* abstract appeared in the 1990s.

The few economists who have written prominently about animal spirits have tended (like Keynes himself) to view them as exogenous perturbations rather than as systematically explicable regularities (Howitt and McAfee 1992). And even some economists whose work echoes Keynes's insights fail to claim their intellectual patrimony. In his best-selling analysis of the late 1990s stock-market bubble, *Irrational Exuberance*, economist Robert Shiller describes the cognitive and affective factors that render equity markets far more volatile than they would be if investors behaved with synoptic rationality. But he takes his lead (and his title) from Alan Greenspan (Uchitelle 1997): neither "Keynes" nor "animal spirits" appears in the book's index.

Shiller's skepticism about the link between equity prices and economic fundamentals places him in a small, if growing, minority of finance economists. Costas Azariadis (1981) called attention to the role in equity markets of self-fulfilling prophecies (an idea about the relevance of which to animal spirits I shall have more to say). Kenneth Arrow (1986) likewise questioned neoclassical orthodoxy, endorsing the position that Knightian uncertainty generates multiple equilibria. In an empirical paper, Edoardo Gaffeo and Marco Gallegati (2000) claim that an "animal spirits" dynamic explains fluctuation in investment regimes in Italy during the past two decades. Economists more typically deny the influence of animal spirits, however, preferring to depict even apparent manias and bubbles as explicable in terms of rational expectations based on market fundamentals (Garber 2000).

If the economic mainstream has neglected Keynes, however, applied economists and investment advisers who make their living trying to forecast the economy's gyrations think about emotional factors a lot. They have translated animal spirits into the more dignified notion of "economic confidence," of which they have identified three kinds.

The first is *consumer confidence*, as measured by two competitive sources, the University of Michigan Survey Research Center's Consumer Sentiment Index and the Consumer Confidence Index of the Conference Board, a big-business research and advocacy organization. Consumer confidence makes consumers want to buy durables and other goods, thus diminishing inventories, sparking employment, and ending (or preventing) recessions. Forecasters have demonstrated that people who think their jobs are secure and their economic prospects promising are more willing to take on debt to satisfy their cravings than people who feel poised at the edge of the abyss (Fuhrer 1988).

The second variety of economic confidence is *business confidence,* also measured by the Conference Board. Measures of business confidence indicate the extent to which executives believe that sales, earnings, and profits will increase and that it is therefore sensible, possible, and necessary for them to hire more workers, order more capital goods, or spend more money on research and development. Consumer and business confidence are, of course, closely related. When consumers are confident, they spend more, increasing demand and making business confident. When business is confident, it hires more workers, who use their wages to buy more goods. This close relationship between consumer and business confidence is one reason economies fall into vicious and virtuous cycles.

A third type of confidence, measured in many ways, is *investor confidence,* the conviction that equities are a sound investment. Just as there are different kinds of investors, so there are different kinds of investor confidence. The emotional horizons of day-traders are measured in minutes and hours. By contrast, dollar-cost-averaging value investors have so much faith in the stock market's long-term soundness that they view market declines as opportunities rather than threats. More so than the other forms, investor confidence, then, seems to oscillate in both short and long cycles, the former defined by quarterly earnings projections, the latter marked by such historical events as the Great Depression and the expansion of the 1990s (and the bursting of the tech-stock bubble), events that define the fundamental expectations of the birth cohorts that experience them.

Researchers have demonstrated that confidence matters. But thus far, economists—even those who recognize the influence of emotions on decisionmaking—have failed to develop powerful models to explain the social dynamics by which confidence is generated and diffused. Sociologists, I believe, have a contribution to make in this regard, for understanding the dynamics of animal spirits—not just their effects, but the mechanisms behind them—engages precisely the kind of reasoning and modeling at which sociologists enjoy a comparative advantage.

Animal Spirits, Rationality, Risk, and Uncertainty

There is nothing inherently irrational about the way in which most investors *approach* stock markets. The stakes are high, the players are committed, the issues are salient, and the analytic technologies are fairly well developed. This combination makes equity markets contexts for rational action par excellence.

Animal spirits matter not because people are irrational but because information is scarce. Think for a moment of the role of confidence in a market with perfect information. That role would be nonexistent. Actors' states of mind would reflect the state of the world as clearly as mirrors reflect the appearance of whomever stands before them. When economic conditions were bad, confidence would be low; when conditions were good, confidence would be high. But an analyst would not care about confidence, because the economic conditions themselves would be all he or she needed to know.

Under conditions of rationality, confidence becomes important only when future states of the world are sufficiently uncertain to invite differences in interpretation. Insofar as confidence routinely biases expectations upward or downward, variations in confidence influence the cost of financial instruments in a manner unrelated either to their underlying value or to the future state of the world.

Note that the problem is uncertainty, not risk. An investor can know two kinds of things about the likely results of an investment: she or he can know the precise payoff, as one does when one buys a Treasury bill guaranteed by the U.S. government, or she or he can know the probability distribution of payoffs of differing magnitudes (that is, the degree of risk). If one has only enough money to buy one or two stocks, this distinction matters. But if one manages a portfolio containing dozens of securities, knowing the degree of risk is almost as good as knowing the payoff. (For an accessible discussion of portfolio management, see Bernstein 1992.) As Jens Beckert (1996) has argued, confidence becomes an interesting sociological issue only when the degree of risk—the variance or probability distribution—is itself unknown.

But why would one turn to a sociologist rather than a psychologist for guidance in such matters? After all, terms like "uncertainty" and "confidence" evoke individual states of mind. Indeed, if variation in confidence were simply individual and adventitious, sociologists would have little to say about it. It is the *nature* of economic uncertainty (and, as I shall argue, of other kinds of uncertainty as well) that makes sociology indispensable.

Three points are critical here. The first is that expectations under uncertainty are socially constructed. The question is not whether investors are rational. Rather, the question is: How are investors rational together? Veblen's "buoyancy" captures this notion better than either "confidence" or "animal spirits" in that it connotes an attribute of a social system—a rising tide that lifts all boats—rather than of isolated persons.

A second point follows from this one: expectations, decisions, and economic outcomes are all interdependent. To form rational expectations, each decisionmaker must take into account the decisions that all others are likely to make. As Keynes (1936, 156) put it when he likened the stock market to a newspaper beauty contest in which a prize goes to the readers who pick the faces deemed "prettiest" by the greatest number of other entrants, the goal is not just guessing what others think, but "anticipating what average opinion expects the average opinion to be."

A third point follows from the first two: actors in market situations must deal with two kinds of uncertainty—uncertainty about the future state of the world and uncertainty about other investors' beliefs about the future state of the world, as these reflect varying degrees of confidence. Particularly in speculative markets, the latter may be more problematic than the former: like hardened convicts playing the prisoners' dilemma, a rational actor may on the basis of experience decide that a certain daring course of action is doomed to failure, but if all actors decide on that course of action at once, then the action will succeed.

Sociologists have an advantage in dealing with this collective aspect of market behavior. Whereas economists' models aggregate the behavior of isolated individuals, sociologists are used to studying situations in which actions are interdependent. Moreover, as I shall argue, sociologists have a rich theoretical vocabulary for analyzing such phenomena.

Animal Spirits in Investment Markets

These observations apply to all three forms of economic confidence—to the animal spirits of investors, consumers, and business executives. But investor confidence is a particularly useful case to examine, both because the relative role of the social component in uncertainty is particularly strong in speculative markets, and because theories of investment behavior are so well developed.

Investors and their advisers fall roughly into three camps. Technical analysts treat the market as if it had a life of its own, reading charts of equity price changes like tea leaves to divine where they will go next. Stock-pickers believe that they can outwit the market: they search for equities that are undervalued, hoping to invest in them before the rest of the market catches on.

Most finance economists reside in a third camp occupied by the theory of "perfect markets" (for an engaging introduction, see Malkiel 1985). According to proponents of perfect-market theory, market prices incorporate instantaneously all available information about the state of the economy (and the state of particular firms). All information is reflected in prices. The strong, nearly theological, version of this theory brooks no exceptions. The weak version admits to numerous exceptions, but none of these mitigate the two main lessons. First, do not bother trying to pick stocks. Just decide how much risk you are willing to absorb and create a balanced portfolio of investments that reflects that decision. Second, the best way to get rich is to buy the stock market itself (through an equity index fund) and hold on to it.[5]

The weak version of perfect-market theories has received empirical support (Malkiel 1989), although how much support remains controversial (Shiller 2000). Insofar as the theory is right (and the weak form appears to have merit), then there are only three reasons prices can depart from a full-information equilibrium. The first consists of exogenous shocks. Insofar as these can be factored into risk estimates, they pose no problem. The second is insider information, but if the market gets good enough at reading and following the lead of insider traders, these effects are brief. The third, and most sociologically interesting, consists of changes in investor confidence that are orthogonal to information about the state of the world—that is, changes in the liveliness of animal spirits. Because animal spirits reflect dynamic patterns of social interaction, they give sociologists the key to understanding what may be the major factor rendering stock markets unpredictable.

Consider two examples: Wayne Baker's (1984) research on stock option trading demonstrated that imperfections in information increase variability in expectations and volatility in outcomes (see also Smith 1981). The larger and more complex the system, the greater the volatility. This is because larger systems have more dissensus, less social control, and greater uncertainty. Under such conditions, they are more susceptible to the effects of animal spirits than are smaller, face-to-face systems.

An anecdotal example comes from the experience of a stockbroker I interviewed several years ago. This successful investment adviser derived much of his short-term strategy from weekly briefings at the New York offices of a large mass-market brokerage house. It was not that the pundits who held forth had stunning insights into the market; indeed, my informant claimed that he had never gotten a good idea from them. Rather, he went to the briefings and counted the house. When attendance was sparse, he concluded that the market's momentum and direction would continue unbroken. When attendance was high, he took this as a sign of investor anxiety and assumed that the market's direction would change as a new collective judgment emerged. Usually, he claimed, this was the case.

If expectations about the future under conditions of uncertainty are socially constructed, whoever can best understand the laws of their construction can predict the (short-term) future best. Moreover, policymakers who learn to intervene in the process of social construction can exert leverage on such obdurate economic variables as consumer savings and business investment. Clearly, understanding the mechanisms that shape animal spirits is an analytic problem for which the stakes are high.

What Sociology Can Provide

The question is this: Under what conditions do groups generate a positive affect that cannot be explained simply by changes in the state of the world? And under what conditions does this positive affect color expectations about the future, independent of "hard" information? This is an important question for understanding financial markets. It is also germane to predicting changes in consumer spending and business investment patterns. And as I argue later, many significant non-economic phenomena are also analogous.

Let us consider five sets of ideas—four from sociology and one from cognitive psychology—that can help us address this question: Daniel Kahneman and Amos Tversky's studies of decision heuristics (Kahneman, Slovic, and Tversky 1982); Robert K. Merton's notions of self-fulfilling prophecy (1948) and pluralistic ignorance (Merton 1957, 336ff; Allport 1924); Mark Granovetter's work on threshold and diffusion models (1978); Randall Collins's theory of interaction ritual chains (1981, 1998); and Harrison White's ideas about social action and collective identity (1992).

Kahneman and Tversky's Decision Heuristics Because Kahneman and Tversky, the only psychologists on our list, share economics' focus on individual decisionmaking, their work has already been influential in that field. And because the parameters they have identified are likely to be shaped by social factors, their work links economic and sociological concerns.

Kahneman and Tversky focus on the manner in which various hard-wired tricks that people use to solve problems efficiently lead to systematic departures from synoptic rationality. Several such "decision heuristics," as they call these mischievous shortcuts, are especially relevant for present purposes (Kahneman, Slovic, and Tversky 1982).

The "recency heuristic" refers to people's tendency to place more weight on new information than on old information. Imagine, for example, that on Wednesday I must decide whether to buy a new computer or keep my old one. If I hear a rumor on Monday that faculty salaries are going down, and on Tuesday a rumor that salaries are going up, the probability that I will make the purchase is greater than it would be if I had heard equally reliable rumors in the reverse order.

The "salience heuristic" refers to the tendency to place more weight on information that fits into existing cognitive frameworks than on information that does not. Conservative economists who worry a lot about cost-push inflation, for example, interpret unemployment declines as dark clouds on the economic horizon likely to lower stock prices, either through the effects of inflation or through the steps that the Federal Reserve takes to prevent inflation (see also "self-fulfilling prophecies"). Liberals (economists or not) are more likely to interpret lower unemployment rates as evidence of economic vitality.

In research on memory, Redelmeier and Kahneman (1996) found that patients experiencing painful medical procedures recalled the pain's severity as the mean of its most painful and last moments. (Doctors can lead patients to remember the procedure as less painful by prolonging the pain as it declines in severity.) If this "most-and-last" dynamic can be generalized to historical experience, it may help us predict the economic behavior of people in societies that have been subject to economic shock treatment if and when their economies recover.

Work in cognitive decision theory is stimulating and often persuasive. It is natural, however, for psychologists to beg certain questions in which sociologists are particularly interested. How do patterns of communication influence the timing with which information is received? How do communities establish, reinforce, and modify cognitive frameworks? How do groups and networks collectively define the boundaries of events? For answers to these questions, we must move to work by sociologists.

Merton on the Self-fulfilling Prophecy and Pluralistic Ignorance   Robert K. Merton's notion of "self-fulfilling prophecy" calls attention to the processes by which predictions about the future shape the behavior of those exposed to such predictions by influencing their perceptions of risk. Merton (1948, 194–95) gave the example of an economic downturn in which depositors at a local bank come to believe that the bank will fail, withdraw their money in response to this expectation, and therefore bring about the very consequence they fear. Citing Merton's use of the idea, Arrow (1986) applied it to changes in financial markets. There are many other examples: the political contest in which the prediction that one candidate has the race locked up leads supporters of other candidates to withdraw their energies; or the investors who rush to invest based on the prediction of a famous stockpicker, thus causing the prediction to become a reality.

The concept of "pluralistic ignorance," with which Merton (1957) is associated (he attributes it to Allport 1924), is related to that of self-fulfilling prophecy. It provides a framework for understanding the ways in which people's own behaviors or preferences are shaped by their often erroneous beliefs about the behavior or preferences of those around them. The townspeople in the children's story "The Emperor's New Clothes" exemplify pluralistic ignorance. Providing a contemporary example are college students who believe that their friends enjoy drinking alcoholic beverages more than they do. As a result, they consume more alcohol than they would like, though not as much as they think their friends want them to drink (Miller and Prentice 1994). Similarly, investment counselors with reservations about economic fundamentals may profess optimism if they believe that their peers are much more bullish than they are, either for fear of losing business or because they gamble that collective expectations will pull the market through.

Whereas the self-fulfilling prophecy is an insight about mass behavior, the notion of pluralistic ignorance introduces structure, underscoring the dependence of collective action on the distribution of beliefs across the opinion spectrum *and* across social space. Pluralistic ignorance can persist for a long time, but whether it is established in the first place depends a great deal on the patterns by which people with different attitudes and preferences, and different propensities to reveal their attitudes and preferences, enter into regular communication.

Granovetter on Bandwagon Effects   Mark Granovetter has developed the combinatorial argument implicit in Merton's work in two essays (Granovetter 1978; Granovetter and Soong 1986) that present models of situations in which people's willingness to act depends on the behavior of others. In each case, system outcomes are driven by the distribution of thresholds at which each person will act. The models are social because these thresholds are activated based on information gained through interaction with, or observation of the behavior of, others. In the tradition of Harvey Leibenstein's (1950) work on bandwagons, Elizabeth Noelle-Neumann's (1993 [1980]) on the "spiral of silence," and Anthony Downs's (1973) on residential segregation,

Granovetter models such systems as patronage at Chinese restaurants and voice-exit decisions in politics as the result of variation in the thresholds at which different people will take action (and the effect of such differences on popular perceptions).

There is a parallel here to economic confidence. Economic growth (or, in less developed economies, economic takeoff), requires a collective definition of the future as full of potential. Because the future is an ambiguous canvas capable of multiple interpretations, this definition depends in large degree on animal spirits. These models enable us to endogenize the emotional tone, confidence, or animal spirits of economic actors as a function of the distribution of levels at which each will take a leap of faith from conservatism and risk-averseness to expansiveness and risk-tolerance.

How might this work? Imagine that every consequential economic actor (business executives, if we are interested in capital investments; consumers if we are concerned with purchases of durables) has some threshold at which she or he will shift from cautious pessimism to engaged optimism. Where the distribution is relatively normal, optimism can pass through the system in gentle waves, reaching a takeoff point at fairly low levels. Where the distribution is discontinuous or bimodal, barriers to diffusion or actively antagonistic emotional countercultures may stymie economic recovery.

The question, of course, is, where do such distributions of propensities come from? Animal spirits may reflect an increased willingness to accept risk under conditions of stable expectations. Or they may represent a rosier interpretation of data about the future under conditions of stable risk-averseness. In either case, we need a theory of how social interactions generate optimism and high spirits.

Collins and Interaction Ritual Chains   Randall Collins's theory of "interaction ritual chains" (1981, 1998) gives us a purchase on this question by proposing that one's propensity to optimism is a function of one's position in a series of linked interactions. Collins's work is critically important for identifying collective affect, or ritual well-being, as an important dimension on which groups and communities vary, and for developing the elements of a model of how such variation emerges. Following Durkheim (1995 [1912]) and Goffman (1967), Collins argues that face-to-face interactions, whatever else they may be, are rituals that reinforce the sacredness of the participating selves. Interaction rituals succeed when participants are well matched in cultural endowments and seek to affirm shared identities rather than to dominate one another. Participants emerge from successful interaction rituals with higher levels of emotional energy, which they may pass on in turn to subsequent interaction partners. (Where the parties in an interaction ritual are hierarchically unequal, the dominant party's energy level is enhanced and the dominated party's is sapped.) Actors whose interaction ritual chains leave them with high levels of emotional energy are more buoyant in their view of the future.

The theory of interaction ritual chains suggests how social processes exogenous to the economic system may influence the buoyancy of economic actors. Some sample hypotheses that come out of this perspective are:

1. Executives who initiate wide-scale efforts at organizational change that require collective action predicated on positive expectations about the behavior of others are more likely to succeed in organizations with low levels of formal inequality.

2. Executives in firms with high levels of inequality are more likely, other things being equal, to feel buoyant and therefore to pursue expansionary policies.

3. Business confidence is higher during periods in which state actors defer to corporate executives than in periods in which state bureaucrats are less deferential, independent of the content of state policies.

Keynes (1936, 162) recognized this last possibility when he wrote that

> economic prosperity is excessively dependent on a political and social atmosphere which is congenial to the average business man. If the fear of a Labour Government or a New Deal depresses enterprise, this need not be the result either of a reasonable calculation or of a plot with political intent; it is the mere consequence of upsetting the delicate balance of spontaneous optimism.

The interaction ritual chain provides a more innocent, if even more obdurate, mechanism behind the structural influence of business on the state than the political-interest based processes that Charles Lindblom identified in *Politics and Markets* (1978).

Social Movement Theory and Collective Identity In *Identity and Control*, Harrison White (1992) underscores the problematic nature of actor identity and calls attention to the processes by which identity is determined. In highlighting the similarities between markets and other forms of social organization, his framework reminds us that markets are concrete sets of actors jockeying for position in a social space, and that when these efforts succeed, niches and identities co-evolve (White, this volume).

The relationship between identity and capacity for action was opened by Marx (1963 [1847]), for whom a question of paramount importance was: When does a *class-in-itself* become a *class-for-itself*? Students of contemporary social movements have generalized Marx's question to racial, gender, and religious identities as well. David Snow (Snow et al. 1986) and William Gamson (1992), for example, have developed the notion of social movement frames, which consist of a collective identity, an affective belief that a condition is unjust, and a cognitive belief (itself shaped by affective buoyancy) that collective action can bring about change. For social movements to succeed, large numbers of potential participants must come to accept such frames as applicable to their own conditions.

What do social movements have to do with markets? The bases of success are very similar. For markets to increase in value, the following conditions must prevail: a collective perception that prices improperly reflect the future value of assets (parallel to the perception of injustice); a belief that mass action will occur to rectify matters (parallel to collective action); and a collective identity that permits investors or purchasers to choose expansive roles under conditions of ambiguity. In the rest of this chapter, I develop these parallels with specific examples.

Politics as a Market Phenomenon

Many social processes have this in common: people make investments based on their expectations about payoffs, where payoffs are a function of the investments of others and expectations therefore are themselves based on expectations about the expectations of others. Although I have used examples from economic markets, there are as many examples among political phenomena.[6]

Note that I am suggesting that many aspects of politics and markets operate through parallel processes, not that they are identical. Animal spirits in economic markets entail a cognitive belief that an asset is undervalued. In politics, collective action requires an affective conviction that some set of persons with whom one identifies is undervalued. Animal spirits in economic markets raise estimates of the probability of mass action, whereas in collective political behavior they raise estimates of the probability that collective action will succeed. In economic markets the key commodity is information; animal spirits derive their influence from the absence of this commodity. In politics the key currency is culture, which, as Kathleen Carley (1991) has demonstrated, can be treated formally as information and which, when shared, lowers costs of transacting and raises the likelihood that interaction rituals will enhance the energy levels of participants (Collins 1998).

Uncertainty and risk are central to economic models and important to collective action in politics. Risk in economics is analogous to dissensus in politics: it provides a basis for discounting the probability of successful collective action. By contrast, the political analogue to economic uncertainty is multivocality: the capacity of political actors to speak in multiple registers, invoking varying orders of value (Boltanski and Thévenot 1991; Stark 2001) in the hope of building coalitions. Because multivocality provides elbow room for skill and happenstance, it renders many political outcomes unpredictable through the ordinary calculus of interest and political preference.

A few examples should help illuminate these speculations. I have already mentioned Granovetter's threshold models of collective action and their applicability to economic markets. As Granovetter himself has noted (1978), bandwagon effects are common not just in economic life but in politics, where collective mobilization is self-propelling in much the same way that economic booms are. If each individual has a threshold—for example, the number of committed participants a social movement must have before he or she will consider participating—then with each new participant the probability that nonparticipants will commit increases. The scale of the ensuing collective action depends on the distribution of thresholds within the population at risk to take part.

A rather different example comes from Pierre Bourdieu's (1974) work on what he calls "the causality of probability." Employing a version of Merton's self-fulfilling prophecy, Bourdieu argues that individuals aspire to futures that are statistically open to members of their social category. That is, members of categories that face discrimination will accommodate such discrimination by tending to develop lower aspirations as they approach the labor force. Bourdieu notes that so-called low aspirations do not "cause" individual underachievement so much as they reflect group-level barriers.

At certain times, however, the causality of probability is suspended. Bourdieu has explored the case of the children of French peasants who in the 1960s began to leave the farms and aspire to roles that had previously been closed to them. A familiar case in the United States is that of African Americans, whose educational aspirations, and eventually educational achievements, came in the 1960s and 1970s to approximate those of Euro-Americans. In both cases groups struggled collectively to change their members' estimates of what was possible, and in each case it was the simultaneous change in many interacting persons' probability estimates that led to systematic change.

My third and final example is Charles Sabel's research (1994) on the dynamics of community development projects in which antagonistic partners (labor, capital, local and state governments) must build trust if they are to cooperate successfully. In this case, uncertainty about the outcome of any strategy is linked to uncertainty about the probability that other participants will cooperate. What is striking about Sabel's work is his depiction of the process through which probability estimates of trustworthy behavior increase and animal spirits are generated. In the cases he has studied, participants accomplish this in part by creating collective narratives that both define a shared identity and explain away prior failures and antagonisms. Sabel calls the outcome of this process "vigilant trust": players trust one another enough to cooperate, but not enough to let down their guard against possible defections.[7]

In drawing these parallels between politics and markets, I describe something quite different from public-choice models of electoral systems (Hotelling 1928; Downs 1957) or game-theoretic approaches to group behavior. Whereas public-choice theory represents a theory of mass (that is, atomistic) behavior, at the core of the models I have described is the assumption that choices are interdependent. Whereas game-theoretic models of politics posit strategy as predictable when groups are given and interests and preferences are known, my examples treat interests, preferences, and group identities as *the product of endogenous social processes.* The assumption here is that analogies between political and economic behavior will be most fruitful once the latter is firmly situated in a social context.

Markets as Social Movements

What can we learn from these political examples about animal spirits in the economic realm, and how can such learning inform macroeconomic policy? Let me switch from investor confidence, where the dynamics of expectations are relatively clear, to consumer and business confidence. I do so, first, because macroeconomic policy focuses on the behavior of consumers and businesses, which fuel economic recoveries and long-term growth, and second, because these forms of confidence may have more in common with the political examples I have described.

Consumer decisions to purchase goods and business decisions to invest in the economy are both likely to be shaped by the same types of interactions that influence decisions to participate in collective political movements. Consumers are influenced not only by their own economic circumstances but by the economic welfare of their peers: people whose friends have new cars are more likely to want a new car themselves, and people whose friends are being laid off are less likely to buy cars than people whose peers are getting raises.

Consumer decisions are shaped by social interactions in another way. When goods and services are complex and their quality is not directly observable, people are more likely to purchase them if they trust their purveyors. People prefer to purchase such goods and services from their friends and relatives, and they find the results more satisfactory when they do (DiMaggio and Louch 1998). When friends or relatives are not available, it seems reasonable to expect that people are more likely to purchase goods when they share a common categorical identity with the seller and when they have higher levels of generalized trust (as defined by Yamigishi and Yamigishi 1994; on "catnets," see White 1992, 62). Common identities are rarely given; more frequently they emerge as a part of efforts to make interaction rituals succeed (Erickson 1975).

From this, I hypothesize that:

1. When animal spirits are high, participants in commercial transactions are more likely to define themselves as sharing a common identity.

2. Animal spirits covary positively with generalized trust.

3. When people are likely to succeed in establishing shared identities and where generalized trust is high, they are more likely to complete purchases of optional complex and expensive goods and services (like real estate, automobiles, home improvement services, and noncommodity consumer durables).

In this way, animal spirits contribute to economic prosperity, which, in a virtuous cycle, enhances the conditions for the production of positive flows of emotional energy.

Similar processes may influence business confidence. As economic and organizational scholars have demonstrated, business executives interact constantly in formal and informal settings in which opinions are formed, moods are engaged, and expectations are molded (Useem 1984; Galaskiewicz 1985; Vogel 1989). When executives are hopeful, they invest. When they turn dolorous (other things being equal), they withhold investment. Given this fact, any lever that can influence the process of corporate elite opinion formation may have significant macroeconomic consequences.

Such understandings seem to enter into government policies. Since the 1980s we have seen a proliferation of symbolic gestures of honor and deference toward business executives (for example, the Malcolm Baldridge Awards for social responsibility). Insofar as the animal spirits of business executives are excited by deference and bestowals of prestige, the cultivation of rewarding interaction rituals may contribute to economic expansion. Perhaps a clever administration could use the elite network analysis techniques that sociologists have developed to identify central players in corporate networks and cultivate them selectively, because their spirits disproportionately affect those of less central players.

Conclusion

Where uncertainty is so high that actors have little informational basis for calculating risk, the flow of emotional energy—what Keynes identified as animal spirits and Veblen referred to as buoyancy and the spirit of confident adventure—plays a determinative role in human affairs. Economists have neglected this insight. Sociologists should not.

Economic markets, no less than political phenomena or innovation diffusion, involve processes of collective mobilization in which actors shape one another's estimates of risk under conditions of uncertainty. Research by sociologists and social psychologists on mood formation and by sociologists on network effects on collective action provides a fundamental basis for understanding such phenomena.

The point is not simply to understand the effects of animal spirits, although this is a worthy goal. It is necessary as well to *endogenize* emotional buoyancy in order to explain its ebbs and flows. Animal spirits matter precisely because they are social. The challenge is to understand the social organization of emotion, not just its social psychology. If this challenge can be met, sociological models of social interaction may hold the keys to Keynes's neglected insights.

Notes

1. These ideas are not original. At the most general level, this chapter is about the self-fulfilling prophecies to which Robert Merton (1948) alerted us years ago. Other points in my argument have been developed theoretically by Randall Collins (1981) and Mark Granovetter (1978; Granovetter and Soong 1986) and empirically by such students of markets as

Wayne Baker (1984) and Charles Smith (1981). My goal is simply to hold familiar prisms up to new light, calling attention to some valuable insights that have not been fully exploited and thus bear repetition.

2. I am indebted to Mark Granovetter and Charles Sabel for alerting me to this part of Keynes's work.

3. Although I have seen no evidence that Keynes had either interest in or knowledge of sociology, neither was he narrowly economistic. Keynes's mind was exceptionally well furnished by his long-standing relationships with the literary and philosophical figures of the Bloomsbury Group, associations that ensured his familiarity with the ideas of Freud, Wittgenstein, and other modernist thinkers. Piero Mini (1993) contends that Keynes's concept of animal spirits reflects the influence of Nietzsche and proto-existentialist philosophy. Rossana Bonadei (1994) asserts a strong affinity between the intellectual views and projects of Keynes and Freud. John Davis (1994) discerns Wittgenstein's influence in Keynes's constructivism and appreciation of the role of convention and also reports an intellectual link between Keynes and Gramsci through Keynes's close associate Piero Sraffa. Whatever the channels of influence, Keynes was much more constructivist and historicist, and less confident in formal models of rational action, than many of his contemporaries and most of his successors.

4. To be sure, other economists acknowledged the economic role of collective sentiments, but without drawing on Keynes's work. Albert Hirschman (1958), for example, noted that entrepreneurial confidence is a positive externality produced by appropriate investment strategies in developing economies.

5. Perfect-market theory is best summed up by the story of two economists walking side by side down a city street. "Look," shouts the younger, pointing to the pavement, "someone dropped a ten-dollar bill." "Keep walking," says his companion. "If the bill had been there, someone else would have picked it up by now."

6. Note that although such phenomena constitute a large class, they are not exhaustive of economic or political decision situations. In some cases, returns to investment are a negative function of the extent to which others view the world the same way. Contrarian stock market investors know this. So did Bill Clinton, who was the only prominent Democrat willing to run against George Bush in the wake of the latter's popularity at the end of the Gulf War.

7. Note that a focus on animal spirits leads us to take a different approach to trust than that typical of economic sociology, which focuses on structural preconditions for the emergence of trust (see, for example, Granovetter, this volume). I would suggest that we also ask how social interactions shape the estimates that people make about the trustworthiness of others (or the extent to which they believe their designs will suffer from deficits

in trustworthiness). In particular, we should attend to the conditions under which interactional processes engender trusting behavior by creating emotional buoyancy where the structural preconditions for trust do not yet fully exist, and to the role of such processes in the takeoff stage of such vigorous microeconomies as Silicon Valley's.

References

Allport, Floyd H. 1924. *Social Psychology.* Boston: Houghton Mifflin.
Arrow, Kenneth J. 1986. "Rationality of Self and Others in an Economic System." *Journal of Business* 59(4): S386–99.
Aspinwall, Lisa G. 1998. "Rethinking the Role of Positive Affect in Self Regulation." *Motivation and Emotion* 22(1): 1–32.
Azariadis, Costas. 1981. "Self-Fulfilling Prophecies." *Journal of Economic Theory* 25: 380–96.
Baker, Wayne. 1984. "The Social Structure of a National Securities Market." *American Journal of Sociology* 89(4): 775–811.
Beckert, Jens. 1996. "What Is Sociological About Economic Sociology?: Uncertainty and the Embeddedness of Economic Action." *Theory and Society* 25(6): 803–40.
Bernstein, Peter L. 1992. *Capital Ideas: The Improbable Origins of Modern Wall Street.* New York: Free Press.
Boltanski, Luc, and Laurent Thévenot. 1991. *De la justification: Les economies de la grandeur.* Paris: Gallimard.
Bonadei, Rossana. 1994. "John Maynard Keynes: Context and Methods." In *John Maynard Keynes: Language and Method*, edited by Alessandra Marzoli and Francesco Silva. Brookfield, Vt.: Edward Elgara.
Bourdieu, Pierre. 1974. "Avenir de classe et causalité du probable." *Revue Française du Sociologie* 15: 3–42.
Carley, Kathleen. 1991. "A Theory of Group Stability." *American Sociological Review* 56: 331–54.
Collins, Randall. 1981. "On the Microfoundations of Macrosociology." *American Journal of Sociology* 86: 984–1014.
———. 1998. *The Sociology of Philosophies.* Cambridge, Mass.: Harvard University Press.
Davis, John. 1994. *Keynes's Philosophical Development.* Cambridge: Cambridge University Press.
DiMaggio, Paul, and Hugh Louch. 1998. "Socially Embedded Consumer Transactions: For What Kinds of Purchases Do People Use Networks Most?" *American Sociological Review* 63(5): 619–37.
Downs, Anthony. 1957. *An Economic Theory of Democracy.* New York: Harper & Row.
———. 1973. *Opening up the Suburbs.* New Haven, Conn.: Yale University Press.
Durkheim, Emile. 1995 [1912]. *The Elementary Forms of Religious Life*, translated by Karen Fields. New York: Free Press.
Erickson, Fred. 1975. "Gatekeeping in the Melting Pot: Interaction in Counseling Encounters." *Harvard Educational Review* 45: 44–70.

Farmer, Roger E. A., and Jang-Ting Guo. 1994. "Real Business Cycles and the Animal Spirits Hypothesis." *Journal of Economic Theory* 63(1): 42–72.

Fuhrer, Jeffrey C. 1988. "On the Information Content of Consumer Survey Expectations." *Review of Economics and Statistics* 70(1): 140–44.

Gaffeo, Edoardo, and Marco Gallegati. 2000. "Investments, Animal Spirits, and Regime Switching: Some Evidence from Italy." Series in Economics Working Paper 02-00-eco. Udine, Italy: University of Udine. Available at: *www.uniud.it/dse/working—papers/2000/wp02—00—eco.pdf* (Accessed December 2, 2001).

Galaskiewicz, Joseph. 1985. "Interorganizational Networks and the Development of a Single Mind-set." *American Sociological Review* 50(5): 639–58.

Gamson, William A. 1992. *Talking Politics.* New York: Cambridge University Press.

Garber, Peter M. 2000. *Famous First Bubbles.* Cambridge, Mass.: M.I.T. Press.

Goffman, Erving. 1967. *Interaction Ritual.* New York: Vintage.

Granovetter, Mark. 1978. "Threshold Models of Collective Behavior." *American Journal of Sociology* 83(6): 1420–43.

Granovetter, Mark, and Roland Soong. 1986. "Threshold Models of Interpersonal Effects in Consumer Demand." *Journal of Economic Behavior and Organization* 7: 481–510.

Hirschman, Albert O. 1958. *The Strategy of Economic Development.* New Haven, Conn.: Yale University Press.

Hotelling, Harold. 1928. "Stability in Competition." *Economic Journal* 39: 467–84.

Howitt, Peter, and R. Preston McAfee. 1992. "Animal Spirits." *American Economic Review* 82(3): 493–507.

Kahneman, Daniel, Paul Slovic, and Amos Tversky. 1982. *Judgment Under Uncertainty: Heuristics and Biases.* Cambridge: Cambridge University Press.

Keynes, John Maynard. 1936. *General Theory of Employment, Interest, and Money.* New York: Harcourt Brace.

Koppl, Roger. 1991. "Animal Spirits." *Journal of Economic Perspectives* 5: 203–10.

Lane, Robert E. 1991. *The Market Experience.* New York: Cambridge University Press.

Leibenstein, Harvey. 1950. "Bandwagon, Snob, and Veblen Effects in the Theory of Consumers' Demand." *Quarterly Journal of Economics* 64(2): 183–207.

Levin, Lee. 1995. "Toward a Feminist, Post-Keynesian Theory of Investment: A Consideration of the Socially and Emotionally Constituted Nature of Agent Knowledge." In *Out of the Margin: Feminist Perspectives on Economic Theory,* edited by Edith Kuiper, Jolande Sap, Susan Feiner, Notburga Ott, and Zafiris Tzannatos. London: Routledge.

Lindblom, Charles E. 1978. *Politics and Markets.* New York: Basic Books.

Malkiel, Burton G. 1985. *A Random Walk down Wall Street.* New York: Norton.

———. 1989. "Is the Stock Market Efficient?" *Science* 243(4896): 1313–18.

Marchionatti, Roberto. 1999. "On Keynes's Animal Spirits." *Kyklos* 52(3): 415–40.

Marx, Karl. 1963 [1847]. *The Poverty of Philosophy.* New York: International Publishers.

Merton, Robert K. 1948. "The Self-fulfilling Prophecy." *Antioch Review* 8: 193–210.

———. 1957. *Social Theory and Social Structure.* Glencoe, Ill.: Free Press.

Miller, Dale T., and Deborah A. Prentice. 1994. "Collective Errors and Errors About the Collective." *Personality and Social Psychology Bulletin* 20: 541–50.

Mini, Piero V. 1993. *John Maynard Keynes: A Study in the Psychology of the Original Work.* New York: St. Martins.

Noelle-Neumann, Elizabeth. 1993 [1980]. *The Spiral of Silence: Our Social Skin.* 2nd ed. Chicago: University of Chicago Press.

Redelmeier, D. A., and Daniel Kahneman. 1996. "Patients' Memories of Painful Medical Treatments: Real-time and Retrospective Evaluations of Two Minimally Invasive Procedures." *Pain* 66(1): 3–8.

Sabel, Charles. 1994. "Learning by Monitoring: The Institutions of Economic Development." In *The Handbook of Economic Sociology,* edited by Neil Smelser and Richard Swedberg. Princeton, N.J. and New York: Princeton University Press and Russell Sage Foundation.

Shiller, Robert. 2000. *Irrational Exuberance.* Princeton, N.J.: Princeton University Press.

Smith, Charles W. 1981. *The Mind of the Market.* Totowa, N.J.: Rowman and Littlefield.

Snow, David A., E. Burke Rochford Jr., Steven K. Worden, and Robert D. Benford. 1986. "Frame Alignment Processes, Micromobilization, and Movement Participation." *American Sociological Review* 51(4): 464–81.

Stark, David. 2001. "Ambiguous Assets for Uncertain Environments: Heterarchy in Postsocialist Firms." In *The Twenty-first Century Firm: Changing Economic Organization in International Perspective,* edited by Paul DiMaggio. Princeton, N.J.: Princeton University Press.

Uchitelle, Louis. 1997. "Irrational Exuberance." *New York Times,* April 21.

Useem, Michael. 1984. *The Inner Circle.* New York: Oxford University Press.

Veblen, Thorstein. 1967 [1923]. *Absentee Ownership and Business Enterprise in Recent Times: The Case of America.* Boston: Beacon Press.

Vogel, David. 1989. *Fluctuating Fortunes: The Political Power of Business in America.* New York: Basic Books.

White, Harrison C. 1992. *Identity and Control: A Structural Theory of Social Action.* Princeton, N.J.: Princeton University Press.

Yamagishi, Toshio, and Midori Yamagishi. 1994. "Trust and Commitment in the United States and Japan." *Motivation and Emotion* 18: 129–66.

= Chapter 5 =

Enter Culture

VIVIANA A. ZELIZER

I N JULY 1999, Hewlett-Packard surprised the corporate world by
appointing a woman, Carleton Fiorina, as its president and CEO.
Fiorina, the third woman to lead a Fortune 500 company, was
hired away from AT&T and Lucent Technologies, the equipment and
research division of the Bell system. At Lucent, Fiorina, dubbed the
most powerful U.S. businesswoman by *Fortune* in 1998, had become
famous for connecting innovative technologies to new markets. Com-
menting on her appointment, Mark Anderson, president of Technology Alliance Partners, a consulting firm, explained: "Hewlett-Packard
has an engineering culture, and it tends to be slow. Carly has seen the
dark side of being slow at the old AT&T and also the benefits of
speed at Lucent. Picking her is not about technology or strategy. It's
about culture" (Lohr 1999, 6).

The corporate world seems to have discovered culture. Two leading interpreters of the subject, Terrence Deal and Allan A. Kennedy
(1999, 1, 40), confirm that "corporate culture" is now "a widely accepted term in mainstream business." Executives, they note, "pay as
much attention to culture as strategy in shaping a business plan.
Some mergers are shunned because of cultural differences; others
proceed because the cultures of the merging partners line up." Deal
and Kennedy warn their corporate audience: "Managers uncomfortable with the idea of culture beware. Culture, not official rules or
policies, ultimately dictate what you can do and what you can't" (see
also Kotter and Heskett 1992; Schein 1999). In corporate culture they
include such diverse elements as shared history, values and beliefs,
ritual and ceremony, stories, heroic figures, and a cultural network of

101

what they describe as corporate storytellers, gossips, priests and priestesses, whisperers, and spies.

Deal and Kennedy are riding a twenty-year wave in corporate analysis. During the early 1980s business leaders and analysts began to speak of a robust corporate culture as crucial to economic success. At that time best-selling books such as Thomas Peters and Robert Waterman's *In Search of Excellence* (1982) placed the formation of effective culture high on the national business agenda. (For an analysis of the growing interest in organizational culture, see Barley and Kunda 1992; for an ethnographic account, see Kunda 1992; see also Dobbin 1994, and Nippert-Eng and Fine 1999.) By the year 2000 many business leaders were speaking of corporate culture as a crucial component of their own strategies. At least 75 publications bearing the phrase "corporate culture" in the title were available for sale at Amazon.com, and in fact, Amazon listed a full 595 books on the subject.

Professional economists have also been paying increased attention to culture, with Gary Becker now *Accounting for Tastes* (1996) and Amartya Sen winning the Nobel Prize (see, for example, Bowles 1998; Greif 1994; Klamer 1996). "The subject of values," Avner Ben-Ner and Louis Putterman observe (1998, 3), "has begun seeping into economic discourse." They go on to distinguish three ways in which economic models can incorporate culture, which in their terms reduces chiefly to values:

> First, we argue that the stock of values helps determine the cost of operating the economy, and even the economic transactions that take place. Second, we point out that value considerations are likely to be crucial to the solution of impasses in the theory of strategic interactions—that is, of games. Third, we consider the evidence that contemporary society is suffering from a "crisis of values." (6)

This relatively narrow definition of culture is consistent with economists' attempt to preserve the centrality of choice according to utility function.

Outside the world of business and economics, many social scientists have recently taken a "culturalist turn" (see Bonnell and Hunt 1999; on culturalist analyses in state studies, see Steinmetz 1999; for a statement of anthropologists' view of culture, see Kuper 1999). That turn, however, has barely brushed economic sociology. On the whole, economic sociologists have recognized the presence of culture but have not integrated its analysis effectively into their own work. Although Neil Fligstein (this volume) claims that economic sociology has formed from an amalgam of political economy, development, organizational theory, stratification, network theory, and the sociology of culture, he fails to add that the blending in of culture has hardly begun. As Richard Swedberg (1997, 168) notes in an authoritative survey of the "new economic sociology," the cultural approach remains "a minority perspective." This chapter examines reasons for and consequences of that neglect.

Although some sociologists have inserted culture directly into the study of economic processes, more commonly, as Paul DiMaggio (1994, 27) has remarked, scholars are "accustomed to the view . . . that economic relations influence ideas, worldviews, and symbols. That the reverse is true, that aspects of culture shape economic institutions and affairs, is less well understood" (see also DiMaggio 1990). It was not always so. After all, with such classics as Weber's *The Protestant Ethic and the Spirit of Capitalism* (1958 [1904]), the junction between economic change and culture once seemed to be a major focus of sociology as a whole. Indeed, such pivotal figures as economist-sociologist Charles Horton Cooley, who founded Michigan's Department of Sociology, were persuaded that the study of social interaction addresses problems central to economic analysis (see Yonay 1998, 52). Cooley (1913, 546) argued, for instance, that "the market . . . is as much an institution as the state or the church. . . . I mean that it is a vast and complicated social system, rooted in the past . . . and though manned by individuals like other institutions, by no means to be understood from a merely individual point of view." "Custom," insisted Cooley, "is as great a factor in the market now as it ever was. Now as always it is the main source of the habits of thought that control demand and supply and so value" (544). For "custom," read "culture"; Cooley's institutions and customs came close to what this chapter means by culture: shared understandings and their representations in objects and practices.

More recently, Talcott Parsons and Neil Smelser (1956) did try to create a culturally informed synthesis of economics and sociology. Their model of societal integration depended ultimately on the supremacy of cultural values. Parsons and Smelser's preaching, however, fell mostly on deaf ears. In the semi-official compendium *Sociology Today* (Merton, Broom, and Cottrell 1959), published three years after the Parsons-Smelser treatise, the only article devoted to what we now would recognize as economic questions is a piece on occupations by Everett Hughes. It does not mention culture at all. In the rest of the volume, "culture" appears rarely, and when it does, it is used almost exclusively as a synonym for values or as a description of variation among peoples. At that time, not only sociological study of economic processes but sociology in general gave little explicit place to culture.

Only in the 1980s did sociologists start forming a specialty explicitly called "economic sociology." Initially, economic sociology, seeking dialogue with professional economists, deliberately marginalized cultural phenomena. Yet culture kept seeping into its analyses in the form of vaguely defined norms, commitments, ideologies, and values.

At the same time, ironically, a distinct group of other sociologists were creating a specialty they called "cultural sociology," a subfield devoted to the study of meanings, representations, symbols, practices, and beliefs. Unlike their colleagues in economic sociology, cultural sociologists deliberately marked their distance from rationalist and economic explanations. Yet by investigating such empirically tinged phenomena as consumption and the arts, they repeatedly cast their eyes across to their neighbors' terrain.

Now it is time to end the flirtatious segregation of culture and economic sociology. Both sides will gain from closer cooperation—students of culture from more systematic analysis of culture's location within organizational processes, and economic sociologists from recognition of culture as a constitutive element of economic transactions. Specialists in what Diana Crane (1994, 2) calls the new "sociologies of culture" can sharpen their analytical tools by taking on the seemingly flat zone of economic life. Economic sociologists will profit from extending their work into those areas of economic activity that they have neglected but that have attracted extensive attention from cultural analysts. Both will gain from the interchange (for a similar argument, see Spillman 1999).

This chapter seeks to promote the integration of cultural concerns into economic sociology by pursuing the following argument:

- As a discipline, economics focuses its explanations of phenomena on individual choice within constraint. As a result, mainstream economics either excludes culture from consideration as a cause of economic behavior or reduces it to an aspect or determinant of preferences.

- Eager for dialogue with economists and influence over the economists' agenda, economic sociologists have generally accepted that explanatory priority, while hoping to broaden the range of phenomena studied and the sorts of causes taken into consideration.

- Such an approach has produced a division between three different explanatory strategies within economic sociology: first, the extension of essentially economic models to subjects not considered central by economists; second, the provision of context for individual decisions within constraint; and third, the search for alternative descriptions and explanations of economic phenomena, thus challenging the focus on individual decisions within constraint. The third alternative approach occupies a marginal position in economic sociology as conventionally conceived.

- For this and other reasons, a notable division has arisen between, on the one hand, economic sociologists' analyses of phenomena that fall clearly within the standard economists' purview of firms and markets, and on the other hand, culturalist analyses of equally economic phenomena (for example, household labor, ethnic niches, the sexual economy) that are not on the standard economists' agenda. In general, economic sociologists have not recognized these culturalist analyses as belonging to their specialty.

- Existing studies of economic activities within the spheres of gender and of consumption illustrate this segregation strikingly.

- The same studies illustrate the possibility of integration between cultural and economic analysis, on condition that economic sociologists undertake genuinely alternative or complementary explanations rather than accept the centrality of individual decision-making under constraint.

- A more, not less, fruitful dialogue between economics and sociology could emerge from such an effort.

After exploring and explaining economic sociology's uneasiness with culture, this chapter proposes ways to integrate culture more directly into analyses of economic phenomena. It takes on the challenge of connecting two topics in which cultural analysis has thrived—gender and consumption—with the main problems of economic sociology. To repeat, for the purposes of this analysis, culture means *shared understandings and their representations in objects and practices.* Such a definition will, of course, elicit objections from theorists who conceive of culture as a feature of individual consciousness or as an autonomous realm. Nevertheless, it offers two significant benefits: relative observability and plausible connection with economic processes.

Situating Culture in Economic Life

Documenting the "embeddedness" of economic activities within institutional structures, tracing the grounding of economic action in social networks, or analyzing the social organization of markets, the field called economic sociology has vigorously shaken some of the fundamental tenets of orthodox economic models. For example, economic sociologists have made a strong case that supposedly transparent and efficient economic markets rest as much on social ties and their understandings as do bazaars or informal economies. Yet, perhaps in their concern to keep up the dialogue with economists, economic sociologists still often cling to economics' explanatory agenda. (For confirmation of the significance of this dialogue with economists, see the Granovetter interview in Swedberg 1990, 105, as well as Granovetter, this volume.) They center explanation on individual choice within constraint, thereby marginalizing culture as either causally irrelevant or determining preferences.

As a result, mainstream economic sociologists have only reluctantly integrated culture into their analyses; they have not quite known what to do with it. Indeed, twenty years ago Mark Granovetter (1981, 37) made an explicit point of differentiating then-current sociological concerns with structure and process from the value-laden Parsonian sociology of an earlier generation. "Sociologists," he declared, "are much more interested in social structure, flows of information and influence, networks of social relations, and the exercise of power" (37). More recently, in an interview with Richard Swedberg, Granovetter recalled:

> I and others who worked with Harrison White as his graduate students in the 1960s were in rebellion against the dominant Talcott Parsons framework, which looked like a rather elaborate taxonomy and did not pay enough attention to concrete social relations and networks of relations. It seems to me that in what you might call a sort of over-reaction to this very abstract argument, we were aggressively uninterested in cultural or mental states. (Quoted in Swedberg 1999, 12)

In the same interview, however, Granovetter noted his own growing interest in cultural and semiotic analysis.[1]

More generally, work in the field recognized as economic sociology falls into three categories, which we can call *extension, context,* and *alternative.* (For a more extensive discussion of these approaches, see Zelizer, forthcoming). They vary with respect to economics in two regards: their proximity to standard economic explanations and their proximity to conventional economic subject matters.

Extension consists of applying relatively standard economic models to phenomena that economists have not treated extensively or effectively, such as household behavior or religious recruitment. James Coleman's (1994) contribution to *The Handbook of Economic Sociology,* for example, lays out a broad program of economically inspired rational-choice analysis ranging over a wide expanse of social experience. (For examples of efforts to forward this program, see Brinton and Nee 1998.)

Context focuses on features of social organization that work as facilitators or constraints on economic action. Borrowing inspiration from Karl Polanyi and following the lead of Mark Granovetter, advocates of context often speak of the embeddedness of economic phenomena in social processes, often referring to organizational structure and interpersonal networks when they do so. Areas for analysis have typically consisted of firms and various forms of markets. As Granovetter states:

> What I mean by "embeddedness" is that the economic action of individuals as well as larger economic patterns, like the determination of prices and economic institutions, are very importantly affected by networks of social relationships. I think that for the economic action of individuals the embeddedness of individuals in networks of social relations is in most contexts extremely important, and you rarely see this taken into account in economic arguments. (1981, 100; for a more recent statement along the same lines, see Granovetter 1999, 161–62; see also Callon 1998, 10–11; Carruthers and Uzzi 2000)

In the third *alternative* category of analysis, sociologists develop competing accounts of economic transactions. Drawing on different combinations of cultural, structural, and relational analysis, those alternatives necessarily vary more (and contradict each other more often) than current extension and context analyses. Rather than expanding, complementing, or correcting economics by adding previously neglected features, this chapter argues that in all areas of economic life people are creating, maintaining, symbolizing, and transforming meaningful social relations. As a result, the economic subject matter, while including firms and markets, also ranges over households, immigrant networks, informal economies, welfare transfers, and organ donations.

The first two approaches, extension and context, have predominated in the agenda of what people have called the "new economic sociology." Granovetter's chapter in this volume clearly states the twofold agenda for economic sociology: showing how the immediate social context affects economic transactions and explaining where those contexts come from. As a consequence, relations between investigators pursuing alternatives and other economic sociologists have been uneasy. In this perspective, such figures as Harrison White (1992) and Charles Smith (1989) appear to be peripheral. Canny British observer Geoffrey Ingham (1996, 561) even remarks: "Both Smith and White are marginal figures, but it is perhaps this kind of approach which might lead to the recasting of intellectual orientation in economic sociology that is advocated by the 'New Economic Sociology'" (for a similar critique, see Callon 1998). From the perspective of the new economic sociology, of course, my own work also stands in a peripheral position.

Here at the margins a good deal of interesting work has been going on. A full survey of alternatives would include, among others, the outstanding efforts of Mitchell Abolafia (1996, 1998), Richard Biernacki (1995), Nicole Woolsey Biggart (1989), Bruce Carruthers (1996), Frank Dobbin (1994), Michel Callon (1998), Wendy Espeland (1998), and Calvin Morrill (1995). However, the point of this chapter is not to survey the whole literature but to identify problems posed by integrating cultural analysis with the study of economic phenomena.

Although it is convenient to distinguish between the extension, context, and alternative approaches, we should not exaggerate the rigidity of the boundaries between them. Indeed, in recent sociology lines of investigation that began as attempts to provide contexts for economic analysis—for example, in studies of informal economies and gender inequality—have repeatedly developed into alternatives to standard economic analyses.[2] Nor should we imagine that economists have stood still in these regards: institutional economists have also been moving into an intensive conversation with economic sociologists of all three persuasions.

Where does culture fit into the extension, context, and alternative approaches? In their attempt to match economists' parsimonious explanations, extension analysts typically treat culture as preferences, which remain exogenous to economic activity as such. Context theorists meanwhile incorporate culture as another instrument or constraint in economic processes. In both cases, economic sociologists hold cultural complexity safely at bay.

The alternative view tackles the difficult challenge of detecting culture—shared meanings and their representations in objects and practices—in the very social relations we call economic, then integrating culture into explanations of economic phenomena. Examining culture as a dynamic, contingent element of economic processes rather than as a mere constraint, the alternative model thus shifts from context to content. For example, instead of treating "the market" as an autonomous realm, alternative analysts of markets chart their variability and identify the shared understandings that occur within and behind every market, shared understandings that underlie the very possibility of market activity.

Analysts of culture who take this approach, however, run the risk of veering into cultural reductionism. It will not do either merely to insist that we can see culture everywhere we look or to reduce economic transactions to simple expressions of meanings, values, and norms. The problem is to identify the place of variable meanings and social relations in ostensibly rational economic transactions.

This step has been difficult for economic sociology to take. The difficulty stems from an intellectual strategy we have already seen at work: economic sociologists on the whole have accepted the explanatory agenda of economics. That strategy has had two deleterious consequences for the integration of culture: first, a concentrated focus on the conditions that affect choices between alternatives in situations of constraint; and second, the excessive attention paid to standard substantive areas of economic analysis such as firms and markets. As a result of tying its agenda so closely to that of economics, mainstream economic sociology has excluded most of the areas in which extensive cultural analysis has been conducted in recent years. The study of inequality, which plays a surprisingly minor part within economic sociology as currently constituted, is one striking example of omission. Within the zone of inequality, perhaps the most dramatic example is the neglect of gender.

The Case of Gender

Feminist scholars have rightly complained that mainstream economic sociology has neglected their concerns. As Ruth Milkman and Eleanor Townsley (1994, 614) observe:

> Economic sociology as a field has yet to be truly sensitized to the gender dimension of economic life. The recent flurry of attention to the Polanyian concept of embeddedness, which has striking gender implications, has yet to persuade most sociologists of the economy to seriously integrate gender concerns into their analyses. Gender-centered research, although plentiful, remains essentially ghettoized and ignored by the mainstream.

The result is to treat gender as one more attribute of single, decisionmaking economic actors instead of as an organizing principle in economic life. In fact, feminist economists agree with that judgment. Since the late 1980s a group of critical scholars has been waging a vigorous campaign against gender-biased traditional economic models and methodologies. More forcefully than their sociological counterparts, feminist economists, with their own organization and a special journal (*Feminist Economics*), have boldly criticized economics' main tenets. As Julie Nelson (1998, 36), a leading figure of this movement, states, economists' "exclusive focus on the individuality, autonomy and agency of the economic actor ignores the social and physical nature and familial upbringing and responsibilities of actual human beings, as it does the possibility of relationships of control and coercion." (See also Folbre and Hartmann 1988; Ferber and Nelson 1993; Nelson 1996; Seguino, Stevens, and Lutz, 1996; for a feminist sociological critique of the economic model, see England 1993.)

Within economic sociology, the exclusion of gender as subject matter has had a remarkable consequence for recruitment into the field. When Richard Swedberg (1990) interviewed seventeen leading economists and sociologists about their common areas of concern in the late 1980s, every respondent was male. That ratio has not changed substantially in the past decade. Some examples:

- The field's most prominent reader, *The Sociology of Economic Life* (Granovetter and Swedberg 1992, 20), with fifteen selections of what the two editors define as "the most interesting work done in modern economic sociology and related disciplines," includes only two women. (The 2001 edition increases the feminine representation to a grand total of four, for an increase from 12.5 to 16 percent of the contributors.)

- Of the forty-five authors in Neil Smelser and Richard Swedberg's *Handbook of Economic Sociology* (1994), only nine are women.

- Of the thirty-four economic sociologists identified in Swedberg's (1997) overview of the field as "key people," only four are women.

We find the same gendered pattern when it comes to who teaches economic sociology courses: only two of the twenty-two economic sociology syllabi published by the American Sociological Association came from women (Green and Myhre 1996). In comparison, of the ten syllabi included in the set on gender and work, every single one came from a woman (Winfield 1999).

These American examples should not mislead us; a similar pattern has appeared among Europe's economic sociologists. When French sociologist Michel Callon (1998) assembled a book of readings in the field, for example, only one of the twelve contributors was a woman. All of the authors of articles in the first two issues of the *European Electronic Newsletter* on economic sociology were male. Another form of evidence comes from scholarly organizations and meetings: for instance, most members and paper givers of the European Sociological Association's economic sociology group are men (Richard Swedberg, personal communication, August 1999).

Let's be clear about what is going on. It is emphatically not that gender is intrinsically a more cultural phenomenon than, say, markets and money; that women instinctively pay more attention to cultural affairs than do men; or even that male economic sociologists deliberately exclude females from their deliberations. Instead, the gendered division of labor emerges as a by-product of subject-matter specialization. Students of gender are predominantly female, more often self-consciously concerned about culture than are most economic sociologists, and more likely to identify themselves with specialties other than economic sociology. Plenty of scholars are investigating gender in economic processes. (For representative work, see the contributions to this volume by Bielby and Bielby, by Reskin, and by Baron, Hannan, Hsu, and Kocak.) The majority of those scholars are women. The point is that most of them are conducting their investigations outside the perimeter of economic sociology, as participants currently define the field. As a consequence, their work has less influence on mainstream economic sociology than it would if scholars recognized them as engaged in the same enterprise.

Why should we care? Why should gender make a difference for economic sociology? First, gender expands definitions of economic activity. Most economic sociology follows economics' concentration on production markets while treating as peripheral a wide range of other economic processes in which women predominate, most notably nonmarket economic activity. Second, attention to gender challenges assumptions of single-utility functions in units, such as households, that are in fact gender-differentiated. Third, a focus on gender raises more general questions concerning the place of categorical differentiation—not only gender but race and ethnicity—in economic processes. These differentiations form barriers to organizational activities that genderless, efficiency-driven models cannot account for. Fourth, the presence of gender multiplies the social work going on in ostensibly purely economic transactions. Where economic analysis postulates only the importance of interests and resources, by recognizing gender, we can see instead how people are creating, maintaining, and transforming social relations.

To be sure, students of gender themselves differ considerably in how much they attend to culture. Specialists in gender inequality with respect to employment or compensation, for instance, have commonly adopted a very thin conception of culture; they have treated it as an attribute of persons on the basis of which discrimination occurs.

Students of gender in employment experience and organizational life, on the other hand, have characteristically adopted richer notions of culture; they have portrayed shared meanings as governing existing practices.[3]

Christine Williams (1995, 9), for instance, proposes a theory of "gendered organizations"; she argues that "cultural beliefs about masculinity and femininity are built into the very structure of the work world." "Organizational hierarchies, job descriptions, and informal workplace practices," Williams states, "all contain deeply embedded assumptions about the gender and gendered characteristics of workers." In her studies of men employed in traditionally female jobs, Williams repeatedly ran into expectations of gender differences or resistance to the men's claims that they were committed to their occupations. For example, male kindergarten teachers or librarians specializing in children's collections reported their supervisors' unsubtle pressures to move them up into more "male-appropriate" specialties.

We find evidence of such culturally produced gender expectations even in Rosabeth Moss Kanter's pathbreaking *Men and Women of the Corporation* (1977, 233–36). While stressing emphatically the priority of structural location to explain organizational gender patterns, Kanter still calls attention to categorizations of female managers into four stereotypical cultural roles: mother, seductress, pet, and iron maiden.

The task of integrating gender, culture, and economic processes will take us much further. Two major challenges await us. The first is to examine how the presence of and change in categorical divisions by gender affect the operation of production, consumption, distribution, and finance as such. The best-documented examples come from occupational segregation by gender, but similar categorical divisions appear within households, informal economies, and financial transfers (see, for example, Zelizer 1994). Both the categorical segregation of economic activities and the maintenance of categorical boundaries demand significant social effort, an effort that itself becomes part of the economic process. Exactly how does that work? What are its consequences for industrial organization, efficiency, and technological innovation? Solid answers with regard to gender will shed light on the operation of categorical differentiation by race, ethnicity, age, or class of origin.[4]

The second challenge is more subtle and troubling. It is to determine what differences in culture—in shared understandings and their representation in objects and practices—characterize males and females in different settings, then to investigate the impact of such differences on production, consumption, distribution, and financial transactions. Feminist literature is rich in contradictory assertions on these fronts, but we will sort out reliable causes and effects only through close collaboration among economic sociologists, specialists in gender, and students of culture.

How can we move toward a richer examination of culture in economic processes? Each area of economic activity incorporates its own versions of culture. The full agenda of integrating culture, therefore, would take us across a number of fields, such as labor markets, finance, firms, industries, informal economies, and welfare economies. For purposes of clarification, however, let us concentrate on consumption.

Consumption

Why consumption? Here we find a critical zone of economic activity that is well established as a secondary pursuit among economists but largely ignored by economic sociologists. (For examples of recent economic forays into consumption, see Frank 1999; Schor 1998.) Within self-defined economic sociology, explicit studies of consumption have taken second place to the study of production (see Frenzen, Hirsch, and Zerrillo 1994). To be sure, for half a century sociologists and economists have collaborated in surveys of consumer expenditures and behavior, a line of work that has significantly influenced market research. Yet that nucleus excluded many aspects of consumption, such as the family dynamics of consumption and the social connections among consumers. On their own, sociologists have related consumption to inequality and class position. In general, those sociological studies have gone on outside of economic sociology as conventionally defined.

The best-documented cases describe the acquisition of goods as a cultural marker of class position, one aspect of which Thorstein Veblen (1953 [1899]) treated as "conspicuous consumption" and another aspect of which Pierre Bourdieu (1984) has identified as the formation of "cultural capital."[5] Work on inequality and consumption maintains at least a nodding acquaintance with self-conscious economic sociology—not as part of its main agenda but at least as a recognizable adjacent field. Outside of economic sociology as currently constituted we find that consumption studies are remarkably fragmented, with various sociological specialties taking them up as part of other inquiries and a whole literature on consumption growing up quite outside the mainstream of North American sociology.

Within sociology, other dimensions of consumption have become mainly the province of specialists in family, class, gender, ethnicity, race, religion, community, the arts, and popular culture. As a result, the recent proposal to form a network within the American Sociological Association on the sociology of consumers, commodities, and consumption draws on an entirely different constituency from organized economic sociologists (Cook 2001; Ritzer 2000).

Major efforts, moreover, have gone into studies of consumption that are centered outside of North American sociology altogether. For the past two decades anthropologists, historians, and cultural studies specialists have pushed consumption to the top of their research agendas. This thriving cross-disciplinary literature strongly emphasizes consumption's cultural features, with investigations into the origins and causes of a culture of consumption, the meaning of commodities, the practices of shopping, advertising, credit, and marketing; this literature pays close attention to gender, but also to racial, ethnic, and class variation.[6] As it happens, British sociologists, unlike their American counterparts, have affiliated quite closely with this research.[7] Still, the British sociology of consumption remains disconnected from economic sociology, even as practiced in Great Britain.

A partial exception to the alienation of consumption studies and economic sociology is the analysis of immigrant communities. The exception is only partial because economic sociologists studying these communities have stressed production. Nevertheless, sociologists, anthropologists, and historians have repeatedly discovered dynamic interaction among new groups of consumers, ethnic entrepreneurs, changing tastes, active marketers, and producers who discover that mainstream products do not sell well in what they call "niche" markets (see, for example, Cohen 1986, 1990; Heinze 1990; Holt 1997; Joselit 1994; Light and Gold 2000; Mahler 1995; Nightingale 1993; Patillo-McCoy 1999; Sanchez 1993).

For instance, Alejandro Portes and Alex Stepick (1993) show that in Miami the Cuban and Nicaraguan communities have created their own segregated economies, retailing goods from the homeland and creating new forms of émigré culture in the process. As consumers, Portes and Stepick report, "new refugees created a growing demand for culturally defined goods . . . that only enclave firms could provide" (145). They point to the case of Nicaraguans who in their homeland had shopped for European and American clothing but now eagerly sought out ostentatiously indigenous items sold by Miami's Nicaraguan stores. For example, *cotonas*, the cotton shirts worn primarily by Indians in Nicaragua, were newly retailed as a fashionable outfit. In exile, Portes and Stepick explain, such goods acquire a "new symbolic significance" that serves to differentiate Nicaraguans from Americans as well as Cubans (169).

Elsewhere, both sides of this academic divide would greatly benefit from a connecting bridge. Economic sociologists could not only begin paying closer attention to consumption markets but more generally get insights into the place of shared meanings and practices in economic life, while cultural specialists of consumption could integrate their thick descriptions of meaning into more sophisticated understandings of how markets actually work as social structures. As with gender, systematic attention to consumption as an economic process expands definitions of economic activity, challenges the imputation of exogenously determined single-utility functions to social units, forces attention to be paid to categorical differentiation, and explicitly incorporates the work of creating, maintaining, and transforming social ties into economic analysis.

Let us single out two controversial but promising problems in the field of consumption for special attention. One concerns variation in the organization and operation of different kinds of consumption markets, the other the impact of participation in those markets. As in the study of markets more generally, the range of available positions around the issue of market variation goes from the argument that all consumption markets are essentially the same to the opposite notion that every combination of commodity, consumers, producers, and social setting creates its own particular form of market.

Cultural analysts can make two significant contributions to this debate: first, by comparing how shared understandings form, change, and constrain exchange in different kinds of consumption markets; and second, by examining how producers, distributors, and consumers actually interact within frames of shared understanding. The study of transnational communities, for example, accomplishes both purposes. It provides a splendid opportunity to study how members of different transnational migrant groups vary and change along a continuum: from importing goods, such as food or clothing, for the exclusive use of their own community to commercializing an ostensibly ethnic genre that appeals to the general non-ethnic public at the point of destination. For instance, Luis Eduardo Guarnizo, Arturo Ignacio Sánchez, and Elizabeth Roach (1999) have investigated the differences between Colombian immigrant businesses in New York City and Los Angeles. In New York, businesses span from serving primarily Colombian immigrants (with restaurants, clothing stores, grocery stores, and bakeries) to providing services such as travel agencies, money transfers, and long-distance telephone to all Spanish-speaking immigrants. Except for food services, in contrast, Colombian-owned businesses in Los Angeles either are generally non-ethnic or appeal to other ethnic groups. At the commercialized extreme of our continuum in consumption markets, we find the remarkable case of the indigenous north Ecuadorian Otavalan merchants, who, as David Kyle

(1999) has shown, have been exceptionally successful at marketing their own and other inexpensive Latin American handicrafts to non-Ecuadorian consumers in Europe, North America, and Asia.

Turning to the impact of consumption, extremes run from views of entirely passive, "defenseless" consumers, as Michael Schudson (1984, 160) puts it (see also Schudson 1991), to views of an active consumer creating and shaping consumer transactions. (For an example of the first position, see Ritzer 1996; for an example of the second, see Cohen 1986, 1990.) Reflecting on the passive end of this continuum, anthropologist Daniel Miller (1995, 21–28) identifies the following four myths in culturally oriented studies of consumption:

1. Mass consumption causes global homogenization or global heterogenization.

2. Consumption is opposed to sociality.

3. Consumption is opposed to authenticity.

4. Consumption creates particular kinds of social being.

Many cultural analysts have accepted one or more of these myths without sufficient observation of the actual social processes in which consumption occurs (see Watson 1997; Zelizer 1999). A large agenda for research opens up. In the long run, research on what effects different sorts of consumption produce on participants, and how they produce those effects, will require that economic sociologists rethink the standard reduction of consumers to disembodied preference schedules.

Gender and consumption are not alone in their marginalization. Other examples of economic processes in which scholars have paid significant attention to culture but that likewise fall outside the standard agenda of economic sociology are households, gift economies, and the sexual economy. We thus arrive at a general problem. By and large economic sociologists, cleaving to the agenda of economics, have excluded cultural processes from their vision. At the same time students of cultural processes have not engaged in dialogue with economic sociologists, even when they have dealt with economic organizations and transactions.

A case in point is the process of gift giving. Here the standard treatments of gender and consumption converge, for analysts have not only generally excluded gifts from the world of truly economic transactions but also relegated gift giving to a feminized world of consumption, or to the even more separate world of primitive peoples (for some exceptions, see Akerlof 1982; Cheal 1988; Davis 1992).

Conclusions

Two of sociology's most influential specialties, culture and economic sociology, are ready for productive confrontation. Cultural sociologists face a great opportunity to explain fundamental processes that previously appeared foreign to their analyses. As we have seen with gender and consumption, economic sociologists stand to gain through a great expansion of their empirical range. Instead of huddling in the corner designated for them by conventional economic analysis, economic sociologists should move freely through the whole range of economic life. For both sets of theorists, the theoretical challenge will be stimulating and profitable.

The current division between economistic and culturalist analyses results in part from understandable processes of disciplinary recruitment and specialization. But it also reflects a widespread belief in a real-world division between the spheres of instrumental rationality and of cultural expression, as well as a fear that in close contact each will corrupt the other. Any new integration of economic and cultural analysis will require not only the transformation of disciplinary practices but also the revision of deep assumptions about the incompatibility of rationality and sentiment, of achievement and ascription, of individualism and solidarity.

Anyone who seeks a greater integration of culture into economic analysis, however, must at all costs avoid three temptations:

- Cultural reductionism of economic phenomena, which can take the form of either mapping economic activity into consciousness or reducing economic life to meaning, discourse, and symbolism

- Insistence on a separate, autonomous sphere for culture that somehow produces its effects separately from the economic process under analysis

- The argument that some social phenomena are more cultural than others—for example, by accepting that full-fledged markets have little or no place for culture

All three fallacies actually fortify the claim that the economy constitutes a separate sphere that therefore deserves its own noncultural science, whether economics or economic sociology.

The proper integration of culture into economic analysis treats shared understandings and their representations in objects and practices as part and parcel of economic activity.

This chapter adapts materials prepared for the conference "Toward a Sociology of Culture and Cognition," Rutgers University, November 1999; the *Newsletter of the Organizations, Occupations, and Work Section of the American Sociological Association* (Fall 1999); and the *European Economic Sociology Newsletter* (June 2000). I thank Bernard Barber, Paul DiMaggio, Alexandra Kalev, Richard Swedberg, Charles Tilly, and this book's editors for their comments and suggestions on earlier drafts.

Notes

1. Bernard Barber (1995) has had reservations about Granovetter's earlier treatment of culture. For Barber's own earlier integration of cultural and social structural accounts of market processes, see Barber (1977).

2. Examples of authors whose work overlaps the context and alternative positions include Wayne Baker (1987); Jens Beckert (1996); Fred Block (1990); Pierre Bourdieu (1997, 2000); Ronald Burt (1998); Randall Collins (1997); Dobbin 1995; Nigel Dodd (1994); Paula England (1992); M. Patricia Fernández-Kelly (1995); Neil Fligstein (1996); Mauro Guillén (2001); Jan Pahl (1999); Alejandro Portes (1995); Walter Powell and Paul DiMaggio (1991); Barbara Reskin and Patricia Roos (1990); William Roy (1997); Supriya Singh (1997); David Stark (1990); Arthur Stinchcombe (1983); Chris Tilly and Charles Tilly (1998); Brian Uzzi (1997); Bruce Western (1997); Robert Wuthnow (1996); and Sharon Zukin and Paul DiMaggio (1990).

3. There are, of course, some exceptions. An interesting middle ground between standard economic sociology work and gender studies appears in Burt (1998) and Ibarra and Smith-Lovin (1997).

4. My arguments here derive from Charles Tilly's (1998) probing analysis of categorical inequality.

5. More recently, Paul DiMaggio and Hugh Louch (1998) have made a novel and significant contribution to the study of how social relations shape the acts of consumption (see also DiMaggio, this volume).

6. See, for example, Brewer and Porter (1993); Calder (1999); Chin (2001); De Grazia with Forlough (1996); Goodwin, Ackerman, and Kiron (1997); Horowitz and Mohun (1998); Jacobs (1997); Miller (1998); Strasser, McGovern, and Judt (1998). Meanwhile, social and economic historians have regularly connected changing patterns of consumption to macro-economic transformations or shifts in public policy such as the New Deal; see, for example, Zunz (1998). For an interesting recent effort to reintegrate studies of class and consumption, see De Grazia and Cohen (1999).

7. See, for example, Campbell (1995); Slater (1997); Warde (1997). Significantly, a single syllabus on consumer culture included in the American Sociological Association's syllabi set (Green and Myhre 1996) is by Don Slater, a sociologist at the University of London.

References

Abolafia, Mitchel Y. 1996. *Making Markets.* Cambridge, Mass.: Harvard University Press.

———. 1998. "Markets as Cultures: An Ethnographic Approach." In *The Laws of the Markets,* edited by Michel Callon. Oxford: Blackwell.

Akerlof, George A. 1982. "Labor Contracts as Partial Gift Exchange." *Quarterly Journal of Economics* 97: 543–69.

Baker, Wayne. 1987."What is Money? A Social Structural Interpretation." In *Intercorporate Relations,* edited by M. S. Mizruchi and M. Schwartz. Cambridge: Cambridge University Press.

Barber, Bernard. 1977. "Absolutization of the Market: Some Notes on How We Got from There to Here." In *Markets and Morals,* edited by Gerald Dworkin, Gordon Bermant, and Peter Brown. Washington, D.C.: Hemisphere.

———. 1995. "All Economies Are 'Embedded': The Career of a Concept, and Beyond." *Social Research* 62: 387–413.

Barley, Stephen R., and Gideon Kunda. 1992. "Design and Devotion: Surges of Rational and Normative Ideologies of Control in Managerial Discourse." *Administrative Science Quarterly* 37: 363–99.

Becker, Gary S. 1996. *Accounting for Tastes.* Cambridge, Mass.: Harvard University Press.

Beckert, Jens. 1996. "What Is Sociological About Economic Sociology?: Uncertainty and the Embeddedness of Economic Action." *Theory and Society* 25–26: 803–40.

Ben-Ner, Avner, and Louis Putterman, eds. 1998. *Economics, Values, and Organizations.* Cambridge: Cambridge University Press.

Biernacki, Richard. 1995. *The Fabrication of Labor.* Berkeley: University of California Press.

Biggart, Nicole Woolsey. 1989. *Charismatic Capitalism: Direct Selling Organizations in America.* Chicago: University of Chicago Press.

Block, Fred. 1990. *Postindustrial Possibilities.* Berkeley: University of California Press.

Bonnell, Victoria E., and Lynn Hunt, eds. 1999. *Beyond the Cultural Turn.* Berkeley: University of California Press.

Bourdieu, Pierre. 1984. *Distinction.* Cambridge, Mass.: Harvard University Press.

———. 1997. "Le champ economique." *Actes de la recherche en sciences sociales* 119: 48–66.

———. 2000. *Les structures sociales de l'économie.* Paris: Éditions du Seuil.

Bowles, Samuel. 1998. "Endogenous Preferences: The Cultural Consequences of Markets and Other Economic Institutions." *Journal of Economic Literature* 36: 75–111.

Brewer, John, and Roy Porter. 1993. *Consumption and the World of Goods.* London: Routledge.

Brinton, Mary C., and Victor Nee, eds. 1998. *The New Institutionalism in Sociology.* New York: Russell Sage Foundation.

Burt, Ronald S. 1998. "The Gender of Social Capital." *Rationality and Society* 10: 5–46.

Calder, Lendol. 1999. *Financing the American Dream: A Cultural History of Consumer Credit.* Princeton, N.J.: Princeton University Press.

Callon, Michel. 1998. "The Embeddedness of Economic Markets in Economics." In *The Laws of the Markets,* edited by Michel Callon. Oxford: Blackwell.

Campbell, Colin. 1995. "The Sociology of Consumption." In *Acknowledging Consumption,* edited by Daniel Miller. London: Routledge.

Carruthers, Bruce G. 1996. *City of Capital: Politics and Markets in the English Financial Revolution.* Princeton, N.J.: Princeton University Press.

Carruthers, Bruce G., and Brian Uzzi. 2000. "Economic Sociology in the New Millennium." *Contemporary Sociology* 29: 486–94.

Cheal, David. 1988. *The Gift Economy.* London: Routledge.

Chin, Elizabeth. 2001. *Purchasing Power: Black Kids and American Consumer Culture.* Minneapolis: University of Minnesota Press.

Cohen, Lizabeth. 1986. "Embellishing a Life of Labor: An Interpretation of the Material Culture of American Working-class Homes, 1885–1915." In *Common Places: Readings in American Vernacular Architecture,* edited by Dell Upton and John Michael Vlach. Athens: University of Georgia Press.

———. 1990. *Making a New Deal: Industrial Workers in Chicago, 1919–1939.* Cambridge: Cambridge University Press.

Coleman, James. 1994. "A Rational Choice Perspective on Economic Sociology." In *The Handbook of Economic Sociology,* edited by Neil Smelser and Richard Swedberg. Princeton, N.J., and New York: Princeton University Press and Russell Sage Foundation.

Collins, Randall. 1997. "Religious Economy and the Emergence of Capitalism in Japan." *American Sociological Review* 62: 843–65.

Cook, Dan. 2001. "Consumers, Commodities, and Consumption." Prospective American Sociological Association section-in-formation. Available at: *socrates.berkeley.edu/~nalinik/ccc.html* (June 20, 2001).

Cooley, Charles H. 1913. "The Institutional Character of Pecuniary Valuation." *American Journal of Sociology* 18: 543–55.

Crane, Diana. 1994. "Introduction: The Challenge of the Sociology of Culture to Sociology as a Discipline." In *The Sociology of Culture,* edited by Diana Crane. Cambridge, Mass.: Blackwell.

Davis, John. 1992. *Exchange.* Minneapolis: University of Minnesota Press.

Deal, Terrence E., and Allan A. Kennedy. 1999. *The New Corporate Cultures.* New York: Perseus Books.

De Grazia, Victoria, and Lizabeth Cohen. 1999. "Class and Consumption." *International Labor and Working-class History* (special issue) 55(spring).

De Grazia, Victoria, with Ellen Forlough. 1996. *The Sex of Things.* Berkeley: University of California Press.

DiMaggio, Paul. 1990. "Cultural Aspects of Economic Action and Organization." In *Beyond the Marketplace,* edited by Roger Friedland and A. F. Robertson. New York: Aldine.

———. 1994. "Culture and Economy." In *The Handbook of Economic Sociology,* edited by Neil Smelser and Richard Swedberg. Princeton, N.J., and New York: Princeton University Press and Russell Sage Foundation.

DiMaggio, Paul, and Hugh Louch. 1998. "Socially Embedded Consumer Transactions: For What Kinds of Purchases Do People Most Often Use Networks?" *American Sociological Review* 63: 619–37.

Dobbin, Frank. 1994. "Cultural Models of Organization: The Social Construction of Rational Organizing Principles." In *The Sociology of Culture*, edited by Diana Crane. Cambridge, Mass.: Blackwell.

———. 1995. *Forging Industrial Policy: The United States, Britain, and France in the Railway Age.* Cambridge: Cambridge University Press.

Dodd, Nigel. 1994. *The Sociology of Money.* New York: Continuum.

England, Paula. 1992. *Comparable Worth: Theories and Evidence.* New York: Aldine.

———. 1993. "The Separative Self: Androcentric Bias in Neoclassical Assumptions." In *Beyond Economic Man: Feminist Theory and Economics*, edited by Marianne A. Ferber and Julie A. Nelson. Chicago: University of Chicago Press.

Espeland, Wendy. 1998. *The Struggle for Water.* Chicago: University of Chicago Press.

Ferber, Marianne A., and Julie A. Nelson, eds. 1993. *Beyond Economic Man: Feminist Theory and Economics.* Chicago: University of Chicago Press.

Fernández-Kelly, M. Patricia. 1995. "Social and Cultural Capital in the Urban Ghetto: Implications for the Economic Sociology of Immigration." In *The Economic Sociology of Immigration*, edited by Alejandro Portes. New York: Russell Sage Foundation.

Fligstein, Neil. 1996. "Markets as Politics: A Political-Cultural Approach to Market Politics." *American Sociological Review* 61: 656–73.

Folbre, Nancy, and Heidi Hartmann. 1988. "The Rhetoric of Self-interest: Ideology of Gender in Economic Theory." In *The Consequences of Economic Rhetoric*, edited by Arjo Klamer, Donald N. McCloskey, and Robert M. Solow. Cambridge: Cambridge University Press.

Frank, Robert H. 1999. *Luxury Fever.* New York: Free Press.

Frenzen, Jonathan, Paul M. Hirsch, and Philip C. Zerrillo. 1994. "Consumption, Preferences, and Changing Lifestyles." In *The Handbook of Economic Sociology*, edited by Neil Smelser and Richard Swedberg. Princeton, N.J., and New York: Princeton University Press and Russell Sage Foundation.

Goodwin, Neva R., Frank Ackerman, and David Kiron. 1997. *The Consumer Society.* Washington, D.C.: Island Press.

Granovetter, Mark. 1981. "Toward a Sociological Theory of Income Differences." In *Sociological Perspectives*, edited by Ivar Berg. New York: Academic Press.

———. 1999. "Coase Encounters and Formal Models: Taking Gibbons Seriously." *Administrative Science Quarterly* 44: 158–62.

Granovetter, Mark, and Richard Swedberg. 1992. *The Sociology of Economic Life.* Boulder, Colo.: Westview Press.

———. 2001. *The Sociology of Economic Life.* 2d edition. Boulder, Colo.: Westview.

Green, Gary P., and David Myhre. 1996. *Economic Sociology: Syllabi and Instructional Materials.* Washington, D.C.: American Sociological Association.

Greif, Avner. 1994. "Cultural Beliefs and the Organization of Society: A Historical and Theoretical Reflection on Collectivist and Individualist Societies." *Journal of Political Economy* 102: 912–50.

Guarnizo, Luis Eduardo, Arturo Ignacio Sánchez, and Elizabeth M. Roach. 1999. "Mistrust, Fragmented Solidarity, and Transnational Migration: Colombians in New York City and Los Angeles." In "Transnational Communities," *Ethnic and Racial Studies* (special issue edited by Alejandro Portes, Luis E. Guarnizo, and Patricia Landolt) 22: 367–96.

Guillén, Mauro F. 2001. *The Limits of Convergence: Globalization and Organizational Change in Argentina, South Korea, and Spain.* Princeton, N.J.: Princeton University Press.

Heinze, Andrew R. 1990. *Adapting to Abundance.* New York: Columbia University Press.

Holt, Douglas B. 1997. "Postructuralist Lifestyle Analysis: Conceptualizing the Social Patterning of Consumption in Postmodernity." *Journal of Consumer Research* 23(March): 326–50.

Horowitz, Roger, and Arwen Mohun, eds. 1998. *His and Hers: Gender, Consumption, and Technology.* Charlottesville: University Press of Virginia.

Ibarra, Herminia, and Lynn Smith-Lovin. 1997. "New Directions in Social Network Research on Gender and Organizational Careers." In *Creating Tomorrow's Organizations: A Handbook for Future Research in Organizational Behavior,* edited by Cary L. Cooper and Susan Jackson. Sussex: Wiley.

Ingham, Geoffrey. 1996. "The 'New Economic Sociology.'" *Work, Employment, and Society* 10(September): 549–64.

Jacobs, Meg. 1997. "'How About Some Meat?': The Office of Price Administration, Consumption Politics, and State Building from the Bottom Up, 1941–1946." *Journal of American History* 84: 910–41.

Joselit, Jenna Weissman. 1994. *The Wonders of America.* New York: Hill and Wang.

Kanter, Rosabeth Moss. 1977. *Men and Women of the Corporation.* New York: Basic Books.

Klamer, Arjo, ed. 1996. *The Value of Culture.* Amsterdam: Amsterdam University Press.

Kotter, John P., and James L. Heskett. 1992. *Corporate Culture and Performance.* New York: Free Press.

Kunda, Gideon. 1992. *Engineering Culture.* Philadelphia: Temple University Press.

Kuper, Adam. 1999. *Culture: The Anthropologists' Account.* Cambridge, Mass.: Harvard University Press.

Kyle, David. 1999. "The Otavalo Trade Diaspora: Social Capital and Transnational Entrepreneurship." In "Transnational Communities," *Ethnic and Racial Studies* (special issue edited by Alejandro Portes, Luis E. Guarnizo, and Patricia Landolt) 22: 422–46.

Light, Ivan, and Steven J. Gold. 2000. *Ethnic Economies.* San Diego: Academic Press.

Lohr, Steve. 1999. "Setting Her Own Precedents." *New York Times,* July 23.

Mahler, Sarah J. 1995. *American Dreaming.* Princeton, N.J.: Princeton University Press.

Merton, Robert K., Leonard Broom, and Leonard S. Cottrell Jr. 1959. *Sociology Today.* New York: Basic Books.

Milkman, Ruth, and Eleanor Townsley. 1994. "Gender and the Economy." In *The Handbook of Economic Sociology,* edited by Neil Smelser and Richard Swedberg. Princeton, N.J., and New York: Princeton University Press: Russell Sage Foundation.

Miller, Daniel, ed. 1995. *Acknowledging Consumption.* London: Routledge.

———. 1998. *A Theory of Shopping.* Ithaca, N.Y.: Cornell University Press.

Morrill, Calvin. 1995. *The Executive Way: Conflict Management in Corporations.* Chicago: University of Chicago Press.

Nelson, Julie A. 1996. *Feminism, Objectivity, and Economics.* London: Routledge.

———. 1998. "Labor, Gender, and the Economic-Social Divide." *International Labor Review* 137: 33–46.

Nightingale, Carl H. 1993. *On the Edge.* New York: Basic Books.

Nippert-Eng, Christena, and Gary Alan Fine. 1999. "The Pursuit of Workplace Culture." *Newsletter of the Sociology of Culture Section of the American Sociological Association* 13: 1, 6–9.

Pahl, Jan. 1999. *Invisible Money: Family Finances in the Electronic Economy.* Bristol: Policy Press.

Parsons, Talcott, and Neil J. Smelser. 1956. *Economy and Society.* New York: Free Press.

Patillo-McCoy, Mary. 1999. *Black Picket Fences: Privilege and Peril Among the Black Middle Class.* Chicago: University of Chicago Press.

Peters, Thomas, and Robert H. Waterman Jr. 1982. *In Search of Excellence: Lessons from America's Best-Run Companies.* New York: Harper & Row.

Portes, Alejandro. 1995. *The Economic Sociology of Immigration.* New York: Russell Sage Foundation.

Portes, Alejandro, and Alex Stepick. 1993. *City on the Edge: The Transformation of Miami.* Berkeley: University of California Press.

Powell, Walter W., and Paul J. DiMaggio, eds. 1991. *The New Institutionalism in Organizational Analysis.* Chicago: University of Chicago Press.

Reskin, Barbara, and Patricia Roos. 1990. *Job Queues, Gender Queues: Explaining Women's Inroads into Male Occupations.* Philadelphia: Temple University Press.

Ritzer, George. 1996. *The McDonaldization of America.* Thousand Oaks, Calif.: Pine Forge.

———. 2000. "A Subfield in Search of Discovery." *Footnotes* (February): 6.

Roy, William G. 1997. *Socializing Capital.* Princeton, N.J.: Princeton University Press.

Sanchez, George. 1993. *Becoming Mexican American: Ethnicity, Culture, and Identity in Chicano Los Angeles, 1900–1945.* New York: Oxford University Press.

Schein, Edgar H. 1999. *The Corporate Culture.* San Francisco: Jossey-Bass.

Schor, Juliet B. 1998. *The Overspent American.* New York: Basic Books.

Schudson, Michael. 1984. *Advertising: The Uneasy Persuasion.* New York: Basic Books.

———. 1991. "Delectable Materialism: Were the Critics of Consumer Culture Wrong All Along?" *American Prospect* 2(spring): 26–35.

Seguino, Stephanie, Thomas Stevens, and Mark A. Lutz. 1996. "Gender and Cooperative Behavior: Economic Man Rides Alone." *Feminist Economics* 2: 1–21.

Singh, Supriya. 1997. *Marriage Money: The Social Shaping of Money in Marriage and Banking.* St. Leonards, Aust.: Allen & Unwin.

Slater, Don. 1997. *Consumer Culture and Modernity.* Cambridge: Polity Press.

Smelser, Neil, and Richard Swedberg. 1994. *The Handbook of Economic Sociology.* Princeton, N.J., and New York: Princeton University Press and Russell Sage Foundation.

Smith, Charles W. 1989. *Auctions: The Social Construction of Value.* New York: Free Press.

Spillman, Lyn. 1999. "Enriching Exchange: Cultural Dimensions of Markets." *American Journal of Economics and Sociology* 58: 1047–71.

Stark, David. 1990. "Work, Worth, and Justice in a Socialist Mixed Economy." Series on Central and Eastern Europe, Working Paper 5. Cambridge, Mass.: Harvard University, Center for European Studies.

Steinmetz, George, ed. 1999. *State/Culture: State-Formation After the Cultural Turn.* Ithaca, N.Y.: Cornell University Press.

Stinchcombe, Arthur L. 1983. *Economic Sociology.* New York: Academic Press.

Strasser, Susan, Charles McGovern, and Matthias Judt. 1998. *Getting and Spending.* Cambridge: Cambridge University Press.

Swedberg, Richard. 1990. *Economics and Sociology.* Princeton, N.J.: Princeton University Press.

———. 1997. "New Economic Sociology: What Has Been Accomplished, What Is Ahead?" *Acta Sociologica* 40: 161–82.

———. 1999. "Mark Granovetter on Economic Sociology in Europe." *Economic Sociology: European Electronic Newsletter* 1: 10–12.

Tilly, Charles. 1998. *Durable Inequality.* Berkeley: University of California Press.

Tilly, Chris, and Charles Tilly. 1998. *Work Under Capitalism.* Boulder, Colo.: Westview Press.

Uzzi, Brian. 1997. "Social Structure and Competition in Interfirm Networks: The Paradox of Embeddedness." *Administrative Science Quarterly* 42: 35–67.

Veblen, Thorstein. 1953 [1899]. *The Theory of the Leisure Class.* New York: Mentor.

Warde, Alan. 1997. *Consumption, Food, and Taste.* London: Sage.

Watson, James L. 1997. *Golden Arches East: McDonald's in East Asia.* Stanford, Calif.: Stanford University Press.

Weber, Max. 1958 [1904]. *The Protestant Ethic and the Spirit of Capitalism.* New York: Charles Scribner's Sons.

Western, Bruce. 1997. *Between Class and Market: Postwar Unionization in the Capitalist Democracies.* Princeton, N.J.: Princeton University Press.

White, Harrison C. 1992. *Identity and Control: A Structural Theory of Social Action.* Princeton, N.J.: Princeton University Press.

Williams, Christine L. 1995. *Still a Man's World: Men Who Do Women's Work.* Berkeley: University of California Press.

Winfield, Idee. 1999. *Gender and Work: Syllabi and Other Instructional Materials.* Washington, D.C.: American Sociological Association.

Wuthnow, Robert. 1996. *Poor Richard's Principle.* Princeton, N.J.: Princeton University Press.

Yonay, Yuval P. 1998. *The Struggle over the Soul of Economics.* Princeton, N.J.: Princeton University Press.

Zelizer, Viviana A. 1994. *The Social Meaning of Money.* New York: Basic Books.

———. 1999. "Multiple Markets, Multiple Cultures." In *Diversity and Its Discontents: Cultural Conflict and Common Ground in Contemporary American Society,* edited by Neil Smelser and Jeffrey Alexander. Princeton, N.J.: Princeton University Press.

———. Forthcoming. "Economic Sociology." In *International Encyclopedia of the Social and Behavioral Sciences.* Oxford: Elsevier.

Zukin, Sharon, and Paul DiMaggio. 1990. "Introduction." In *Structures of Capital,* edited by Sharon Zukin and Paul DiMaggio. Cambridge: Cambridge University Press.

Zunz, Olivier. 1998. *Why the American Century?* Chicago: University of Chicago Press.

= Part II =

Social Networks and Economic Sociology

= Chapter 6 =

Markets and Firms: Notes Toward the Future of Economic Sociology

Harrison C. White

P ERSISTENT directionality in continuing flows is the most striking characteristic of the present economy, which has evolved around repetitive production by organizations that are each invested in some considerable specialization, in a layered system of intermediate goods or services, with a recognizable upstream and downstream. Within each market each producing organization learns to seek a distinctive niche for its output commitments among a nest of peers able to establish themselves jointly as an industry or market that has become taken for granted in the perceptions of other markets and firms up- and downstream of them. The market interface shields the firms from uncertainty in the flows. An ordering by quality disciplines the niches.

These markets are social constructions. Active guidance comes from watching the actions of the other peers as signals of that market. They reproduce themselves as molecules built from these firms as atoms. Each molecule arrays its atoms linearly.

The settings of these markets in flows of intermediate products are what distinguish them from older sorts of markets that deal in given stocks. Economists take markets as fundamental, but as yet they have no way to characterize the process and structure through which particular firms actually constitute a market; so economists largely pass over particular *firms* by settling for a stylized story of pure competition. On the other hand, analysts of firms' histories, strategies, and structures usually pass over particular *markets* and focus on the various relations between firms and the orientations of firms. Neither of these approaches has been able to provide a plausible account of a production economy, because neither explains how markets and firms interdigitate as they co-evolve.

A main goal of economic sociology is to integrate the two framings by markets and firms and thereby achieve a more complete realism. Together these two framings not only offer a richer basis for understanding the cultural and psychological dynamics and styles that cross-cut economic action but also sustain more incisive analyses that are larger-scale and longer-term with respect to capitalization and business cycle.

This chapter provides a partial overview, largely qualitative, of a family of mathematical models (White, 2001).[1] Distinct varieties of these production markets are located on a map according to valuation sensitivities. The models thus uncover commonalities despite diversity—in era and industry as well as in sizes, numbers, and locations of firms.

The first sections describe the general setting and the signaling mechanism around which the market molecule builds. Then I present the core results for the equilibrium model and its path dependencies. In the final section, I explore possible switches in orientation along stream and more general evolutions over time.

Asymmetric Setting

Firms add value by transforming the inputs they buy and incorporate into their own product, which in turn may become input to further transformation by industries downstream. Determining the set of firms that find niches in, and thus constitute, a particular market are the histories of substitutabilities across firms and markets. Unlike familiar markets of haggle and exchange, markets for production firms necessarily implicate not two but three roles: supplier, producer, and purchaser. Thus, producers must look upstream as well as downstream when deciding on an optimal commitment given the discernible signals.

Some form of comparability across producers is the prerequisite. It is simplest to achieve in a linear ordering such as a pecking order (Chase 1974; Podolny 1993). Quality is imputed according to this ordering. Profit maximization is certainly sought by firms, quite rationally, but it finds stable grounds as a business practice only during operation *within* a quality framing as a recognized industry *within* economic networks.[2] Quality need not be calibrated by explicit index.

The producers thus can sidestep the need to estimate directly the potential valuation that purchasers assign to each producer's flow of product or service. The trade-off, of course, is that they have to toe the line of equal valuation insisted upon by purchasers, expressed as a common deal ratio theta.

This production economy consists in disparate market interfaces. Each is based on some matching of local variances; each orients the producers toward the direction of greater uncertainty. Production flows do not course through anonymous market intersections, as hypothesized in economists' pure competition. Commonplace notions of supply and demand become contingent and relativized, since it is matchings of local variabilities that establish the viability of market profiles.

Supply and demand simply emerge as by-products of the interactive process of establishing market and thence product. As just one example, consider the Scottish knitwear sector in textiles. Social scientists have studied current operation intensively (Porac et al. 1995; see also White, 2001, ch. 6), and there is also a published history (Gulvin 1984). A higher standard of "fully fashioned" wear evolved in Scotland as several distinct markets in this sector, many centered in hand production. Together they generate about one-third as much product as the mass-produced English knitwear. Each of these Scottish markets must continue to earn recognition and identity for its product, an evolution in which "demand" and "supply" co-invent each other.

Market Mechanism

Production flows in monetarized economies have been greatly augmented by decades-old specialization in dedicated production facilities. Therein lies the conundrum. In the face of risks and uncertainties in placement and procurement, commitments are required, period by period, to sizes of flows in the next period. There is a crucial distinction between assessable risk and uncertainty, as argued long ago by the economist Frank Knight (1977 [1921]). Producers seek footings in the direction where they perceive Knightian uncertainty.

Only one axiom is required for modeling: *The principal business of any actor is finding footing in interactions with other actors who are also seeking footings in what thereby becomes a sustained course of action.* Each producer looks to a market profile, which translates present indefiniteness from across the market into a definite menu. Observability governs the mechanism of such a market, which constitutes a molecule with firms as atoms.

To estimate the rival profile in which it is caught up, each competitor scans the market positions of its peers. Concretely, it scans the volume and price of other producers in order to find apt footing for itself by making a suitable commitment to a volume of its own. This commitment in turn signals to the other producers its location on this rival profile, which they are thereby together constituting, in continuing reenactment of last month's or last quarter's pattern of commitments. Buyers, on their side, insist with every producer on the same ratio, theta, of perceived value to amount paid.

It proves feasible to set all this up mathematically using elegantly simple approximations—known as Cobb-Douglas functions (Nerlove 1965)—to the contextual facts of valuations. This yields explicit models calibrated around two ratios from four parameters (a, b, c, d), each of which summarizes (exponentially) the reaction tendencies of the various producers as to volume and quality in their two contexts—one as supplier and one as customer. Explicit solutions are obtained, although extensive numerical computations and simulations usually are required to establish predictions when parameter values are inserted into the equations. Simulations also are needed for exploring strategic manipulations (Bothner and White, 2001).

Model and Context for Mechanism

An explicit formula is derived for $W(y)$, the profile that can reproduce itself, in worth W for volume y produced by a representative firm.

$$W(y) = (A\ y^g + k)^f \qquad (6.1)$$

Here the only descriptors of this "representative" firm are y, its volume of product, and W, its revenue and thence market share. Only the reaction ratios appear in g and in f, whereas they are folded into A, along with the deal ratio theta. This profile must be consistent both with the ordering of producers from the cost structure that each perceives and with their ordering by relative satisfactoriness to buyers of a given amount of product. This implies a common ordering by quality of one producer's distinctive product vis-à-vis that of another. None of the participants measure quality explicitly, and so values of the index n for particular producers should not figure in equation 6.1. The equation simulates how the perceptions and calculations of participants interact through a market profile, the $W(y)$. It is only we analysts who stipulate quality as explicit values of some index n.

The performances of firms in the market depend on context—as sensitivity ratios—in addition to the particular quality levels of member firms. With the description of this market context kept simple yet realistic, the W(y) model can highlight it as the crux of market survival and performances, which are the dependent variables. The particular niche a firm achieves on quality does, of course, seem crucial to it. But understanding and predicting outcomes for the market and its array of firms depends not on the particular values of n but only on the existence of some appreciable range in quality. One can show in detail how to work back from observed outcomes for all firms in a market to the set of n values (White, 2001, ch. 8), but these can be put on the shelf for present purposes.

In actual observation the "profile" for a market joins a few points in the W and y plane, one for each of the firms. Besides the quality index, the market is indexed as a whole configuration doubly within the formula. One indexing is by the shift constant k shown in equation 6.1. Each value of k specifies a different member of the family of similar profiles of formula 6.1. It is an index of the history or path of interactive jockeying by firms and buyers from which the profile emerged. The second indexing is by the buyer's deal-criterion, theta, which is incorporated into A. It may depend on the particular path or history but will tend to be set by the standards that have emerged across markets in that sector of the economy as to how good a deal buyers expect to settle for. That requires paying attention to influences from whole other markets around the given one; those influences will be captured later in another exponentiated parameter, gamma.

The shape of the market profile proves to depend primarily on context, expressed in the two ratios a/c and b/d. However, the market profile is also subject to decomposition and unraveling by competitive pressures within the market. Unraveling depends on history or path dependency, as summarized for the profile as a whole in theta and k. For some contexts, the profile can unravel for any values of shift constant k, and for most contexts this is so for some values of k. Yet the unraveling may be contingent on the qualities of producers seeking to be in the market. The shift constant k is held to be more labile than quality locations, and these in turn are less stable than the main features of context for the whole market represented by the valuation parameters.

Valuation Parameters

The real crux lies in two trade-offs in valuations across the three layers of actors. The first trade-off is with respect to how the valuation of sheer volume grows for producers as compared with growth from the buyers' perspective. The modeling strategy is to estimate each of these growths in valuation by a *single* number, which is in fact the exponent of a power function (c for producer side, a for buyer side). That is what greatly simplifies the portrayal and hence yields an explicit formula as a solution. It can be justified as an approximation on those pragmatic grounds, but this is also the assumption natural in an account of what these businesspersons are themselves jointly constructing out of their own ongoing perceptions and assessments.

A market profile W(y) is not, after all, the work of some mathematician or a bunch of engineers. It is more like the discipline observable in conversations (Sacks 1995; Gibson 1999), or the discipline observable in greetings among kinfolk (White 1963), or the discipline seen in vacancy chains (White 1970; Stewman and Konda 1983) or in residential segregation (Schelling 1978). These interactions are intricate and involve subtleties, but commitments can issue only on the basis of approximations that are spontaneously workable in the field. In the same spirit, the first trade-off of the two sides' valuations is taken to be simply the ratio of these two numbers: exponent a, for growth in buyer satisfaction with volume, to exponent c, for growth in costs that the producers anticipate from volume growth given their procurement arrangements.

Such a number that stably characterizes some situation, process, or entity deserves special recognition. If such a number is not just an idiosyncrasy but rather can be applied across some determinate family of instances, it is called a *parameter* (White 2000). For the family of production markets and their members, a and c are parameters.

If that were enough, varieties of markets could be mapped into points along a line that measures context by the size of a/c. Indeed, this calculation (allowing for theta, but not k) is close to the claim that orthodox theorists make for their dream world of pure competition (see White, 2001, chs. 5 and 11).

Instead, turn to the second trade-off, which is between how the buyer side valuates quality growth and how the producers' side valuates quality growth in their cost built from relations with suppliers. Again, a single parameter, an exponent, is used for each valuation, b and d, respectively. And again, the trade-off is equated with the ratio b/d. The W(y) model argues that the distinctiveness of the various firms and their products within a market can be captured in their order by the quality portrayed by n.[3] But the particular values of n for a market have been put on the shelf as secondary. What really counts for market survival and firm performances is some balance between the second trade-off and the first trade-off.

Figure 6.1   Market Place

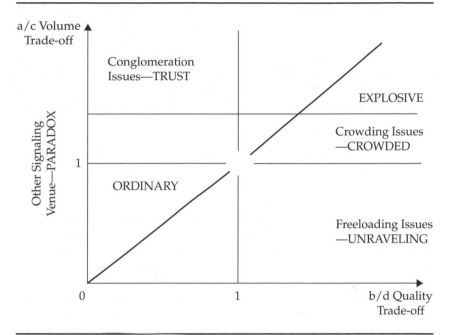

Source: Author's configuration.
a = Buyer demand for volume.
b = Buyer demand for quality.
c = Supplier cost per volume.
d = Supplier cost by quality.

Market Plane

Figure 6.1 locates varieties of markets in a plane. One dimension is a/c, the other is b/d. The plane assigns a niche to a market as a whole according to these two trade-off ratios governing the balancing of its firms' niches into a viable profile. The main payoff from the whole model is this state space.

Performances can be characterized in terms of quadrants, of rays, and of subregions. Price variations can be predicted from equation 6.1 using the two ratios of the four valuation parameters. Differences in patterns of profit follow, along with market size and the relative shares of firms in it. This all follows from the market's construction through niche-seeking and through searchings for identity by firms in terms of the signalings validated in aggregate by buyers.

So the performance of markets can be distinguished crudely according to a split into four quadrants around the point (1,1) shown at the center. The quadrants are constructed by crossing the two regions in which a/c is less than 1 or greater than 1 with the two regions in which b/d is less than 1 or greater than 1. In other words, a/c < 1 is where, for any growth in volume, demand goes up more slowly than producers' costs, whereas a/c > 1 is the region where demand goes up more rapidly with volume than do producers' costs. On the other dimension, similarly, b/d < 1 is where, for any increase in quality, demand goes up more slowly than do producers' costs, whereas b/d > 1 is the region where demand goes up more rapidly with quality than do producers' costs. Quite different histories are characteristic for the markets in the different quadrants, and also different tendencies to turn into nonmarket forms of one sort or another.

The two lines splitting the plane at the unity ratio cross, of course, at the center point (1,1). This crossing is left blank in figure 6.1 because performances predicted for a market are extreme for either ratio being unity but in opposite ways, so that the predictions break down when they intersect. Right around the central point is a black hole of contexts that will not support a W(y) market. This is just as we should expect, since the market interface equilibrates itself by trading off variation in volume valuation with variation in quality valuation; this trade-off becomes difficult as sensitivities on the two sides tend toward equality.

Two of these quadrants tend toward symmetry: in the lower left, the upper hand is held by buyers as to both volume and quality increases. Here producers vie for buyers who are relatively limited in their demand for volume and quality relative to what they cost producers. High-volume production is lower-quality, lower-cost. Here it seems hard for producers to grow, and there may tend to be more of them in a market, in conditions similar to those in population ecology theories of organization (Carroll and Hannan 1995). And this is closest to pure competition, the idealized model convenient for orthodox economic theory in which buyers see no differences in quality.

But we need to probe within each quadrant. Also shown in figure 6.1 is the diagonal ray running from the origin through the center point (1,1). The profit rate tends toward equality and at a very high value among firms in a market near this diagonal, while at the same time the absolute volumes and revenues of the firms are shrunken. By contrast, near the splitting line at a/c = 1, the market tends to be swallowed up into one large firm that is not profitable at all.

Equation 6.1 suggests some similarity in performances for the markets lying along any ray through the central point. When we put together rays within quadrants, we also identify wedge sectors. On one side of unity, the triangle between the diagonal and the horizontal ray is labeled ORDINARY, and on the other side, the triangle is labeled EXPLOSIVE. Equilibrating the market profile in ORDINARY depends on the volume valuation trade-off ratio a/c between the two sides being *larger* than the quality valuation trade-off ratio b/d. Exactly the opposite statement holds with respect to the triangle EXPLOSIVE.

Thus, the lower left quadrant contains the ORDINARY triangle, where producers vie for buyers who are relatively limited in their demand for volume and quality relative to what they cost producers. The upper left quadrant contains TRUST, an asymmetrical region, where there is high demand per volume cost (favoring mass production) but lagging demand for quality relative to its cost of production. This tends toward a nonmarket form in which firms either conglomerate or divide up markets by volume shares. In the lower right quadrant, another asymmetrical region, there is high demand for quality relative to cost, but lagging demand for volume relative to cost. The key dynamic is the undercutting of quality by low-quality producers who all choose the same volume-revenue position, driving out layer after layer of higher-quality producers and making the market unsustainable: call it UNRAVELING. The tendency is toward a guild arrangement, which fixes quality levels and restricts market entry.

The upper right quadrant contains the NOVEL triangle, which becomes split between EXPLOSIVE and CROWDED. Here there are increasing returns to scale. The entire market becomes more profitable the bigger it is; this has the character of waves of buyer enthusiasm, something like social movements taking place in the economic realm, or bandwagon effects in the popularity of products. These are most characteristic of novelties that catch on and become defined as the cutting edge of fashionability or respectability or technology. With such a basis of quality, buyer enthusiasm grows faster than producer cost with quality.

This is where we can exercise intuition but at the same time concede that *guidance from the explicit mathematics of the W(y) model is essential.* In the dull contexts where valuations by buyers of both volume increases and quality increases are below the costings of these by producers, the two sides will not come to agreement on a profile of compensating payments W to producers *unless* the volume valuation sensitivity ratio is more nearly even than that for quality (the ORDINARY triangle). In those dull, ordinary contexts, quality difference cannot play as much of a role as relative sensitivity to volume shipped if a market is to sustain itself as a viable profile. The real test of intuition is then to reason out why the opposite balance between volume and quality sensitivity ratios applies when both instead are high—in hot markets, so to speak, where buyers pressure harder. The crux is that in this quadrant of contexts a market is more vulnerable to other markets located cross-stream from it and will thereby splinter into subregions of different viability and performance, according to substitutability with other markets.

For this quadrant, it is important to introduce a third dimension, gamma: the substitutability of one market's producers for those of another. In this third dimension, which can also affect how good a deal the buyers get, the NOVEL region divides into two. CROWDED is where the optimum number of firms is rather small and the aggregate market size decreases if more competitors are added. This fits the case of high-prestige novelties: imitators reduce the economic social movements' enthusiasm and dry up demand. CROWDED occurs with relatively more substitutability of other industries, as in very novel and especially faddish products. More well-established industries have smaller gamma as substitutabilities are discovered. With somewhat less substitutability, profitability grows along with market revenue and the number of firms in the EXPLOSIVE subregion. Markets in each subregion may witness collusive efforts, but toward higher quality spread in the former versus reduced quality spread in the latter.

Path Dependence

Performance in fact depends on k, as is obvious from equation 6.1. Each firm in a market has its own volume and revenue, and it is only in the special case that they all have the same relative performance (profitability) that closed formulas are obtained for a market solution. This is the special case of $k = 0$. Then a mathematical formula enables one to see just how markets straddle between the two extreme performance packages described earlier for the diagonal ray and horizontal splitter, according to the intermediate ray they lie along. This is indicated in figure 6.2.[4]

The results in figure 6.2 guided my previous qualitative claims. But the special case of $k = 0$ does not yield viable market profiles in the other two quadrants, TRUST and UNRAVELING, where firms cannot exhibit the same relative performances and numerical solutions are required. What we do see is that almost everywhere in the market plane one can expect a great deal of path dependence. That is a fundamental prediction from this family of models. The extreme region is CROWDED where any value of k—positive, 0, or negative—indexes a path yielding a viable profile; earlier the richness of these contexts was emphasized.

Figure 6.2 **Dependency of Firm Profitability on Location Along Rays in Market Space: Ratio of W over Cost C**

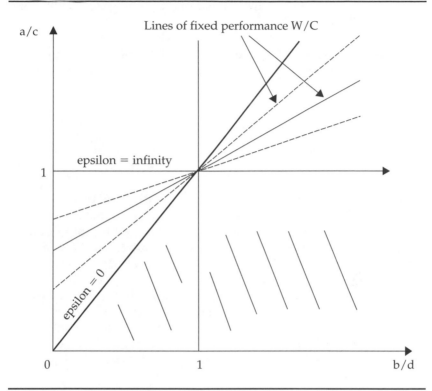

Source: Author's configuration.

At most points on the map any positive value of k can yield a viable market profile but only positive values. One can see from equation 6.1 that this means it is the market profile offering higher ranges of revenues that is robust dynamically. At the same time this market profile tends to enable member firms to cover any fixed costs over and above the variable costs that enter into their optimization choices, as Favereau and his colleagues (forthcoming) have pointed out. And in the rich CROWDED region, covering fixed costs would not be a focus.

Return now to ORDINARY. The other triangle making up the quadrant with ORDINARY is made up of contexts that *cannot* sustain a market for any value of k. Numerical, and thus messier, solutions of the W(y) model are needed to guide interpretation here, as is also true for the other two whole quadrants in which profiles with k = 0 cannot yield viable markets. In fact, markets from this bottom triangle are much like those for the whole UNRAVELING quadrant.

It becomes most obvious in this region that testing the viability of a market profile requires looking at the particular spread of locations of firms on quality. In fact, some points in UNRAVELING can yield viable market profiles—only for positive k, as in other quadrants. But now that will be true only if no firms are seeking niches from lower quality.

Orientation and Evolution

Unraveling invokes strategic moves by individual firms, but there may also be strategic moves by a whole market. Boundary changes may be induced.

Intrinsic to the production economy is the distinction between upstream and downstream. This is little noted in economic theories and business analyses but is foundational to my theory. One implication is so basic that the W(y) theory falls if it is invalidated. Each market must exhibit an orientation either upstream or downstream. Upstream or downstream orientations can be seen as historical outcomes of an evolutionary sifting process, just like memberships in the production markets themselves. But orientation may be switched.

The account so far has presupposed downstream orientation. Orientation in fact constructs itself in the most problematic direction; the unproblematic direction is left to habitual ties (White, 2001, chs. 9 and 10). An orientation upstream for markets generally may be produced by inflation or war shortages, during which times downstream prices are left as calculable and emphasis is turned to coaxing suppliers. Another version of an upstream orientation is that taken by colonial producers of raw materials with high overseas demand, who concentrate on exploiting their own suppliers. Former Soviet state enterprises might have been yet another version: their barter network with counterparts was focused on procurement rather than marketing.[5]

Within the U.S. economy, an upstream orientation can be indexed for some particular market by the relative prestige and size of sales and advertising relative to procurement departments. A set of discount supermarket stores may come to constitute just itself as a market oriented upstream seeking bargains from suppliers while confident of tailoring sales. Bothner and White (2001) exploit the W(y) model to examine strategic uses of switches in orientation. Matthew Bothner's simulations point to great potentials for gain from switching.

Orientation possibilities direct attention to questions about the actual process over time through which such a W(y) market comes to establish itself with its profile. Each production market gets itself together as a collection of peers only amid other like nuclei for other markets. Markets come out of networks of firms, but the primary question is not the formation of cliques and dense clusterings along stream. On the contrary, firms in search of protection against the winds of Knightian uncertainty are shying away from reliance on clusterings along habitual ties, which, although comfortable in the short run, can inhibit scanning and adaptation to changes and opportunities. The effect is to group together firms that have little direct connection but rather are in structurally equivalent positions, upstream and down, with respect to the networks of flows.

This is how some set of producers, amid a partitioning with other such sets, comes to key on one another in establishing differentiated niches as a set. This set comes to be recognized as the place to go for a whole line of goods that have come to be seen as differentiated varieties of that industry. This means that an industry derives from structural equivalence rather than cliquing (Burt 1987; Burt and Carlton 1989).

The exact paths of evolution are endlessly variable; dependent on contingent incident, they are also affected by variation in what neighbor markets are up to. How can one understand these evolutions? Turn, first, to an analogy from network modeling of other social contexts where actors are coming to cue on one another in some mobilization as they seek guidance on sources and sinks of services amid a flux of contingencies.

The analogy is to the work of Douglas Heckathorn (1997) on evolution. He has developed and empirically implemented network modelings. His target population is people who are drug injectors and who may thus be exposed to the HIV virus. They seek one another out for information on and access to drug sources as well as lifestyle. This information seeking is usually divorced from their ordinary lives— much as the market ordering of producers is divorced from their own primary individual operations in producing. Heckathorn's actual design is for users to track other users, thereby constituting a representative population for his analysis.

He specifies Markov Chain models with estimates of fixed transition probabilities between subsets of the resulting population, such as by gender and ethnicity and town. The point is that this is a plausible model not just of his specific process of target acquisition, which was motivated in part by offering reward coupons for each referral of a new subject. It can more generally model the process of self-constitution of a set out of a preexisting network population and thus serve as a prototype for market formation.

Heckathorn's further key idea is the role of homophily in biasing the coagulation out of sets around similarities in orientation. This is akin to distinct industries forming within an overall sector of inputs and outputs according to the propensities and identities of the actors who are searching. In both applications there is sifting by similarity that complements the striving for a distinct niche in the overall final grouping.

Heckathorn finds that attribute types seem to dominate path dependencies. He analyzes self-aggregating clusters of users that are only partially correlated by town of residence, an analogue to industry for firms. The key additional step is to invoke a generalization of the Markov Chain to a "mover-stayer" model (see also White 1970). This offers a paradigm for investigating market dynamics.

A second guide to understanding evolution comes from examining how boundaries emerge and are maintained. The Burt and Carlton (1989, 723) paper is entitled "Another Look at the Network Boundaries of American Markets," and it seeks "clearer distinctions among the market environment in which organizations operate." They argue that structural equivalence within the networks plays a greater role than connectivity, but they have to reason from census data that are aggregated across the many markets that make up an SIC category.

From less aggregated data, Ezra Zuckerman (1999, 2000) distinguishes the market memberships of individual firms. He also lacks data on evolution, but he does propose and validate a boundary-maintaining mechanism for markets. Investment analysts have considerable impact on a corporation's worth through their advice to investors, much of it based on discussions with executives of those corporations. What Zuckerman hypothesizes is that these analysts, like the participants themselves, have trouble understanding and following firms whose market membership is not clear-cut. Zuckerman shows that analysts tend to downgrade stocks of such firms. He goes on to show that the corporate executives thereupon take corrective action. The analysts thus are acting as gatekeepers for these markets as social constructions.

Boundary breakings of various sorts nonetheless may be key to strategic maneuvers. Simulations show that they can have significant impacts on performance (see White, 2001, ch. 9). Changes in the boundaries of markets are also a major avenue for the impact of the state on the economy. Neil Fligstein (2001) offers theoretical framing;

for case studies of industries, see Campbell, Hollingsworth, and Lindberg (1991).

Conclusion and Discussion

The market is like a social molecule of firms rather than a mere abstraction called up in some string-maze of firms in a sea of perfect competition. Producers seek shelter from uncertainty together under a market umbrella induced through their own actions as a set who have come to eye each other and be eyed by others as structurally equivalent in networks of business relations (Burt 1992). The present model offers a story to displace the pure competition story about markets involved in production.

Firms come to make some product X in an evolving economy as and only as they form a new type of tie with peers, not with suppliers or buyers. They form these ties on the basis of structural equivalence within existing networks of procurement and sales. Such a set of peers becomes known jointly as a package. As each firm jockeys for a distinctive niche within the resulting market, the set thereby spreads knowledge of, encouraging demand for, product X, in part by inducing comparisons of quality and price trade-offs that support the observed volume-price profile of the market. This array of niches on quality becomes established as the place to go for X, that is, as the market for X.

The array settles out because buyers insist on a quality-price trade-off, and thereby producers settle into an ordering by volume with the niche of each maximizing its profit (revenue minus cost). The array becomes established as the place to go for X; the very boundaries of the market for X are established in the formation of the market. Push and pull interact in building each other up through this market pump that runs on differentiation. The curvature of the price profile is what disciplines this market. Supply equaling demand is a by-product rather than a driver.

This model of social construction derives from central sociological theories of roles, identities, and network embeddings (Granovetter 1985; Nohria and Eccles 1992, White 1963). Yet it is also germane to the relational theory of contracting, to principal-agent theory, to transaction-cost economics, to rational-choice theory, and to industrial organization theory. A W(y) market is both a construct, analogous to a grammar, and a tangible system of discourse, as well as an actor with ties to other markets.

This model offers an alternative approach to that of orthodox microeconomics, which offers little guidance to empirical studies of production markets. Applied work is energetic in its detailed case studies, speculations, and statistical surveys but has no central unifying models applicable across observable market situations. The W(y) model answers a seventy-year-old call by the economist Edwin Chamberlin (1962 [1933]) for an operational and behavioral microeconomics.

The principal aim, however, is to join the refounding of economic sociology that has been under way since 1990 (Swedberg 1993, 1997). Investigators must pick their way through bewildering congeries of common sense and stereotypical accounts that variously distort the realities of social constructions. Parametric frameworks established by mathematical models can greatly enhance interpretability amid such complexity. Extensive simulations can be combined with numerical calculations to enlarge and refine these mathematical solutions and extend them to dynamics.

Most markets today regulate production flows, of goods or services, rather than exchanges of existing stocks, as in traditional sorts of markets. Three roles, not just buyer and seller, are involved. Putting-out systems of production were precursors of the production market economy, and today's trends toward greater subcontracting point back to that. I argue that economic action increasingly is becoming incorporated into such network systems of production markets. Edge markets that deal with services are becoming more prominent, bringing more social activity into the economy. Large production organizations are being unpacked into congeries of smaller organizations linked together in such production markets. The parametric mapping of contexts in the market plane can site a variety of these distinct types of market construction. Newly concrete predictions in case studies as well as fresh policy implications can result.

This chapter is a revision of a presentation at the Second Annual Conference on Economic and Organizational Sociology, University of Pennsylvania, March 4, 2000. I am indebted to the editors, and especially to Randall Collins for his continuing advice on presenting the models. I gratefully acknowledge partial support from the Council for Behavioral and Social Research (CBSRC) under a grant co-directed with Kathryn Neckerman, "Cooperation, Conflict, and Network Change," and from the National Science Foundation under grant SBR-982014 for a joint project with Ann Mische, "Dynamics from Social Settings." The Columbia University International Institute for Scholars and Mihaela Bacou provided help with and a setting for the final revision.

Notes

1. The first publications of the core model (White 1981a, 1981b) attracted little notice, but a decade later Richard Swedberg (1990) brought it to attention as part of his effort to renew economic sociology. Then, beginning in 1995, the French economist Olivier Favereau organized a series of workshops in Paris that related the first papers, and also White (1998 [1988]), to findings from the Economics of Convention School in France. This motivated me to write a book to develop the models further. Through meetings and their numerous publications, Richard Swedberg and Mark Granovetter helped with the retooling on the sociological side; on the economics side, there had providentially appeared in 1989 the authoritative *Handbook of Industrial Economics* in two volumes. Alas, neither side likes the way I meld them, in both qualitative phenomenology and mathematical framing.

2. In some lines of business, accolades for *higher* quality in a firm's product accompany a cost structure *lower* than that of any peer judged to be of lesser quality. The signaling mechanism as originally proposed by Michael Spence (1974) refers only to this paradoxical situation, which I also include in my forthcoming book, *Markets from Networks* (White 2001, ch. 5.)

3. Such assignment of quality is justified and explicated by the Economics of Convention School; for a penetrating analysis and direct application to the W(y) model, see Favereau, Biencourt, and Eymard-Duvernay (forthcoming).

4. Figure 6.2 derives from later discussion in my forthcoming book (White 2001) than figure 6.1, and it provides for the paradoxical situations of note 2: figure 6.2 is rotated ninety degrees from figure 6.1 to accommodate extension of the b/d axis to allow negative values.

5. Randall Collins suggested these last two illustrations.

References

Bothner, Matthew S., and Harrison C. White. 2001. "Market Orientation and Monopoly Power." In *Dynamics of Organizations,* edited by Alessandro Lomi and Erik Larsen. Cambridge Mass.: MIT Press.

Burt, Ronald S. 1987. "Social Contagion and Innovation: Cohesion Versus Structural Equivalence." *American Journal of Sociology* 92: 1287–1335.

———. 1992. *Structural Holes.* Cambridge, Mass.: Harvard University Press.

Burt, Ronald S., and Debbie S. Carlton. 1989. "Another Look at the Network Boundaries of American Markets." *American Journal of Sociology* 94: 723–53.

Campbell, John L., J. Rogers Hollingsworth, and Leon N. Lindberg, eds. 1991. *Governance of the American Economy.* New York: Cambridge University Press.

Carroll, Glenn R., and Michael Hannan. 1995. *Organizations in Industry: Strategy, Structure, and Selection.* New York: Oxford University Press.

Chamberlin, Edwin H. 1962 [1933]. *The Theory of Monopolistic Competition.* Cambridge, Mass.: Harvard University Press.

Chase, Ivan D. 1974. "Models of Hierarchy Formation in Animal Societies." *Behavioral Science* 19: 374–82.

Favereau, Olivier, Olivier Biencourt, and François Eymard-Duvernay. Forthcoming. "Where Do Markets Come From?—From (Quality) Conventions!" In *Conventions and Structures,* edited by Emmanuel Lazega and Olivier Favereau. London: Arnold.

Fligstein, Neil. 2001. *The Architecture of Markets.* Princeton, N.J.: Princeton University Press.

Gibson, David. 1999. "Taking Turns in Business Talk." Preprint 225. New York: Columbia University, Center for the Social Sciences.

Granovetter, Mark. 1985. "Economic Action and Social Structure: The Problem of Embeddedness." *American Journal of Sociology* 91: 481–510.

Gulvin, Clifford. 1984. *The Scottish Hosiery and Knitwear Industry: 1680–1980.* Edinburgh: John Donald.

Heckathorn, Douglas D. 1997. "Respondent-Driven Sampling: A New Approach to the Study of Hidden Populations." *Social Problems* 44: 172–99.

Knight, Frank. 1977 [1921]. *Risk, Uncertainty, and Profit.* Boston: Houghton Mifflin.

Nerlove, Marc. 1965. *Estimation and Identification of Cobb-Douglas Production Functions.* Chicago: Rand McNally.

Nohria, Nitin, and Robert G. Eccles. 1992. *Networks and Organizations: Structure, Form, and Action.* Boston: Harvard Business School Press.

Podolny, Joel M. 1993. "A Status-Based Model of Market Competition." *American Journal of Sociology* 98: 829–72.

Porac, Joseph F., Howard Thomas, Fiona Wilson, Douglas Paton, and Alaina Kanfer. 1995. "Rivalry and the Industry Model of Scottish Knitwear Producers." *Administrative Science Quarterly* 40: 203–27.

Sacks, Harvey. 1995. *Lectures on Conversation.* Oxford: Blackwell.

Schelling, Thomas. 1978. *Micromotives and Macrobehavior.* New York: Norton.

Spence, A. Michael. 1974. *Market Signaling: Informational Transfer in Hiring and Related Screening Processes.* Cambridge, Mass.: Harvard University Press.

Stewman, Shelby, and S. L. Konda. 1983. "Careers and Organizational Labor Markets: Demographic Models of Organizational Behavior." *American Journal of Sociology* 88: 637–85.

Swedberg, Richard. 1990. *Economics and Sociology: Redefining Their Boundaries—Conversations with Economists and Sociologists.* Princeton, N.J.: Princeton University Press.

———. 1993. *Explorations in Economic Sociology.* New York: Russell Sage Foundation.

———. 1997. "New Economic Sociology: What Has Been Accomplished, What Is Ahead?" *Acta Sociologica* 40: 161–82.

White, Harrison C. 1963. *An Anatomy of Kinship: Mathematical Models for Structures of Cumulated Roles.* Englewood Cliffs, N.J.: Prentice-Hall.

———. 1970. *Chains of Opportunity: System Models of Mobility in Organizations*. Cambridge, Mass.: Harvard University Press.

———. 1981a. "Production Markets as Induced Role Structures." In *Sociological Methodology*, edited by Samuel Leinhardt. San Francisco: Jossey-Bass.

———. 1981b. "Where Do Markets Come From?" *American Journal of Sociology* 87: 517–47.

———. 1992. *Identity and Control*. Princeton, N.J.: Princeton University Press.

———. 1998 [1988]. "Varieties of Markets." In *Social Structures: A Network Approach*, edited by Barry Wellman and S. D. Berkowitz. New York: Cambridge University Press.

———. 2000. "Parameterize!: Notes on Mathematical Modeling in Sociology." *Sociological Theory* 18: 505–9.

———. 2001. *Markets from Networks: Socioeconomic Models of Production*. Princeton, N.J.: Princeton University Press.

Zuckerman, Ezra W. 1999. "The Categorical Imperative: Securities Analysts and the Illegitimacy Discount." *American Journal of Sociology* 104: 1398–1438.

———. 2000. "Focusing the Corporate Product: Securities Analysts and De-diversification." *Administrative Science Quarterly* 45: 591–619.

Chapter 7

The Social Capital of Structural Holes

RONALD S. BURT

T HIS CHAPTER, drawn in large part from a lengthy review elsewhere (Burt 2000) of the arguments and evidence on social capital, is about current work on the social capital of structural
holes. I begin broadly with social capital in metaphor, get more specific with four network mechanisms that define social capital in theory (contagion, prominence, closure, and brokerage across structural
holes), then focus on three categories of empirical evidence on the
fourth mechanism: evidence of the rewards and achievement associated with brokerage, evidence of the creativity and learning associated with brokerage, and evidence on the process of bridging structural holes.

Social Capital Metaphor

Figure 7.1 is an overview of social capital in metaphor and network
structure. The diagram is a road map through the next few pages, and
a reminder that beneath general agreement about social capital as a
metaphor lies a variety of network mechanisms that can lead to contradictory predictions about social capital.

Cast in diverse styles of argument (Coleman 1990; Bourdieu and
Wacquant 1992; Burt 1992; Putnam 1993), social capital is a metaphor
about advantage. Society can be viewed as a market in which people
exchange all variety of goods and ideas in pursuit of their interests.
Certain people, or certain groups of people, do better in the sense of
receiving higher returns to their efforts. Some people enjoy higher

Figure 7.1   Social Capital in Metaphor and Network Structures

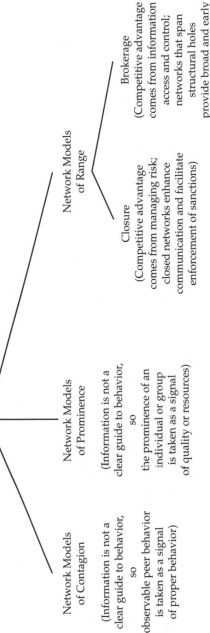

Bourdieu and Wacquant (1992, 119): "Social capital is the sum of the resources, actual or virtual, that accrue to an individual or group by virtue of possessing a durable network of more or less institutionalized relationships of mutual acquaintance and recognition."

Coleman (1990, 302): "Social capital is defined by its function. It is not a single entity but a variety of different entities having two characteristics in common: They all consist of some aspect of social structure, and they facilitate certain actions of individuals who are within the structure. Like other forms of capital, social capital is productive, making possible the achievement of certain ends that would not be attainable in its absence."

Social Capital Metaphor
(Advantages that individuals or groups have because of their location in the social structure)

Network Models of Contagion
(Information is not a clear guide to behavior, so observable peer behavior is taken as a signal of proper behavior)

Network Models of Prominence
(Information is not a clear guide to behavior, so the prominence of an individual or group is taken as a signal of quality or resources)

Network Models of Range

Closure
(Competitive advantage comes from managing risk; closed networks enhance communication and facilitate enforcement of sanctions)

Brokerage
(Competitive advantage comes from information access and control; networks that span structural holes provide broad and early access to, and entrepreneurial control over, information)

Source: Author's configuration.

incomes. Some more quickly become prominent. Some lead more important projects. The interests of some are better served than the interests of others. The human capital explanation of these inequalities is that the people who do better are more able individuals—they are more intelligent, more attractive, more articulate, more skilled, and so on.

Social capital is the contextual complement to human capital. The social capital metaphor is that the people who do better are somehow better connected. Certain people or certain groups are connected to certain others, trusting certain others, obligated to support certain others, dependent on exchange with certain others. Holding a certain position in the structure of these exchanges can be an asset in its own right. That asset is social capital, in essence, a concept of location effects in differentiated markets. For example, Pierre Bourdieu is often quoted, as in figure 7.1, for defining social capital as the resources that result from social structure (Bourdieu and Wacquant 1992, 119, expanded from Bourdieu 1980). James Coleman, another frequently cited source (as in figure 7.1), defines social capital as a function of social structure producing advantage (Coleman 1990, 302; from Coleman 1988, S98). Robert Putnam (1993, 167) grounds his influential work in Coleman's metaphor, preserving the focus on action facilitated by social structure: "Social capital here refers to features of social organization, such as trust, norms, and networks, that can improve the efficiency of society by facilitating coordinated action." I echo these definitions with a social capital metaphor to begin my argument about the competitive advantage of structural holes (Burt 1992, 8, 45).

So there is a point of general agreement from which to begin a discussion of social capital. The cited perspectives on social capital are diverse in their origin and style of accompanying evidence, but they agree on a social capital metaphor in which social structure is a kind of capital that can create for certain individuals or groups a competitive advantage in pursuing their ends. Better-connected people enjoy higher returns.

Network Mechanisms

Disagreements begin when the social capital metaphor is made concrete in terms of the network mechanisms that define what it means to be "better connected." Connections are grounded in the history of a market. Certain people have met frequently. Certain people have sought out specific others. Certain people have completed exchanges with one another. There is at any moment a network, as illustrated in

Figure 7.2   Social Organization

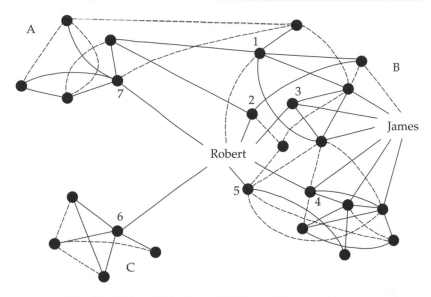

Density Table of Relations Within and Between Groups

.65			Group A (5 people and 8 ties; 5 strong, 3 weak)
.05	.25		Group B (17 people and 41 ties; 27 strong, 14 weak)
.00	.01	.65	Group C (5 people and 8 ties; 5 strong, 3 weak)

Source: Author's configuration.

figure 7.2, in which individuals are variably connected to one another as a function of prior contact, exchange, and attendant emotions. Figure 7.2 is a generic sociogram and density table description of a network. People are dots. Relations are lines. Solid (dashed) lines connect pairs of people who have a strong (weak) relationship.

In theory, the network residue from yesterday should be irrelevant to market behavior tomorrow: I buy from the seller with the most attractive offer, who may or may not be the seller I often see at the market, or the seller from whom I bought yesterday. So viewed, the network in figure 7.2 would recur tomorrow only if buyers and sellers come together as they have in the past. The recurrence of the network would have nothing to do with the prior network as a causal factor. Continuity would be a by-product of buyers and sellers seeking one another out for personal best exchanges.

Selecting the best exchange, however, requires that each person have information on the available goods, sellers, buyers, and prices.

This is the point at which network mechanisms enter the analysis. The structure of the relationships between people and organizations in a market can affect, or replace, information.

Network Contagion and Prominence as Social Capital

Replacement happens when market information is so ambiguous that people use network structure as the best available information. This assumption underlies the discussion of network contagion and prominence as social capital (to the left in figure 7.1).

For example, transactions may be so complex that the available information cannot be used to make a clear choice between sellers, or the available information may be ambiguous such that no amount of it can be used to pick the best exchange. Harrison White (1981) argues that information is so ambiguous for producers that competition is more accurately modeled as imitation. Producers in White's model deal with the ambiguity of market information by focusing on their position relative to other producers. Markets emerge as separate cliques of interdependent producers. White (this volume) provides a sketch of the broader argument, and empirical support can be found for even simple versions of the argument (Burt 1992, 197–208; see Baker 1984).

More generally, presumptions about the ambiguity inherent in market information underlie social-contagion explanations of firms adopting policies in imitation of other firms (Greve 1995; Davis and Greve 1997; for a review, see Strang and Soule 1998; on network mechanisms that drive contagion, see Burt 1987). Ezra Zuckerman's (1999) market model is an important new development in that it goes beyond predicting where producer conformity is most likely to describe the penalties that producers pay for deviating from accepted product categories and the audience (mediators) that enforces penalties.

Information quality is also the problem addressed in Joel Podolny's concept of status as market signal (Podolny 1993; Podolny, Stuart, and Hannan 1997; Podolny 2001). Podolny (1993) describes how investors who cannot get an accurate read on the quality of an investment opportunity look to an investment bank's standing in the social network of other investment banks as a signal of bank quality. Banks higher in status are able therefore to borrow funds at lower cost and enjoy higher margins.

Network contagion and prominence could be studied as social capital, but they are more often discussed as other concepts. Contagion can be an advantage in that social structure facilitates the transmission of beliefs and practices between certain people and organizations (a theme in Bourdieu's discussion of cultural capital), but it is more familiar as the mechanism for imitation in institutional theory (Strang and Soule 1998). Network prominence has long been studied as an advantage for people (Brass 1992) and organizations (Podolny 1993), but it is more often discussed in contemporary economics and sociology as reputation or status.

Network Closure as Social Capital

The network mechanisms typically discussed as social capital are the last two in figure 7.1: closure and brokerage. In these mechanisms, networks do not replace information so much as they affect the flow of information and what people do with it.

Closure and brokerage both begin with the assumption that communication takes time, so prior relationships affect who knows what early. Information can be expected to spread across the people in a market, but it circulates within groups before it circulates between groups. A generic research finding is that information circulates more within than between groups—within a work group more than between work groups, within a division more than between divisions, within an industry more than between industries. (Often cited as an early exemplar in this research is Festinger, Schachter, and Back 1950.) For example, the sociogram in figure 7.2 shows three groups (A, B, C), and the density table at the bottom of the figure shows that the generic pattern of ingroup relations is stronger than relations between groups in that diagonal elements of the table are higher than the off-diagonals. (Each cell of a density table is the average of relations between individuals in the row and individuals in the column.) The result is that people are not simultaneously aware of opportunities in all groups. Even if information is of high quality and eventually reaches everyone, individuals informed early or more broadly have an advantage because diffusion requires an interval of time.

Networks with closure—that is to say, networks in which everyone is connected such that no one can escape the notice of others (a dense network usually, in operational terms)—create advantage by lowering the risk of cooperation. The argument is associated with Coleman (1988, 1990), but Putnam's (1993) application to community development greatly expanded the audience for the argument. (For a review, see Portes 1998; Woolcock and Narayan 2001; for a review and comparative analysis of three communities that illustrates the potential contingency of the social capital of closure on other material and institutional resources, see Portes and Mooney, this volume.)

Coleman's argument (1990, 310; see Coleman 1988, S104) is that closure does two things for people in the closed network. First, it affects access to information (Coleman 1990, 310; see 1988, S104):

> An important form of social capital is the potential for information that inheres in social relations. . . . A person who is not greatly interested in current events but who is interested in being informed about important developments can save the time required to read a newspaper if he can get the information he wants from a friend who pays attention to such matters.

For example, noting that information quality deteriorates as it moves from one person to the next in a chain of intermediaries, Wayne Baker (1984; Baker and Iyer 1992) argues that markets with networks of more direct connections improve communication between producers, thus stabilizing prices. This is the central finding in his analysis of a securities exchange (Baker 1984).

Second—and this is the benefit that Coleman emphasizes—network closure facilitates sanctions that make it less risky for people in the network to trust one another. Illustrating the trust advantage with rotating-credit associations, Coleman (1988, S103) notes:

> But without a high degree of trustworthiness among the members of the group, the institution could not exist—for a person who receives a payout early in the sequence of meetings could abscond and leave the others with a loss. For example, one could not imagine a rotating-credit association operating successfully in urban areas marked by a high degree of social disorganization—or, in other words, by a lack of social capital. (See also Coleman 1990, 306–7; for a closer look at how such associations operate, see Biggart 2000.)

With respect to norms and effective sanctions, Coleman (1990, 310–11) says: "When an effective norm does exist, it constitutes a powerful, but sometimes fragile, form of social capital. . . . Norms in a community that support and provide effective rewards for high achievement in school greatly facilitate the school's task" (see Coleman 1988, S104). Coleman (1988, S107–8) summarizes: "The consequence of this closure is, as in the case of the wholesale diamond market or in other similar communities, a set of effective sanctions that can monitor and guide behavior. Reputation cannot arise in an open structure, and collective sanctions that would ensure trustworthiness cannot be applied."

Coleman's closure argument is prominent with respect to social capital, but it is not alone in predicting that dense networks facilitate trust and norms by facilitating effective sanctions. In sociology, Mark Granovetter (1985; 1992, 44) argues that the threat of sanctions makes trust more likely between people who have mutual friends (mutual friends being a condition of structural embeddedness): "My mortification at cheating a friend of long standing may be substantial even when undiscovered. It may increase when the friend becomes aware of it. But it may become even more unbearable when our mutual friends uncover the deceit and tell one another." An analogous argument in economics is that the threat of sanctions creates a reputation effect (Tullock 1985; Greif 1989). Mutual acquaintances observing two people make behavior between the two people public, thus increasing the salience of reputation for entry to future relations with the mutual acquaintances and making the two people more careful about displaying cooperation, consequences that lower the risk of trusting the other to cooperate.

Structural Holes as Social Capital

Where closure creates advantage by lowering the risk of cooperation, the fourth network mechanism in figure 7.1, brokerage, creates advantage by increasing the value of cooperation. The argument draws on network concepts that emerged in sociology during the 1970s: most notably, the strength of weak ties (Granovetter 1973), betweenness centrality (Freeman 1977), the benefits of exclusive exchange partners (Cook and Emerson 1978), and the autonomy created by complex networks (Burt 1980). More generally, sociological ideas elaborated by Simmel (1955 [1922]) and Merton (1968 [1957]) on the autonomy generated by conflicting affiliations are combined in the hole argument with concepts of monopoly power and oligopoly to produce network models of competitive advantage.

The weaker connections between groups in figure 7.2 are holes in the social structure of the market. These holes in social structure—or more simply, structural holes—create a competitive advantage for an individual whose network spans the holes (Burt 1992). The structural hole between two groups does not mean that people in the groups are unaware of one another. It only means that the people are focused on their own activities and do not attend to the activities of people in the other group. Holes are buffers, like an insulator in an electric circuit. People on either side of a structural hole circulate in different flows of information. Structural holes are an opportunity to broker the flow of *information* between people and *control* the projects that bring together people from opposite sides of the hole.

Information Benefits of Bridging
Structural Holes

Structural holes separate nonredundant sources of information, that is, sources that are more additive than overlapping. There are two network indicators of redundancy: cohesion and equivalence. Cohesive contacts (contacts strongly connected to each other) are likely to have similar information and so provide redundant information. Structurally equivalent contacts (contacts who link a manager to the same third parties) have the same sources of information and so provide redundant information.

Robert and James in figure 7.2 have the same volume of connections—six strong ties and one weak tie—but Robert has something more. James is connected to people within group B, and through them to friends of friends all within group B. James can be expected to be well informed about cluster B activities. Robert is also tied through friends of friends to everyone within group B, but in addition, his strong relationship with contact 7 is a conduit for information on group A, and his strong relationship with contact 6 is a conduit for information on group C. His relationship with contact 7 is for Robert a network bridge in that the relationship is his only direct connection with group A. Moreover, his relationship with contact 6 meets the graph-theoretic definition of a network bridge: break the relationship and there is no connection between groups B and C. More generally, Robert is a broker in the network. Network constraint is an index that measures the extent to which a person's contacts are redundant (Burt 1992). James has a constraint score that is twice Robert's (30.9 versus 14.8), and Robert is the least constrained of the people in figure 7.2. Network betweenness, proposed by Freeman (1977), is an index that measures the extent to which a person brokers indirect connections between all other people in a network. Robert's betweenness score of 47.0 shows that almost half of indirect connections run through him. His score is the highest score in figure 7.2, well above average (47.0 is a 4.0 z-score), and much higher than James's 5.2 score, which is below average.

Robert's bridge connections to other groups give him an advantage with respect to information access. He reaches a higher volume of information because he reaches more people indirectly. Further, the diversity of his contacts across the three separate groups causes his higher volume of information to contain fewer redundant bits of information. Further still, Robert is positioned at the crossroads of social organization, so he is early to learn about activities in the three groups. He corresponds to the opinion leaders proposed in the early diffusion literature as the individuals responsible for the spread of new ideas and behaviors (Burt 1999). Moreover, Robert's more diverse contacts make him more likely to be a candidate discussed for inclusion in new opportunities. These benefits are compounded by the fact that having a network that yields such benefits makes Robert more attractive to other people as a contact in their own networks.

Control Benefits of Bridging Structural Holes

The information benefits make Robert more likely to know when it would be valuable to bring together certain disconnected contacts, and this knowledge gives him disproportionate say in whose interests are served when the contacts do come together. In addition, the holes between his contacts enable him to broker communication while displaying different beliefs and identities to each contact ("robust action" in Padgett and Ansell 1993; on the connection with structural holes, see Breiger 1995; on knowledge brokers, see Hargadon 1998). Simmel and Merton introduced the sociology of people who derive control benefits from structural holes: the ideal type is the *tertius gaudens* (literally, "the third who benefits"; for a review, see Burt 1992, 30–32).

Robert in figure 7.2 is an entrepreneur in the literal sense—a person who adds value by brokering connections between others (see Burt 1992, 34–36, and the section "Adaptive Implementation" later in this chapter). Bringing together separate pieces is the essence of entrepreneurship. There is no value to a venture if it only connects people who are already connected. As Alex Stewart (1990, 149) reports from economic anthropology, entrepreneurs focus on

> those points in an economic system where the discrepancies of evaluation are the greatest, and . . . attempt to construct bridging transactions. Bridging roles are based on the recognition of discrepancies of evaluation, which requires an edge in information about both sides of the bridge. Because this requires an information network, bridgers will commit time, energy, travel, and sociability to develop their personal networks. For many entrepreneurs, their most significant resource is a ramifying personal network.

In terms of the structural hole argument, structures rich in holes are entrepreneurial networks, and network entrepreneurs are people who build interpersonal bridges across structural holes. Speeding the process toward equilibrium, network entrepreneurs operate somewhere between the force of corporate authority and the dexterity of markets, building bridges between disconnected parts of markets and organizations where it is valuable to do so.

There is tension here, but it is not the hostility of combatants so much as the uncertainty of change. In the swirling mix of preferences characteristic of social networks, value is created by network entrepreneurs strategically moving accurate, ambiguous, or distorted information between people on opposite sides of structural holes in the routine flow of information. The information and control benefits of bridging the holes reinforce one another at any moment in time and accumulate together over time. Thus, individuals with networks rich in structural holes are the individuals who know about, have a hand in, and exercise control over, more rewarding opportunities. The behaviors by which they develop the opportunities are many and varied, but opportunity itself is defined by a hole in social structure.

Hole Hypothesis

In sum, the hypothesis is that in comparisons between otherwise similar people like James and Robert in figure 7.2, it is Robert who has more social capital. Specifically, using figure 7.3 as a frame of reference for the next few pages, the hole hypothesis has three components: Robert has an advantage in seeing productive new ideas, bringing these ideas to fruition, and so obtaining higher returns to his efforts.

First is the question of what to do. What projects are available? On which should we focus? With early access to diverse, often contradictory, information and interpretations, people whose networks span structural holes can expect to find themselves synthesizing new understandings as they seem to others to be gifted with creativity. Putting aside the individuals involved, creativity and learning occur more often where relationships bridge structural holes.

Next is the question of implementation. Established ideas have a ready constituency and an allocated budget. New ideas typically have neither. The more innovative the idea, the lower the probability that a constituency or a budget exists a priori. Social capital offers an advantage in knowing which parties to connect for support, how to connect them, and when. Implementation that is responsive to new and changing circumstances can be distinguished as adaptive implementation, and social capital facilitates it. Networks rich in structural holes provide a broad base of referrals to customers, suppliers, alliances, and employees for a project; improve due diligence on potential customers, suppliers, alliances, employees, financing, and alternative organization models; and increase the probability of knowing which way to pitch the project will most appeal to specific potential customers, suppliers, or other sources of support. Thus, in-

Figure 7.3   Evidence Categories for the Hole Hypothesis

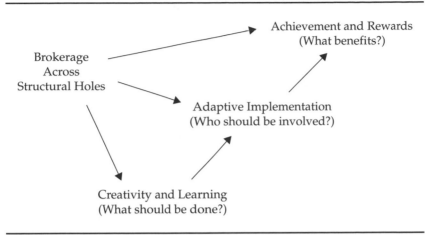

Source: Author's configuration.

dividuals rich in the social capital of structural holes are not only more likely to be creative in seeing opportunities but also more likely to launch projects to take advantage of the opportunities. Finally, the projects they launch are more likely to reach fruition because network entrepreneurs are more likely to anticipate and adapt to the problems that will inevitably arise. They become aware of trouble sooner, and they are more flexible in reshaping a project to adapt to exogenous change (as is vividly illustrated in drug traffic networks; see Williams 1998; Morselli 2001; on health insurance fraud, see Tillman and Inder- gaard 1999). They are also better able to control the interpretations that others give to the project by tailoring solutions to the specific individuals brought together for it.

The third category in figure 7.3 is about benefits—achievements and rewards as a result of action taken. Adaptive implementation, and the creativity and learning associated with it, creates an associa- tion between brokerage and benefits. In fact, studying the association with benefits is a logical place in which to begin research on the social capital of structural holes because the first two component effects in figure 7.3 are implicit in the association. There is little incentive to look for brokerage effects on creativity, learning, or adaptive imple- mentation if brokerage has no association with achievement and re- wards. I begin my review with benefits. There is evidence of an asso- ciation between brokerage and more positive evaluations, more successful teams, faster promotion, and higher compensation.

Individual and Group Benefits

Three categories of evidence show that achievement and rewards are associated with brokerage. Lab experiments with small-group exchange networks show that resources accumulate in brokers: people with exclusive exchange relations to otherwise disconnected partners (Cook and Emerson 1978; Cook et al. 1983; Markovsky, Willer, and Patton 1988; for a review, see Willer 1999).

Census data on economic transactions have been used to describe how producer profit margins increase with structural holes in the networks of transactions with suppliers and customers. Burt (1983) described the association in 1967 with profits in American manufacturing markets defined at broad and detailed levels of aggregation, and he extended the results to include nonmanufacturing through the 1960s and 1970s (Burt 1988, 1992). Burt, Guilarte, Raider, and Yasuda (forthcoming) refined the nonlinear form of the model to describe more accurately the association between performance and market network and extended the results through the early 1990s. Using profit and network data on markets in other countries, similar results have been found in Germany during the 1970s and 1980s (Ziegler 1982), Israel in the 1970s (Talmud 1994), Japan in the 1980s (Yasuda 1996), and Korea in the 1980s (Jang 1997).

Third, archival and survey data on interpersonal relations have been used to describe the career advantages of having a contact network rich in structural holes. An early, widely known study is Granovetter's (1995 [1974]) demonstration that white-collar workers find better jobs faster through weak ties that bridge otherwise disconnected social groups (on weak ties across structural holes, see Burt 1992, 25–30). Nan Lin worked with several colleagues to present evidence of the importance of ties to distant contacts for obtaining more desirable jobs (Lin, Ensel, and Vaughn 1981; Lin and Dumin 1986; Lin 1999). Similar empirical results appear in Campbell, Marsden, and Hurlbert (1986), Marsden and Hurlbert (1988), Flap and De Graaf (1989), Boxman, De Graaf, and Flap (1991), Lin and Bian (1991), Wegener (1991), Bian (1994, ch. 5), and in more recent empirical studies (Leenders and Gabbay 1999; Lin, Cook, and Burt 2001). Lin (1999, 2001) provides an integrative review of such research through a focus on networks as a resource for status attainment.

In particular, organizations have been a fruitful site for network studies of social capital. Burt (1992, 1995, 1997, 1998) and Joel Podolny and James Baron (1997) present survey evidence from probability samples of managers in two high-technology electronics firms showing that senior managers with networks richer in structural holes are more likely to get promoted early (for a data graph and discussion, see Burt 2000, fig. 3C). Ronald Burt, Robin Hogarth, and Claude Michaud (2000) present evidence from a French chemical firm of salary increasing with the structural holes in a manager's network, and Burt (1997, 2002) presents evidence of higher bonus compensation to investment officers with networks richer in structural holes (for data graphs and discussion, see Burt 2000, figs. 3D and 3E). Ajay Mehra, Martin Kilduff, and Daniel Brass (2000) find that supervisors in a small high-technology company give higher performance evaluations to employees whose networks bridge otherwise disconnected parts of their organization. Mark Mizruchi and Linda Brewster Sterns (2001), studying loan officers in a large commercial bank, show that the officers whose networks span structural holes in the firm (in the sense of being less dense and less hierarchical) are more likely to be successful in bringing a deal to closure. Working with more limited data, Raymond Sparrowe and Pamela Popielarz (1995) innovatively reconstruct past networks around managers to estimate the effects of holes in yesterday's network on promotion today (see Hansen 1999, 93). Shaul Gabbay (1997) shows that promotions occur more quickly for salespeople with strong-tie access to structural holes (see Meyerson 1994, on manager income as a function of strong ties), and Gabbay and Zuckerman (1998) show that expectations of promotion are higher for research and development (R&D) scientists whose networks are richer in spanning structural holes.

Information and control benefits to individuals aggregate to the management teams on which they serve. For example, Elizabeth Rosenthal (1996) studied the performance of teams in several Midwest manufacturing plants. Troubled by the variable success of total quality management (TQM) teams, and inspired by Deborah Ancona and David Caldwell's (1992a) demonstration that networks beyond the team are associated with team performance, Rosenthal wanted to see whether the structure of external relationships had the effect predicted by the hole argument. Studying TQM teams across plants operated by a midwestern manufacturing company, she shows that more successful teams are composed of people with less constrained networks beyond the team (for a data graph and discussion, see Burt 2000, fig. 3B). Morten Hansen (1999) studied new-product teams in one of America's leading electronics and computer firms, a firm segmented by geography and product lines into forty-one divisions. The network data are aggregate in that Hansen asked the R&D manager in each division to describe the extent to which people in his or her division had frequent and close working relationships with other divisions. Team performance is measured by the relative speed with which a team moves from initiation (first employee dedicated to the project) to completion (product released to shipment). Faster solutions are to be expected from teams with the social capital of bridge relationships that span the structural holes between divisions, and Hansen finds that teams reached completion more quickly when they were in divisions with frequent and close relations to other divisions. Morten Hansen, Joel Podolny, and Jeffrey Pfeffer (2000) studied the interpersonal networks around the teams. Each team member was asked to name intradivision contacts from whom he or she had regularly sought information and advice, then asked about relations between the contacts. The teams that completed their assigned task more quickly contained people with more nonredundant contacts beyond the team (measured by "advice size" and "sparseness").

Related results are reported by David Krackhardt and Robert Stern (1988) on higher performance in student groups with cross-group friendships, and in numerous studies of interorganization networks (on corporate social capital, see also Leana and Van Buren 1999): Fernandez and Gould (1994) on organizations in broker positions within the national health policy arena being perceived as more influential; Provan and Milward (1995) on higher-performing mental health systems that have a hierarchical network structure rather than a dense one; Geletkanycz and Hambrick (1997) on better company performance when top managers have boundary-spanning relationships beyond their firm and beyond their industry; Pennings, Lee, and Witteloostuijn (1998) on the survival of accounting firms as a function of strong partner ties to client sectors; Stuart and Podolny (1999) on the higher probability of innovation from semiconductor firms that establish alliances with firms outside their own technological area; McEvily and Zaheer (1999) on the greater access to competitive ideas enjoyed by small job manufacturers with more nonredundant sources of advice beyond the firm (on the lower absorptive capacity of these organizations when their sales network is concentrated in a single customer, see also McEvily and Marcus 2000); Sørensen (1999) on the negative effect on firm growth of redundant networks beyond the firm; Llobrera, Meyer, and Nammacher (2000) on the importance of nonredundant networks to the development of Philadelphia's biotechnology district; Ahuja (2000) on the higher patent output of organizations that hold broker positions in the network of joint ventures or alliances at the top of their industry; Baum, Calabrese, and Silverman (2000) on the faster revenue growth and more patents granted to biotechnology companies that have multiple kinds of alliance partners at start-up; Koput and Powell (2000) on the higher earnings and survival chances of biotechnology firms with more kinds of activities in alliances with more kinds of partner firms; and Podolny (2001) on the higher probability of early-stage investments surviving to IPO for venture capital firms with joint investment networks of otherwise disconnected partners.

Suggestive results come from research in which networks beyond the team are inferred from the demography of the people within the team. Ancona and Caldwell (1992b) provide a study of this type describing 409 individuals from 45 new-product teams in 5 high-technology companies. Teams were distinguished by managerial ratings of innovation, member reports on the volume of communication outside the team (on distinguishing types of communication, see Ancona and Caldwell 1992a), functional diversity (members from multiple functions), and tenure diversity (members vary in their length of time with the firm). Structural holes are implicit in the boundaries between corporate divisions and the boundaries between cohorts of employees in that each division or cohort is presumed to have its own unique perspectives, skills, or resources. A team composed of people from diverse corporate functions spans more structural holes in the firm and so has faster access to more diverse information and more control over the meaning of the information than a team composed of people from a single function. For tenure diversity, we can replace the timing and control advantages of access to more functionally diverse information with the same advantages stemming from access to information that differs between longtime employees who are familiar with how things have worked before and newer employees who are more familiar with procedures and techniques outside the firm.

More innovative solutions are to be expected from teams with the social capital of bridge relationships that span the structural holes between divisions (see the section "Creativity and Learning" later in the chapter for a detailed discussion), and Ancona and Caldwell report higher managerial ratings of innovation for teams with more external communication, and more external communication by teams drawn from diverse functions.

Tenure diversity has the opposite effect. Ancona and Caldwell report that some benefits of tenure diversity are associated with higher evaluations of team performance, but the aggregate direct effect of tenure diversity is lower performance. Presumably people drawn from widely separate employee cohorts have more difficulty with communication and coordination within the team.

The conflicting results are brought together in a productive way by Reagans and Zuckerman (2001) in their study of performance in 223 corporate R&D units within 29 major American firms in 8 industries. They report higher levels of output from units in which scientists are drawn from widely separate employee cohorts (implying that their networks reach diverse perspectives, skills, and resources outside the team) *and* there is a dense communication network within the unit. In other words, the negative association between performance and tenure diversity reported by Ancona and Caldwell could have been positive if the density of communication within the team had been held constant. Tenure diversity (or other kinds of diversity; see Williams and O'Reilly 1998) can be disruptive because of the difficulties associated with communicating and coordinating across different perspectives, but when communication is successful (as implied by a dense communication network within the team), team performance is enhanced by the timing and control advantages of the team having access to more diverse information. This is as Ancona and Caldwell initially predict, and as predicted by the hole argument. (See also Dyer and Nobeoka 2000, a case study of Toyota's supplier network in which Toyota promotes coordination among diverse suppliers by investing in infrastructure to facilitate knowledge transfer between suppliers and emphasizing the identity that suppliers share as members of the network.)

This is a productive interpretation of Reagans and Zuckerman's analysis because it links team networks and performance with the performance effects of structural holes in market networks. The aggregate profit margin for a market increases with the organization of producers in the market and the disorganization of suppliers and customers (Burt 1992, 91–97). The market model applied to team performance predicts that high-performance teams will be those in which member networks beyond the team span structural holes (giving the team access to diverse perspectives, skills, and resources), and that strong relations within the team will provide communication and coordination so that the team can take advantage of its access to diverse perspectives, skills, and resources. (On the complementary social capital of network closure and structural holes, see Burt 2000, fig. 5.)

At the same time that group performance is enhanced by the social capital of its members, organizational social capital can enhance employee performance. For example, William Bielby and Denise Bielby (1999) describe a decade of data on the careers of almost 9,000 film and television writers. Social capital in their study is held by the talent agency that represents a writer. About half of the writers (52 percent) had no representation in 1987, a figure that fell to 38 percent in 1992 (73). One-quarter had the traditional representation of an agency that "finds work . . . and in exchange it receives a 10-percent commission from the client's earnings" (66). The remaining one-quarter of the writers enjoyed the advantage of having what Bielby and Bielby describe as "core" representation (66–67): representation by an agency that brokers connections between functional areas to propose whole projects in which the writer is a component. "Instead of seeking out projects for their clients, they initiate projects on their own. They negotiate unique arrangements with the talent guilds and cultivate long-term relationships with those who finance, produce, and distribute new projects." Bielby and Bielby do not have network data, so they reduce social capital to binary distinctions between those who have it and those who do not (70, 72); nevertheless, they obtain strong evidence of more likely employment and higher compensation for writers affiliated with the agencies that have it. (On the social capital of songwriters attributable to their country's network position among other countries, see Yair and Maman 1996; on the more accurate company earnings predictions from analysts employed in brokerage houses that provide the information advantages of many other analysts and specialists in the company's industry, see Jacob, Lys, and Neale 1999.)

Creativity and Learning

Anecdotal evidence of brokerage-enhancing creativity can be found in the remarks of prominent creators. In a frequently cited lecture on the influence of commerce on manners, Adam Smith (1982 [1766], 539) noted that, "when the mind is employed about a variety of objects it is somehow expanded and enlarged." Richard Swedberg (1990, 3) begins his book of interviews with leading academics who work across the boundary between economics and sociology with John Stuart Mills's (1987 [1848], 581) opinion:

> It is hardly possible to overrate the value . . . of placing human beings in contact with persons dissimilar to themselves, and with modes of thought and action unlike those with which they are familiar. . . . Such communication has always been, and is peculiarly in the present age, one of the primary sources of progress.

Moving to more contemporary and practical creators, Jean-René Fourtou, as CEO of the French chemical and pharmaceutical company Rhône-Poulenc ($17 billion in annual sales), has observed that top scientists are stimulated to their best ideas by people outside their own discipline. Fourtou emphasizes that le vide—literally, "the emptiness," what I have discussed as structural holes—is essential to creative work (quoted in Stewart 1996, 165):

> *Le vide* has a huge function in organizations. . . . Shock comes when
> different things meet. It's the interface that's interesting. . . . If you don't
> leave *le vide*, you have no unexpected things, no creation. There are two
> types of management. You can try to design for everything, or you can
> leave *le vide* and say, "I don't know either; what do you think?"

Similarly, Mary Jo Hatch 1999 discusses the importance of empty
places to the integrated improvisation among jazz musicians playing
together, and by analogy to the integrated improvisation of managers
working together. An analogy can also be drawn to Merton's (1968
[1948]) view of serendipity in science. Expanding on research's familiar passive role in testing theory, Merton discusses the active roles
that research can play in shaping theory, one of which is the serendipity pattern in which an "unanticipated, anomalous, and strategic
datum exerts pressure for initiating theory" (158). Serendipity must
involve an unanticipated result (datum) that is inconsistent with established facts or the theory being tested, but the third attribute of the
datum, being strategic, is the key that distinguishes Merton's view.
The strategic value of a research result lies in its implications for generalized theory (159), which refers to "what the observer brings to the
datum rather than to the datum itself." Strategic value is created
when the observer sees how a research result has implications for
what seems to other people to be unrelated theory. The creative spark
on which serendipity depends, in short, is to see bridges where others
see holes.

A more explicit network perspective underlies Gad Yair and Daniel
Maman's (1996) conclusion that certain songwriters had a better
chance of winning the Eurovision Song Contest because of their country's network position among other countries. Bonnie Erickson (1996)
innovatively measured network diversity for a cross-section of people
in the security industry (guards, not financial analysts) by asking
whether they had friends and acquaintances in nineteen disparate occupations. The more diverse their non-kin contacts were (that is, the
more occupations in which they had friends and acquaintances), the
broader their knowledge of diverse cultural genres—sports, art,
books, restaurants, and business magazines. (For the method applied
to an informal local economy showing that participants with more
diverse contact networks enjoy higher earnings, see Erickson 2001.) In
his panoramic analysis of the history of philosophy, Randall Collins
(1998) presents sociograms of the intergenerational social networks
among philosophers to illustrate his argument that the philosophers
of greatest repute tend to be personal rivals who represent conflicting
schools of thought for their generation.

The famous names, and the semi-famous ones as well who hold the
stage less long, are those persons situated at just those points where the
networks heat up the emotional energy to the highest pitch. Creativity
is the friction of the attention space at the moments when the structural
blocks are grinding against one another the hardest. (Collins 1998, 76)

Brainstorming groups are another source of evidence. Laboratory
and field studies show two things: groups generate fewer ideas, and
fewer of high quality, than the same number of people working separately; yet people in these studies report that groups generate more
ideas and higher personal performance within groups (Diehl and
Stroebe 1987; for a review, see Mullen, Johnson, and Salas 1991; for
field illustration in an organization, see Paulus, Larey, and Ortega
1995). The connection to social capital is that performance is significantly improved if individuals come to the brainstorming group from
heterogeneous backgrounds (Stroebe and Diehl 1994, 293–97). The
value of group brainstorming depends on the group facilitating the
exchange of ideas across the structural holes that separate members
in the absence of the group. This is a useful analogy for two reasons.
First, it fits with the story emerging that the social capital of groups
increases as a function of network density inside the group combined
with bridge relationships spanning structural holes outside the group
(see the section "Individual and Group Benefits" earlier in the chapter). Second, the usefulness of this analogy means that the brainstorming studies that analyze group process can be used to better
understand the process of brokerage. For example, Robert Sutton and
Andrew Hargadon (1996) describe the processes by which a firm,
IDEO, uses brainstorming to create product designs; they clarify in
Hargadon and Sutton (1997) the brokerage function served by the
brainstorming. The firm's employees work for clients in diverse industries. In the brainstorming sessions, technological solutions from
one industry are used to solve client issues in other industries where
the solutions are rare or unknown. The firm profits, in other words,
from employee bridge relationships through which they broker the
flow of technology between industries. (For comparative analysis of
other organizations that similarly profit from being "knowledge brokers," see Hargadon 1998; on gatekeepers, see Allen and Cohen 1969;
on network management of the status auction, see Lazega and Pattison 2001.)

Detailed network data underlie Katherine Giuffe's (1999) analysis
of photographers who received National Endowment for the Arts
photography grants or had solo shows in a New York City gallery.
Studying the network of gallery affiliations among the photographers

over time, she finds three structurally distinct careers; peripheral careers of photographers who drop in and out of the gallery world; "long unbroken careers" in a "tight knit clique" of densely interconnected photographers; and "long unbroken careers" in "loose knit networks" of sparsely interconnected photographers. In terms of structural holes, the peripheral photographers had the least social capital, those with a clique career had little, and those with a career in loose-knit networks had the most (see Sediatis 1998, 373–74, on the greater flexibility, adaptability, and volume of business in Russian commodity markets created by organizers who had little previous contact with one another). Relative social capital has a statistically significant association with relative success measured by critical attention to a photographer's work. Giuffe (1999) counted the number of reviews received by each photographer over the study decade in the two major trade magazines, *Art News* and *Art in America*. The peripheral photographers received the least attention, photographers with a clique career received slightly more, and those with a career in a loose-knit network received the most.

Experience seems to be the answer to questions about where, when, or how people learn about brokering connections across structural holes. Evidence comes from experiments with people learning social structures. Using Clinton DeSoto's (1960) experimental design for measuring the difficulty of learning a social structure, Freeman (1992) asked college students to learn the relationships in a small network that contained a structural hole (a missing connection between persons 1 and 4). Errors occurred when students failed to recall a relationship that existed, but the most frequent error was to fill in the structural hole by saying that the two disconnected people were connected. Gregory Janicik (1998) also used DeSoto's design, but with older (MBA) students; he also added a control for the network around each student in his or her most recent or current job. Students who held a job in which they were exposed to structural holes learned the network significantly faster, in particular because they quickly recognized the structural hole in the network. If Freeman's undergraduates lived in small, dense friendship networks, as is typical of college students, then the summary conclusion from Freeman's and Janicik's experiments is that experience matters: people who live in a network that contains structural holes are more likely to recognize the holes in their next network.

There is related evidence from fieldwork. Martin Gargiulo and Mario Benassi (2000) describe managers in the research consulting unit of a large Italian firm. They measure "coordination failure" as the extent to which a manager consults with people not relevant to his or her assigned projects. They show that coordination failures are significantly more likely for managers with small, dense networks (see Barker 1993). Shawn Lofstrom (2000) asked key individuals (scientists, physicians, and engineers) how much they learned from their firm's participation in an alliance intended to develop or extend a medical device technology. Individuals with a higher number of nonredundant contacts, especially contacts within their own firm, were more likely to report that they had "learned a great deal" in the alliance. Burt (2002) describes change in the colleague networks of bankers over a four-year period, focusing on the decay of the relationships that span structural holes (bridges). The rate of decay is high (nine out of ten disappear from one year to the next), but significantly lower for bankers who have more experience with such relationships. Inasmuch as the bridges are social capital associated with bonus compensation, and bridge relationships are less subject to decay when they involve people more experienced with bridges, the conclusion is that social capital accrues to those who already have it.

There is also indirect evidence at the level of organizations. Granted that technological change can affect social structure (for a clear illustration with network data, see Barley 1990, 92–95), social structure has its own effects on an organization's ability to manage technological change productively. Electronics and biotechnology have been favored research sites for studying such network effects, with Walter Powell (Powell and Brantley 1992; Powell, Koput, and Smith-Doerr 1996; Powell et al. 1999; Koput and Powell 2000) and Toby Stuart (Stuart 1998; Stuart, Hoang, and Hybels 1999; Stuart and Podolny 1999; Stuart and Robinson, 2000) providing prominent ports of entry into the work. More generally, Bruce Kogut (2000) builds on a series of studies (Shan, Walker, and Kogut 1994; Zander and Kogut 1995; Kogut and Zander 1996; Walker, Kogut, and Shan 1997) to propose a network theory of the firm in which value is derived from a firm's ability to create and lay claim to knowledge derived from its membership and participation in networks. (On social capital and knowledge, see Nahapiet and Ghoshal 1998; on information issues in the economic sociology of networks, especially with respect to inter-organizational networks, see Powell and Smith-Doerr 1994.)

More specifically, accumulating empirical research shows that structural holes are a correlate of organizational learning, often discussed in terms of an organization's ability to learn—what Wesley Cohen and Daniel Levinthal (1990, 128) describe as an organization's absorptive capacity: "the ability of a firm to recognize the value of new, external information, assimilate it, and apply it to commercial ends," which can be studied in terms of industry factors that facilitate absorption (Cohen and Levinthal 1990) and external networks that enhance an organization's absorptive capacity (Cockburn and Henderson 1998; for a secondary review, see Knoke 2001, 362ff). To the extent that the information and control benefits of bridging structural holes enhance organizational learning, the following hypothesis should be true: organizations with management and collaboration networks that more often bridge structural holes in their surrounding market of technology and practice will learn faster and be more productively creative. This is the hypothesis that Lofstrom (2000) uses to interpret her observation that people in medical-device alliances report more learning when they have a broader network of nonredundant contacts. The hypothesis is related to Ancona and Caldwell's (1992b) report that teams judged more innovative had more external communication with contacts in diverse corporate functions. (See also the evidence on group brainstorming in the next section.) The hypothesis is explicit in several studies cited in the previous section: Bill McEvily and Akbar Zaheer (1999) report greater access to competitive ideas for small job manufacturers with more nonredundant sources of advice beyond the firm. (For a demonstration of the lower absorptive capacity for these organizations when their sales network is concentrated in a single customer, see McEvily and Marcus 2000.) Stuart and Podolny (1999) report a higher probability of innovation from semiconductor firms that establish alliances with firms outside their own technological area. Comparing the biotechnology districts in Minneapolis and Philadelphia, Joseph Llobrera, David Meyer, and Gregory Nammacher (2000) attribute the growth and adaptation of Philadelphia's district to its many overlapping but nonredundant networks around organizations in the district. Gautam Ahuja (2000) reports higher patent output for organizations that hold broker positions in the network of joint ventures or alliances at the top of their industry. Joel Baum, Tony Calabrese, and Brian Silverman (2000) have studied Canadian biotechnology companies for their growth in revenues, number of patents granted, and the extent to which a company had multiple kinds of alliance partners at start-up. Companies with a heterogeneous mix of alliance partners tend to enjoy faster revenue growth and a dramatic advantage in obtaining patents. Kenneth Koput and Walter Powell (2000) report higher earnings and survival chances of biotechnology firms with more kinds of activities in alliances with more kinds of partner firms. Joel Podolny (2001) argues that the information and control advantages of structural holes should be a competitive advantage for venture capital firms that detect and develop ventures at an early stage of development. He has studied panel data on investments from 1981 through 1996 to distinguish venture capital firms that span structural holes in the sense that they bring together as co-investors other firms that are not investing together. Under attractively stringent controls for autocorrelation, Podolny (2001, 56) finds that, "as a venture capital firm acquires a 'deal-flow' network that is characterized by numerous structural holes, the firm makes a greater proportion of its investments in the earlier stages." This finding echoes the finding cited earlier that more early-stage investments survive to IPO for the venture capital firms whose co-investment network spans structural holes.

Whatever the explanation for these results—that bridging structural holes enhances an individual's ability to learn, or that more intelligent people learn faster and so make better reports on holes in the social structure around them—there is an association between structural holes and learning. The implication is that the social capital of structural holes accumulates over a career so that it is critical to encounter holes early in one's career (Burt 2002; on the cumulative effects of social heterogeneity on mobility, see Sørensen 2000). Managers with experience of structural holes are more likely to see the holes in a new situation and thus enjoy the enhanced performance associated with spanning the holes. They are also more likely to be promoted to senior positions, which will broaden their opportunities to add value by brokering connections across structural holes.

Adaptive Implementation

Evidence on this category in figure 7.3 is primarily in the form of episodic anecdotes, in part because the many different processes by which people bridge structural holes are sensitive to context. Still, the available evidence is suggestive of general processes and consistent with other evidence of value created by brokerage across structural holes.

Illustrative Cases

The case materials developed for business education are a rich source of information on bridging holes because much of business leadership is about bringing together ill-connected functions, organizations, or market segments—in other words, it is about building bridges across structural holes. Almost no cases discuss social capital per se (lack of academic jargon is a feature of the materials), and not all are about network entrepreneurs (many are about routine business practices). Where change is intended to create value, however, there is always a story—richer in some cases than others, of course—about brokerage and network entrepreneurs.

For example, a case of Harvard Business School's John Clendenin describes a middle manager making more efficient the flow of components between Xerox's regional operations in the late 1980s (Eisenstat 1993). Regional operations had evolved independently such that each region had its own inventory system. The independence made sense in Xerox's early days. By the time of the case, however, logistics technology had progressed to the point where it was more efficient to ship components in a just-in-time production system rather than leave components on shelves as inventory. There was now value to bridging the structural holes between the regional operations. The problem was that regional leaders had good reasons to prefer the status quo. The case is about how Clendenin overcame resistance to bridge the disconnected regional operations, adding substantial value to Xerox and growing his group in proportion.

Brokerage processes in a larger organizational perspective are described in a complement of INSEAD cases on strategic alliances involving the visionary biochemist Alejandro Zaffaroni. The earlier of the two cases describes interests over the course of the 1977 to 1982 alliance between the Swiss pharmaceutical giant Ciba-Geigy and ALZA, a California company that Zaffaroni founded in 1968 to develop products involving controlled-release drug delivery (Doz and Angelmar 1991; see also Doz 1988; Doz and Hamel 1998). The more recent case consists of videotaped interviews with key people at a California company, Affymax, founded by Zaffaroni in 1988 to develop products to accelerate the drug-discovery process, and at the British pharmaceutical giant Glaxo-Wellcome, which purchased Affymax in 1995. (The case was still in production when this chapter was written.) In both cases, Zaffaroni's small, thriving, entrepreneurial company created new products, and the large, bureaucratic partner commercialized them; Ciba-Geigy did clinical tests and marketing for ALZA drugs, and Glaxo-Wellcome integrated Affymax discovery products into its large-scale drug development.

Zaffaroni is precisely a network entrepreneur as discussed in this chapter, and the cases describe how he does it. One of the Affymax leaders interviewed in the more recent case describes Zaffaroni's critical value to the enterprise:

> He is reading and thinking very widely. He is totally unafraid of any new technology in any area of human creativity. He has wonderful contacts with people in many different areas, so *he sees the bridges between otherwise disparate fields.* Then he places them in front of you. The way

he works is to give it to you—and instantly you can see what he is driving at; there is some potential technology synergy or some business opportunity. Then he leaves it with you. He trusts. The wonderful thing I like about him is that he trusts you to see whether there is value or not. He delegates responsibility, scientific and managerial, to people. You know that he has picked you. You know that he trusts you, he has picked you to have certain qualities, and he is not going to second-guess you.

Moreover, Zaffaroni institutionalizes his bridges with inter-disciplinary workshops involving prominent outsiders, as well as his own reputation for success and high moral standards in bringing people together. In fact, one of the Affymax leaders praises Zaffaroni as a source of instruction precisely on the adaptive implementation variable depicted in figure 7.3: "So, at a personal level, he [Zaffaroni] is very good to be around, because you learn how to deal with people, get the best out of them, and how to deal with problems when they inevitably arise."

The communication and trust processes with which Zaffaroni establishes bridges across disciplinary lines within his companies carry over to bridges with outside partners. The Ciba-Geigy alliance failed. The Glaxo-Wellcome merger works. Both interorganizational bridges were strategically sound in the value they could provide, and both linked a small, entrepreneurial firm with a large and bureaucratic partner. Implementation differed. Communication and trust were not strategic issues in planning the Ciba-Geigy alliance, in part because such issues were deemed irrelevant: ALZA was to discover products, then hand them over to Ciba-Geigy for commercialization. Over the course of the alliance, however, it became clear that the alliance required coordination between the firms before and after the ALZA product was handed over to Ciba-Geigy. Made wiser by the Ciba-Geigy experience, Zaffaroni and his counterparts in Glaxo-Wellcome took communication and trust as central issues in planning the merger between Affymax and Glaxo-Wellcome. An organization was created inside Glaxo-Wellcome that was a clone of Affymax. The clone was integrated into Glaxo-Wellcome's production operations, and Affymax was left to run as it had outside the company as a source of insider knowledge about how to operate the clone.

The virtues of the business-education case materials are interpersonal detail and case variety. To describe brokerage in wider perspective, if less detail, one can turn to archives on historical figures. For example, Robert Caro (1982, ch. 15) describes Lyndon Johnson's creation of a Washington power base in 1933 from the "Little Congress," through which he brokered connections between journalists and prominent people in government. Robert Dalzell (1987, pt. 1) describes Francis Lowell's role as a broker in creating the American cotton industry. Paul DiMaggio (1992, 129–30) describes Paul Sachs's role as a broker in establishing the Museum of Modern Art in New York: "Sachs could employ his talents precisely because his strong ties to sectors that had previously been only weakly connected—museums, universities, and finance—placed him at the center of structural holes that were critical to the art world of his time." John Padgett and Christopher Ansell (1993) describe Cosimo de Medici's use of his contacts with opposing elite family factions to establish his Medicean political party in Renaissance Florence. Patrick McGuire and Mark Granovetter (2000) describe Samuel Insull's use of his network of contacts in finance, politics, and technology to shape the electric utility industry at the turn of the century. (On polycentric networks that facilitate economic cooperation, see Granovetter, this volume; for an account of Russian commodity markets created by organizers who had little previous contact with one another, see Sediatis 1998.)

These several cases could have been cited in the section "Creativity and Learning" inasmuch as the cases describe people using brokerage to create a new organization or industry. In the same vein, much of the work I cite in the section "Creativity and Learning" could have been cited in this section as descriptions of how bridges are built across structural holes. The distinction is a fine line since creativity, learning, and adaptive implementation are so interwoven in practice. The case examples cited in this section simply provide more detail on the process of bridging structural holes.

Bridge Processes

The question remains of how to generalize across the cases. There are two directions in which to proceed. One is to generalize case content to describe the ways in which brokerage occurs. See Hargadon (1998) for an example, Aldrich (1999, ch. 4) and Thornton (1999) for a broad review, and Aldrich in particular for intuitions about the changing role of networks over the course of a venture (see Doz and Hamel 1998; Van de Ven et al. 1999; for case-study description with respect to structural holes, see Steier and Greenwood 2000; for results across cases, see Podolny 2001). Although an obvious site for research on the network forms of social capital, quantitative research on networks in entrepreneurship has been limited to the most rudimentary of network data (with rare exceptions such as Stuart, Hoang, and Hybels's

1999 analysis of how prominent affiliations speed a venture's time to IPO in biotechnology). I discuss elsewhere the potential value, and current shortcomings, of network data in entrepreneurship (Burt 2000, 370–72). At the risk of oversimplifying the case-specific details on brokerage, I conclude from the casework that successful network entrepreneurs excel at certain skills: communicating across differences of opinion; reasoning from the interests of the other; establishing mechanisms that build trust and reputation; and restructuring the organization or market where the current structure is a problem.

Hole Processes

A second direction of generalization is to leave open the question of how bridges get established and instead study process in terms of the structural hole being bridged.

There is abundant evidence of the achievement and rewards associated with brokerage, but the value created by a bridge can be expected to decrease as more bridges are built across the same structural hole. When the first entrepreneurs benefit from synthesizing information across a structural hole, others join them and the value of bridging the hole decreases. If figure 7.2 were an academic market, for example, and Robert had produced a useful idea because of a group A technology he discovered from contact 7, other academics in Robert's line of work would be expected to develop relationships with contacts in group A, eventually eliminating the structural hole between the two groups. (For example, contacts 1 and 2 are positioned to draw quickly on their ties to group A.)

The rate of decline in value is a question for future research, but the functional form of the decline is probably nonlinear. Imagine X-Y coordinates where Y is the value of building a strong relationship across a structural hole and X is the number of such relations that exist. The value of Y at $X = 1$ would be the value of the first bridge across the hole, the value at $X = 2$ would be the value of the second bridge, and so on. No one knows how Y decreases across increasing X, but it seems likely that the decrease is steeper for the first few bridges than for the last few. Value is certainly eliminated long before everyone eligible to span the hole has done so. Holes are closed by individuals, not populations. (Or, in network jargon, a high density of bridges is not required to close a hole; the first few bridges suffice.) To cite familiar academic work, the acclaim that Michael Hannan and John Freeman (1977) received for synthesizing organization theory from sociology and population biology was much higher than the acclaim accorded to subsequent elaborations within the population ecology of organizations. The acclaim that Mark Granovetter (1985) received for so clearly making the case that economic transactions are contingent on their sociological context was higher than the acclaim accorded to subsequent elaborations within the embeddedness metaphor. In fact, the nonlinear decline in value is probably a non-monotonic decline in benefits. Whatever the functional form of decline in value with additional entrants, cost must decrease more quickly because the first entrant has to create both product and market. Problems revealed by the first entrant can be anticipated and avoided by subsequent entrants. Whatever the benefits to the first who bridges a structural hole, benefits are probably higher for the next few entrants, then decreasing for subsequent entrants.

The Social Order of Equilibrium

Value declines with subsequent entrants down to some equilibrium level at which value is marginally higher than the cost of bridging the hole. Regardless of the rate of decline in value, there is no competitive advantage at system equilibrium to a network that spans structural holes because there are enough people with networks across the structural holes to eliminate the value of additional people spanning them. Network entrepreneurs have moved the market to equilibrium by eliminating holes in the market where it was valuable to do so. So viewed, the social capital of structural holes is about a short-run advantage on the path to equilibrium. At equilibrium, the advantage is gone.

The Social Order of Disequilibrium

That is, unless the system is forever on its way to equilibrium. The short-run advantages of brokerage could be a long-run advantage—for example, if information grows quickly out of date, as seems to be the case for senior managers (see Mintzberg 1973; on the short half-life of information in organizations, see Stinchcombe 1990). The process could run as follows: as an industry of managers and organizations moves toward equilibrium, managers with more social capital have an advantage in identifying and developing the more rewarding opportunities. Technological change and events create new priorities, so the industry begins moving toward a new equilibrium. Again, managers with more social capital have an advantage in identifying and developing the more rewarding opportunities. If the industry is subject to repeated change such that information grows quickly out of date, then managers with more social capital have a continuous competitive advantage, which would be visible as the association between brokerage and benefits illustrated in figure 7.3.

Further, a short-run brokerage advantage can become a long-run advantage if bridges are not absorbed into the social structure around a hole. Here it is useful to distinguish between passive and active structural holes. A hole is passive if bridges across it are readily absorbed into the surrounding social structure. The previous subsection on the social order of equilibrium assumes passive holes. Each bridge is secure in that information flows freely across it, thereby diminishing the value of subsequent bridges across the same structural hole.

A structural hole is active if interests attached to it resist bridges. For example, interests can be configured such that in the competition to bridge the hole a bridge established by one group is subject to erosion by the other groups. Progress toward equilibrium with the establishment of a bridge is destabilized, resulting in a continuous disequilibrium around the structural hole. There are numerous illustrations in the sociological literature, such as Georg Simmel's (1902, 185–86) brief descriptions of Incan rule over subject provinces and Venetian expansion onto the mainland, or Karen Barkey's (1994) description of local governors competing against bandits to be the legitimate representative of Turkish rule. For this chapter, consider William Finlay and James Coverdill's (1999, 2000) work on structural holes among managers, human resources (HR) staff, and executive headhunters. Headhunters offer advantages to a hiring manager: faster search (headhunters have up-to-date data on suitable candidates; "What people are paying me for is somebody with experience to step in to do something right away"), broader search (headhunters know attractive candidates who are happy where they are and would not apply for an advertised job, and they can recruit from customer or supplier organizations from which recruitment by the hiring manager could threaten his organization's relationship with the raided customer or supplier), and more successful search (headhunters put time into selecting candidates suited to the job because their compensation depends on their candidate accepting the job). The complication is that the hiring manager's organization has a human resources staff responsible for recruiting, so brokerage for the headhunter involves matching candidates with the hiring manager while buffering the HR manager. The tension is indicated by the headhunter phrase for HR staff ("weenies") and their characterization by one industry trainer as people who "didn't have the personality to become morticians" (Finlay and Coverdill 1999, 20). Bridging structural holes in this case involves a simultaneous process of creating holes. As Finlay and Coverdill conclude: "When headhunters buffer hiring managers from HR or when they shield a client from a competitor, they open gaps in these relationships that the headhunters themselves then bridge. The success of headhunters, and their attractiveness to employers, rests on this dual function of creating and filling holes" (27).

Then there are the holes around which interests explicitly oppose a bridge and so ensure continuing disequilibrium as new entrants try alternative ways of bridging the hole. Charles Tilly (1998, 8–11, 84–86) provides a richly substantiated overview of the forms that resistance can take when a group is advantaged by a structural hole. He describes the social mechanisms that preserve paired insider-outsider categories, such as legitimate versus illegitimate, our class versus theirs, citizens versus foreigners, and other pairs of asymmetric categories defined by income, education, age, gender, ethnicity, and so on. Tilly's boundaries between social categories are examples of the structural holes discussed in this chapter. His four mechanisms preserving boundaries describe the interests that oppose bridges across structural holes. Adapting the mechanisms to this chapter, a structural hole is active if (1) it provides an opportunity for insiders on one side of the hole to exploit outsiders on the other side; (2) it permits insiders to hoard opportunities, keeping them away from outsiders; (3) it makes it easier for insiders to construct new organizations based on existing models in which insiders are advantaged; or (4) daily routines and valued social ties of aid, influence, and information gathering have adapted to the hole.

The fourth mechanism—"adaptation" in Tilly's analysis—is particularly important because it is a way in which passive structural holes often become active. A passive hole becomes active over time if people and groups invest in behaviors and beliefs adapted to the hole. For example, the Clendenin case cited earlier begins with structural holes between Xerox's regional operations. Initially the holes were passive; no one set out to create them. The holes simply reflected the technological limits of production at the time when the regional operations were created. Over time, however, people adapted to the separate regional operations. Each region developed its own performance benchmarks, financial systems, and production control systems. Clendenin's idea of integrating production across regions required people to give up their local systems in favor of an integrated central system—a change rejected by the regional managers. Managing the resistance was a critical element in Clendenin's successful brokerage.

The Clendenin case illustrates the resistance that occurs when people adapt daily routines and behaviors to otherwise passive structural holes. Resistance is stronger if adaptation moves deeper, to fears and beliefs. Resistance is especially forceful against bridges between groups

with conflicting beliefs, or between one group and another that prohibits relationships of the kind represented by a proposed bridge (on
network indicators of the depth of a structural hole, see Burt 1992,
42–44). For example, Maryann Keller (1989, ch. 6) describes how se-
nior-level distrust between General Motors and the United Auto
Workers reversed successful labor-management collaboration in the
Van Nuys plant in California to establish a team-based production
system.

One way to think about active structural holes is to ask why a hole
observed is not already closed. If there is value to bridging the hole,
why has someone not already done so? Consider two companies,
MY-CD.com and Musicmaker.com, founded in 1998 to bridge the
structural hole between music producers and customers. Instead of a
system in which producers guess demand, press a batch of CDs, and
distribute them through retail stores, the idea was that a customer
goes to a website, selects music, and has it pressed on a CD made just
for him or her. Implementation differed between the two companies.
MY-CD focused on assembling the technological and financial resources needed to create and operate the site, treating as passive the
hole between producers and customers. Even before Napster
emerged as a challenge, MY-CD was, in the words of one observer, "a
forlorn-looking site that seems to be barely alive." The problem was
getting record companies to release current popular titles. Producers
feared the Internet as a threat to property rights. Musicmaker, in contrast, focused on assuaging record company concerns about the Internet; the founders were senior people from record companies, and the
company was largely owned by record companies. Between personal
ties and ownership control, Musicmaker was given access to current
hits. At the end of 1999 a senior Musicmaker officer explained that
"we've been able to do business on terms that the record companies
could accept."

Eventually bridges can emerge across active holes. Fredrik Barth
(1967) describes a structural hole in the economy of a tribe, the Fur, in
central Africa. The Fur had a prohibition against exchanging labor or
beer for money; it was shameful to work for a wage ("though some
men have worked as migrant labor elsewhere" [153]; on socially enforced conceptual boundaries between kinds of money, see Zelizer
1994) and shameful to sell beer: "Some women also brew beer and
bring it for sale in the market-place. Though there is no dearth of
buyers, especially as the afternoon wears on, the sale of beer is regarded as immoral and the women who do so are looked upon as
immodest" (155–56). The Fur adapted beer parties as a conversion
medium: "In the simplest form, two more friends may decide to work

together for company, in which case they jointly cultivate each other's field in turn, he whose field is being cultivated providing a pot of beer for their joint consumption" (153). Barth tells of an entrepreneur, an Arab from the north, who made a profit from the hole in the Fur economy. (Outsiders often play this role; see, for example, Siamwalla 1978, on Chinese middlemen in the Thai economy; Light and Karageorgis 1994, on socially excluded ethnicities for whom entrepreneurial activities are a route into society.) The Arab entrepreneur purchased grain in an area where the price was low, brewed beer from the grain, used the beer to pay for Fur labor on his tomato crop, and sold the tomato crop for a substantial profit. "On an investment of ¥5 worth of millet, he obtained a return of more than ¥100 for his tomatoes." His success drew others over the next two years: "More merchants, and some local people, adopted the strategy with results nearly as spectacular" (171–72). The Fur had social sanctions with which they could have thwarted the entrepreneurs, but after three years of activity, at the close of Barth's fieldwork with the Fur, no such reaction had emerged to block them. In the terms of this chapter, it looked as though a bridge had been absorbed into the surrounding social structure.

Active structural holes illustrate how the information and control benefits of brokerage can be such a competitive advantage in adaptive implementation: network entrepreneurs are more likely to know through their personal contacts who would benefit from a proposed bridge, whose interests would be hurt, and who would be likely to react. In other words, when people with little social capital try to establish bridge relationships across active structural holes, their bridges are more likely to collapse from resistance and so continue the disequilibrium of the hole. More broadly, the social capital of structural holes is about change—about discovering and developing opportunities to add value with bridges across holes in the existing structure. It is, in short, a story about the social order of disequilibrium. (Note the economist Leonard Joy's [1967, 184–85] effort to analyze Barth's work on the Fur in terms of an equilibrium model in preference to the anthropologist Barth's "straight observation of disequilibrium conditions.")

Conclusions

Empirical evidence on the social capital of structural holes comes from research on diverse substantive questions, and the evidence is expanding quickly. Much of the work reviewed here is new, either published in the last couple years or not yet published, and much of it is at a preliminary stage of development. Accordingly, the evidence reviewed here is based on network data of uneven quality. However, the one consistent finding from comparative study across populations with detailed network data (Burt 2000) is that dense networks are associated with substandard performance. A general conclusion from the review here, and from review elsewhere of detailed network data, is that brokerage across structural holes is social capital. For individuals and groups, networks that span structural holes are associated with creativity and learning, adaptive implementation, more positive evaluations, more successful teams, early promotion, and higher compensation.

The review has touched on two qualifications. First, brokerage appears to be the source of value added, but network closure can be critical to realizing the value. As evidence, brokerage across structural holes is more valuable to people who have few competitors, more valuable for groups within which people are closely interconnected, and more valuable in markets within which organizations are closely interconnected (Burt 2000, fig. 5). Second, only insiders, "the right kind of people," have direct access to the social capital of brokerage. Outsiders have to borrow. Among senior managers, for example, insiders are typically older men, and outsiders include women and young men (Burt 1998; Burt 2000, table 2). The outsider proposing an idea that bridges groups has to borrow social capital in the sense that she has to work through a strategic partner, a person who has the social capital of a network that spans structural holes.

References

Ahuja, Gautam. 2000. "Collaboration Networks, Structural Holes, and Innovation: A Longitudinal Study." *Administrative Science Quarterly* 45: 425–55.

Aldrich, Howard E. 1999. *Organizations Evolving.* Thousand Oaks, Calif.: Sage Publications.

Allen, Thomas J., and Saul Cohen. 1969. "Information Flow in R&D Labs." *Administrative Science Quarterly* 14: 12–19.

Ancona, Deborah G., and David F. Caldwell. 1992a. "Bridging the Boundary: External Activity and Performance in Organizational Teams." *Administrative Science Quarterly* 37: 634–65.

———. 1992b. "Demography and Design: Predictors of New Product Team Performance." *Organization Science* 3: 321–41.

Baker, Wayne E. 1984. "The Social Structure of a National Securities Market." *American Journal of Sociology* 89: 775–811.

Baker, Wayne E., and Ananth Iyer. 1992. "Information Networks and Market Behavior." *Journal of Mathematical Sociology* 16: 305–32.

Barker, James R. 1993. "Tightening the Iron Cage: Concertive Control in Self-managing Teams." *Administrative Science Quarterly* 38: 408–37.

Barkey, Karen. 1994. *Bandits and Bureaucrats.* Ithaca, N.Y.: Cornell University Press.

Barley, Stephen R. 1990. "The Alignment of Technology and Structure Through Roles and Networks." *Administrative Science Quarterly* 35: 61–103.

Barth, Fredrik. 1967. "Economic Spheres in Darfur." In *Themes in Economic Anthropology*, edited by Raymond Firth. London: Tavistock.

Baum, Joel A. C., Tony Calabrese, and Brian S. Silverman. 2000. "Don't Go It Alone: Alliance Network Composition and Start-ups' Performance in Canadian Biotechnology." *Strategic Management Journal* 21: 267–94.

Bian, Yanjie. 1994. *Work and Inequality in Urban China*. Albany: State University of New York Press.

Bielby, William T., and Denise D. Bielby. 1999. "Organizational Mediation of Project-based Labor Markets: Talent Agencies and the Careers of Screenwriters." *American Sociological Review* 64: 64–85.

Biggart, Nicole Woolsey. 2000. "Banking on Each Other: The Situational Logic of Rotating Savings and Credit Associations." Paper presented to the Organization Science Winter Conference, Denver (February 10–12).

Bourdieu, Pierre. 1980. "Le capital social: Notes provisoires." *Actes de la recherche en sciences sociales* 3: 2–3.

Bourdieu, Pierre, and Loïc J. D. Wacquant. 1992. *An Invitation to Reflexive Sociology*. Chicago: University of Chicago Press.

Boxman, Ed A. W., Paul M. De Graaf, and Hendrik D. Flap. 1991. "The Impact of Social and Human Capital on the Income Attainment of Dutch Managers." *Social Networks* 13: 51–73.

Brass, Daniel J. 1992. "Power in Organizations: A Social Network Perspective." In *Research in Politics and Society*, edited by Gwen Moore and J. A. Whitt. Greenwich, Conn.: JAI Press.

Breiger, Ronald L. 1995. "Socioeconomic Achievement and the Phenomenology of Achievement." *Annual Review of Sociology* 21: 115–36.

Burt, Ronald S. 1980. "Autonomy in a Social Topology." *American Journal of Sociology* 85: 892–925.

———. 1983. *Corporate Profits and Co-optation*. New York: Academic Press.

———. 1987. "Social Contagion and Innovation, Cohesion Versus Structural Equivalence." *American Journal of Sociology* 92: 1287–1335.

———. 1988. "The Stability of American Markets." *American Journal of Sociology* 93: 356–95.

———. 1992. *Structural Holes*. Cambridge, Mass.: Harvard University Press.

———. 1995. "Le capital social, les trous structuraux, et l'entrepreneur." Translated by Emmanuel Lazega. *Revue française de sociologie* 36: 599–628.

———. 1997. "The Contingent Value of Social Capital." *Administrative Science Quarterly* 42: 339–65.

———. 1998. "The Gender of Social Capital." *Rationality and Society* 10: 5–46.

———. 1999. "The Social Capital of Opinion Leaders." *Annals* 566: 37–54.

———. 2000. "The Network Structure of Social Capital." In *Research in Organizational Behavior*, edited by Robert I. Sutton and Barry M. Staw. Greenwich, Conn.: JAI Press.

———. 2002. "Bridge Decay." *Social Networks* 23.

Burt, Ronald S., Miguel Guilarte, Holly J. Raider, and Yuki Yasuda. Forthcoming. "Competition, Contingency, and the External Structure of Markets." In

Advances in Strategic Management, vol. 19, edited by Paul Ingram and Brian Silverman. Greenwich, Conn.: JAI Press.

Burt, Ronald S., Robin M. Hogarth, and Claude Michaud. 2000. "The Social Capital of French and American Managers." *Organization Science* 11: 123–47.

Campbell, Karen E., Peter V. Marsden, and Jeanne Hurlbert. 1986. "Social Resources and Socioeconomic Status." *Social Networks* 8: 97–117.

Caro, Robert A. 1982. *The Path to Power.* New York: Knopf.

Cockburn, Iain M., and Rebecca M. Henderson. 1998. "Absorptive Capacity, Coauthoring Behavior, and the Organization of Research in Drug Discovery." *Journal of Industrial Economics* 64: 157–82.

Cohen, Wesley M., and Daniel A. Levinthal. 1990. "Absorptive Capacity: A New Perspective on Learning and Innovation." *Administrative Science Quarterly* 35: 128–52.

Coleman, James S. 1988. "Social Capital in the Creation of Human Capital." *American Journal of Sociology* 94: S95–120.

———. 1990. *Foundations of Social Theory.* Cambridge, Mass.: Harvard University Press.

Collins, Randall. 1998. *The Sociology of Philosophies.* Cambridge, Mass.: Harvard University Press.

Cook, Karen S., and Richard M. Emerson. 1978. "Power, Equity, and Commitment in Exchange Networks." *American Sociological Review* 43: 712–39.

Cook, Karen S., Richard M. Emerson, Mary R. Gillmore, and Toshio Yamagishi. 1983. "The Distribution of Power in Exchange Networks: Theory and Experimental Results." *American Journal of Sociology* 89: 275–305.

Dalzell, Robert F. 1987. *Enterprising Elite.* New York: Norton.

Davis, Gerald F., and Heinrich R. Greve. 1997. "Corporate Elite Networks and the Governance Changes in the 1980s." *American Journal of Sociology* 103: 1–37.

DeSoto, Clinton B. 1960. "Learning a Social Structure." *Journal of Abnormal and Social Psychology* 60: 417–21.

Diehl, Michael, and Wolfgang Stroebe. 1987. "Productivity Loss in Brainstorming Groups: Toward the Solution of a Riddle." *Journal of Personality and Social Psychology* 53: 497–509.

DiMaggio, Paul. 1992. "Nadel's Paradox Revisited: Relational and Cultural Aspects of Organizational Structure." In *Networks and Organizations,* edited by Nitin Nohria and Robert G. Eccles. Boston: Harvard Business School Press.

Doz, Yves. 1988. "Technology Partnerships Between Larger and Smaller Firms: Some Critical Issues." *International Studies of Management and Organization* 17: 31–57.

Doz, Yves, and Reinhard Angelmar. 1991. *Ciba-Geigy/ALZA Series.* Fontainebleau, France: INSEAD.

Doz, Yves, and Gary Hamel. 1998. *Alliance Advantage.* Boston: Harvard Business School Press.

Dyer, Jeffrey H., and Kentaro Nobeoka. 2000. "Creating and Managing a High-Performance Knowledge-Sharing Network: The Toyota Case." *Strategic Management Journal* 21: 345–67.

Eisenstat, Russell A. 1993. *Managing Xerox's Multinational Development Center.* Harvard Business School Case 9–490–029. Boston: Harvard Business School Press.

Erickson, Bonnie H. 1996. "Culture, Class, and Connections." *American Journal of Sociology* 102: 217–51.

———. 2001. "Good Networks and Good Jobs: The Value of Social Capital to Employers and Employees." In *Social Capital,* edited by Nan Lin, Karen S. Cook, and Ronald S. Burt. New York: Aldine de Gruyter.

Fernandez, Roberto M., and Roger V. Gould. 1994. "A Dilemma of State Power: Brokerage and Influence in the National Health Policy Domain." *American Journal of Sociology* 99: 1455–91.

Festinger, Leon, Stanley Schachter, and Kurt W. Back. 1950. *Social Pressures in Informal Groups.* Stanford, Calif.: Stanford University Press.

Finlay, William, and James E. Coverdill. 1999. "The Search Game: Organizational Conflicts and the Use of Headhunters." *Sociological Quarterly* 40: 11–30.

———. 2000. "Risk, Opportunism, and Structural Holes: How Headhunters Manage Clients and Earn Fees." *Work and Occupations* 27: 377–405.

Flap, Hendrik D., and Nan D. De Graaf. 1989. "Social Capital and Attained Occupational Status." *Netherlands Journal of Sociology* 22: 145–61.

Freeman, Linton C. 1977. "A Set of Measures of Centrality Based on Betweenness." *Sociometry* 40: 35–40.

———. 1992. "Filling in the Blanks: A Theory of Cognitive Categories and the Structure of Social Affiliation." *Social Psychology Quarterly* 55: 118–27.

Gabbay, Shaul M. 1997. *Social Capital in the Creation of Financial Capital.* Champaign, Ill.: Stipes.

Gabbay, Shaul M., and Ezra W. Zuckerman. 1998. "Social Capital and Opportunity in Corporate R&D: The Contingent Effect of Contact Density on Mobility Expectations." *Social Science Research* 27: 189–217.

Gargiulo, Martin, and Mario Benassi. 2000. "Trapped in Your Own Net: Network Cohesion, Structural Holes, and the Adaptation of Social Capital." *Organization Science* 11: 183–96.

Geletkanycz, Marta A., and Donald C. Hambrick. 1997. "The External Ties of Top Executives: Implications for Strategic Choice and Performance." *Administrative Science Quarterly* 42: 654–81.

Giuffe, Katherine A. 1999. "Sandpiles of Opportunity: Success in the Art World." *Social Forces* 77: 815–32.

Granovetter, Mark S. 1973. "The Strength of Weak Ties." *American Journal of Sociology* 78: 1360–80.

———. 1985. "Economic Action, Social Structure, and Embeddedness." *American Journal of Sociology* 91: 481–510.

———. 1992. "Problems of Explanation in Economic Sociology." In *Networks and Organization,* edited by Nitin Nohria and Robert G. Eccles. Boston: Harvard Business School Press.

———. 1995 [1974]. *Getting a Job.* Chicago: University of Chicago Press.

Greif, Avner. 1989. "Reputation and Coalition in Medieval Trade: Evidence on the Maghribi Traders." *Journal of Economic History* 49: 857–82.

Greve, Heinrich R. 1995. "Jumping Ship: The Diffusion of Strategy Abandonment." *Administrative Science Quarterly* 40: 444–73.

Hannan, Michael T., and John H. Freeman. 1977. "The Population Ecology of Organizations." *America Journal of Sociology* 82: 929–64.

Hansen, Morten T. 1999. "The Search-Transfer Problem: The Role of Weak Ties in Sharing Knowledge Across Organization Subunits." *Administrative Science Quarterly* 44: 82–111.

Hansen, Morten T., Joel M. Podolny, and Jeffrey Pfeffer. 2000. "So Many Ties, So Little Time: A Task Contingency Perspective on the Value of Social Capital in Organizations." Paper presented to the Organization Science Winter Conference, Denver (February 10–12).

Hargadon, Andrew B. 1998. "Firms as Knowledge Brokers: Lessons in Pursuing Continuous Innovation." *California Management Review* 40: 209–27.

Hargadon, Andrew B., and Robert I. Sutton. 1997. "Technology Brokering and Innovation in a Product Development Firm." *Administrative Science Quarterly* 42: 716–49.

Hatch, Mary Jo. 1999. "Exploring the Empty Spaces of Organizing: How Improvisational Jazz Helps Redescribe Organizational Structure." *Organization Studies* 20: 75–100.

Jacob, John, Thomas Z. Lys, and Margaret A. Neale. 1999. "Expertise in Forecasting Performance of Security Analysts." *Journal of Accounting and Economics* 28: 51–82.

Jang, Ho. 1997. "Market Structure, Performance, and Putting-out in the Korean Economy." Ph.D. diss., University of Chicago.

Janicik, Gregory A. 1998. "Social Expertise in Social Networks: Examining the Learning of Relations." Ph.D. diss., University of Chicago.

Joy, Leonard. 1967. "An Economic Homologue of Barth's Presentation of Economic Spheres in Darfur." In *Themes in Economic Anthropology*, edited by Raymond Firth. London: Tavistock.

Keller, Maryann. 1989. *Rude Awakening.* New York: Morrow.

Knoke, David. 2001. *Changing Organizations.* Boulder, Colo.: Westview Press.

Kogut, Bruce. 2000. "The Network as Knowledge: Generative Rules and the Emergence of Structure." *Strategic Management Journal* 21: 405–25.

Kogut, Bruce, and Udo Zander. 1996. "What Do Firms Do?: Coordination, Identity, and Learning." *Organization Science* 7: 502–18.

Koput, Kenneth, and Walter W. Powell. 2000. "Not Your Stepping Stone: Collaboration and the Dynamics of Industry Evolution in Biotechnology." Paper presented to the Organization Science Winter Conference, Denver (February 10–12).

Krackhardt, David, and Robert N. Stern. 1988. "Informal Networks and Organizational Crisis: An Experimental Simulation." *Social Psychology Quarterly* 51: 123–40.

Lazega, Emmanuel, and Philippa E. Pattison. 2001. "A Social Mechanism as a Form of Corporate Social Capital: Status Auctions Among Peers." In *Social Capital*, edited by Nan Lin, Karen S. Cook, and Ronald S. Burt. Chicago: Aldine de Gruyter.

Leana, Carrie R., and Harry J. Van Buren III. 1999. "Organizational Social

Capital and Employment Practices." *Academy of Management Review* 24: 538–55.

Leenders, Roger, and Shaul M. Gabbay. 1999. *Corporate Social Capital and Liability.* Amsterdam: Kluwer Academic Publishers.

Light, Ivan, and Stavros Karageorgis. 1994. "The Ethnic Economy." In *The Handbook of Economic Sociology,* edited by Neil J. Smelser and Richard Swedberg. Princeton, N.J.: Princeton University Press.

Lin, Nan. 1999. "Social Networks and Status Attainment." *Annual Review of Sociology* 25: 467–87.

———. 2001. *Social Capital.* New York: Cambridge University Press.

Lin, Nan, and Yanjie Bian. 1991. "Getting Ahead in Urban China." *American Journal of Sociology* 97: 657–88.

Lin, Nan, Karen S. Cook, and Ronald S. Burt. 2001. *Social Capital.* Chicago: Aldine de Gruyter.

Lin, Nan, and Mary Dumin. 1986. "Access to Occupations Through Social Ties." *Social Networks* 8: 365–85.

Lin, Nan, Walter Ensel, and John Vaughn. 1981. "Social Resources and Strength of Ties: Structural Factors in Occupational Status Attainment." *American Sociological Review* 46: 393–405.

Llobrera, Joseph T., David R. Meyer, and Gregory Nammacher. 2000. "Trajectories of Industrial Districts: Impact of Strategic Intervention in Medical Districts." *Economic Geography* 76: 68–98.

Lofstrom, Shawn M. 2000. "Absorptive Capacity in Strategic Alliances: Investigating the Effects of Individuals' Social and Human Capital on Inter-firm Learning." Paper presented to the Organization Science Winter Conference, Denver (February 10–12).

Markovsky, Barry, David Willer, and Travis Patton. 1988. "Power Relations in Exchange Networks." *American Sociological Review* 53: 220–36.

Marsden, Peter V., and Jeanne Hurlbert. 1988. "Social Resources and Mobility Outcomes: A Replication and Extension." *Social Forces* 66: 1038–59.

McEvily, Bill, and Alfred Marcus. 2000. "The Acquisition of Competitive Capabilities as Social Learning." Paper presented to the Organization Science Winter Conference, Denver (February 10–12).

McEvily, Bill, and Akbar Zaheer. 1999. "Bridging Ties: A Source of Firm Heterogeneity in Competitive Capabilities." *Strategic Management Journal* 20: 1133–56.

McGuire, Patrick, and Mark Granovetter. 2000. "The Social Construction of the Electric Utility Industry, 1878–1919." In *Constructing Industries and Markets,* edited by Joe Porac and Marc Ventresca. New York: Elsevier.

Mehra, Ajay, Martin Kilduff, and Daniel J. Brass. 2000. "Combining Personality and Network Theory: The Effects of Self-monitoring and Structural Position on Workplace Performance." University of Cincinnati. Unpublished paper.

Merton, Robert K. 1968 [1948]. "The Bearing of Empirical Research upon the Development of Social Theory." In *Social Theory and Social Structure.* New York: Free Press.

———. 1968 [1957]. "Continuities in the Theory of Reference Group Behavior." In *Social Theory and Social Structure.* New York: Free Press.

Meyerson, Eva M. 1994. "Human Capital, Social Capital, and Compensation: The Relative Contribution of Social Contacts to Managers' Incomes." *Acta Sociologica* 37: 383–99.

Mills, John Stuart. 1987 [1848]. *Principles of Political Economy.* Fairchild, N.J.: Augustus M. Kelley.

Mintzberg, Henry. 1973. *The Nature of Managerial Work.* New York: Harper & Row.

Mizruchi, Mark S., and Linda Brewster Sterns. 2001. "Getting Deals Done: The Use of Social Networks in Bank Decision Making." American Sociological Review 66: 647–71.

Morselli, Carlo. 2001. "Structuring Mr. Nice: Entrepreneurial Opportunities and Brokerage Positioning in the Cannabis Trade." *Crime, Law, and Social Change* 35: 203–44.

Mullen, Brian, Craig Johnson, and Eduardo Salas. 1991. "Productivity Loss in Brainstorming Groups: A Meta-analytic Integration." *Basic and Applied Social Psychology* 12: 3–24.

Nahapiet, Janine, and Sumantra Ghoshal. 1998. "Social Capital, Intellectual Capital, and the Organization Advantage." *Academy of Management Review* 23: 242–66.

Padgett, John F., and Christopher K. Ansell. 1993. "Robust Action and the Rise of the Medici, 1400–1434." *American Journal of Sociology* 98: 1259–1319.

Paulus, Paul B., Timothy S. Larey, and Anita H. Ortega. 1995. "Performance and Perceptions of Brainstormers in an Organizational Setting." *Basic and Applied Social Psychology* 17: 249–65.

Pennings, Johannes M., Kyungmook Lee, and Arjen van Witteloostuijn. 1998. "Human Capital, Social Capital, and Firm Dissolution." *Academy of Management Journal* 41: 425–40.

Podolny, Joel M. 1993. "A Status-based Model of Market Competition." *American Journal of Sociology* 98: 829–72.

———. 2001. "Networks as the Pipes and Prisms of the Market." *American Journal of Sociology* 107: 33–60.

Podolny, Joel M., and James N. Baron. 1997. "Relationships and Resources: Social Networks and Mobility in the Workplace." *American Sociological Review* 62: 673–93.

Podolny, Joel M., Toby E. Stuart, and Michael T. Hannan. 1997. "Networks, Knowledge, and Niches: Competition in the Worldwide Semiconductor Industry, 1984–1991." *American Journal of Sociology* 102: 659–89.

Portes, Alejandro. 1998. "Social Capital: Its Origins and Applications in Modern Sociology." *Annual Review of Sociology* 24: 1–24.

Powell, Walter W., and Peter Brantley. 1992. "Competitive Cooperation in Biotechnology: Learning Through Networks?" In *Networks and Organizations,* edited by Nitin Nohria and Robert G. Eccles. Boston: Harvard Business School Press.

Powell, Walter W., Kenneth W. Koput, and Laurel Smith-Doerr. 1996. "Interorganizational Collaboration and the Locus of Innovation: Networks of Learning in Biotechnology." *Administrative Science Quarterly* 41: 116–45.

Powell, Walter W., Kenneth W. Koput, Laurel Smith-Doerr, and Jason Owen-Smith. 1999. "Network Position and Firm Performance: Organizational Returns to Collaboration." In *Research in the Sociology of Organizations,* edited by Steven Andrews and David Knoke. Greenwich, Conn.: JAI Press.

Powell, Walter W., and Laurel Smith-Doerr. 1994. "Networks and Economic Life." In *The Handbook of Economic Sociology,* edited by Neil J. Smelser and Richard Swedberg. Princeton, N.J.: Princeton University Press.

Provan, Keith G., and H. Brinton Milward. 1995. "A Preliminary Theory of Inter-organizational Network Effectiveness: A Comparative Study of Four Community Mental Health Systems." *Administrative Science Quarterly* 40: 1–33.

Putnam, Robert D. 1993. *Making Democracy Work.* Princeton, N.J.: Princeton University Press.

Reagans, Ray, and Ezra W. Zuckerman. 2001. "Networks, Diversity, and Performance: The Social Capital of Corporate R&D Units." *Organization Science* 12: 502–17.

Rosenthal, Elizabeth A. 1996. "Social Networks and Team Performance." Ph.D. diss., University of Chicago.

Sediatis, Judith. 1998. "The Alliances of Spin-offs Versus Start-ups: Social Ties in the Genesis of Post-Soviet Alliances." *Organization Science* 9: 368–81.

Shan, Weijian, Gordon Walker, and Bruce Kogut. 1994. "Interfirm Cooperation and Start-up Innovation in the Biotechnology Industry." *Strategic Management Journal* 15: 387–94.

Siamwalla, Ammar. 1978. "Farmers and Middlemen: Aspects of Agriculture Marketing in Thailand." *Economic Bulletin for Asia and the Pacific* 29: 38–50.

Simmel, Georg. 1902. "The Number of Members as Determining the Sociological Form of the Group, II." Translated by A. Small. *American Journal of Sociology* 8: 158–96.

———. 1955 [1922]. *Conflict and the Web of Group Affiliations.* New York: Free Press.

Smith, Adam. 1982 [1766]. *Lectures on Jurisprudence.* Indianapolis: Liberty Fund.

Sørensen, Jesper B. 1999. "Executive Migration and Interorganizational Competition." *Social Science Research* 28: 289–315.

———. 2000. "The Longitudinal Effects of Group Tenure Composition on Turnover." *American Sociological Review* 65: 298–310.

Sparrowe, Raymond T., and Pamela A. Popielarz. 1995. "Weak Ties and Structural Holes: The Effects of Network Structure on Careers." University of Illinois, Chicago. Unpublished paper.

Steier, Lloyd, and Royston Greenwood. 2000. "Entrepreneurship and the Evolution of Angel Financial Networks." *Organization Studies* 21: 163–92.

Stewart, Alex. 1990. "The Bigman Metaphor for Entrepreneurship: A 'Library Tale' with Morals on Alternatives for Further Research." *Organization Science* 1: 143–59.

Stewart, Thomas A. 1996. "The Great Conundrum: You Versus the Team." *Fortune* 134(November): 165–66.

Stinchcombe, Arthur L. 1990. *Information and Organizations.* Berkeley: University of California Press.

Strang, David, and Sarah A. Soule. 1998. "Diffusion in Organizations and Social Movements." *Annual Review of Sociology* 24: 265–90.

Stroebe, Wolfgang, and Michael Diehl. 1994. "Why Groups Are Less Effective Than Their Members: On Productivity Losses in Idea-generating Groups." In *European Review of Social Psychology*, edited by Wolfgang Stroebe and Miles Hewstone. London: Wiley.

Stuart, Toby E. 1998. "Producer Network Positions and Propensities to Collaborate: An Investigation of Strategic Alliance Formations in a High-technology Industry." *Administrative Science Quarterly* 43: 668–98.

Stuart, Toby E., Ha Hoang, and Ralph C. Hybels. 1999. "Interorganizational Endorsements and the Performance of Entrepreneurial Ventures." *Administrative Science Quarterly* 44: 315–49.

Stuart, Toby E., and Joel M. Podolny. 1999. "Positional Causes and Correlates of Strategic Alliances in the Semiconductor Industry." In *Research in the Sociology of Organizations*, edited by Steven Andrews and David Knoke. Greenwich, Conn.: JAI Press.

Stuart, Toby E., and David T. Robinson. 2000. "Network Effects in the Governance of Strategic Alliances in Biotechnology." Paper presented to the Organization Science Winter Conference, Denver (February 10–12).

Sutton, Robert I., and Andrew B. Hargadon. 1996. "Brainstorming Groups in Context: Effectiveness in a Product Design Firm." *Administrative Science Quarterly* 41: 685–718.

Swedberg, Richard. 1990. *Economics and Sociology*. Princeton, N.J.: Princeton University Press.

Talmud, Ilan. 1994. "Relations and Profits: The Social Organizations of Israeli Industrial Competition." *Social Science Research* 23: 109–35.

Thornton, Patricia H. 1999. "The Sociology of Entrepreneurship." *Annual Review of Sociology* 25: 19–46.

Tillman, Robert, and Michael Indergaard. 1999. "Field of Schemes: Health Insurance Fraud in the Small Business Sector." *Social Problems* 46: 572–90.

Tilly, Charles. 1998. *Durable Inequality*. Berkeley: University of California Press.

Tullock, Gordon. 1985. "Adam Smith and the Prisoners' Dilemma." *Quarterly Journal of Economics* 100: 1073–81.

Van de Ven, Andrew H., Raghu Garud, Douglas E. Polley, and Sankaran Venkataraman. 1999. *The Innovation Journey*. New York: Oxford University Press.

Walker, Gordon, Bruce Kogut, and Weijian Shan. 1997. "Social Capital, Structural Holes, and the Formation of an Industry Network." *Organization Science* 8: 109–25.

Wegener, Bern. 1991. "Job Mobility and Social Ties: Social Resources, Prior Job, and Status Attainment." *American Sociological Review* 56: 60–71.

White, Harrison C. 1981. "Where Do Markets Come From?" *American Journal of Sociology* 87: 517–47.

Willer, David. 1999. *Network Exchange Theory*. New York: Praeger.

Williams, Katherine Y., and Charles A. O'Reilly III. 1998. "Demography and Diversity in Organizations: A Review of Forty Years of Research." In *Research in Organizational Behavior*, edited by Barry M. Staw and Larry L. Cummings. Greenwich, Conn.: JAI Press.

Williams, Phil. 1998. "The Nature of Drug-Trafficking Networks." *Current History* 97: 154–59.

Woolcock, Michael, and Deepa Narayan. 2001. "Social Capital: Implications for Development Theory, Research, and Policy." *World Bank Research Observer* 15: 225–49.

Yair, Gad, and Daniel Maman. 1996. "The Persistent Structure of Hegemony in the Eurovision Song Contest." *Acta Sociologica* 39: 309–25.

Yasuda, Yuki. 1996. *Network Analysis of Japanese and American Markets.* Tokyo: Bokutaku-sha.

Zander, Udo, and Bruce Kogut. 1995. "Knowledge and the Speed of the Transfer and Imitation of Organizational Capabilities: An Empirical Test." *Organization Science* 6: 76–92.

Zelizer, Viviana. 1994. *The Social Meaning of Money.* New York: Basic Books.

Ziegler, Rolf. 1982. "Market Structure and Co-optation." Universität München. Unpublished paper.

Zuckerman, Ezra W. 1999. "The Categorical Imperative: Securities Analysts and the Legitimacy Discount." *American Journal of Sociology* 104: 1398–1438.

= Part III =

Gender Inequality and Economic Sociology

= Chapter 8 =

Telling Stories About Gender and Effort: Social Science Narratives About Who Works Hard for the Money

WILLIAM T. BIELBY AND DENISE D. BIELBY

W HO WORKS hard, and are there differences by gender? Is part of the earnings gap between men and women attributable to gender differences in the allocation of effort to work and family roles? What kind of theories do social scientists offer about whether and why men work harder than women (or vice versa)?

The review presented here was motivated by our plan to replicate and extend our research published in 1988 testing the theory of gender differences in the allocation of effort offered by the Nobel Prize–winning economist Gary Becker (Bielby and Bielby 1988). In returning to this line of scholarship, we discovered that labor economists had developed a new story about who works hard and why, with implications for gender differences in work intensity and wages that were at odds with empirical findings by organizational sociologists. In attempting to reconcile economic theory with sociological data, we made two discoveries: that both economists and sociologists had been remarkably casual about how key constructs like work effort and organizational commitment are conceptualized and measured; and that each camp had largely overlooked a rich body of scholarship by social psychologists that might clarify the underlying mechanisms that determine how, why, and when individuals withhold effort or work harder than is required by their employers. In this chapter, we first summarize labor economists' accounts of the allocation of work effort from the human capital and efficiency-wage perspectives. We then attempt to make sense of the different ways in which economists and organizational sociologists have conceptualized and measured work effort and related constructs and summarize scholarship that challenges simplistic notions of the relationship between earnings and effort in modern work contexts. We conclude by addressing the implications of social-psychological research on "social loafing" and on competitive versus cooperative behavior in social dilemmas for understanding similarities and differences between men and women in the allocation of work effort and organizational commitment.

Gender, Human Capital, and the Allocation of Effort

In an elegant elaboration of human capital approaches to earnings inequality, Becker (1985) has proposed a formal model of the allocation of effort that explains gender differences in labor market outcomes solely on the basis of the utility-maximizing choices of job-seekers. In the standard human capital model, women who are burdened by family responsibilities and anticipate intermittent employment seek jobs that are compatible with the demands of family life. Such jobs rely more on general training than on firm-specific training, and they involve lower wage penalties for leaving and reentering the paid labor force than do the jobs most likely to appeal to individuals who anticipate continuous labor force participation (Polachek 1981; Tam 1997). According to this model, a substantial portion of the gender gap in earnings is attributable to the fact that women have fewer years of labor market experience and acquire different kinds of human capital (more general, less specific) than do men.

In Becker's elaboration of this model, the earnings of men and women are expected to differ even when they have the same amount and type of investments in human capital. According to his model, women with family responsibilities allocate less effort to their jobs outside the home than do men with comparable skills and labor market experience. Therefore, hour for hour, men are more productive than are women (who have greater household responsibilities), and men receive more pay and better career opportunities as a result. Moreover, gender segregation results because "married women seek occupations and jobs that are less effort intensive and otherwise more compatible with their home responsibilities" (Becker 1985, S52).

The findings of two recent studies are consistent with Becker's reasoning. The labor economists Joni Hersch and Leslie Stratton (1997) rely on the Panel Study of Income Dynamics (PSID) to estimate wage penalties for time spent on housework. The results obtained under a variety of specifications and estimation techniques suggest that gender differences in housework time explain as much as 30 percent of the wage gap, comparable to the fraction explained by gender differences in organizational tenure. Largely consistent with these results are Michelle Budig and Paula England's (1999) estimates of the wage penalty for motherhood, based on fixed-effects models using the National Longitudinal Study of Youth (NLSY). They report a wage penalty of approximately 5 percent per child, net of labor market experience. (The effect is about 10 percent without controlling experience.)

Both of these analyses pose the allocation of effort and discrimination (not against women as a class but against those who somehow signal a greater commitment to household work) as alternative explanations for the wage penalties, and neither study is able to differentiate definitively between the two. Hersch and Stratton's findings suggest that the wage penalty for housework is greater for women than for men. This could indicate that men are allocating less effort than women to each hour of housework (and conversely for effort allocations for paid work), or it could indicate that employers discriminate against women who signal a commitment to household responsibilities.[1] Budig and England included some indirect measures of job effort in their specification (the Dictionary of Occupational Titles [DOT] measures of skill and training requirements and occupational averages of measures of effort from the 1977 Quality of Employment Survey [QES]), and neither these nor any other job-level measures mediated the wage penalty for motherhood.[2] Although Budig and England can rule out any explanation based on the idea that mothers choose "motherhood-friendly" jobs, they conclude that both gender differences in the allocation of effort and employer discrimination may account for the wage penalty, with employers practicing statistical discrimination against mothers, based on their perception that on average mothers are less productive than nonmothers. However, a recent study that corrects for endogeneity in household hours in estimates of wages and for heterogeneity among women fails to find significant effects of housework on wages for women or for men (McLennan 2000).

The notion that women's productivity suffers from family demands is at odds with several lines of empirical research. Our research (Bielby and Bielby 1988), using self-reports of effort expended on the job from the 1973 and 1977 Quality of Employment Surveys, showed that on average employed women allocate just as much if not more effort to work than do men. In fact, our results showed that compared to men with similar household responsibilities, human capital, and work contexts, women allocate substantially *more* effort to outside employment. We found that to the extent that women do allocate effort away from the workplace in order to meet family demands, those trade-offs bring their work effort back to the level of the typical male with no such family responsibilities. Overall, however, the impact of household and family arrangements on work effort was small, a finding we have replicated with the data from the 1991 National Organizations Study (NOS) (Bielby et al. 1995).

Marsden, Kalleberg, and Cook (1993), also using the 1991 NOS, found a similar pattern with organizational commitment as the dependent variable: slightly higher commitment among women compared to men in comparable jobs and organizational settings, and virtually no effects of family circumstances on commitment. Other research on organizational commitment tells a similar story. Two meta-analyses show either no relationship between gender and commitment or a slight tendency for women to exhibit higher levels of commitment than men (Mathieu and Zajac 1990; Aven, Parker, and McEvoy 1993). Given the inconsistencies between the human capital model of effort allocation and empirical studies of gender differences in effort and commitment, we decided to take a closer look at the other stories in social research about who works hard and who does not, and under what circumstances.

A New Twist in the Story of Gender and Effort: Efficiency Wages, Monitoring Costs, and Gift Exchange

In the mid-1980s economists began writing about the concept of "efficiency wages"—above-market wages that elicit greater effort and commitment from employees. The basic efficiency wage model is based on the notion that under some circumstances, employers pay a wage premium to reduce shirking among workers employed in jobs for which performance is costly to monitor (Bowles 1985; Bulow and Summers 1986). Labor economists who apply this model to gender differences in earnings assume that women have a higher propensity to leave a firm than do men and therefore anticipate a lower return for a given wage over the course of their tenure with the employer. One implication of this model is that the marginal gain in work intensity from a given wage premium is greater for men than for women (Goldin 1986; Robinson and Wunnava 1991). One version of this model also assumes that the costs of supervision are greater for men than for women (that is, that women are more "docile"; see Robinson and Wunnava 1991, 57). In any case, to optimize the trade-off between efficiency wages and supervision, women are expected to be assigned to jobs in which effort is monitored through direct supervision, whereas men's jobs of comparable work intensity elicit effort through wage premiums. In Becker's model, women earn less because they do not work as hard as men. In contrast, these versions of efficiency wage models suggest that men work hard because they have been "bought off" with a wage premium, whereas women work hard because they are closely supervised. The efficiency wage model implies that job segregation mediates the relationship between gender, work effort, and earnings, and if it is based on employers' beliefs about gender differences in monitoring costs or turnover rates, it is also fully consistent with statistical discrimination as an underlying mechanism.

A variation of the efficiency wage model places less emphasis on worker discipline and focuses instead on a "gift exchange" between employer and employee (Akerlof 1982). An above-market wage is part of the employer's side of an implicit contract whereby firms agree to provide high wages and favorable working conditions in exchange for high effort norms among employees in jobs that are difficult to monitor (Belman, Drago, and Wooden 1992). According to this model, the trust generated from the implicit contract is an efficient way to economize on monitoring costs. Mark Granovetter (1988) adds sociological content to the model, emphasizing that trust and reputability grow out of stable networks of social relations. Thus, structural features of the workplace that promote long job tenures, embedded social relationships among workers and between workers and employers, and perceptions of fairness are likely to lead to a workplace culture that can sustain the implicit contract. Workers who are in jobs that are difficult to monitor or that require traits that are difficult to observe, such as loyalty, commitment, or initiative, receive a wage premium relative to workers who have otherwise identical observable traits but are in jobs that do not have these properties (Kirchler, Fehr, and Evens 1996). The gift exchange model is designed to explain differences in work effort and wages that occur across firms or industries, not variation across individuals who are employed in the same work setting. The model seems to be based on differences across work contexts in norms about a fair day's work, not on differences in the extent to which individuals depart from those norms.

In one sense, the gift exchange model represents a radical departure from the neoclassical model of the labor market, in which each party to the exchange is strictly opportunistic and "seeks to maximize their egoistic interests without considering the other's outcome." In the neoclassical model, "comparisons between one's own and the other's outcome are not supposed to influence the [buyer's or seller's] choices" (Kirchler et al. 1996, 328). Of course, the idea that people will cheat if not watched closely is fully consistent with the neoclassical view of human behavior. But with the concept of gift exchange, labor market economists embrace social psychology, albeit in a characteristically "stylized" form: under norms of reciprocity, the recipient of a gift from an employer is obliged to do a favor in return. Although a move away from economic reductionist approaches, this line of scholarship does not attempt to undertake empirical research of the type called for by Viviana Zelizer (ch. 11, this volume) in her exploration of the circumstances under which social ties between economic actors become infused with distinctive meanings and obligations.

Remarkably, outside of some areas of game theory, labor economists rarely examine the basic premise of efficiency wage theory, namely, that higher wages elicit greater effort. Moreover, when applying the concept of efficiency wages to explain gender differences in labor market outcomes, labor economists sometimes draw on stereotypes (or in their jargon, "stylized facts") about gender differences in work commitment and other-regarding behavior.

Again, given the shortcomings of what was found in the labor markets literature, we were motivated to look at other areas of social research for work designed to test more directly the relationship between work context and work effort. As it turns out, several somewhat related lines of inquiry in social psychology suggest alternative frameworks for understanding the relationships among gender, effort, and labor market outcomes and for rethinking human capital and efficiency wage models of effort allocation. One is social-psychological research on "social loafing," which is defined as the reduction in motivation and effort when individuals work collectively on a joint task, compared to when they work individually or co-actively. (The textbook example is not pulling as hard on a rope when one is part of a group compared to when one pulls alone; see Karau and Williams 1995.) A second line of research is looking at the circumstances under which individuals pursue competitive versus cooperative strategies in "social dilemma" settings, that is, contexts where individual incentives for not cooperating are greater than those for cooperating, but the group is better off if all cooperate (Yamagishi 1995). But before turning to these lines of research, we describe two other sources of frustration in attempting to make sense of scholarship on gender and work effort. One lies in the many inconsistencies and contradictions in how effort is conceptualized and operationalized, and the other is the remarkably weak evidence supporting the notion that higher wages elicit greater work effort.

Ways of Conceptualizing and Operationalizing Effort and Commitment

Becker (1985) uses "effort" and "energy" interchangeably and attributes different energy intensities to different activities, such as employment, housework, leisure, and sleep. An individual's stock of energy is allocated across activities, and it is also allocated over time and across the life cycle. For example, workaholics who experience burnout are assumed to have borrowed against future stocks of energy. According to Becker, the stock of energy "varies enormously" across individuals, so a "slacker" could be either a person with a stock of energy that is far below average or a person who is saving it up for later. Becker writes that the dimensions of energy stock include ambition and motivation as well as mental and physical energy, although the formal properties of his model require no disaggregation of effort into its component dimensions, and no such aggregation has ever been attempted in this line of research.

Becker assumes that firms can indeed monitor the amount of work effort, but the basic "worker discipline" efficiency wage model relaxes that assumption: workers naturally and rationally withhold effort when there is a reasonable probability that they can get away with it—that is, effortful work is seen to bring disutility (Becker 1985, S43–44). However, with the appropriate incentive in the form of a wage premium, the worker sees that he or she is actually better off by working to full potential, rather than risk termination and banishment to the low-wage sector. This version of the efficiency wage model requires nothing in the way of other-regarding behavior on the part of the worker, and the decision about whether or not to shirk, viewed as one of optimal allocation of effort, is fully consistent with Becker's assumption about workers' decisionmaking calculus. Shirking is a decision to allocate effort (but not time) away from work and to other activities. In the efficiency wage model, effort is unidimensional, and a single process governs the decision about whether to devote as little energy to work as one can get away with or to work harder than that.

Both Becker's allocation model and the "worker discipline" efficiency wage model are concerned with what has been called the "propensity to withhold effort" (PWE), which Roland Kidwell and Nathan

Bennett (1993, 429) define as "the likelihood that an individual will give less than full effort on a job-related task." Kidwell and Bennett make an important distinction between PWE, which they argue is the common concern of models of shirking, social loafing, and free-riding, and the propensity of employees to provide *extra* effort on behalf of the organization, or what is sometimes called "organizational citizenship behavior" (OCB). PWE, they note, can be discussed in terms of doing less work than is required or expected, whereas OCB can be viewed as doing work beyond what is required or expected. Kidwell and Bennett observe that PWE is usually framed in terms of a rational, cost-benefit calculus, whereas OCB has been defined as the informal contributions to an organization that employees choose to give or withhold *without regard to formal sanctions or incentives;* in other words, OCB is a form of other-regarding behavior or altruism (Organ 1988; Kidwell and Bennett 1993).

The distinction between PWE and OCB implies that there is some widely understood normative level of effort associated with a job in a specific work setting. It also seems to imply that one set of processes applies to the decision to reduce effort below some normative level and another set of processes applies to the decision to exert effort beyond the norm. However, this need not be the case. Rather, it could be that the processes operate in parallel: under some circumstances an individual makes rational calculations to allocate effort above or below the norm according to a cost-benefit calculus, while under other circumstances that choice is made with less deliberation and is more sharply shaped by social identity and social influences. Indeed, the circumstances under which either of these processes is operative is the focus of some of the research in the social loafing literature, described later in the chapter.

Kidwell and Bennett's distinction between rational approaches to PWE versus social-psychological approaches to OCB is relevant to the ways in which gender differences in effort have been conceptualized theoretically. Models that address gender differences in the PWE realm, like Becker's effort allocation and "worker discipline" efficiency wage models, typically emphasize differences in the incentives that men and women face by virtue of structural locations (primarily differences in family roles and obligations) rather than gender differences in social-psychological orientations toward work. In contrast, models that attempt to account for gender differences in organizational citizenship or commitment tend to pose social-psychological orientations and structural locations as competing explanations—for example, "gender models" (or gender role socialization models) versus "job models" of organizational commitment (Marsden et al.

1993; Aven et al. 1993). However, much *empirical* work (including our own) on gender differences and similarities in effort and commitment tends to confound PWE and OCB in both conceptualization and measurement and fails to consider that the determinants of each may be quite different.

In our 1988 article, which was formulated as a test of Becker's model, we measured work effort with three items. Two items measured perceptions of the effort requirements of the job and addressed the implication of Becker's model that women avoid effort-intensive jobs. The third measured perceptions of the effort put into the job *beyond what is required;* this is perhaps more appropriately viewed as a measure of OCB. We used the latter item because it was less likely to be subject to attribution biases. (In other words, on the other items a job with given energy requirements might *seem* more demanding to someone facing heavy family demands than to someone with no such responsibilities.) However, we offered no explanation for the finding that women report more of what could be seen as organizational citizenship behavior. Moreover, none of our measures tapped the propensity to shirk ("less than none" was not an option on the item measuring "how much work do you put into your job beyond what is required?").

The research that focuses specifically on gender differences in organizational commitment (OC) suffers from similar problems of conceptualization and measurement. Most studies rely on some subset of items on the Organizational Commitment Questionnaire (OCQ) developed by Richard Mowday, Lyman Porter, and Richard Steers (1982). The OCQ scale combines three conceptually distinct dimensions: loyalty (sometimes called attachment or "continuance commitment"), defined as the desire to remain with an organization; identification, defined as acceptance of the organization's values; and involvement, which is similar to organizational citizenship behavior and is defined as the willingness to exert effort on behalf of the organization (Bar-Hayim and Berman 1992). Based on patterns of covariation (for example, as demonstrated by factor analysis and similar scaling techniques), it is often argued that the three dimensions reduce to two empirically based dimensions: passive versus active commitment. The former is organizational loyalty, and the latter is involvement-identification. Women's commitment is often argued to be passive: because they have fewer alternatives, women develop loyalty to the organizations that employ them through a process of retrospective, dissonance-reducing rationalization (Bar-Hayim and Berman 1992; Marsden et al. 1993; Aven et al. 1993). However, these arguments are unsatisfactory on several grounds. First, there is no research that attempts to assess retrospective rationalization processes explicitly. Second, findings of no difference or a slight difference favoring females on organizational commitment appear to apply equally to measures of active and passive commitment. Third, the collapsing of identification and involvement into a single dimension of active commitment fails to consider the suggestion in some theoretical accounts that the underlying processes generating each are distinct.

In sum, social scientists tell four stories about gender and work effort. One explains why women allocate less effort than men to paid employment; a second explains why they earn less than men who work at the same level of intensity; and two others explain why women are more committed to their employers than men. The most common story told by social scientists about gender and effort is that women do not work as hard as men because household responsibilities limit the amount of energy and commitment they can devote to paid employment. Another story is that employers find it efficient to elicit greater effort from men by offering them higher wages while using supervision to reduce shirking among women, so for a given expenditure of effort men are paid more than women. Some social scientists say that compared to men, women are more loyal to their employers, and this is because they are rationalizing their lack of alternatives and the barriers they have overcome to sustain their careers. Finally, some argue that women are more "other-regarding" than men and therefore more likely to engage in organizational citizenship behaviors.

The empirical evidence regarding any of these stories is mixed at best, and just as important, social scientists have been remarkably careless about what it means to work hard on behalf of one's employer. Is shirking—not working as hard as is expected—simply the flip side of working harder than is required? Is working harder than required a form of altruistic organizational citizenship, and is it generated by the same process that builds agreement in values between employers and their employees? Without greater clarity about the concept of work effort and the underlying mechanisms, it will be impossible to make sense of the seemingly contradictory findings about gender and effort.

Does Anyone Work Hard for the Money?

In our 1988 article using the 1977 Quality of Employment Survey data, we found only a marginal effect of earnings on effort. If anything, the likelihood of simultaneity bias (that is, people earn more because they work hard, as well as vice versa) probably caused us to overstate the effect of earnings relative to other determinants of work effort. Nevertheless, the impact of job autonomy on effort (as measured by both the three-item scale and the "beyond what is required" item) was roughly three times as strong as the effect of earnings (as measured by the impact of a one-standard-deviation difference on each variable on effort). John Walsh and Shu-Fen Tseng (1998), using survey data collected in the Chicago area in 1992, found a strong effect of worker participation in decisionmaking on "active effort" (effort beyond what is required on the job) and no effect of wages. (Indeed, the point estimate of the wage effect is negative.) Similarly, Marsden and his colleagues (1993), using the 1991 National Organizations Study, found a substantial effect of job autonomy on organizational commitment but no effect at all of earnings, and Karen Loscocco (1990) reports a virtually identical pattern with data on workers employed in a midwestern manufacturing plant.

Although this pattern of results seems at odds with the basic premise of efficiency wage models, there may be a way to make it partially consistent with that story. The usual interpretation of these findings—that allowing workers greater autonomy elicits higher levels of effort and commitment—may have the causality running in the wrong direction. That is, some workers may be closely supervised (allowed little discretion in how they do their work) precisely because they tend not to work hard at the job. But since the relationship between autonomy and effort is strongest when the outcome measure taps organizational citizenship behavior or commitment (as opposed to the tendency not to shirk), this interpretation seems implausible.

Social-psychological research on the "overjustification effect" suggests a more plausible interpretation. Experimental studies show that individuals often lose interest in intrinsically engaging tasks when they are subsequently given an external reward for accomplishing the task. "Once an activity is categorized as one associated with an extrinsic orientation, it is less likely to be chosen in a free choice period because the reason for engaging in the activity . . . is no longer available and because it is less likely to be seen as the sort of thing one does in one's free time" (Pittman 1998, 567). This mechanism would seem particularly relevant to organizational citizenship behavior, which we defined earlier as the informal contributions to an organization that employees choose to make without regard to formal sanctions or incentives. The overjustification effect suggests that it may be counterproductive to attempt to induce such behavior with higher wages when it might otherwise be provided voluntarily for intrinsically interesting tasks (Frey 1997).[3] In any case, in attempting to make sense of the consistent empirical findings of the relationship between autonomy and commitment, we once again conclude that scholars studying the allocation of effort in work settings need to be much more careful about conceptualization and operationalization of the outcome and about specification of the social-psychological mechanisms presumed to be operating. In the sections that follow, we draw from recent research in two somewhat related areas of social psychology for insights into the mechanisms that may explain similarities and differences between men and women in work effort and organizational citizenship behavior.

Social Loafing and Social Compensation: Gender, Work Context, and Effort in Collective Versus Co-Active Tasks

"Social loafing" (SL) (Karau and Williams 1993, 1995) refers to the reduction in motivation and effort that occurs when working collectively on a group task, compared to working on one's own (though possibly in the presence of others). Research in this tradition examines the features of the task and social context that encourage or inhibit the tendency to reduce effort in group contexts, as well as the factors that facilitate the allocation of extra effort or "social compensation." Strictly speaking, SL applies only to situations in which output is measured at the group level and cannot be observed at the level of individual contributions, although some research examines the circumstances under which individuals reduce effort when working co-actively, that is, in the presence of others, but where individual output can be measured (see, for example, Schnake 1991).

As in efficiency wage models, monitoring of performance is key to the concept of social loafing. Called the "hide-in-crowd" effect in the SL literature, the idea is that monitoring individual contributions to the performance of a collective task becomes increasingly difficult as the size of the group increases (Kidwell and Bennett 1993). However, SL scholarship assumes that in a group context, minimizing effort is just one of several motivations; it also assumes that social influence and evaluation can occur in ways other than having a supervisor observe one's specific contribution to a group task. In short, how a person actually responds when it is possible to "hide in a crowd" depends on what she or he believes about the relationship of self to others in the group (Huguet, Charbonnier, and Monteil 1999). Steven Karau and Kipling Williams (1993, 686) summarize the research showing that individuals respond to any of three motivational dimensions: a public self that responds to external evaluation; a private self that responds mainly to internal values; and a collective self oriented toward "fulfilling one's role within the context of the goals of important reference groups." Their meta-analysis of mostly laboratory studies as well as considerable experimental research published since the early 1990s points to several key factors that are relevant to the allocation of work effort in real-world settings. Among them are the complexity and meaningfulness of the task, work group cohesion, equity norms, and the perception of one's own competence relative to that of others in the work group. Later we discuss how these factors, along with the gender label of a task and the gender composition of a work group, may illuminate the social-psychological mechanisms that generate gender differences and similarities in the allocation of work effort.

One particular focus of social loafing research explores how individuals adjust their contributions based on their perceptions of the competencies and contributions of others. Individuals tend to withhold effort if they feel their contributions are redundant with those of others in the work group. The converse is also true: an individual who perceives that his or her contribution is unique and indispensable tends to compensate for the shortcomings of others by expending greater effort, but only under certain circumstances. If the task is complex and difficult, making a unique contribution adds to a positive self-evaluation, eliminating the motive to shirk (Charbonnier et al. 1998; Huguet et al. 1999).[4] However, that is not the case if the task is easy (since competent performance is not self-validating), or if one believes that coworkers are in fact capable of contributing but are withholding their effort. The withholding of effort when one believes others are capable of performing the task is called the "sucker effect," since individuals are motivated to avoid "being played for a sucker" when others violate equity norms.[5] Group cohesiveness also shapes the dynamics of the processes described earlier. A feeling of belonging or being attracted to a group heightens concern with self-evaluation in a group task (Karau and Hart 1998). For that reason, social ostracism—being ignored by coworkers—can lead to compensatory efforts, that is, to working harder to regain a sense of belonging to the group (Williams and Sommer 1997).

Obviously, both the gender label of the task and the gender composition of the work group can be relevant to the processes described here. For example, men typically assume that women are less competent in a mixed-sex work group engaged in "masculine" tasks (or they attribute women's successful performance to luck rather than competence), and the "provider role" would reinforce the tendency toward social compensation described earlier. Moreover, men would have a greater incentive to withhold effort on a feminine task, since competent performance would not enhance self-evaluation. In other words, traditional sex roles and group gender composition can shape both the perception of whether one's competence is in question and of whether the group can succeed without one's own best efforts (Ridgeway 1997). Consistent with this reasoning, Kerr and his colleagues (1985) found that on a group task requiring physical strength, men exerted greater effort in mixed-sex than in single-sex groups and that both men and women were willing to compensate for a free-riding female partner. Jeffrey Vancouver, Beth Rubin, and Norbert Kerr (1991) performed a similar experiment with a stereotypically feminine task and hypothesized that both men and women engaged in a group sewing task would socially loaf when they believed they had been partnered with a woman, and both men and women would socially compensate when led to believe they had been partnered with a man. The hypothesis was confirmed for male subjects, suggesting that men are not inclined to take on a "provider role" and socially compensate when engaged in "feminine" tasks. However, contrary to their hypothesis, women exerted greater effort when they believed they were in a single-sex group.

It also seems plausible to hypothesize that responses to social ostracism depend on the extent to which group cohesion is gender-based. For example, when male bonding is the basis for group cohesion, an ostracized female is probably less likely to compensate socially to gain acceptance (because she perceives that doing so is futile) and more likely to respond by disengaging and withholding effort. To date, however, the only study of gender differences in responses to ostracism has been with single-sex groups—that is, male subjects' responses to ostracism by other men, and women subjects' responses to ostracism by other women. That study (Williams and Sommer 1997) found that women tend to respond to ostracism by socially compensating, whereas men respond by reducing effort. In a highly speculative vein, the authors suggest that men and women experience ostracism in the same way but respond with different coping mechanisms—men by withdrawing and masking their feelings, and women by compensating, thereby signaling to others their emotional connection to the group. Perhaps the most straightforward conclusion one can draw from this interpretation is that even social psychologists can fall back on stereotypes for ad hoc explanations of gender differences in social interaction.

Indeed, it is remarkable how readily social psychologists embrace assumptions about differences between men and women in competitive versus cooperative behavior when hypothesizing about the main effect of gender on social loafing. For example, in their meta-analysis of social loafing studies, Karau and Williams (1993, 686) offer two citations to support the claim that "research conducted in small group settings has found that men tend to specialize in activity oriented toward task completion, whereas women tend to specialize in activity oriented toward meeting interpersonal demands within the group."[6] One of the cited studies is an unpublished manuscript written over a decade earlier, and the other is a literature review by Lynn Anderson and Nick Blanchard (1982) that actually concludes that sex differences in task and socioemotional behavior are quite small and highly contingent on the task and sex composition of the group. Anderson and Blanchard also warn that social psychologists tend to be careless in citing the conclusions of this literature and often let stereotypes shape which studies they cite. As if to prove their point, a study published last year in the *Journal of Social Psychology* cites Anderson and Blanchard in support of the assertion that "women in Western countries are considered generally more oriented to maintaining group coordination and human relations, that is, toward consideration—whereas men are more oriented toward achievement" (Kugihara 1999, 517).

Gross generalizations about gender aside, we feel that the social loafing literature is quite useful for understanding the social-psychological mechanisms that can lead to both similarities and differences between men and women in the allocation of work effort. In search of similar insights into the social-psychological mechanisms that generate gender differences and similarities in competitive-selfish versus cooperative–other-regarding behavior, we turn to a rich literature on experimental studies of the strategies that men and women use in the "prisoners' dilemma," in public-goods provision, and in other social dilemma contexts.

Cooperation and Competition in Social Dilemmas—Are Women More Other-Regarding and Less Competitive Than Men?

Social dilemmas are group decisionmaking contexts in which pursuing self-interest is rational for individuals, but greater benefits are achieved by all if everyone cooperates. The provision of public goods is one example of a social dilemma. A public good is something that is beneficial to everyone in a group, regardless of individual contributions (for example, a pollution-free environment, or public broadcasting).[7] The propensity to contribute to the provision of a public good can be studied in the context of game theory experiments. In one version, for example, each game player decides privately how much of an initial endowment he or she is willing to contribute to a group fund. The total in the group fund is multiplied by some fixed amount, and the total is divided evenly among group members, so that higher contributions in the aggregate leave everyone better off but individuals have an incentive to free-ride (Brown-Kruse and Hummels 1993; Nowell and Tinkler 1994; for a brief review, see Ortmann and Tichy 1999, 329). The prisoners' dilemma game is a two-person version of the public goods game—each person is better off if both cooperate, but individually there is incentive to pursue self-interest.

Experiments with social dilemma games have been used to test the hypothesis that women are less competitive than men in social interaction and more concerned with the welfare of others. (Support for this hypothesis could explain why women often score slightly higher than men on measures of organizational citizenship behavior.) Motivation for this hypothesis comes from literatures as diverse as functionalist sex role theory and feminist standpoint theory (Stockard, Can De Kragt, and Dodge 1988; Sell 1997). Based on both meta-analyses and review articles, the bottom line regarding overall gender differences is easy to summarize: on average, women are slightly more likely to cooperate in social dilemmas than are men, but small variations in context can eliminate or reverse this pattern (Stockard et al. 1988; Walters, Stuhlmacher, and Meyer 1998; Ortmann and Tichy 1999; Eckel and Grossman 2000).

Particularly relevant to the issue of gender differences in orientations toward work are the mechanisms that mediate gender effects in social dilemma experiments. One is the impact of stereotypical beliefs in evoking stereotype-confirming behavior. When led to believe that they are partnered with a female, participants in social dilemma games tend to assume that she will be cooperative and adjust their own strategies accordingly, regardless of the partner's actual strategy (Sell 1997; Walters et al. 1998). Moreover, Stockard and her colleagues (1988) found that even when women behave as competitively as men in a social dilemma experiment, women tend to justify their behavior as altruistically motivated and oriented toward harmonious group relations. The authors draw on the concept of self-schema—the application of cultural stereotypes to oneself—to explain this finding. They suggest that "females' view of themselves as cooperative and group-oriented may be so closely linked with their gender identity—their view of themselves as female—that when their behavior contradicts this 'self schema' they may be less likely to recognize it and may justify it with notions that conform to their self-concept and their view of socially defined roles" (Stockard et al. 1988, 162).

Although the constructs of stereotypes, self-schema, and gender role may explain gender-based rationalizations and attributions, they are static concepts that do not contribute to understanding change, in particular how cumulative experiences in decisionmaking contexts can erode gender differences in choice behavior. Andreas Ortmann and Lisa Tichy (1999), building on a tradition of research on learning in social dilemmas, explore whether men's and women's strategies converge across repeated exposure to a prisoners' dilemma game. They assigned subjects to a multiple-round prisoners' dilemma game in which each person is assigned to a different partner in the new round, and subjects record their own and their partner's choices after each of the seven rounds. In the first round, females were significantly more likely to cooperate than men (62 percent versus 41 percent), but cooperation rates declined across trials, and by the final round there were no significant gender differences. Ortmann and Tichy conclude that men and women approach the laboratory environment with different subjective expectations about how others will behave, and those expectations apparently generated the first-round differences in behavior choices. However, as the experiment progressed, men and women reacted similarly in response to their experiences in the previous round, and by the final round both their understandings of the context and their responses were virtually identical. In other words, given the opportunity to have the same experiences, women and men eventually came to understand their self-interests and group interests in a similar manner, and having achieved a common understanding, men and women made similar choices about strategies to pursue in social interaction.

Ortmann and Tichy's results parallel the findings of a substantial body of research on gender differences in personal entitlement. Both experimental and survey designs have been used to demonstrate that men and women tend to rely on both their own personal experiences and comparisons with others believed to be similarly situated to form beliefs about what constitutes fair pay (for a review, see Major 1994). As a result, sex segregation tends to sustain gender differences in entitlement norms. Brenda Major's experimental studies (Major, McFarlin, and Gagnon 1984; Blysma and Major 1992) show that either exposing men and women to equivalent social comparison standards (by allowing them to see how others have been compensated for the same task) or providing them with comparable explicit performance feedback eliminates gender differences in perceptions of entitlement. Similarly, Ortmann and Tichy's experiment suggests that exposing

under which work effort is responsive to wage premiums. Also, is it indeed the case that workers who anticipate short firm tenure are less responsive to above-market wages? Are incentive schemes and workplace effort norms in fact shaped by monitoring costs and employers' expectations about turnover, as hypothesized by efficiency wage models? Are employers' beliefs about gender differences in turnover accurate (compare Sicherman 1996; Royalty 1998)? From a social-psychological perspective, more research is needed on the circumstances under which social identity and social influence processes are more important than prospectively rational calculation of a course of action based on personal gain, and vice versa. Again, for the most part these research questions are not about gender at all.

Experimental research from the social loafing and social dilemma paradigms emphasizes the importance of the relationship between self and others in shaping strategic orientations and behavioral choices. The more sophisticated work exploring gender issues suggests that the gender composition of a work group, the gender label of a task, and gender schemata and stereotypes have an impact on the relationship between self and other generally, and more specifically on an individual's propensity to be self-regarding versus other-regarding, to free-ride on the contributions of others, and to "socially compensate" in a manner that makes up for the limited contributions of coworkers. However, only a handful of studies have been published to date, and much more research is needed that studies these relationships in contexts that systematically vary the gender composition of task groups, the gender label of the task, and the extent and basis of work-group social cohesion. Research along these lines could bring together theory and methods from experimental economics and experimental social psychology in a way that has direct relevance to the issues usually studied on a more macro level by stratification scholars interested in gender and work.

Support for this research was provided by a grant from the National Science Foundation (SBR–9511572). We wish to thank Paula England, Cathy Weinberger, and the members of the University of California, Santa Barbara, Comparative Institutions Seminar for their helpful comments on an earlier draft.

Notes

1. Hersch and Stratton (1997) also note that any effect of housework on wages for men is more difficult to detect in their fixed-effects specification because of weak instruments, low variance in hours of housework for

men, and possibly greater measurement error in reporting of hours of housework.

2. Budig and England (1999) find a greater wage penalty for married mothers than for single or divorced mothers, a finding that on its face would seem not to support an explanation based on the allocation of effort. One might presume that single mothers who balance the demands of parental responsibilities and paid work without the ability to draw on the contributions of a spouse are expending more effort on child-rearing than are mothers who can rely on the contributions of a spouse. If so, the wage penalty should be greater for single mothers than for married mothers. On the other hand, the presence of a husband may simply add to the burdens of motherhood, requiring a greater expenditure of energy on household work by married mothers compared to single mothers.

3. In a clever test that assesses this effect by using true randomization in a natural setting, Barry Staw (1974) found support for his hypothesis that ROTC cadets who drew low numbers in the draft lottery (so that military service was no longer a voluntary act) would exhibit lower subsequent commitment to the ROTC program.

4. Note that this is not an instance of altruistically motivated behavior. The purpose of such compensating behavior is not to improve the well-being of others in the group but rather to validate one's own sense of competency and mastery.

5. Mel Schnake (1991) hypothesized that "vicarious punishment"—observing negative social cues given by a supervisor to a shirking coworker—should reduce the sucker effect, since it directly addresses the cause of the problem (the coworker's violation of equity norms). However, he found that setting difficult performance goals was more effective than vicarious punishment in reducing the sucker effect, apparently because the former increases intrinsic motivation while the latter reduces it.

6. Similarly, Emmanuelle Charbonnier and her colleagues (1998, 330) assert, without qualification, that "women tend to be more group- or collectively-oriented than men and are generally characterized by an emphasis on their interrelatedness to others and to the environment."

7. Technically, a public good is one for which consumption is "nonexcludable": "A group member can be excluded from partaking of the good, regardless of his or her individual level of participation" (Sell 1997, 253).

8. The legal scholar Vicki Schultz (1990) shows how the same stereotypes enter into legal discourse about gender differences in orientations toward work.

References

Akerlof, George. 1982. "Labor Contracts as Partial Gift Exchange." *Quarterly Journal of Economics* 97: 543–69.

Anderson, Lynn R., and P. Nick Blanchard. 1982. "Sex Differences in Task and Social-emotional Behavior." *Basic and Applied Social Psychology* 3: 109–39.

Aven, Forrest F., Jr., Barbara Parker, and Glenn McEvoy. 1993. "Gender and Attitudinal Commitment to Organizations: A Meta-analysis." *Journal of Business Research* 26: 63–73.

Bar-Hayim, Aviad, and Gerald S. Berman. 1992. "The Dimensions of Organizational Commitment." *Journal of Organizational Behavior* 13: 379–87.

Becker, Gary S. 1985. "Human Capital, Effort, and the Sexual Division of Labor." *Journal of Labor Economics* 3: S33–58.

Belman, Dale, Robert Drago, and Mark Wooden. 1992. "Work Groups, Efficiency Wages, and Work Effort." *Journal of Post-Keynesian Economics* 14: 497–520.

Bielby, Denise D., and William T. Bielby. 1988. "She Works Hard for the Money: Household Responsibilities and the Allocation of Work Effort." *American Journal of Sociology* 93: 1031–59.

————. 1992. "I Will Follow Him: Family Ties, Gender-role Beliefs, and Reluctance to Relocate for a Better Job." *American Journal of Sociology* 97: 1241–67.

Bielby, William T., Denise D. Bielby, Matt Huffman, and Steven Velasco. 1995. "Who Works Hard for the Money?: 'Efficiency Wages,' Work Organization, and Gender Differences in the Allocation of Work Effort." Paper presented at the annual meeting of the American Sociological Association, Washington (August 19–23).

Blysma, Wayne H., and Brenda Major. 1992. "Two Routes to Eliminating Gender Differences in Personal Entitlement." *Psychology of Women Quarterly* 16: 193–200.

Bowles, Samuel. 1985. "The Production Process in a Competitive Economy: Walrasian, Neo-Hobbesian, and Marxian Models." *American Economic Review* 75: 16–36.

Brown-Kruse, Jamie, and David Hummels. 1993. "Gender Effects in Laboratory Public Goods Contribution." *Journal of Economic Behavior and Organization* 22: 255–67.

Budig, Michelle, and Paula England. 1999. "The Wage Penalty for Motherhood." Paper presented at the annual meeting of the American Sociological Association, Chicago (August 9).

Bulow, Jeremy, and Lawrence H. Summers. 1986. "A Theory of Dual Labor Markets with Application to Industrial Policy, Discrimination, and Keynesian Unemployment." *Journal of Labor Economics* 4: 376–414.

Charbonnier, Emmanuelle, Pascal Huguet, Markus Brauer, and Jean-Marc Monteil. 1998. "Social Loafing and Self-beliefs: People's Collective Effort Depends on the Extent to Which They Distinguish Themselves as Better Than Others." *Social Behavior and Personality* 26: 329–40.

Eckel, Catherine C., and Philip J. Grossman. 2000. "Differences in the Economic Decisions of Men and Women: Experimental Evidence." In *Handbook of Results in Experimental Economics,* edited by Charles Plott and Vernon L. Smith. New York: North Holland.

Frey, Bruno S. 1997. *Not Just for the Money: An Economic Theory of Personal Motivation.* Cheltenham, Eng., and Lyme, N.H.: Elgar.

Goldin, Claudia. 1986. "Monitoring Costs and Occupational Segregation by Sex: A Historical Analysis." *Journal of Labor Economics* 4: 3–27.

Granovetter, Mark. 1988. "The Sociological and Economic Approaches to Labor Market Analysis: A Social Structural View." In *Industries, Firms, and Jobs: Sociological and Economic Approaches*, edited by George Farkas and Paula England. New York: Plenum.

Hersch, Joni, and Leslie S. Stratton. 1997. "Housework, Fixed Effects, and the Wages of Married Workers." *Journal of Human Resources* 32: 285–307.

Huguet, Pascal, Emmanuelle Charbonnier, and Jean-Marc Monteil. 1999. "Productivity Loss in Performance Groups: People Who See Themselves as Average Do Not Engage in Social Loafing." *Group Dynamics* 3: 118–31.

Karau, Steven J., and Jason W. Hart. 1998. "Group Cohesiveness and Social Loafing: Effects of a Social Interaction Manipulation on Individual Motivation Within Groups." *Group Dynamics* 2: 185–91.

Karau, Steven J., and Kipling D. Williams. 1993. "Social Loafing: A Meta-analytic Review and Theoretical Integration." *Journal of Personality and Social Psychology* 65: 681–706.

———. 1995. "Social Loafing: Research Findings, Implications, and Future Directions." *Current Directions in Psychological Science* 5(October): 134–39.

Kerr, Norbert L., Raymond H. Bull, Robert J. MacCoun, and Harriet Rathborn. 1985. "Role Expectations in Social Dilemmas: Sex Roles and Task Motivation in Groups." *Journal of Personality and Social Psychology* 49: 1547–56.

Kidwell, Roland E., Jr., and Nathan Bennett. 1993. "Employee Propensity to Withhold Effort: A Conceptual Model to Intersect Three Avenues of Research." *Academy of Management Review* 18: 429–56.

Kirchler, Erich, Ernst Fehr, and Robert Evens. 1996. "Social Exchange in the Labor Market: Reciprocity and Trust Versus Egoistic Money Maximization." *Journal of Economic Psychology* 17: 313–41.

Kugihara, Naoki. 1999. "Gender and Social Loafing in Japan." *Journal of Social Psychology* 139: 516–26.

Loscocco, Karen A. 1990. "Career Structures and Employee Commitment." *Social Science Quarterly* 71: 53–68.

Major, Brenda. 1994. "From Social Inequality to Personal Entitlement: The Role of Social Comparisons, Legitimacy Appraisals, and Group Membership." *Advances in Experimental Social Psychology* 26: 293–355.

Major, Brenda, Dean B. McFarlin, and Diana Gagnon. 1984. "Overworked and Underpaid: On the Nature of Gender Differences in Personal Entitlement." *Journal of Personality and Social Psychology* 47: 1399–1412.

Marsden, Peter V., Arne L. Kalleberg, and Cynthia R. Cook. 1993. "Gender Differences in Organizational Commitment: Influences of Work Positions and Family Roles." *Work and Occupations* 20: 368–90.

Mathieu, John E., and Dennis M. Zajac. 1990. "A Review and Meta-analysis of the Antecedents, Correlates, and Consequences of Organizational Commitment." *Psychology Bulletin* 108: 171–94.

McLennan, Michele C. 2000. "Does Household Labor Impact Wages?" *Applied Economics* 3: 1541–57.

Mowday, Richard T., Lyman W. Porter, and Richard M. Steers. 1982. *Employee-Organization Linkages: The Psychology of Commitment, Absenteeism, and Turnover.* New York: Academic Press.

Nowell, Clifford, and Sarah Tinkler. 1994. "The Influence of Gender in the Provision of a Public Good." *Journal of Economic Behavior and Organization* 25: 25–36.

Organ, Dennis W. 1988. *Organizational Citizenship Behavior.* Lexington, Mass.: Lexington Books.

Ortmann, Andreas, and Lisa K. Tichy. 1999. "Gender Differences in the Laboratory: Evidence from Prisoners' Dilemma Games." *Journal of Economic Behavior and Organization* 39: 327–39.

Pittman, Thane S. 1998. "Motivation." In *Handbook of Social Psychology,* 4th ed., edited by Daniel T. Gilbert, Susan T. Fiske, and Gardner Lindzey. New York: Oxford University Press.

Polachek, Solomon W. 1981. "Occupational Self-selection: A Human Capital Approach to Sex Differences in Occupational Structure." *Review of Economics and Statistics* 63: 60–69.

Ridgeway, Cecilia L. 1997. "Interaction and the Conservation of Gender Inequality: Considering Employment." *American Sociological Review* 62: 218–35.

Robinson, Michael D., and Phanindra V. Wunnava. 1991. "Discrimination and Efficiency Wages: Estimates of the Role of Efficiency Wages in Male/Female Wage Differentials." In *New Approaches to Economic and Social Analyses of Discrimination,* edited by Richard R. Cornwall and Phanindra V. Wunnava. New York: Praeger.

Royalty, Anne Beeson. 1998. "Job-to-Job and Job-to-Nonemployment Turnover by Gender and Education Level." *Journal of Labor Economics* 16: 392–443.

Schnake, Mel E. 1991. "Equity in Effort: The 'Sucker Effect' in Co-acting Groups." *Journal of Management* 17: 41–55.

Schultz, Vicki. 1990. "Telling Stories About Women and Work: Judicial Interpretations of Sex Segregation in the Workplace in Title VII Cases Raising the Lack of Interest Argument." *Harvard Law Review* 103: 1749–1843.

Sell, Jane. 1997. "Gender, Strategies, and Contributions to Public Goods." *Social Psychology Quarterly* 60: 252–65.

Sicherman, Nachum. 1996. "Gender Differences in Departures from a Large Firm." *Industrial and Labor Relations Review* 49: 484–505.

Staw, Barry M. 1974. "Attitudinal and Behavioral Consequences of Changing a Major Organizational Reward: A Natural Field Experiment." *Journal of Personality and Social Psychology* 6: 742–51.

Stockard, Jean, Alphons J. C. Can De Kragt, and Patricia J. Dodge. 1988. "Gender Roles and Behavior in Social Dilemmas: Are There Sex Differences in Cooperation and Its Justification." *Social Psychological Quarterly* 51: 154–64.

Tam, Tony. 1997. "Sex Segregation and Occupational Gender Inequality in the United States: Devaluation or Specialized Training?" *American Journal of Sociology* 102: 1652–92.

Vancouver, Jeffrey B., Beth Rubin, and Norbert L. Kerr. 1991. "Sex Composition of Groups and Member Motivation: III. Motivational Losses at a Feminine Task." *Basic and Applied Social Psychology* 12: 133–44.

Walsh, John P., and Shu-Fen Tseng. 1998. "The Effects of Job Characteristics on Active Effort at Work." *Work and Occupations* 25: 74–96.

Walters, Amy E., Alice F. Stuhlmacher, and Lia L. Meyer. 1998. "Gender and Negotiator Competitiveness: A Meta-analysis." *Organizational Behavior and Human Decision Processes* 76: 1–29.

Williams, Kipling D., and Kristin L. Sommer. 1997. "Social Ostracism by Co-workers: Does Rejection Lead to Loafing or Compensation?" *Personality and Social Psychology Bulletin* 23: 693–706.

Yamagishi, Toshio. 1995. "Social Dilemmas." In *Sociological Perspectives on Social Psychology,* edited by Karen S. Cook, Gary Alan Fine, and James S. House. Boston: Allyn and Bacon.

= Chapter 9 =

Rethinking Employment Discrimination and Its Remedies

BARBARA F. RESKIN

D ISCRIMINATION in market transactions falls squarely within the rubric of economic sociology. Yet economic sociology has given scant attention to employment discrimination (see, for examples, Smelser and Swedberg 1994, and most of the chapters in this volume). Having borrowed from economics a preference for explaining phenomena in terms of individuals' rational choices within constraints (see Zelizer, ch. 5, this volume), economic sociology has available only two theoretical approaches to discrimination by individuals (whether acting on their own behalf or as agents): intentional discrimination and statistical discrimination. Each of these approaches attributes discrimination to individuals' economic calculations—decisions to pay to indulge a taste for persons from certain groups or to pursue or avoid those from certain groups to minimize economic costs (Tilly and Tilly 1994, 305). That neither approach provides an innovative lens for understanding ongoing labor market discrimination may help to explain economic sociology's lack of interest in discrimination.

I hope to make a case in this chapter for placing the problem of employment discrimination on economic sociology's agenda. The chapter's argument is as follows: Existing theories of individual-level discrimination that emphasize people's conscious choices do not encompass common sources of micro acts of discrimination. We need to theorize discrimination more broadly to include automatic cognitive processes that distort information processing and decisionmaking by individuals in ways that—unless checked—lead to micro (and sometimes macro) acts of discrimination. However, the sociologically interesting and practically meaningful variation is not in individuals' propensities to automatic cognitive distortions (hypothetically all human brains are subject to these distortions), but in whether, when, and with what results organizations implement personnel practices that can check the discriminatory effects of automatic cognitive biases. Put differently, I propose that variability across organizations in personnel practices and work arrangements plays a nontrivial role in workers' exposure to discrimination, and that workers' risk is greater than suggested by conventional approaches to discrimination, which fail to recognize discrimination that originates in the nonconscious, automatic cognitive processes to which all individuals are subject.

I begin by summarizing the limitations of the paradigmatic definition of discrimination. I then argue that this conception of discrimination as intentional and the dominant theoretical explanation of employment discrimination as motivated by negative sentiment—while applicable to some contemporary acts of discrimination—are incomplete because they exclude discrimination that stems from *un*intended differential treatment. I argue further that our too-narrow conception of individual discrimination prevents the implementation of existing remedies for most employment discrimination.[1] Next I review social cognition research that suggests that automatic cognitions are an important source of *unintentional* differential treatment based on sex and race—in other words, of discrimination. I conclude by discussing the impact of work structures and employment practices on whether the cognitive distortions stemming from automatic cognitive processes produce discriminatory outcomes.

Retheorizing Employment Discrimination

Paradigmatic Conception of Individual Discrimination

The paradigmatic definition of discrimination is the differential treatment of persons because of status characteristics that are functionally irrelevant to the outcome in question (Merton 1972; see also Allport 1954, 51).[2] Implicit in this definition is the proposition that individuals discriminate because of their negative feelings (antipathy, distaste, fear) toward or negative beliefs (social stereotypes) about members of a status group (Allport 1954, 14; Becker 1957). Media accounts of whites' hostility toward blacks prior to and during the civil rights movement lent face validity to an antipathy-based theory of discrimination. Although the success of the civil rights movement depended partly on its ability to expose the antagonism that many whites harbored toward blacks, it simultaneously reinforced the theory that discrimination resulted from the deliberate efforts of individual whites to harm blacks because of their hostility to them.

In emphasizing differential treatment *based on* or *because of* an irrelevant characteristic, social scientists construed discrimination as *intentional* behavior.[3] So too did the major antidiscrimination law, Title VII of the 1964 Civil Rights Act. Although the statute did not explicitly define discrimination, it conceptualized it as an intended and consciously motivated act (Stryker 2001, 18). Thus, the law operationalized illegal employment discrimination as intentional.[4]

Non-Animus-Based Intentional Discrimination   Economists have theorized that employers may also intentionally discriminate against individuals on the rational rather than emotional ground that they belong to a race or sex thought to be less productive or more costly to employ, or that they will otherwise adversely affect business because of customers' or coworkers' prejudices (Phelps 1972; Bergmann and Darity 1981). Economists term this intentional, non-animus-based discrimination "statistical discrimination."[5] The Equal Employment Opportunity Commission (EEOC) and the Supreme Court (*Los Angeles Department of Water and Power v. Manhart* 1978; 435 U.S. 702)—the federal agencies charged with enforcing and interpreting Title VII— have interpreted the law as prohibiting intentional, non-animus-based discrimination, including statistical (stereotype-based) discrimination. The law prohibits employers from *deliberately* using race and sex in personnel decisions, regardless of their motive (except to redress egregious discrimination of the past; see Reskin 1998).[6] Thus, the major U.S. antidiscrimination law bans individuals—whether acting on their own behalf or as agents of their employer—from intentionally discriminating regardless of whether their motives derive from negative sentiments toward a group or from concerns about the economic ramifications of employing members of that group.

Reconceptualizing Discrimination

There is ample evidence that individuals continue to engage in intentional acts that conform to the paradigmatic definition of discrimination (Kirschenman and Neckerman 1991; Kasinitz and Rosenberg 1996; Browne and Kennelly 1999; U.S. Equal Employment Opportunity Commission 2001a-g). However, both the paradigmatic theory of intentional disparate treatment and the theory of statistical discrimination ignore another important source of employment discrimination: automatic, nonconscious cognitive processes.[7] In this chapter, I review research that implies that employment decisions are routinely biased as a result of normal cognitive processes. If nonconscious cognitive processes—unless checked by employment structures—regularly contribute to discrimination, our theoretical approach to discrimination needs to be modified.

In the years since the animus theory of discrimination gained paradigmatic status, social cognition researchers have established that automatic cognitive processes give rise to cognitive errors whose results are likely to be discriminatory. Largely outside individual control, these processes are marked by a cognitive efficiency that makes them generally adaptive. Because of their automaticity, neither intention nor antipathy is a necessary condition for discriminatory outcomes. The role of automatic cognitive processes in discrimination means that we also cannot continue to view discrimination as anomalous acts by a few biased individuals within an otherwise fair system of employment opportunities (Black 1989). Instead, we must recognize that discriminatory outcomes—many of them involving micro acts of discrimination—are pervasive, permitting members of favored groups to accumulate advantages while members of disfavored groups accumulate disadvantages.

Social Cognitive Processes and Employment Discrimination

Categorization

The core cognitive process that links gender and race to workplace outcomes is categorization. We automatically categorize the people we encounter into ingroups and outgroups, into "we" and "they" (Rothbart and Lewis 1994; Brewer and Brown 1998). In 1908 Georg Simmel wrote that we necessarily think of others in terms of general categories (1971 [1908], 10–12). Almost half a century later Gordon Allport (1954, 19) echoed this insight, asserting that "the human mind must think with the aid of categories." Recent research supports these claims: we understand the social world in terms of categorical distinctions and readily categorize others into ingroups and outgroups, on the basis of both highly visible as well as arbitrary and trivial characteristics (Brewer 1997, 200; Brewer and Brown 1998, 566; Fiske 1998, 364, 375).[8]

A critical concomitant of categorization is the generalization of similarity and difference. Having categorized others on trait A, we infer both that ingroup members resemble us and that outgroup members differ from us on traits B, C, D, and so on. As a result, we systematically underestimate within-group differences and exaggerate between-group differences on a variety of characteristics (Brown 1995, 78).[9] Categorization also affects how and how quickly we encode and recall information about others, thereby (unbeknownst to us) distorting our perceptions and shaping our preferences (Perdue et al. 1990).

It is important to note that we automatically prefer ingroup members to outgroup members. We are more comfortable with them, feel more obligated and loyal to them,[10] impute to them positive attributes, trust them, remember their positive traits while forgetting their negative ones, are predisposed to cooperate with them, and favor them when distributing rewards (Perdue et al. 1990; Baron and Pfeffer 1994; Rothbart and Lewis 1994, 369; Brown 1995; Brewer 1997, 201; Brewer and Brown 1998, 567; Fiske 1998, 361).[11]

Although we tend to distrust and depersonalize outgroup members and see them as competitors (Brewer 1997, 201), laboratory research indicates that we apparently do not automatically see them in negative ways (Perdue et al. 1990, 482) or discriminate against them when allocating negative outcomes (Brewer and Brown 1998, 559). Together, this body of research suggests that automatic categorization gives rise to discrimination primarily through pervasive ingroup favoritism rather than pervasive outgroup antipathy.

Automatic categorization is not inevitably group-serving. We categorize others into ingroups and outgroups largely independently of our conscious feelings toward the groups or our desire to protect our own status (Fiske 1998, 364). Nonetheless, ingroup preferences reinforce dominant groups' privileges. For example, group status affects whether people infer "illusory correlations" between positive traits and group membership. Members of high-status ingroups show more ingroup favoritism than do members of low-status ingroups (Brewer and Brown 1998, 570). Also, ingroup attachment is especially strong among people who think that group membership affects their opportunities or risks, both among competing groups and among ingroups in a numerical minority (Weber 1994).

Group membership is often based on ascribed characteristics. Ingroup favoritism cannot operate unless we can readily distinguish who is "us" and who is "them" (Brewer 1997, 205). Given its cultural salience and socially exaggerated visibility, we habitually use sex in assigning others to ingroups or outgroups (Brewer and Brown 1998). Because sex and race are strongly correlated with control over workplace opportunities, with white men monopolizing these roles, ingroup preference favors whites, men, and especially white men. Thus, ingroup favoritism produces status-group discrimination.

In sum, concomitant to our automatic sorting of people into categories are automatic biases in our feelings toward others based on whether we see them as "us" or "them." The effects of such biases are discriminatory, although they are neither intended nor even known to us as we perpetrate them (Fiske 1998, 362). In addition, they apparently operate more through our automatic inclination to favor others like ourselves than to deprive or punish those who differ (Brewer and Brown 1998; DiTomaso 2000).

Stereotyping

Categorization leads to a second automatic cognitive process with potentially discriminatory effects: stereotyping. Stereotyping is an inferential process in which we attribute traits that we habitually associate with a group to individuals who belong to that group.[12] Although *conscious* stereotypes can culminate in intentional statistical discrimination (see, for example, Wilson 1996, ch. 5; Moss and Tilly 1996, 264), here I address the *unintentional* discriminatory effects of *nonconscious* stereotypes.[13] Almost invariably, noticing that a "target" belongs to a stereotyped group automatically brings to mind characteristics that are stereotypically linked to that group, even when we consciously reject those stereotypes as false (Bodenhausen, Macrae, and Garst 1998, 316).[14] In fact, we automatically pursue, prefer, and remember "evidence" that supports our stereotypes (including untrue "evidence") and ignore, discount, and forget facts that challenge them. Stereotypes have been described as "hypotheses in search of evidence" (Brown 1995) because we are predisposed toward behavioral interpretations that conform to our stereotypes, blind to stereotype-inconsistent interpretations, and cognitively better able to find stereotype-consistent than -inconsistent evidence (Fiske 1998, 367). This selectivity means that our nonconscious stereotypes include a confirmatory bias (Brown 1995).

Given our cognitive capacity to override evidence with stereotypes, it stands to reason that we invoke stereotypes when we lack complete information about others. For example, given the stereotype of blacks as lazy (Bobo 2001), an employer who is choosing between a black applicant and a white applicant and has limited information about the black is likely to assume automatically that the black applicant is lazy. Stereotypes also distort our recollections of others. We more readily remember stereotypical than nonstereotypical descriptions—

an attractive flight attendant, for example, is more memorable than an unattractive flight attendant (Brown 1995, 96). As discussed later, stereotypes also bias the attributions we automatically construct for others' behavior; these attribution errors in turn distort our assessments of others and our expectations of their future behavior.

Automatic stereotypes often prevail even when we are consciously motivated not to stereotype. For instance, experimental subjects asked to judge the heights of women and men from photographs routinely underestimated women's height relative to same-height men, although they had been instructed to judge each photograph as an individual and they knew that accurate judgments could yield a substantial payoff (Brown 1995, 92). Subjects in another study who were instructed to suppress their stereotypes were able to do so, but in a subsequent task they expressed stronger stereotypes than members of a control group who had not been told to avoid stereotyping (Bodenhausen et al. 1998, 326).

Automatic stereotyping is tenacious because it is cognitively efficient (Fiske 1998, 366; Fiske, Lin, and Neuberg 1999, 237, 244). We can process information that supports our stereotypes more quickly than inconsistent information. Time pressure, information overload, mental busyness, and pressure to make a decision—conditions that characterize the work lives of many decisionmakers—increase our likelihood of stereotyping and exacerbate the effects of stereotypes on judgment and memory, presumably because these situations require cognitive efficiency (Bodenhausen et al. 1998: 319; Fiske 1998, 389; Goodwin, Operario, and Fiske 1998, 694). For example, subjects in a sentence-completion task could refrain from making sexist statements when they had ample time; given time limits, however, their statements were more sexist than those of members of a control group (Bodenhausen et al. 1998, 326).

Any attribute that is stereotypically linked to a status characteristic can activate (or "prime") group stereotypes (Heilman 1995; Fiske 1998, 366). For example, research subjects who were subliminally exposed to the words "black" and "white" were more likely to link negative traits to blacks and positive traits to whites than those who were not subliminally exposed (Dovidio et al. 1997), and men who were primed with stereotypic statements about women were more likely to ask a female job applicant sexist questions than were non-primed men, and they took longer to recognize nonsexist words (Fiske et al. 1999). These findings imply that an idle remark can activate sex or race stereotypes that in turn affect how decisionmakers assess job or promotion candidates or other workers (Heilman 1995).

Importantly, by priming race or sex stereotypes, diversity training may actually foster distorted impressions and differential treatment based on sex or race.[15]

Status affects the propensity to automatic stereotyping. Subordinates are less likely to stereotype members of dominant groups than the reverse, presumably because they need to make accurate assessments of the people who control their work environment and rewards (Fiske et al. 1999, 241). In addition, dominant-group members appear to have greater confidence in their stereotyped assessments than do members of subordinate groups, probably both because their dominant-group status gives them confidence *and* because being wrong is less likely to have negative consequences.

In sum, social cognition research suggests that unconscious sex and race stereotyping can lead to discrimination by distorting our impressions of individuals based on group membership. This occurs, unless checked, when group-based stereotypes automatically are applied to individuals, replace missing information about individuals, distort what we recall of others' behavior, bias our attributions of others' success and failures, and influence our predictions of others' future behavior.

Attribution Error

How we expect others to perform affects the meaning we assign to their behavior. When people's performance conforms to our expectations, we attribute it to their stable, internal traits (for example, ability); when it contradicts our expectations, we attribute it to transient, external causes (for example, task difficulty or luck). Both ingroup versus outgroup membership and sex and race stereotypes influence our expectations about others' performance. We expect members of socially preferred groups to succeed and members of devalued groups to fail.[16] Thus, we tend to chalk up successes by ingroup members and white men and failures by outgroup members, minorities, and white women to their stable predispositions, while we attribute failures by ingroup members and white men and successes by outgroup members, minorities, and white women to external (and hence, unstable) factors (Crocker, Major, and Steele 1998, 539). For example, we credit a man's talents for his success in a customarily male job, while we attribute a woman's success to situational factors, such as help from others. Importantly, we do not see successes or failures that we have attributed to external causes as predicting future success (Swim and Sanna 1996; Brewer and Brown 1998, 560).

Moreover, our brains tend to encode behavior that conforms to our expectations in terms of abstract traits (intelligence, honesty, laziness) and encode unexpected behavior in concrete terms (his car would not start; she took the class twice). Thus, we attribute an ingroup member losing his temper to provocation and the same behavior by an outgroup member to personality. Attributions in abstract terms are more likely than ones in concrete terms to affect our global evaluation of others as well as our predictions of their future performance, and they are more resistant to challenge by counterevidence. As a result, these cognitive propensities give ingroup members and persons from socially valued groups the benefit of the doubt, while preventing new data on outgroup members and persons in socially subordinate status groups from dispelling negative attributions.

Once again, while these propensities are universal, perceptions by members of majority groups are more prone to attribution error than those by minority-group members (Brown 1995, 101–2).

Micro-Macro Links

Automatic categorization, ingroup preference, and stereotyping are cognitively efficient for individuals. Their efficiency frees up cognitive resources for other purposes, making these propensities cognitively adaptive to individuals, especially those who are juggling multiple demands (Brown 1995, 95). Given what seems to be the near-impossibility of suppressing these cognitive propensities, the resulting biases are pervasive and predictable. Because they link employment outcomes to functionally irrelevant group membership, they are also discriminatory.

In addition, although many of the daily discriminatory events stemming from cognitive biases such as excluding someone from a project or denying them credit for a success may seem trivial (and certainly not legally actionable), over time members of preferred groups accumulate advantages and members of disparaged groups accumulate disadvantages. Eventually group differences emerge that appear to justify unequal career outcomes (Krieger 1995). Thus, unless employers implement structures to check the biasing effects of these microlevel processes, their long-term consequences create or exacerbate macrolevel disparities across race and sex groups in their economic and social fates.

In view of the automaticity of these cognitive processes,[17] the proximate cause of employment discrimination becomes whether employers' personnel practices prevent or permit these cognitive propensities from linking workers' status characteristics to their employment outcomes (Bielby 2000; Reskin 2000). In the next section, I discuss employment structures and practices that can reduce their discriminatory impact.

Organizational Practices, Cognitive Biases, and Discriminatory Outcomes

Work organizations cannot stamp out our propensities to categorize others automatically or to treat ingroup members more favorably than outgroup members. As we have seen, attempts to repress stereotyping can backfire. But employment structures can curb the *biasing effects* of these cognitive processes, thus inhibiting the discrimination that would otherwise result (Fiske 1998, 375). The impact of audition practices on women's share of positions in major symphony orchestras illustrates my point. With the adoption in the 1970s and 1980s of blind auditions that physically screened the musician from the auditors, women's odds of being selected rose sharply (Goldin and Rouse 2000). Screens that concealed the sex of the candidates circumvented intentional discrimination and obviated the discriminatory consequences of nonconscious sex stereotyping and ingroup favoritism. Social cognition and organizational research points to employment practices or structures that can arrest—or activate—the biasing effects of cognitive processes. Based on that scholarship, this section proposes organizational practices that mitigate the biasing effects of automatic cognitive processes.

Organizational Practices and Categorization

The automaticity of ingroup preference probably plays an important role in producing disparate employment outcomes for different race or sex groups. One way to minimize its discriminatory effects is to dissociate ingroup membership from ascribed statuses. As Marilynn Brewer (1997, 205) observes, a precursor of ingroup favoritism is the identification of who is "us" and who is "them." Employers can take advantage of this fact by discouraging ingroups based on race or sex through *decategorization* and *recategorization*.

Decategorization conveys individuating information about workers to decisionmakers (which in turn reduces stereotyping). Recategorization recognizes that people have many characteristics that compete to serve as the basis of categorization. According to Galen Bodenhausen and her colleagues (1998, 316), "the stereotypes associated with the category that 'wins' the competition" are activated, while we suppress the "losing" stereotype. Consider, for example, an experiment in which exposure to a photograph of a Chinese woman activated sub-jects' stereotypes about women, while inhibiting their stereotypes about Asians, but exposure to a picture of the same woman eating noodles with chopsticks triggered stereotypes about Asians, while suppressing stereotypes about women (Bodenhausen et al. 1998, 317). In general, recategorization exploits people's readiness to categorize others on the most trivial criteria by encouraging the categorization of workers on characteristics that are independent of their sex and race (Brewer and Brown 1998, 583). Employers can encourage recategoriz-ation based on work-related functions, for example. Function-based categories such as teams, projects, and divisions are cognitively avail-able and exploitable by employers through work-group culture and structured competition. Firms can also emphasize recategorization to a "superordinate category" such as an officer of the law or a UPS employee (Brewer 1997, 202).

Demographically heterogeneous work groups facilitate both de- and recategorization. In heterogeneous groups, sex and race are less likely to serve as bases for ingroup-outgroup status. Also, because decisionmakers are more likely to vary on sex and race in hetero-geneous groups, favoritism toward ingroups based partly on sex or race is less likely to disadvantage women and men of color and white women. Organizations can exploit the advantage of a heterogeneous workforce in recategorization through task-based groups, and they can decategorize through job rotation that prevents stable ingroups from forming. Interdependence in task groups should particularly foster recategorization.

Organizational Practices and Stereotyping

Although the propensity to automatic stereotyping is universal, whether we stereotype others varies, and whether our stereotypes give rise to biased cognitions depends on several factors, such as the type and quality of information that is available to decisionmakers about "targets"; whether the decisionmaking process highlights sta-tus-group membership and hence primes stereotyping; decision-makers' awareness of potential biases and their motivation to per-ceive others accurately; and whether decisionmakers have the cognitive resources to consciously minimize stereotype-based distor-tions (Bodenhausen et al. 1998, 330).

Making available accurate individuating information about per-sons from negatively stereotyped groups can prevent stereotyping. (But feeling informed in the absence of objective information may promote stereotyping; see Fiske 1998, 387.) When we lack information

that we need to make employment decisions, our descriptive stereotypes automatically provide it. Because stereotypes about socially devalued groups tend to be negative and those about socially favored
groups to be positive, the effect is usually discriminatory.[18] In addition,
because multiple bases for categorizing a person compete for activation, providing relevant information (Is the applicant a college graduate? An experienced manager?) about members of stereotyped groups
can prevent their being stereotyped by sex, race, and other ascribed
characteristics (Bodenhausen et al. 1998, 316). Thus, employment practices that increase the amount of unambiguous, relevant information
available to decisionmakers may suppress stereotyping (Heilman 1995,
12). By compiling and disseminating to decisionmakers standardized
information for all candidates on all the criteria relevant to a personnel
decision, organizations can reduce stereotyping.

The assumption that individuating information discourages stereotyping is the basis for the "contact" hypothesis that holds that intergroup contact can improve intergroup relations (Allport 1954). But for
interaction to prevent stereotyping, intergroup contact must be close,
sustained, and among equal-status persons (Brewer and Brown 1998,
576–78). Implicitly, then, effective contact requires interdependence.
Interdependence discourages stereotyping by motivating us to seek
accurate information about others, sensitizing us to counter-
stereotypic information about others, and encouraging us to see
others as individuals rather than as members of a group. In hierarchical employment relations, 360-degree evaluation fosters interdependence: supervisors who know that their salary may depend on their
subordinates' evaluations are motivated to individualize their subordinates (Goodwin et al. 1998, 694). However, the suppressing impact
on stereotyping of such evaluations lasts only as long as the interdependent contact does (Brewer and Brown 1998, 582–83). Genuine,
long-term interdependence almost certainly entails genuine job integration.

Although the desire not to stereotype is not sufficient to suppress
automatic stereotyping, motivation to perceive others accurately does
make a difference (Brown 1995, 105). When each team member's productivity depends on other group members, as in competitive sports
(Blalock 1962), group members invest cognitive resources in obtaining
accurate information about the members of their team (Fiske et al.
1999, 241–42).

In contrast, because anything that makes a status characteristic
cognitively salient can prime unconscious stereotypes, employers
need to safeguard against priming. For example, instructing a search
committee to look closely at female or minority male candidates can

backfire, eliciting sex and race stereotypes and thus tainting the evaluation of minority and white female candidates. Similarly, diversity training may activate stereotypes (Heilman 1995).[19] It is important to note, however, that priming can also suppress the effects of stereotyping, according to research that showed that decisionmakers primed with egalitarian values were more attentive to information that contradicts outgroup stereotypes than members of a control group (Operario, Goodwin, and Fiske 1998, 172–73).

The demographic context of a work unit affects both the amount of information that majority-group members have about persons from minority groups and the visibility of minority groups. The larger the size disparity between the two groups, the less contact members of the numerical majority have with minorities, and the less information they have about minorities, the greater their reliance on stereotypes (Blau 1977). Skewed group composition can also trigger stereotyping. Members of a numerical minority have heightened visibility, making their category membership contextually salient and thereby activating stereotypes (Kanter 1977; Bodenhausen et al. 1998, 317). In more balanced groups, in contrast, decisionmakers are more likely to view minority-group members as individuals (Blau 1977, 78–83).

Finally, because time pressure, multiple demands, and information overload exacerbate the effects of stereotypes on judgment and memory (Bodenhausen et al. 1998, 319), making adequate time available for personnel decisions will reduce bias.

Decisionmakers' Discretion

Discretion is an important perquisite for managers. It not only permits autonomy but allows decisionmakers to control the amount of effort they must expend. Although organizational members tend to assume that managers' decisions are rational (Baron 1984, 56), discretion invites unconscious and conscious biases to influence their decisions, thus spawning discriminatory treatment. Employment decisions that are based on unstructured observations are especially vulnerable to cognitive biases (Fiske et al. 1991). The key to preventing such automatic biases from giving rise to unintended micro acts of discrimination lies in curbing decisionmakers' discretion by requiring specific procedures for distributing opportunities.[20]

Consider the case of Home Depot (for a detailed account, see Sturm 2001). Home Depot began as a close-knit, predominantly male company that retained its informal employment practices as it grew.[21] Although Home Depot is hardly exceptional in its reliance on informal networks to fill jobs and in the segregative consequences of that reliance (Marsden and Gorman 2001), its segregated workforce and barriers to managerial jobs for women led to a discrimination lawsuit. As a result of the consent decree that settled the suit, Home Depot restructured its personnel practices and completely revamped its human resources system. It developed minimum qualifications for each position[22] and installed computer or telephone kiosks in every store through which applicants could indicate job preferences and qualifications. Applicants automatically became part of the pool for any position that matched their preferences and qualifications; when managers posted openings, the computer automatically listed all qualified applicants. Home Depot also standardized interviews to ensure that managers asked all job candidates the same questions. In curtailing managers' discretion, these practices reduced the likelihood that they would unconsciously or consciously favor their buddies or make assignments based on stereotypes.

Home Depot responded to problems associated with unchecked managerial discretion the same way firms routinely do: through bureaucratization (Edwards 1979). When candidates' qualifications are ambiguous, experimental subjects are more likely to recommend persons of their own race and sex than when the criteria are clear (Salancik and Pfeffer 1978). Employers can reduce the discriminatory effects of cognitive biases by insisting that decisionmakers use only job-relevant criteria in evaluations and that they have valid, complete, objective, and timely information for all evaluatees. Decisions based on this kind of information are less vulnerable to automatic cognitive distortion (Heilman 1995; Krieger 1995, 1246). Thus, it is not surprising that formalized practices enhance outgroup members' access to attractive jobs (Reskin and McBrier 2000), and that consent decrees in class action lawsuits often entail massively revamping employers' personnel practices (McKay 2000).[23]

Reducing discretion by formalizing personnel practices is not enough, however. As Susan Sturm (2001, 161) observes, "Some form of pressure had to be built in . . . to assure that, once identified, problems were . . . addressed." "Accountability," she adds, "is the key to the long term viability of these problem-solving systems." Sturm's conclusion from three case studies corroborates what cognitive psychology has taught us: organizations can reduce the biasing effects of stereotyping, ingroup preference, and other cognitive distortions on decisionmakers' evaluative judgments by holding them accountable for the criteria they use, the accuracy of the information upon which they base their decisions, the procedures by which they reach their decisions, and the consequences of their decisions for race and gender equality (Salancik and Pfeffer 1978; Konrad and Linnehan 1995; Tetlock and Lerner 1999).[24] Being informed—before being exposed to the information on which they will base their judgment—that one is going to be held accountable for one's decision reduces both the expression of biases and the way we encode information (Tetlock 1992; Pendry and Macrae 1996). Experimental subjects who were recommending whom to hire as teaching assistants and who had been told that the decisionmaking process would be public were less likely to recommend candidates of their own race and sex than were those who thought their decisions would be kept secret. The former but not the latter presumably wished to avoid being seen as biased (Salancik and Pfeffer 1978).

Of course, visibility is a necessary condition for accountability. Home Depot's computer system provided data to store managers on individual managers' hiring decisions so that regional managers could monitor compliance and deal with managers accordingly (Sturm 2001, 157). Deloitte & Touche's initiative to address the problems faced by its female workers mandated reviews in which the managing partner at each branch listed all assignments and their desirability by worker's sex and tied their performance to managers' compensation (Sturm 2001, 138–39). These examples illustrate both the need for maintaining and circulating data on rewards and opportunities by group membership and the importance of genuine accountability for decisionmakers (Heilman 1995).

Conclusion

In keeping with the paradigmatic conception of discrimination as conscious invidious treatment motivated by antipathy, Congress outlawed intentional discrimination in Title VII of the 1964 Civil Rights Act. Although the enforcement of Title VII has reduced employment discrimination (Burstein 1989; Burstein and Edwards 1994), decades after the enactment of Title VII the careers of thousands of Americans continue to be stunted by employment discrimination (Blumrosen et al. 1998; Reskin 2001). Discrimination persists partly because antidiscrimination remedies misconstrue discrimination as based in antipathy toward a group. Despite the applicability of the paradigmatic construction of discrimination in many instances, that construction ignores an even more important reason individuals' sex and race are routinely and illegitimately linked to employment rewards: automatic nonconscious cognitive processes that distort our perceptions and treatment of others.

Categorization, ingroup preference, stereotyping, attribution error—all part of the normal information processing that occurs largely outside our conscious control—bias our perceptions, evaluations, and treatment of people because of their sex, color, accent, and other discernible characteristics that signal membership in more or less valued groups. They engender biases because we automatically categorize others into ingroups and outgroups—often based on these same characteristics. Moreover, we prefer ingroup members to outgroup members, evaluate them more favorably, treat as factual impressions that are based on stereotypes, and make erroneous inferences about the successes or failures of ingroup and outgroup members.

These cognitive biases occur during interpersonal relations, and interpersonal relations are an intrinsic part of most jobs. Thus, ordinary, everyday cross-sex and cross-race interactions elicit automatic ingroup favoritism, stereotyping, and attribution biases. These cognitive distortions lead on a daily basis to micro acts of discrimination: omitting a qualified but female inside candidate from the short list for a top position because no one thinks of her; not recognizing the contribution that a Japanese woman makes to a project; assuming that women do not want challenging assignments; not inviting a black man to a meeting of his specialty group; being confused about which black worker made a suggestion; giving a white male a tip on a job opening (Cose 1993; Fiske 1998, 371–72; Catalyst 1999; Barrett 1999; DiTomaso 2000; Reskin and McBrier 2000, 224; Sturm 2001, 113, 136).

At the individual level, these "countless small acts by a changing cast of characters . . . *incrementally* and consistently limit the employment prospects of one group of workers compared with those of another" (Nelson and Bridges 1999, 241–43, emphasis added; see also Feagin 2000, 139; Sturm 2001, 113). As a result, workers who regularly benefit from ingroup preference accumulate advantages, and members of disparaged groups who suffer the negative discriminatory effects of cognitive biases accumulate disadvantages. Over time, career disparities between sex- and race-based groups also accumulate. In the aggregate, the unchecked consequences of automatic cognitive biases help to preserve job segregation, promotion differences, and earnings disparities by race and sex. That they result from nonconscious cognitive processes rather than conscious antipathy does not mitigate their impact or reduce the need for more effective policy remedies. The results are the same.[25]

Attribution error by beneficiaries means that they fail to recognize that they enjoy advantages because of automatic ingroup preferences. Meanwhile, victims often are unaware of the biased consequences of stereotyping or ingroup favoritism. Indeed, many are not in a position to know that stereotyping or ingroup favoritism has occurred (Fiske 1998, 384); others learn to disregard their effects (Feagin 2000).

Over time, however, we know that workers react negatively to blocked opportunity (Kanter 1977; Cassirer and Reskin 2000; Sturm 2001, 136), although they may not label it discrimination. It usually takes a calamitous event, like being laid off, to precipitate a discrimination complaint (Krieger 1995). By then, the accumulation of disadvantages to people of color and white women and of advantages to members of favored groups may have made the latter objectively better qualified (Krieger 1998, 1326). Then, since persons from different groups are no longer "similarly situated," organizational logic dictates intentional differential treatment, in both small matters and consequential decisions regarding job assignments, promotions, salaries, layoffs, and downsizings. And legal remedies are not available because Title VII applies only to similarly situated persons.

Research Agenda

Research in social cognition suggests that employers' personnel practices should reduce the discriminatory effects of decisionmakers' cognitive biases (Baron and Pfeffer 1994; Bielby 2000; Reskin 2000). According to my understanding of the underlying cognitive processes, personnel practices can forestall their effects by discouraging categorization and stereotyping based on sex and race and by curtailing individuals' discretion over whom to hire, promote, or provide with other career-enhancing opportunities. However, almost all of the cognitive research cited in this chapter was done in laboratory experiments on the usual pool of subjects—undergraduates. There may be theoretical reasons to agree with William Bielby (2000, 122) when he observes that, "if anything, stereotyping and ingroup bias effects are probably substantially larger in the 'real world' than they are in the laboratory." Nonetheless, we need research in real work settings to determine their strength, scope, and contextual effects.

Although one reason to study real work organizations is to validate laboratory findings, a more important reason is to establish how workers are affected by personnel practices that, to varying degrees, constrain the discriminatory effects of automatic biases. Both theory and case studies suggest that the accumulation of disparities leads to demoralization and job dissatisfaction among outgroup members. Consider turnover. Industry studies indicate that female managers leave their jobs because they become frustrated when they fail to advance (see, for example, Sturm 2001, 135). Turnover fell sharply in firms that reorganized personnel practices to address "second-generation discrimination" (Sturm 2001), which resembles the cognitive biases considered here.

A related question is whether and why organizations implement personnel practices that minimize the discriminatory effects of cognitive biases. We know that most good-sized U.S. employers have written job descriptions for most jobs and other written personnel procedures, and that almost all have human resources staff who compile data on the qualifications of candidates for positions (Kalleberg et al. 1996; Edelman 1992). Although many organizations formalize personnel practices out of conformity to general business practices, many employers organize work structures and practices to reduce their risk of discrimination. These include firms that are subject to the Federal Contract Compliance Program, which requires federal contractors to take affirmative steps to ensure that they do not discriminate; firms that are subject to court-authorized outcomes in discrimination cases; firms that have been advised to create such structures by human resources or legal staff; and assorted others (Edelman 1992; Bisom-Rapp 1999).

This broader perspective on discrimination raises several important questions for economic sociologists: What prompts employers to consider seriously the need to check unintentional discrimination? Who participates in any discussions? What actions do they decide to take? Inertia is a powerful barrier to altering employment structures and practices, especially when they pass muster in the regulatory community. The adversarial nature of discrimination complaints under the traditional conception of discrimination deters many employers from collecting data on the experiences of their minority and female staff, the first step in modifying personnel practices. Reportedly, some legal advisers counsel a "don't ask, don't tell" strategy with respect to compiling data that could reveal problems, because such information could be used against employers in discrimination lawsuits (Segal 1998, 117; Bisom-Rapp 1999; Sturm 2001, 118). How often does concern about fueling potential litigation dissuade employers from implementing personnel practices that would reduce the discriminatory effects of unconscious (and conscious) cognitive biases?

Because personnel issues are not usually seen by high-level decisionmakers as directly linked to profits, firms may avoid them until a visible discrimination allegation compels them to do so. According to a mediation expert who advises employers on how to address such allegations, "Operations people look at you like you are crazy" (Sturm 2001, 120). Their reactions beg the question of what kinds of organizational structures, decisionmaking systems, and cultures encourage implementing or ignoring protective personnel practices. And finally, are there detectable effects of such practices on employers' exposure to discrimination complaints and on productivity?

Social psychologists have documented the automatic cognitive processes that can bias information in ways that discriminate against people of color and white women. It is time for sociologists, particularly those interested in how economic institutions make decisions about employment practices, to investigate these processes and their concomitants and to work with employers to shape rational, discrimination-reducing responses.

Several people have helped me to develop the ideas in this chapter. Because I did not take all of their advice, I am solely responsible for all errors and muddy thinking that remain. Nonetheless, I am particularly indebted to William Bielby and Marilynn Brewer for many conversations about these processes, and to Nancy DiTomaso, Paula England, Cecilia Ridgeway, and three anonymous reviewers for their comments on previous drafts. Mary Beth Beasley, James Brudney, and Ruth Colker were among the several faculty members at the Ohio State University College of Law who challenged me to think more clearly about the relevant legal issues. I am particularly grateful to the Center for Law, Policy, and Social Science at the Ohio State University College of Law for its hospitality while I was working on this project. Only through the energy and efficiency of Dorothy Friendly was I able to finish this chapter in time for inclusion in this volume; I have been indeed fortunate to have her assistance.

Notes

1. Because of space constraints, I limit my discussion to discrimination stemming from individuals' feelings and cognitions. Theories of structural and institutional discrimination do not assign a causal role to the actions of individuals. Instead, they focus on discrimination that results from ostensibly neutral structures (such as job requirements or work arrangements) that link more or less desirable outcomes to workers' status-group membership. For a discussion of institutional discrimination, see Stryker (2001).

2. The legal variant recognizes the irrelevance of the status characteristic by defining discrimination as the differential treatment of "similarly situated" persons (Gold 1993, 3).

3. For example, James Heckman (1998, 102, emphasis added) defines discrimination as treating an "otherwise identical person . . . differently *by virtue of* that person's race or gender," and Robin Stryker (2001, 15, emphasis in original) defines it as "behavior that disadvantages members of minority groups . . . *because of* their group membership."

4. This legal theory of discrimination has been dubbed the "disparate-treatment" theory.

5. Statistical discrimination occurs when employers attempt to reduce their information costs by making inferences about individuals' likely produc-

tivity based on statistical generalizations about the productivity of the groups to which they belong (Phelps 1972). Some scholars distinguish *error discrimination,* which involves consciously motivated, non-animus-based differential treatment based on false generalizations about group differences, from statistical discrimination, which is differential treatment based on real group differences (see, for example, England 1994).

6. Throughout this chapter I use "race and sex" as a shorthand for the variety of ascribed characteristics on which systematic discrimination may be based.

7. According to Shiffrin and Schneider (1977), automatic cognitive processes are those that are not effortful, intentional, or consciously controlled.

8. For example, subjects have categorized others into ingroups and outgroups based on whether they over- or underestimated the number of dots on a screen (Tajfel 1970).

9. Although we tend to exaggerate differences between ingroups and outgroups on dimensions that favor ingroup members, we are less likely to do so on traits that do not (Brewer and Brown 1998, 570).

10. Our deference to members of our ingroup predisposes to accede to the conscious prejudices of a member of the ingroup rather than side against him or her on behalf of a member of an outgroup. Thus, automatic ingroup loyalty can permit intentional animus-based discrimination.

11. See DiTomaso (2000) for evidence on the benefits of ingroup preference (which she terms "affirmative inclusion") for white workers' careers.

12. As defined here, stereotypes are descriptive generalizations. Prescriptive stereotypes, in contrast, are normative generalizations about how members of a status group are supposed to be against which we consciously or unconsciously evaluate others' behavior (Fiske 1998). Whether descriptive stereotypes have a basis in fact may be germane for statistical discrimination but is irrelevant for nonconscious stereotyping in which perceivers automatically ascribe stereotyped traits to group members.
    Stereotyping also occurs when jobs are labeled as appropriate for a certain sex or race, and the distortions associated with these stereotypes can contribute to the devaluation of work associated with people of color and white women. This devaluation may also stem from preconscious processes.

13. The ready accessibility of stereotypes makes them frequent tools in other cognitive enterprises. In fact, as William Bielby and Denise Bielby show (this volume), even social psychologists resort to sex stereotypes to explain sex differences in social interaction.

14. The Implicit Association Tests at *www.yale.edu/implicit* allow readers to observe their ability to control their own stereotyping (Greenwald and Banaji 1999).

15. Personnel practices that are explicitly race- or gender-conscious in order to remedy past discrimination can also activate unconscious stereotypes; however, their explicit treatment of sex and race as plus factors should render stereotyping irrelevant in the particular employment action.

16. When our ingroup members are persons of color or white women, these generalizations imply contradictory effects. I could not locate empirical research that addressed what happens when the ingroup comprises men and women of color or white women.

17. As Bielby and Bielby (this volume) observe, the construct of stereotype is a static concept that does not in itself help us understand change. However, the predictability of automatic stereotyping points to the need for structural interventions, whose existence and form help us to understand change.

18. Although our propensity to exceptionalize persons for whom we have counterstereotypical information can prevent our stereotyping them, it nonetheless leaves our stereotypes intact.

19. Remedial race- and sex-conscious affirmative action practices that explicitly treat race and sex as plus factors in choosing among qualified candidates for a position may prime stereotypes (Heilman 1996). Thus, providing individuating information about persons hired under race- or sex-conscious affirmative action is particularly important to reduce stereotyping. However, there is some evidence that evaluators make less biased decisions when employers use identity-conscious structures (Konrad and Linnehan 1995, 795).

20. Reducing discretion can also curb intentional, animus-based discrimination.

21. As William Bielby (1997) wrote in his report as an expert witness for the plaintiffs in *Home Depot v. Stender et al.*:

> There are no written guidelines for making decisions about promotions to department supervisor positions, and the company does not provide training to Store Managers and Assistant Managers on how to select employees for promotion. While Standard Operating Procedures specify the process to be followed in making promotions into salaried assistant manager and store manager positions, they do not specify the criteria to be used in making promotion decisions. Promotion opportunities in existing stores are not posted, and there is no formal procedure for making vacancies known or requesting a promotion. In making decisions about promotion to department supervisor, there is no requirement that the person under consideration meet any minimum rating or recent performance evaluations, or that written performance reviews are consulted at all in making the decision. Nor is there any requirement to record the reasons why an employee is or is not selected for promotion.

22. As Bielby (2000, 124) indicates, what constitutes job-relevant information must be determined through systematic job analysis.

23. Formalization is not a silver bullet. For example, all four of the work organizations that Robert Nelson and William Bridges (1999, 313) studied had bureaucratized personnel systems, but this did not prevent managerial discretion from systematically setting pay lower in predominantly female jobs.

24. See Sessa (1992) on Xerox's successful use of accountability.

25. An employer's undisciplined system of subjective decisionmaking has the same effects as a system pervaded by intentional discrimination, as the Supreme Court recognized in *Watson v. Fort Worth Bank & Trust* (487 U.S. 977, 990–91, 1988).

References

Allport, Gordon W. 1954. *The Nature of Prejudice.* Reading, Mass.: Addison-Wesley.

Baron, James N. 1984. "Organizational Perspectives on Stratification." *Annual Review of Sociology* 10: 37–69.

Baron, James N., and Jeffrey Pfeffer. 1994. "The Social Psychology of Organizations and Inequality." *Social Psychology Quarterly* 57: 190–209.

Barrett, Paul M. 1999. *The Good Black: A True Story of Race in America.* New York: Dutton.

Becker, Gary. 1957. *The Economics of Discrimination.* Chicago: University of Chicago Press.

Bergmann, Barbara R., and William Darity Jr. 1981. "Social Relations, Productivity, and Employer Discrimination." *Monthly Labor Review* 104(April): 47–49.

Bielby, William T. 1997. *Report to U.S. District Court.* U.S. Dist. LEXIS 16296, at *33.

———. 2000. "Minimizing Workplace Gender and Racial Bias." *Contemporary Sociology* 29(1): 120–29.

Bisom-Rapp, Susan. 1999. "Discerning Form from Substances: Understanding Employer Litigation Prevention Strategies." *Employee Rights and Employment Policy Journal* 3: 1–64.

Black, Donald. 1989. *Sociological Justice.* New York: Oxford University Press.

Blalock, Hubert M. 1962. "Occupational Discrimination: Some Theoretical Propositions." *Social Problems* 9(3): 240–47.

Blau, Peter M. 1977. *Inequality and Heterogeneity.* New York: Free Press.

Blumrosen, Alfred W., Mark Bendick, J. J. Miller, and Ruth G. Blumrosen. 1998. "Employment Discrimination Against Women in Washington State, 1997." Employment Discrimination Project Report 3. Newark, N.J.: Rutgers University School of Law.

Bobo, Lawrence D. 2001. "Racial Attitudes and Relations at the Close of the

Twentieth Century." In *America Becoming: Racial Trends and Their Consequences*, vol. 1, edited by Neil J. Smelser, William J. Wilson, and Faith N. Mitchell. Washington: National Academy Press.

Bodenhausen, Galen V., C. Neil Macrae, and Jennifer Garst. 1998. "Stereotypes in Thought and Deed: Social Cognitive Origins of Intergroup Discrimination." In *Intergroup Cognition and Intergroup Behaviors*, edited by Constantine Sedikides, John Schopler and Chester A. Insko. Mahwah, N.J.: Erlbaum.

Brewer, Marilynn B. 1997. "The Social Psychology of Intergroup Relations: Can Research Inform Practice?" *Journal of Social Issues* 53(1): 197–211.

Brewer, Marilynn B., and Rupert J. Brown. 1998. "Intergroup Relations." In *Handbook of Social Psychology*, edited by Daniel T. Gilbert, Susan T. Fiske, and Gardner Lindzey. New York: McGraw-Hill.

Brown, Rupert. 1995. *Prejudice*. Oxford: Blackwell.

Browne, Irene, and Ivy Kennelly. 1999. "Stereotypes and Realities: Images of Black Women in the Labor Market." In *Latinas and African American Women at Work*, edited by Irene Browne. New York: Russell Sage Foundation.

Burstein, Paul. 1989. "Attacking Sex Discrimination in the Labor Market: A Study in Law and Politics." *Social Forces* 67: 641–65.

Burstein, Paul, and Mark E. Edwards. 1994. "The Impact of Employment Discrimination Litigation on Racial Disparity in Earnings: Evidence and Unresolved Issues." *Law and Society Review* 28: 79–111.

Cassirer, Naomi, and Barbara Reskin. 2000. "High Hopes: Organizational Location, Employment Experiences, and Women's and Men's Promotion Aspirations." *Work and Occupations* 27: 438–63.

Catalyst. 1999. "Women of Color Report a 'Concrete Ceiling' Barring Their Advancement in Corporate America." *Catalyst Press Room*, July 13. Available at: *www.catalystwomen.org/press/mediakit/release071399woc.html* (May 20, 2001).

Cose, Ellis. 1993. *Rage of the Privileged Class*. New York: HarperCollins.

Crocker, Jennifer, Brenda Major, and Claude Steele. 1998. "Social Stigma." In *Handbook of Social Psychology*, edited by Daniel T. Gilbert, Susan T. Fiske, and Gardner Lindzey. New York: McGraw-Hill.

DiTomaso, Nancy. 2000. "Why Antidiscrimination Policies Are Not Enough: The Legacies and Consequences of Affirmative Inclusion—for Whites." Rutgers University, Newark. Unpublished manuscript.

Dovidio, John F., Kerry Kawakami, Craig Johnson, Brenda Johnson, and Adaiah Howard. 1997. "On the Nature of Prejudice: Automatic and Controlled Processes." *Journal of Experimental Social Psychology* 33: 510–40.

Edelman, Lauren B. 1992. "Legal Ambiguity and Symbolic Structures: Organizational Mediation of Civil Rights Law." *American Journal of Sociology* 97: 1531–76.

Edwards, Richard. 1979. *Contested Terrain: The Transformation of the Workplace in the Twentieth Century*. New York: Basic Books.

England, Paula. 1994. "Neoclassical Economists' Theories of Discrimination." In *Equal Employment Opportunity*, edited by Paul Burstein. New York: Aldine de Gruyter.

Feagin, Joe R. 2000. *Racist America: Roots, Current Realities, and Future Repara-tions.* New York: Routledge.

Fiske, Susan T. 1998. "Stereotyping, Prejudice, and Discrimination." In *Hand-book of Social Psychology*, edited by Daniel T. Gilbert, Susan T. Fiske, and Gardner Lindzey. New York: McGraw-Hill.

Fiske, Susan T., Donald N. Bersoff, Eugene Borgida, Kay Deaux, and Mad-eline E. Heilman. 1991. "Social Science Research on Trial: Use of Sex Stereo-typing Research in *Price Waterhouse v. Hopkins.*" *American Psychologist* 46: 1049–60.

Fiske, Susan T., Monica Lin, and Steven L. Neuberg. 1999. "The Continuum Model: Ten Years Later." In *Dual Process Theories in Social Psychology*, edited by Shelly Chaiken and Yaacov Trope. New York: Guilford Press.

Gold, Michael E. 1993. *An Introduction to the Law of Employment Discrimination.* New York: New York State School of Industrial Relations/ILR Press.

Goldin, Claudia, and Cecilia Rouse. 2000. "Orchestrating Impartiality: The Impact of 'Blind' Auditions on Female Musicians." *American Economic Re-view* 90: 715–41.

Goodwin, Stephanie A., Don Operario, and Susan T. Fiske. 1998. "Situational Power and Interpersonal Dominance Facilitate Bias and Inequality." *Journal of Social Issues* 54: 677–98.

Greenwald, Anthony, and Mahzarin Banaji. 1999. "Implicit Association Test." IAT Corporation Homepage, June 13. Available at: *www.yale.edu/implicit* (June 20, 2001).

Heckman, James J. 1998. "Detecting Discrimination." *Journal of Economic Per-spectives* 12(2): 101–16.

Heilman, Madeline E. 1995. "Sex Stereotypes and Their Effects in the Work-place: What We Know and What We Don't Know." *Journal of Social Issues* 10: 3–26.

———. 1996. "Affirmative Action's Contradictory Consequences." *Journal of Social Issues* 52: 105–9.

Kalleberg, Arne, David Knoke, Peter Marsden, and Joe Spaeth. 1996. *Organi-zations in America.* New York: Sage Publications.

Kanter, Rosabeth Moss. 1977. *Men and Women of the Corporation.* New York: Basic Books.

Kasinitz, Philip S., and Jan Rosenberg. 1996. "Missing the Connection: Social Isolation and Employment on the Brooklyn Waterfront." *Social Problems* 43: 180–96.

Kirschenman, Joleen, and Kathryn M. Neckerman. 1991. "'We'd Love to Hire Them But . . .': The Meaning of Race for Employers." In *The Urban Under-class*, edited by Christopher Jencks and Paul Peterson. Washington, D.C.: Brookings Institution.

Konrad, Alison M., and Frank Linnehan. 1995. "Formalized HRM Structures: Coordinating Equal Employment Opportunity or Concealing Organiza-tional Practices?" *Academy of Management Journal* 38: 787–820.

Krieger, Laura H. 1995. "The Contents of Our Categories: A Cognitive Bias Approach to Discrimination and Equal Employment Opportunity." *Stanford Law Review* 47: 1161–1248.

————. 1998. "Civil Rights *Perestroika:* Intergroup Relations After Affirmative Action." *California Law Review* 86: 1251–1331.

Marsden, Peter V., and Elizabeth Gorman. 2001. "Social Networks, Job Changes, and Recruitment." In *Sourcebook on Labor Market Research: Evolving Structures and Processes,* edited by Ivar Berg and Arne L. Kalleberg. New York: Plenum.

McKay, Betsy. 2000. "Coca-Cola Agrees to Settle Bias Suit for $192.5 Million." *Wall Street Journal,* November 17.

Merton, Robert K. 1972. "Insiders and Outsiders." *American Journal of Sociology* 78: 9–47.

Moss, Philip, and Chris Tilly. 1996. "Soft Skills and Race: An Investigation of Black Men's Employment Problems." *Work and Occupations* 23: 252–76.

Nelson, Robert L., and William S. Bridges. 1999. *Legalizing Gender Inequality.* New York: Oxford University Press.

Operario, Don, Stephanie A. Goodwin, and Susan Fiske. 1998. "Power Is Everywhere: Social Control and Personal Control Both Operate at Stereotype Activation, Interpretation, and Response." In *Stereotype Activation and Inhibition: Advances in Social Cognition,* vol. 11, edited by Robert S. Wyer Jr. Mahwah, N.J.: Erlbaum.

Pendry, Louise F., and C. Neil Macrae. 1996. "What the Disinterested Perceiver Overlooks: Goal-Directed Social Categorization." *Personality and Social Psychology Bulletin* 22: 249–56.

Perdue, Charles, John F. Dovidio, Michael B. Gutman, and Richard B. Tyler. 1990. "Us and Them: Social Categorization and the Process of Intergroup Bias." *Journal of Personality and Social Psychology* 59: 475–86.

Phelps, Edmund S. 1972. "The Statistical Theory of Racism and Sexism." *American Economic Review* 62: 659–61.

Reskin, Barbara F. 1998. *The Realities of Affirmative Action.* Washington, D.C.: American Sociological Association.

————. 2000. "The Proximate Causes of Discrimination: Research Agenda for the Twenty-First Century." *Contemporary Sociology* 29: 319–29.

————. 2001. "Employment Discrimination and Its Remedies." In *Sourcebook on Labor Market Research: Evolving Structures and Processes,* edited by Ivar Berg and Arne Kalleberg. New York: Plenum.

Reskin, Barbara F., and Debra B. McBrier. 2000. "Why Not Ascription?: Organizations' Employment of Male and Female Managers." *American Sociological Review* 65: 210–33.

Rothbart, Myron, and Susan Lewis. 1994. "Cognitive Processes and Intergroup Relations: A Historical Perspective." In *Social Cognition: Impact on Social Psychology,* edited by Patricia G. Devine and David L. Hamilton. San Diego: Academic Press.

Salancik, Gerald R., and Jeffrey Pfeffer. 1978. "Uncertainty, Secrecy, and the Choice of Similar Others." *Social Psychology* 41: 246–55.

Segal, Jonathan A. 1998. "Kill All Lawyers?" *HR Magazine* 43(February): 117–27.

Sessa, Valerie I. 1992. "Managing Diversity at the Xerox Corporation: Balanced Workforce Goals and Caucus Groups." In *Diversity in the Workplace*, edited by Susan E. Jackson and Associates. New York: Guilford Press.

Shiffrin, Richard M., and Walter Schneider. 1977. "Controlled and Automatic Human Information Processing." *Psychological Review* 84: 127–90.

Simmel, Georg. 1971 [1908]. *On Individuality and Social Forms: Selected Writings.* Edited and with an introduction by Donald N. Levine. Chicago: University of Chicago Press.

Smelser, Neil, and Richard Swedberg, eds. 1994. *The Handbook of Economic Sociology.* New York: Russell Sage Foundation.

Stryker, Robin. 2001. "Disparate Impact and the Quota Debates: Law, Labor Market Sociology, and Equal Employment Policies." *Sociological Quarterly* 42(1): 13–46.

Sturm, Susan. 2001. "Second Generation Employment Discrimination: A Structural Approach." *Columbia Law Review* 101(3): 101–207.

Swim, Janet K., and Lawrence J. Sanna. 1996. "He's Skilled, She's Lucky: A Meta-analysis of Observers' Attributions for Women's and Men's Successes and Failures." *Personality and Social Psychology Bulletin* 22: 507–19.

Tajfel, Henri. 1970. "Experiments in Intergroup Discrimination." *Scientific American* 223: 96–102.

Tetlock, Philip E. 1992. "The Impact of Accountability on Judgment and Choice: Toward a Social Contingency Model." In *Advances in Experimental Social Psychology 23*, edited by Mark P. Zanna. San Diego: Academic Press.

Tetlock, Philip E., and Jennifer S. Lerner. 1999. "The Social Contingency Model: Identifying Empirical and Normative Boundary Conditions on the Error-and-Bias Portrait of Human Nature." In *Dual Process Theories in Social Psychology*, edited by Shelly Chaiken and Yaacov Trope. New York: Guilford Press.

Tilly, Chris, and Charles Tilly. 1994. "Capitalist Work and Labor Markets." In *The Handbook of Economic Sociology*, edited by Neil Smelser and Richard Swedberg. New York: Russell Sage Foundation.

U.S. Equal Employment Opportunity Commission. 2001a. "EEOC and Private Plaintiffs Settle Harassment Suit for $485,000 Against Chicken Processing Plant." *EEOC Press Releases* (April 10). Available at: *www.eeoc.gov/press/4-10-01.html* (June 20, 2001).

———. 2001b. "EEOC Responds to Final Report of Mitsubishi Consent Decree Monitors." *EEOC Press Releases* (May 23). Available at: *www.eeoc.gov/press/5-23-01.html* (June 20, 2001).

———. 2001c. "EEOC Seeks to Join Nationwide Sex Discrimination Suit Against Rent-A-Center." *EEOC Press Releases* (March 12). Available at: *www.eeoc.gov/press/3-12-01.html* (June 20, 2001).

———. 2001d. "EEOC Settles Bias Suit for $2.6 Million Against TWA." *EEOC Press Releases* (May 24). Available at: *www.eeoc.gov/press/5-24-01.html* (June 20, 2001).

———. 2001e. "EEOC Settles Racial Harassment Suit Against Georgia-Pacific Corporation." *EEOC Press Releases* (April 3). Available at: *www.eeoc.gov/press/4-3-01.html* (June 20, 2001).

———. 2001f. "EEOC Sues Two Indiana Employers for Race Harassment." *EEOC Press Releases* (May 22). Available at: *www.eeoc.gov/press/5-22-01.html* (June 20, 2001).

———. 2001g. "Joe's Stone Crab Liable for Intentional Discrimination Court Rules in Sex Bias Suit Brought by EEOC." *EEOC Press Releases* (March 28). Available at: *www.eeoc.gov/press/3-28-01.html* (June 20, 2001).

Weber, Joseph G. 1994. "The Nature of Ethnocentric Attribution Bias: Ingroup Protection or Enhancement?" *Journal of Experimental Social Psychology* 20: 177–94.

Wilson, William J. 1996. *When Work Disappears*. Chicago: University of Chicago Press.

= Chapter 10 =

Gender and the Organization-Building Process in Young High-Tech Firms

JAMES N. BARON, MICHAEL T. HANNAN, GRETA HSU,
AND OZGECAN KOCAK

I N HIGHLIGHTING the social foundations of economic life, economic sociologists tend to emphasize social and cultural influences in firms' environments that affect economic exchange. Yet social forces impinge on economic activity in a manner that is arguably even more fundamental: by shaping the very way in which economic organizations are structured from their inception. This chapter examines one manifestation of that process, namely, how gender shapes the initial structure and early evolution of firms. Drawing on a rich archive of data describing the evolution of emerging technology companies in Silicon Valley, this chapter examines the determinants and consequences of gender composition in young start-up firms. We document that the propensity to hire women into the "core" scientific and engineering roles in these companies depends on a variety of factors, including the particular organizational blueprint envisioned by the founder-architects of new enterprises. Women's early representation in core scientific and technical roles, in turn, has decisive consequences for how emerging companies evolve, including the extent and rate of bureaucratization. The findings suggest that applying such terms as "organizational architects" and "blueprints for organizing" to founders and their activities in building new enterprises may be particularly apt. Like architects, founders of organizations appear to design structures that depend on the social characteristics of—and the relations between—the individuals intended to occupy the structure.

Gender and the Organization-Building Process in Young High-Technology Firms

Quantitative and ethnographic studies have documented extensive gender segregation within work settings, with profound consequences for attainment, opportunity, and psychological experiences on the job (for excellent reviews, see Bergmann 1986; Jacobs 1989; England 1992; Reskin 1993). This has prompted researchers in a variety of disciplines to open up the organizational "black box" in an effort to understand the features of work settings that exacerbate or ameliorate gender inequalities in job assignment, advancement, and compensation. Although their interpretations of causes and effects often differ, economists and sociologists alike have sought to relate gender inequality to aspects of formal structure (including personnel rules and procedures), technology (the division of labor, task interdependencies, and the structure of jobs and job titles), and the current organizational environment (the labor market, regulatory pressures, and so on).

This shift in focus is a welcome corrective to prior work on inequality, which has either focused on supply-side factors or else purported to capture demand-side considerations by comparing patterns across broad categories of occupations, industries, or regions. However, based on our ongoing research into the organization-building process among high-technology companies in California's Silicon Valley, we suspect that focusing on technology, formal structure, and the current environment takes us only so far in understanding organizational inequality. Rather, our prior work suggests that organizational structures and labor force outcomes are profoundly influenced by the *premises* or *cultural blueprints* that organizational architects bring to their nascent enterprises. These assumptions about employment relations and how to manage them are imprinted on organizations at birth and shape their subsequent development.

In previous studies, we have documented that the initial employment blueprints or models embraced by founders have enduring path-dependent effects on organizational evolution, involving such outcomes as bureaucratization and formalization, development of the human resources (HR) function, CEO succession, the likelihood of going public, and employee turnover (Baron, Burton, and Hannan 1996, 1999; Baron, Hannan, and Burton 1998, 2001; Burton and O'Reilly 2000; Hannan, Burton, and Baron 1996). Path dependence is likely to be no less important in understanding the contours and magnitude of gender inequality within organizations. To be sure, organizations can and do alter their job definitions, screening and job assignment processes, and reward allocations—either promptly, in response to rapid shifts in labor markets or the institutional environment, or more gradually, in response to technological changes and changes in the composition of the labor force (see, for example, Reskin and Roos 1990). However, historical research, case studies, and quantitative analyses all suggest that the mechanisms that segregate workers by sex within organizations are quite inert. Organizational structures, processes, and routines, once adopted, display remarkable persistence over time (Hannan and Freeman 1984; Boeker 1988; Barnett and Carroll 1995; Carroll and Hannan 2000), including those that create and sustain a segregated division of labor (Baron and Newman 1990; Reskin 1993; Kim 1989, 1999).

Inattention to founding conditions may help explain why results have not always been consistent in studies seeking to attribute gender inequalities in organizations to formal structure (such as bureaucratization), to particular employment practices, or even to women's relative representation within the labor force. As Paul Adler and Bryan Borys (1996) have noted, for instance, the meaning and impact of a given bureaucratic practice can vary markedly, depending on the larger cultural context and historical evolution of which it is a part. Hence, one reason why "structural effects" on gender inequality might not be stronger or more consistent is that organizational *premises* and *history* are crucial to understanding the impact of formal structures, employment practices, and the current gender mix on patterns of inequality by sex.

This suggests that we may gain considerable insight into the origins, extent, persistence, and effects of gender segregation at work by examining the process of organization building in its early stages. Contemporary organizational theory asserts that the architects of work organizations imprint cultural scripts, models, or templates for organizing on the enterprises they create (Powell and DiMaggio 1991; Fligstein 1987, 1990; Fligstein and Byrkjeflot 1996; Guillén 1994), which become institutionalized in formal structures and informal processes. In a similar vein, contemporary feminist scholars invoke culturally based organizational logics, such as patriarchy and bureaucracy, in seeking to account for women's disadvantaged positions within work enterprises (Ferguson 1984; Ianello 1992; Martin and Knopoff 1997; Martin, Knopoff, and Beckman 1998).

Accordingly, this chapter examines how the organizational logics or models of founders affect the emergence of gender segregation in nascent enterprises within a particular setting: high-technology firms in California's Silicon Valley. Drawing on a rich database of quantitative and qualitative information about the organization-building process in start-up firms, we examine the factors that account for women's representation in the core scientific, technical, and engineering occupations, both at the firm's inception and subsequently. Women's historical underrepresentation in high technology generally, and in scientific and engineering occupations in particular, has been well documented for the economy as a whole (see, for example, McIlwee and Robinson 1992; Hanson, Schaub, and Baker 1996). However, nascent high-tech firms vary considerably in women's representation within the core workforce. After briefly describing this research setting, we develop and test some predictions about the factors that influence women's initial and subsequent representation in the scientific and technical core of high-technology companies.

The Setting: The Stanford Project on Emerging Companies

The Stanford Project on Emerging Companies (SPEC), a panel study of young high-technology firms in California's Silicon Valley begun in 1994, examines the evolution of business strategies, organizational designs, and employment practices among these firms. SPEC seeks to understand how human resources systems get established, and with what effects. The focus on firms in a single region and sector of economic activity holds constant key labor market and environmental conditions, as well as some of the institutional influences asserted to shape organizational structures and labor force dynamics. Within the Silicon Valley region, we sought industries containing sufficient numbers of comparable firms to enable quantitative comparisons; accordingly, we concentrated on firms engaged in computer hardware or software, telecommunications (including networking equipment), medical and biological technologies, and semiconductors. We assumed that organizations must reach a minimum size before they need formal systems or practices, and therefore we required that the firms included in our study have at least ten employees. Because we also wanted to understand how founding conditions and early decisions affect subsequent organizational evolution, we needed to gather information about the earliest days of the organization. We assumed that individuals could reliably recall only fairly recent information; consequently, we limited the sample to firms no more than ten years old when first visited in 1994–95. (The typical firm was about six years old.)

Trained MBA and doctoral students conducted semistructured interviews with the current CEO, who also referred us to the founder (or a member of the founding team) who was best equipped to provide information on the firm's origins, and to the person he or she deemed the best informant regarding human resources practices in the organization. We followed up with these informants about company history and HR, respectively, and asked them to return completed surveys to us prior to being interviewed. The company history survey solicited details about the firm's founding and subsequent milestones. The HR survey sought information about workforce demographics and employment policies and practices. Additional details of the sample and data collection procedures are provided in our previously published papers, cited in the References.

Founders' Organizational Models

As noted earlier, recent neo-institutional work invokes the notion of culturally based logics, blueprints, scripts, or conceptions of control. Yet researchers have seldom operationalized such blueprints directly, tending instead to infer their existence from other sources of information. In designing the SPEC study, we knew from the extant literature that conceptions of employment relationships might vary along numerous dimensions, and we were unsure a priori which dimensions would be most relevant in our setting. Accordingly, we used open-ended interviews to gather information, asking each founder whether he or she had "an organizational model or blueprint in mind when [you] founded the company." (The CEO was asked a parallel question about the period corresponding to the date of the interview.) We inductively analyzed transcripts of interviews with founders and CEOs (Glaser and Strauss 1967). Those analyses indicated that interviewees' images regarding how work and employment should be organized varied along three dimensions, which we term *attachment, coordination-control*, and *selection*. Each is characterized by three or four fairly distinct options or approaches from which organizational architects seemed to be selecting. (For detailed descriptions of these different response categories, see Burton 1995, 2001.)

The first dimension along which founders' models vary concerns attachment and retention of employees—the principal mechanism by which founders sought to bind employees to their nascent enterprises. Founders articulated three different primary bases of employee attachment, which we label *love* (or *affiliation*), *work*, and *money*. The second dimension reflects the founders' thinking about the primary basis of coordinating and controlling work. Here, their implicit or explicit conceptions tended to fall into one of the following categories: *informal control through peers or organizational culture*; *professional control*, that is, an assumption that workers hired through elite recruitment channels are committed to excellence in their work and can perform at high levels because they have been professionally socialized to do so; *formal procedures and systems*; or *direct oversight*, reminiscent of Richard Edwards's (1979) description of the "simple control" paradigm that characterized small capitalist firms in the late nineteenth and early twentieth centuries. Finally, the third dimension concerns the primary basis for selecting employees. Founders' responses tended to cluster into three categories: a view of the firm as a bundle of tasks, causing founders to focus on selecting employees with the *skills and experience needed to accomplish some immediate task(s)*; a view of the firm more as a sequence of (as yet ill-defined) projects, leading to a conception of employee selection focused on *long-term potential*; and a cultural conception of the firm, accompanied by a selection process focused primarily on *values and cultural fit*.

Based on the interview transcripts, members of the research team coded or classified the responses of each founder on these three dimensions, unless missing data precluded doing so. (The interview responses of CEOs regarding their organizational premises at the time of our first visit to the company, rather than at founding, were also coded.) Coders were instructed to classify firms based on the premises espoused by founders or CEOs rather than on the specific HR practices in place.

Relationships Among the Three Dimensions

In previous work, we have shown that these three dimensions cohere and can be used to characterize the implicit organizational model or blueprint espoused by the founder and the model embraced by the CEO at the time our team first visited each firm. (For an overview and additional details, see Burton 1999, 2001; Baron and Kreps 1999, ch. 19). These blueprints can be classified into three types of attachment and selection and four types of control, yielding 36 (3 × 3 × 4) possible combinations. However, the observations cluster into a few cells, which we refer to as the five "basic model types" for employment relations. These basic model types are shown in table 10.1.[1]

The *engineering model* involves attachment through challenging work, peer group control, and selection based on specific task abilities. This model parallels standard descriptions of the default culture among high-tech Silicon Valley start-ups (see, for example, Saxenian 1994), in which loyalties are to specific exciting *projects*, and it is the

Table 10.1   **Five Basic Employment Model Types, Based on Three Dimensions**

Dimensions			Basic Model Type
Attachment	Selection	Coordination-Control	
Work	Potential	Professional	Star
Work	Skills	Peer-cultural	Engineering
Love	Fit	Peer-cultural	Commitment
Work	Skills	Formal	Bureaucracy
Money	Skills	Direct	Autocracy

Source: Authors' configuration.

modal employment blueprint among founders of SPEC firms. The *star model* refers to attachment based on challenging work, reliance on autonomy and professional control, and selecting elite personnel based on long-term potential. The *commitment model* entails reliance on emotional-familial attachments of employees to the organization, selection based on cultural fit, and peer group control. The *bureaucracy model* involves attachment based on challenging work or opportunities for development, selecting individuals based on their qualifications for a particular role, and formalized control. (For further discussion of this model type, see Baron, Hannan, and Burton 1998, appendix.) Finally, the *autocracy model* refers to employment premised on monetary motivations, control and coordination through close personal oversight, and selection of employees to perform prespecified tasks.

We refer to these five blueprints as the basic model types not only because they are the most prevalent combinations observed within this sample, but because they also display several other important properties. First, each of the blueprints exhibits a high degree of *coherence* or *internal consistency* among the three dimensions, suggesting that they complement one another to form an overarching system. Second, these types display *cultural resonance* and *salience* within this population and its setting. In conversations with Silicon Valley employers, employees, and other knowledgeable parties, we find that insiders resonate with these distinctions and can easily classify organizations with which they have experience in these terms. Third, the five basic types reflect different logics of organizing within other institutions that actors in this organizational field have confronted; indeed, the labels for the types are fairly evocative of the characteristics. For instance, the star employment model—particularly prevalent among firms that develop medical technology or pursue research[2]—

resonates closely with the model that underlies academic science, from which many of the founders and key scientific personnel sought for these start-ups are recruited. The commitment model draws instead on familial imagery and the revered Silicon Valley legend of Hewlett-Packard. The engineering model resonates with the socialization that engineers receive in professional school and suits the Valley's highly mobile labor force. The bureaucratic model is readily familiar from encounters with bureaucracies in numerous contexts. Finally, the austere, no-nonsense autocracy model communicates a powerful and consistent message that employees are certain to have encountered elsewhere before: "You work (for me, the founder), you get paid (by me)—nothing more, nothing less."

We make no claim that these basic model types are generic or even generalizable outside this population. Rather, we simply claim that these types capture blueprints for organizing that have a systemic quality and display cultural resonance within this setting.[3]

Literature Review: Organizational Models and Gender Composition in High-Technology Firms

In previous research, we have shown that these founder models, in turn, have profoundly influenced subsequent organizational evolution along various dimensions. In this chapter, we explore whether the cultural models that architects bring to the organization-building process have a bearing on the sexual division of labor within the enterprises they found. In particular, we are interested in how and why technology firms differ in the presence of women in core scientific, technical, and engineering occupations, both during the start-up phase and subsequently.

At one level, perhaps the most plausible hypothesis is that there should be virtually no variation to explain in gender composition among these companies. After all, women are notoriously underrepresented in scientific and technical occupations and in start-ups (McIlwee and Robinson 1992; Hanson, Schaub, and Baker 1996), and our study design attenuates or eliminates variation in a number of organizational and environmental characteristics (such as industry, organizational age and size, region and labor market) that could affect the sexual division of labor within firms. Especially at the start-up phase, a reasonable prediction is that there will be uniformly low representation of women within the scientific and technical core throughout our sample of companies.

Nor are there strong theoretical bases for making precise predictions about the relationship between organizational blueprints and gender mix. After all, the typology of organizational blueprints described earlier was derived empirically, rather than from first principles. Moreover, the different basic model types vary along numerous dimensions. For instance, they could be differentiated in terms of individualism versus collectivism, with the commitment model representing the most collectivistic blueprint and the star, autocratic, and bureaucratic models located toward the individualistic end of the continuum. Alternatively, the blueprints could be distinguished in terms of the formalization they entail, with the bureaucratic model at one extreme, followed by the star and engineering models, then the commitment model, and the autocratic model at the other extreme. Consequently, it is difficult to derive a precise hypothesized ordering of the basic model types in terms of their relative likelihood of favoring the hiring or retention of women in scientific and technical roles. Instead, we simply offer some rival speculations based on existing theory and research.

The first point to emphasize is that much of our previous research based on the SPEC sample finds that the *founder's* organizational blueprint tends to have stronger and more robust effects on present-day features than does the organizational blueprint associated with the present-day CEO (Baron, Hannan, and Burton 1999). This suggests that initial premises become institutionalized in organizational routines and practices, shaping how organizations evolve. Accordingly, we suspect that present-day gender mix is more likely to be associated with the organizational model embraced at the firm's founding than with the present-day model espoused by the current CEO.

Second, there are plausible bases for competing predictions about whether bureaucracy, commitment, and engineering model firms should be especially hospitable or inhospitable to women. On the one hand, some scholars argue that the formalization of rules and procedures governing recruitment, selection, and allocation of rewards in bureaucracies improves opportunities and attainments for historically disadvantaged groups (for instance, see Reskin, this volume). In a comparison of women working in engineering versus law in Australia, Clarissa Cook and Malcolm Waters (1998) attribute the greater representation of women within engineering to the fact that engineering work is usually conducted within bureaucratic organizations, whereas law is practiced in collegial partnerships within which women are subject to greater subjectivity and exclusion. In the same vein, based on their analysis of four biotechnology firms, Susan Eaton and Lotte Bailyn (1998) conclude that exciting work, a project management orientation, and large organizational scale—all factors that tend to be associated with reliance on an engineering or bureaucracy model—are among the key factors that create opportunities for women in high technology. And in her pioneering analysis of these issues within a single large corporation, Rosabeth Moss Kanter (1977) argued that women face the greatest barriers in settings in which trust and fitting in matter most (for example, at higher organizational levels) because it is in these settings that "homosocial reproduction" is most likely to prevail. If the same reasoning applies *across* organizations, it suggests that the commitment model within technology industries could be relatively inhospitable to women. Consistent with that prediction, Judith McIlwee and Gregg Robinson (1992, 138) compared the career mobility of female engineers in two firms—a relatively bureaucratic aerospace firm dependent on government contracts and an innovative computer firm—and concluded that

> women experience the least occupational mobility in environments where the culture of engineering is most extensive. Women's mobility is greatest where the culture of engineering is minimized by bureaucratization and affirmative action. Where engineers as a group are powerful, the culture takes on a form strongly identified by the male gender role.

Yet other scholars have argued that the logic of bureaucratic organization is primarily a male contrivance, often serving to legitimate differential treatment by sex (see, for example, Martin et al. 1998). In contrast, the more affiliative, collaborative nature of commitment model firms might actually be *more* hospitable to women than are bureaucracy or engineering model firms, particularly given stereotypes that tend to devalue women's technical skills relative to their interpersonal skills.

Finally, sensible arguments can also be advanced for an affinity between the other two basic model types—star and autocracy—and the presence of women in core scientific and technical roles. Kanter (1977, 177) argued that power and opportunity accrue from activities that are extraordinary, visible, and organizationally relevant (identified with the solution to a core problem). Recognizing this, many career-oriented women in business and engineering are attracted to those work roles and organizational settings that are most merit-based and in which the ability to demonstrate individual ability is greatest (Cook and Waters 1998). This suggests that the star model may be conducive to the recruitment and retention of women.[4]

Alternatively, it is conceivable that autocracy model firms are particularly likely to hire women for, or retain them in, scientific and technical roles. Neo-Marxists and dual labor market theorists have argued that, even within occupations, women and people of color tend to be concentrated in those firms and industries in which "despotic" control systems are most prevalent (Edwards 1979). In the same vein, queuing models of occupational gender segregation (Reskin and Roos 1990) suggest that women tend to become over-represented in those specialties and work settings that are least remunerative and desirable, with the superior opportunities monopolized by men. Given the intense aversion to autocracy among scientific and engineering professionals, this model is likely to be singularly unattractive to potential employees, suggesting that women may be over-represented in firms founded according to that model relative to their representation within the sample as a whole.[5]

Given these competing predictions, we simply address the issue empirically by summarizing analyses that relate organizational model type to gender mix at the firm's inception and in 1994–1995.

Summary of Findings

Effects of Organizational Blueprints on the Gender Mix in High-Technology Firms

Descriptive Statistics   As background for the multivariate analyses, table 10.2 provides summary descriptive information on selected characteristics of the SPEC firms, including the size and composition of their technical core (scientific and engineering roles).[6]

By the end of the first year of operations, the average SPEC firm had 38.3 percent of its full-time labor force in scientific-engineering occupations (median = 42.6 percent, range = 0 to 78.0 percent). This fraction hardly changed over time: as of 1994–1995, the average was 37.7 percent (median = 38.9 percent, range = 0 to 76 percent). At the end of its first year of operations, the average SPEC company had the equivalent of 10.5 full-time employees employed in engineering and scientific roles (median = 5), of whom 1.3 were female (median = 0). Of the 75 firms that provided an occupational distribution from the first year of operations, 65 had one or more scientist-engineer specialists, with women averaging 11.3 percent of that group (median = 0 percent; range = 0 to 100 percent). By 1994–1995, when the average SPEC enterprise was roughly six years old, women's representation in the technical core had increased somewhat. On average, SPEC firms

Table 10.2 Descriptive Statistics: Selected Characteristics of SPEC Companies

Variable	End of First Year of Operations (N = 75)				1994–95 (N = 74)			
	Mean	Median	Standard Deviation[a]	Minimum, Maximum	Mean	Median	Standard Deviation[a]	Minimum, Maximum
Number of full-time employees (FTEs)	29.43	14.00	66.15	1, 440	132.31	59.50	241.54	6, 1895
FTEs in scientific-engineering occupations	10.47	5.00	26.88	0, 226	49.40	20.00	139.82	0, 1185
Percentage female FTEs (all employees)	22.15	20.00	15.74	0, 64	31.13	30.59	13.44	0, 77
Percentage FTEs in scientific-engineering occupations	38.32	42.62	23.03	0, 78	37.68	38.92	19.75	0, 76
Female FTEs in scientific-engineering occupations	1.29	0.00	4.83	0, 41	9.70	2.00	36.70	0, 314
Percentage females among scientists-engineers[b]	11.26	0.00	20.18	0, 100	16.88	11.76	16.68	0, 100

Founder's employment
model[c] (percentages)

Commitment	13.33	—	—	—
Autocracy	5.33	—	—	—
Star	9.33	—	—	—
Engineering	32.00	—	—	—
Bureaucracy	5.33	—	—	—
Aberrant	34.67	—	—	—
Organizational age in 1994–1995 (years)	—	6.02	5.79	2.88	2.08, 14.58
Public firm in 1994–1995 (1 = yes)	—	0.31	0.00	—	—

Source: Authors' calculations.

[a]Standard deviations not shown for binary variables.

[b]Only for firms having one or more FTE scientist-engineer.

[c]Includes basic model types and near-model cases within each category (see ch. 10, n. 3 for explanation).

in 1994–1995 had 49.4 full-time employees in scientific-engineering roles (median = 20), of which 9.7 were female (median = 2). Of the 74 firms for which we have a 1994–1995 occupational distribution, 71 had one or more scientist-engineer specialists, with women averaging 16.9 percent of that group (median = 11.8 percent; range = 0 to 100 percent).[7]

Multivariate Analyses   Because personnel counts tend to be small in these organizations, the proportion of women in the core technical occupations can be strongly affected by a few entries or exits. Therefore, we opted to model the counts themselves. We relate the count of women in the core to the count of men in the core, to other personnel counts, and to other relevant covariates. We do so using an explicit probability model, the negative binomial, estimating specifications in which the mean of the process depends on the covariates.[8]

Table 10.3 summarizes statistical analyses relating organizational blueprint to gender mix. The analyses report the effects of the founder's blueprint on the representation of women in scientific and technical roles at two points in time: at the end of the firm's first year of operations, and when it was visited by our research team in 1994–1995 (on average, roughly six years after founding; see table 10.2). The analyses control for various factors that would be expected to influence this count, including the (log) number of *men* employed in those same core roles at the same point in time, the (log) number of people employed in all other roles within the firm at the same point in time, and the industry.[9] In addition, for analyses predicting gender mix in 1994–1995, we control for: measures of occupational mix in 1994–1995 and at the end of the first year of operations, including the lagged dependent variable; and measures of organizational age and whether the firm had gone public, both as of the interview date in 1994–1995.

Model 1 in table 10.3 reports negative binomial regressions for the gender mix in each firm's first year of operations. Versions 1a and 1b differ only in the reference (omitted) category for the founder's employment model: the commitment blueprint in model 1a and the bureaucracy blueprint in model 1b. Although there are a few significant zero-order differences among model types with respect to initial gender mix (supplementary regressions not shown in the table), the net differences are modest once we control for the other covariates in table 10.3. Indeed, only the net contrast between the autocracy and bureaucracy blueprints is statistically significant at conventional levels, and the set of variables representing founders' blueprints falls just short of statistical significance as a group.[10] Although this may reflect the fact that there is less variation to explain among firms in gender mix in the first year, this is not the whole story, because the correlations between employment blueprint types and gender mix in 1994–1995 are quite similar in pattern and magnitude as for the first year of operations. Rather, the gross association between employment blueprint and gender mix in the first year apparently reflects the fact that founders' initial choices regarding employment blueprints depended largely on the industry and occupational mix of their nascent firms. Once those latter factors are controlled, the association between blueprint type and gender mix largely vanishes.

The story is quite different, however, when we look at *change* in women's representation within scientific and engineering roles, measured (in model 2) by a specification predicting the number of women in engineering and scientific roles in 1994–1995, net of the number at the end of the first year of operations (and other controls). Model 2 reveals that, relative to the commitment blueprint, all other blueprints displayed more growth in women's representation within the core occupations. (None of the other net contrasts among blueprint types is significant in model 2, although the contrast between the autocracy and star blueprints, on the one hand, and the remaining blueprints, on the other, approaches significance.)[11]

This result is consistent with the conjecture by some scholars that high-commitment cultures may not be conducive to the employment of women and people of color, owing to the high premium placed on trust and fitting in (see, for example, Kanter 1977; McIlwee and Robinson 1992). Supplementary analyses of turnover data suggest that the low representation of women in commitment model firms does not appear to reflect unusually high rates of attrition by employees out of those firms (see Baron, Hannan, and Burton 2001; Baron, Hannan, Hsu, and Kocak 2002). Rather, the effect seems more likely to reflect homosocial reproduction within firms structured along commitment lines, an aversion among technical women to entering such cultures, or both.[12]

The effects of control variables in models 1 and 2 generally conform to intuition. At the end of the first year of operations, women are more highly represented in biotechnology, medical device, and research start-ups (the omitted category) than in any of the other industry groups represented in our sample (see also Eaton and Bailyn 1998). Predictably, the absolute number of women in scientific and engineering roles at the end of the first year of operations is also higher in firms that have hired more men in those same roles and in firms that are larger (that is, that have more employees in nonscientific roles). In model 2, which focuses on change since the first year of

Table 10.3 Determinants of Women's Representations in Scientific, Engineering, and Technical Occupations Within Start-Up Firms

Variable	Gender Mix: End of First Year of Operations (model 1a; N = 75)			Gender Mix: End of First Year of Operations (model 1b; N = 75)			Gender Mix: 1994–1995 (model 2; N = 74)		
	Coefficient	Z	P > |Z|	Coefficient	Z	P > |Z|	Coefficient	Z	P > |Z|
Founder's employment model									
Commitment	—	—	—	-1.342	-1.260	.208	—	—	—
Autocracy	-2.145	-1.339	.181	-3.487	-2.229	.026	2.251	2.696	.007
Star	1.133	1.091	.275	-0.209	-0.240	.810	2.084	3.269	.001
Engineering	0.667	0.747	.455	-0.675	-0.931	.352	1.391	2.857	.004
Bureaucracy	1.342	1.260	.208	—	—	—	1.330	1.952	.051
Aberrant	1.102	1.239	.215	-0.240	-0.331	.741	1.505	3.004	.003
Male scientists-engineers (ln), year 1	0.248	2.020	.043	0.248	2.020	.043	0.031	0.450	.653
Non-engineering employees (ln), year 1	1.000	4.181	.000	1.000	4.181	.000	-0.381	-2.188	.029
Female scientists-engineers (ln), year 1							0.125	3.147	.002
Computer (hardware or software) industry[a]	-1.215	-2.007	.045	-1.215	-2.007	.045	0.072	0.174	.862
Semiconductor industry[a]	-2.290	-2.226	.026	-2.290	-2.226	.026	-0.636	-1.119	.263
Telecommunications/ networking equipment industry[a]	-1.416	-2.058	.040	-1.416	-2.058	.040	-0.485	-1.014	.311

	(1)	(2)	(3)	(4)	(5)	(6)	(7)	(8)	(9)
Manufacturing industry[a]	−1.889	−1.293	.196	−1.889	−1.293	.196	−1.579	−1.467	.142
Male scientists-engineers (ln), 1994–1995							0.050	0.522	.601
Non-engineering employees (ln), 1994–1995							0.714	4.340	.000
Age of organization in 1994–1995							−0.092	−1.518	.129
Public company by 1994–1995							0.886	2.958	.003
Constant	−2.504		.012	−1.370	−1.572	.116	−1.160	−1.453	.146
	−2.712								
Overdispersion (α)	0.521[b]			0.655[b]			0.512[b]		
Mean (maximum) of dependent variable	1.293 (41)			1.293 (41)			9.703 (314)		
Standard deviation of dependent variable	4.834			4.834			36.704		

$\chi^2 = 62.86(16)$; p = .000
Log likelihood = −72.905
Pseudo R^2 = .301

$\chi^2 = 99.54(16)$; p = .000
Log likelihood = −178.520
Pseudo R^2 = .218

Source: Authors' calculations.

Note: The table shows the results of a negative binomial regression predicting the number of full-time equivalent female employees in "engineering and scientific" occupations. Results are based on unweighted data.

[a] Omitted industry category represents companies in biotechnology, medical devices, or research.

[b] For model 1, the likelihood ratio test for overdispersion (that $\alpha = 0$) yields $\chi^2 = 25.53$ (df = 1); p = .000. For model 2, $\chi^2 = 64.63$ (df = 1); p = .000.

operations, the net effects of industry on gender mix are trivial and presumably are already reflected in the lagged dependent variable. Not surprisingly, the absolute number of women in core (scientific or engineering) roles in 1994–1995 was higher in firms that also had a large number of employees in noncore roles. Net of that effect, however, the number of workers in noncore occupations at the end of the first year of operations had a *negative* effect on gender mix within the core. This indicates that women's representation within core occupations increased most rapidly in firms that experienced the greatest employment growth, a finding that is consistent with numerous other studies documenting that organizational growth tends to promote gender integration (Reskin 1993).[13] According to model 2, women were also more highly represented in core occupations within firms that had gone public by 1994–1995, even controlling for employment growth. This suggests that companies anticipating an IPO might have been more proactive in implementing employment policies and practices aimed at diversity than were privately held concerns.

Finally, supplementary analyses provide important evidence about the enduring effects of cultural blueprints on organizations (for details, see Baron, Hannan, Hsu, and Kocak 2002). We estimated versions of model 2 in which comparable dummy variables denoting the organizational blueprint of the *then-current CEO* were either substituted for the founder's blueprint or included along with the vector of variables capturing the founder's blueprint. Not surprisingly, there are significant net associations between the organizational blueprint espoused by the CEO in 1994–1995 and the gender mix in scientific and engineering occupations in 1994–1995. Specifically, firms in which the CEO was characterized as embracing either a star or bureaucratic model had more women in core occupations than did otherwise comparable firms in which the current CEO espoused a commitment model. Moreover, after controlling for the other covariates in model 2, there are significant contrasts between every category of CEO blueprint and the (omitted) commitment category. However, if we include measures of both the founder's and the CEO's blueprint in the same specification, only the contrast between the autocracy and commitment types remain significant among the variables depicting the CEO's blueprint, whereas the magnitude and significance of the coefficients capturing the founder's blueprint are essentially unchanged. In other words, as the SPEC research team has found in analyzing administrative intensity and other outcomes, the founders' initial conceptions seem to do a better job of predicting the current state of affairs in an enterprise than do the conceptions of the then-current CEO.

Effects of Initial Gender Mix on Organization Building in High-Technology Firms

Our results suggest that the premises embraced by organizational architects may be no less important than technology, formal structure, and the like in shaping the gender mix within nascent technology companies. Indeed, whereas much of the literature has sought to link gender segregation to attributes of formal organizational structure (for a review, see Baron 1991), previous analyses of the SPEC sample suggest that the causality may also operate in the opposite direction: the evolution of formal organizational structures and practices may be influenced significantly by the firm's initial gender mix in its core occupations.

For instance, Baron, Hannan, and Burton (1999) reported that firms with a higher initial representation of women in the core scientific and technical roles subsequently remained less administratively intense. (They measured administrative intensity as the log number of full-time managerial or administrative specialists, controlling for the log number of other full-time-equivalent employees in a given enterprise. Their analyses also controlled for firm age, public-private status, industry, strategy, and founders' organizational blueprints.) The effect was large in substantive terms and robust across many different specifications. Baron, Hannan, and Burton (1999) estimate that, relative to an all-male baseline, a firm that was 25 percent female at the end of its first year of operations (which is close to the sample mean) would have had only 80 percent as many full-time administrators by 1994–95. Furthermore, they found that initial gender mix mattered more than contemporaneous gender mix for the growth of administrative overhead: that is, the effect of the contemporaneous gender mix (proportion female) on administrative intensity was weaker than the effect of the initial gender mix, and the latter effect dwarfed the former when both measures were included in the same specification. This evidence supports the notion of path-dependent evolution of organizational structures.

The results indicate that it is the early presence of women *among the firm's core workforce* that matters: the proportion of scientific and engineering jobs held by women within the first year of operations had a significant negative effect on administrative intensity (b = −.629; t = −2.38), whereas women's initial share of other jobs had only a trivial effect (b = −.112; t = −.40). Thus, it is apparently women's early representation in the core scientific and engineering occupations that shapes subsequent bureaucratization within these technology-based companies. This finding provides additional evidence that the effect of gender composition is not spurious but instead captures differences in the propensity to formalize administration and management that depend on the social demography of a firm's core workforce early in its history. This negative effect on bureaucratization of the percentage of females in the core workforce generalizes to another key facet of bureaucratization, namely, the proliferation of specialized senior management roles (Baron, Burton, and Hannan 1999).[14]

Discussion

Based on our ongoing research into organization building within emerging technology companies, we have summarized two sets of findings that we believe have potentially profound implications for economic sociology and for understanding inequality in organizations.

First, we have documented path dependence in the evolution of the gender mix within the core occupations of emerging technology companies. Consistent with the recent emphasis by neo-institutional scholars on the cultural blueprints that shape organization building, we have shown that founders' initial premises regarding employment relations shape their firms' trajectories with respect to the hiring of women in core scientific and engineering roles. Technologically inclined theories of organization, whether propounded by economists or sociologists, tend to presume that formal structure and technology determine the labor force requirements and attributes of enterprises, and that internal arrangements and staffing patterns change over time in response to changes in organizational environments, strategies, and technologies. However, some of our evidence on the early years of start-up companies suggests that such conceptions are limited.

In particular, firms founded along commitment model lines are significantly less likely to add (or retain) women in key scientific and engineering roles, relative to otherwise comparable firms founded according to other blueprints. This result is consistent with the claim of some scholars that strong organizational cultures can be an impediment to the integration of women and people of color, especially in high-technology settings. This effect may be especially pronounced in nascent high-commitment firms like the ones in our sample; these organizations, for the most part, have yet to develop either a formal apparatus or an informal reputation that might allay concerns about inclusiveness and equity among diverse segments of the labor force.

Another key finding, with significant implications for economic sociology, is that organizational architects apparently craft administrative structures and policies that reflect the early social demography of their enterprises. In searching for "structural effects" on gender inequality in organizations, analysts may frequently miss the most profound structural effect of all, namely, that the structures in place have emerged as a consequence of the organization's initial demography. Choices about whether to hire males or females in the early days of an organization certainly have much to do with the industry, strategy, and occupational requirements, but our findings suggest that those variables are hardly determinative, as there is significant variation in gender mix even net of those factors. That variation, in turn, is systematically related to the pace and extent of subsequent bureaucratization in these companies, suggesting that early labor force choices are quite fateful for nascent organizations. The structures, practices, and routines that emerge in enterprises may owe a great deal to early choices (conscious or otherwise) by organizational architects about the kinds of individuals who staff key roles; those choices, in turn, reflect particular organizational blueprints or cultural scripts. If our results prove generalizable to other organizational samples, other aspects of organizational structure, and other dimensions of labor force demography, we believe there are important implications for economic sociology and for our understanding of organizational inequality.

How should we interpret these results regarding the effect of initial gender mix on subsequent organizational design? One possibility, consistent with some feminist scholarship, is that the logic of bureaucracies is fundamentally male and that organizations relying more on female labor require less formal apparatus for coordinating work. A related conjecture is that the creation of specialized administrative roles is a vehicle for creating opportunity chains within emerging organizations (that is, oversight positions into which employees can be promoted as the enterprise grows), and that employers are more likely to create such hierarchies when the labor force consists disproportionately of men. Based on qualitative information gleaned from the companies, however, Baron, Hannan, and Burton (1999) have suggested another intriguing possibility—that the link between gender composition and administrative intensity reflects a network-based hiring effect, whereby women tend to predominate in the early days of high-tech firms when they enter through network ties to the founder.[15] The existence of those network ties ostensibly provides social capital and mechanisms of informal control, enabling the firm subsequently to economize on the administrative overhead needed to coordinate and control activities (Walton 1985). Unraveling the causal mechanisms at work in producing the link between the initial gender mix of firms and their subsequent organization-building activity will require quantitative and qualitative studies that can focus more deeply and directly on the forces at work both inside and outside organizations. Research along these lines should be a high priority for economic sociologists interested in the evolution of organizational structures and routines.

At the broadest level, our results underscore that economic sociology ignores founding conditions, especially the cultural blueprints of organizational architects, at its peril. (For a broader critique, see Zelizer, ch. 5, this volume.) The enduring imprint of founders' premises on the firms they launch—not only on gender composition but on the various other outcomes we have documented in other papers—highlights the point that current organizational arrangements (and, we suspect, labor market structures) cannot be adequately predicted or understood without attention to the ways in which social and cultural conceptions become embedded in structures, processes, and routines in the formative stages of organization building.

This, in turn, has important implications for the sorts of research designs that are likely to be most informative. Economists and economic sociologists alike have tended to pay closer attention to "lock-in" and historical forces when they attempt to chart the social origins of industries, markets, specific technologies, or the structure of economies at the regional or national level than they have in studying *firms*, where their analyses have tended to be more cross-sectional. In part, this no doubt reflects data limitations, but we believe it also reflects a need for economic sociologists to reorient their conceptualizations in studying organizations, as well as to rethink the methods and statistical models they employ. Economic sociology should pay closer attention to specifying the social and cultural factors and institutions that shape organization-building activities in particular eras, regions, and industries, and how those influences become institutionalized within organizations. As we have argued elsewhere (Baron, Hannan, and Burton 2001), understanding the enduring imprint of founding conditions on organizational evolution will also require adjustments to the kinds of data that economic sociologists gather and analyze and the ways in which time-series data on organizations are modeled. For example, the standard approach to studying longitudinal data on organizations—applying fixed-effects estimates to pooled cross-section time-series models—causes founding conditions to drop out of the analysis, because they are by definition time-invariant for every organization.

A reorientation along similar lines is likely to benefit students of labor market inequality. Research on organizational gender inequality has suggested that women tend to fare better in firms in which their relative numbers are greatest. Our preliminary analyses of a sample of high-tech firms suggest, however, that women may have joined the ranks of the scientific and technical core of these companies through quite disparate paths, depending on the organizational blueprint with which their firm was launched. This leads us to speculate that the current extent of gender inequality in attainment and opportunity within a given enterprise may reflect not only the current gender mix in that setting but also the *developmental path* by which the enterprise arrived at that demographic composition. Put differently, students of inequality must recognize that the link between origins and destinations is no less profound for firms than it is for individual employees. Analyses that ignore path-dependent organizational evolution are likely to fall well short of the mark in trying to predict, much less make sense of, existing patterns in the labor market and in the distribution of opportunities within firms.

The authors' names are listed in alphabetical order. An earlier version of this chapter was presented at the Second Annual Conference on Economic and Organizational Sociology at the University of Pennsylvania, March 4, 2000. We gratefully acknowledge helpful assistance and comments from Diane Burton, Paula England, Jerry Jacobs, Barbara Lubben, Joanne Martin, Daniel Stewart, and Jane Wei, and research support from the Stanford Business School, particularly the Center for Entrepreneurial Studies and the Human Resources Research Initiative.

Notes

1. This effort to characterize entrepreneurs' organizational blueprints raises numerous conceptual and methodological issues, such as: the match between what founders-CEOs espouse and organizational reality, retrospection bias, and the validity of our categorization of organizational models. Space limitations preclude consideration of these issues, a number of which are discussed by Baron, Hannan, and Burton (1998, 2001).

2. Among SPEC firms in the medical technology or research sectors (including biotechnology), 42.3 percent were founded along star model lines, compared with only 1.6 percent of firms in other industry sectors.

3. A significant number of companies differed from one (and only one) of the basic model types on only one dimension. We refer to these as "near-model" types. For instance, about 3 percent of founders envisioned basing attachment on love, selecting based on fit, and utilizing direct control. This combination represents a "near-commitment" blueprint: it differs from the basic commitment model firm in terms of control (only)

and is substantially different (that is, on two or more dimensions) from the other four model types. Such an organization suggests an autocratic, cult-like variant of the commitment model. Finally, we use the terms "aberrant" or "non-type" to refer to all other blueprints—firms in which the blueprint either differs from two or more basic model types on one dimension (and does not fall into any of the basic types) or differs along two or more dimensions from every basic model type. The statistical analyses reported in this chapter combine near-model cases with their basic model counterparts in classifying firms into founder and CEO model categories. However, the pattern and magnitude of results do not change materially if near-model cases are grouped instead with the aberrant cases, so that the categories corresponding to the basic model types include only cases that fit perfectly into a given type. (Supplementary results are available on request.)

4. Baron, Hannan, and Burton (1999) suggest another reason for making this prediction. In star model firms—concentrated disproportionately in biotechnology within this sample—early stars are typically recruited to the firm through personal ties to the founder, by virtue of having worked with him or her previously in a company or educational setting. These network ties appear to be more heterophilous with respect to gender than other types of networks and apparently facilitate the entrée of women into core technical roles relative to their prospects in firms founded according to other blueprints.

5. In addition, founder-owners who champion autocracy tend to resist all forms of overhead and infrastructure—they are, in a word, *cheap*. If these employers believe they can hire, retain, or control women at lower wages than otherwise comparable men would command, this belief could provide another affinity between autocracy and the prevalence of women.

6. The (unweighted) descriptive statistics in table 10.2 characterize the subset of SPEC companies having complete data on the variables used to estimate the regression models reported in table 10.3. (For a discussion of missing data issues, see Baron, Hannan, and Burton 1998, appendix.)

7. Not surprisingly, if firms are weighted in proportion to their employment size, women's representation within the technical core is slightly higher: a mean of 13.4 percent (median = 7.7 percent) among firms having one or more scientists or engineers on the payroll at the end of the first year of operations, and a mean of 17.4 percent (median = 16.7 percent) in 1994–1995.

8. A standard way of motivating this choice is to begin with the Poisson model, generalized to express functional dependence of the mean (and variance) of the process on a vector of covariates (Barron 1992). Let Y denote the random variable that expresses the count to be modeled, and y denote a realization of that random variable. The Poisson regression model has the form:

$$\Pr\{Y|x = y\} = \lambda^y e^{-\lambda} / y!,$$

where $\lambda = \exp(x'\beta)$.

Frequently in social science (and other) applications the Poisson assumption does not fit because the (conditional) variance does not equal—even approximately—the (conditional) mean. Rather, data are often over-dispersed in the sense that the variance exceeds the mean, and this is the case in our application. The negative binomial is a standard alternative that allows such overdispersion. This model can be seen as a generalization of the Poisson in which the mean of the process is $\lambda = \exp(x'\beta) \times \varepsilon$, where the disturbance term ε has a gamma distribution. The software package we use to estimate the negative binomial model, NBREG in Stata 6.0 (StataCorp 1999), assumes that this distribution has the form $\Gamma(1/\alpha, 1/\alpha)$, which makes α the overdispersion parameter.

In expressing the dependence of the expected count of women in the technical core on other personnel counts, we adopted the following strategy. Consider the case in which we relate the count of women in the core in 1994–1995 (time 1) to the count of women in the core at time 0 (call these y_1 and y_0, respectively). An appealing specification would have $E(y_1) \propto y_0^{\theta}$. With $\theta = 1$, the relationship is strict proportionality; alternatively, there might be increasing ($\theta > 1$) or decreasing ($0 < \theta < 1$) returns to scale. We impose this kind of power-law relationship by entering the natural log of each personnel count in the vector of covariates (because $\exp[\theta \ln(y_0)] = y_0^{\theta}$).

9. For independent variables in the log metric that had a raw count of 0, we added 0.01 before taking logs.

10. Comparing models with and without the variables representing founders' employment blueprints yields a test statistic (the difference in log likelihoods, multiplied by -2) of 9.736 (p = .083).

11. For instance, if the autocracy and star blueprints (together) are made the reference category, the contrast with engineering yields a coefficient of -0.733 with a t statistic of -1.799 (p = .072).

12. In supplementary regressions (details available on request), we reestimated the models in table 10.3, replacing the measures of the five basic blueprint types with dummy variables characterizing the options on the attachment, selection, and coordination-control dimensions. (With three discrete options for attachment and for selection and four options for coordination-control, seven dummy variables are required to exhaust the possible combinations.) Those analyses reveal significant effects associated with both the selection and attachment dimensions. At the end of the first year of operations, women were more prevalent in firms in which the founder's blueprint emphasized attachment based on challenging work (relative to those emphasizing love) and selection based on potential or talent (relative to skills and fit). Women were also slightly more prevalent in firms whose blueprint emphasized formalized control, relative to the other alternatives. In models predicting the gender mix in

1994–1995, women represented a significantly smaller fraction of the technical core in firms characterized by attachment based on love (relative to attachment based on either work or money) or selection based on fit (relative to selection based on potential or talent). The vector of seven dummy variables was statistically significant as a group in predicting gender mix at both points in time.

13. In other words, the negative effect of time 0 noncore employment on time 1 gender mix, holding constant time 1 noncore employment, means that for two companies with the same number of noncore employees in 1994–1995, women were more highly represented in the core within the firm that was smaller (that is, that had fewer noncore employees) in its first year of operations.

14. Firms with a high initial representation of women were also somewhat less likely to adopt formal HR practices, though the effect was not highly significant.

15. To be sure, it is likely that men benefit more from network-based hiring in Silicon Valley than do women. The claim here is simply that recruitment through personal ties may be one of the few means by which women can gain entrée into the scientific and technical core of start-up firms at the founding stage, and therefore firms with women represented in the technical core early on may rely most on network-based recruitment and social ties.

References

Adler, Paul S., and Bryan Borys. 1996. "Two Types of Bureaucracy: Enabling and Coercive." *Administrative Science Quarterly* 41: 61–89.

Barnett, William P., and Glenn R. Carroll. 1995. "Modeling Internal Organizational Change." *Annual Review of Sociology* 21: 217–36.

Baron, James N. 1991. "Organizational Evidence of Ascription in Labor Markets." In *New Approaches to Economic and Social Analyses of Discrimination*, edited by Richard Cornwall and Phanindra Wunnava. New York: Praeger.

Baron, James N., M. Diane Burton, and Michael T. Hannan. 1996. "The Road Taken: The Origins and Evolution of Employment Systems in Emerging High-Technology Companies." *Industrial and Corporate Change* 5: 239–76.

———. 1999. "Engineering Bureaucracy: The Genesis of Formal Policies, Positions, and Structures in High-Technology Firms." *Journal of Law, Economics, and Organization* 15(spring): 1–41.

Baron, James N., Michael T. Hannan, and M. Diane Burton. 1998. "Determinants of Managerial Intensity in the Early Years of Organizations." Research Paper 1550. Stanford University, Graduate School of Business.

———. 1999. "Building the Iron Cage: Determinants of Managerial Intensity in the Early Years of Organizations." *American Sociological Review* 64: 527–47.

———. 2001. "Labor Pains: Organizational Change and Employee Turnover in Young High-Tech Firms." *American Journal of Sociology* 106: 960–1012.

Baron, James N., Michael T. Hannan, Greta Hsu, and Ozgecan Kocak. 2002. "In the Company of Women: Organization Building and Gender Segregation in Young High-Tech Firms." Unpublished paper. Stanford University, Graduate School of Business.

Baron, James N., and David M. Kreps. 1999. *Strategic Human Resources: Frameworks for General Managers*. New York: Wiley.

Baron, James N., and Andrew E. Newman. 1990. "For What It's Worth: Organizations, Occupations, and the Value of Work Done by Women and Nonwhites." *American Sociological Review* 55: 155–75.

Barron, David. 1992. "The Analysis of Count Data: Overdispersion and Autocorrelation." In *Sociological Methodology 1992*, edited by Peter V. Marsden. Oxford: Blackwell.

Bergmann, Barbara R. 1986. *The Economic Emergence of Women*. New York: Basic Books.

Boeker, Warren. 1988. "Organizational Origins: Entrepreneurial and Environmental Imprinting at the Time of Founding." In *Ecological Models of Organizations*, edited by Glenn R. Carroll. Cambridge, Mass.: Ballinger.

Burton, M. Diane. 1995. "The Evolution of Employment Systems in High-Technology Firms." Ph.D. diss., Stanford University.

———. 1999. "Employment Models in Entrepreneurial Companies." Harvard Business School, Boston. Unpublished paper.

———. 2001. "The Company They Keep: Founders' Models for Organizing New Firms." In *The Entrepreneurship Dynamic: Origins of Entrepreneurship and the Evolution of Industries*, edited by Claudia Bird Schoonhoven and Elaine Romanelli. Stanford, Calif.: Stanford University Press.

Burton, M. Diane, and Charles A. O'Reilly III. 2000. "The Impact of High-Commitment Work Systems on IPOs: Additive or Multiplicative Effects?" Paper presented at the Academy of Management annual meeting, Toronto (August).

Carroll, Glenn R., and Michael T. Hannan. 2000. *The Demography of Corporations and Industries*. Princeton, N.J.: Princeton University Press.

Cook, Clarissa, and Malcolm Waters. 1998. "The Impact of Organizational Form on Gendered Labour Markets in Engineering and Law." *Sociological Review* 46(2): 314–39.

Eaton, Susan E., and Lotte Bailyn. 1998. "Surprising Opportunities: Gender and the Structure of Work in Biotechnology Firms." Paper presented at the New York Academy of Sciences conference "Choices and Successes: Women in Science and Engineering," New York (March 12–13).

Edwards, Richard C. 1979. *Contested Terrain: The Transformation of the Workplace in the Twentieth Century*. New York: Basic Books.

England, Paula. 1992. *Comparable Worth: Theories and Evidence*. New York: Aldine de Gruyter.

Ferguson, Kathy E. 1984. *The Feminist Case Against Bureaucracy*. Philadelphia: Temple University Press.

Fligstein, Neil. 1987. "The Intraorganizational Power Struggle: The Rise of Finance Presidents in Large Corporations." *American Sociological Review* 52: 44–58.

————. 1990. *The Transformation of Corporate Control.* Cambridge, Mass.: Harvard University Press.

Fligstein, Neil, and Haldor Byrkjeflot. 1996. "The Logic of Employment Systems." In *Social Differentiation and Social Inequality,* edited by James N. Baron, David B. Grusky, and Donald J. Treiman. Boulder, Colo.: Westview Press.

Glaser, Barney G., and Anselm L. Strauss. 1967. *The Discovery of Grounded Theory: Strategies for Qualitative Research.* Chicago: Aldine.

Guillén, Mauro F. 1994. *Models of Management: Work, Authority, and Organization in a Comparative Perspective.* Chicago: University of Chicago Press.

Hannan, Michael T., M. Diane Burton, and James N. Baron. 1996. "Inertia and Change in the Early Years: Employment Relations in Young High-Technology Firms." *Industrial and Corporate Change* 5(2): 503–36.

Hannan, Michael T., and John Freeman. 1984. "Structural Inertia and Organizational Change." *American Sociological Review* 49: 149–64.

Hanson, Sandra L., Maryellen Schaub, and David P. Baker. 1996. "Gender Stratification in the Pipeline: A Comparative Analysis of Seven Countries." *Gender and Society* 10(3): 271–90.

Ianello, Kathleen P. 1992. *Decisions Without Hierarchy: Feminist Interventions in Organization Theory and Practice.* New York: Routledge.

Jacobs, Jerry A. 1989. *Revolving Doors: Sex Segregation and Women's Careers.* Stanford, Calif.: Stanford University Press.

Kanter, Rosabeth Moss. 1977. *Men and Women of the Corporation.* New York: Free Press.

Kim, Marlene. 1989. "Gender Bias in Compensation Structures: A Case Study of Its Historical Basis and Persistence." *Journal of Social Issues* 45(winter): 39–50.

————. 1999. "Inertia and Discrimination in the California State Civil Service." *Industrial Relations* 38(1): 46–68.

Martin, Joanne, and Kathleen Knopoff. 1997. "The Gendered Implications of Apparently Gender-Neutral Theory: Rereading Max Weber." In *Women's Studies and Business Ethics,* edited by Andrea Larson and R. Edward Freeman. New York: Oxford University Press.

Martin, Joanne, Kathleen Knopoff, and Christine Beckman. 1998. "Seeking an Alternative to Bureaucratic Impersonality and Emotional Labor: Bounded Emotionality at The Body Shop." *Administrative Science Quarterly* 43: 429–69.

McIlwee, Judith S., and J. Gregg Robinson. 1992. *Women in Engineering: Gender, Power, and Workplace Culture.* Albany: State University of New York Press.

Powell, Walter W., and Paul J. DiMaggio, eds. 1991. *The New Institutionalism in Organizational Analysis.* Chicago: University of Chicago Press.

Reskin, Barbara. 1993. "Sex Segregation in the Workplace." *Annual Review of Sociology* 19: 241–70.

Reskin, Barbara F., and Patricia A. Roos. 1990. *Job Queues, Gender Queues: Explaining Women's Inroads into Male Occupations.* Philadelphia: Temple University Press.

Saxenian, AnnaLee. 1994. *Regional Advantage: Culture and Competition in Silicon Valley and Route 128.* Cambridge, Mass.: Harvard University Press.

StataCorp. 1999. *Stata Statistical Software: Release 6.0.* College Station, Tex.: Stata Corporation.

Walton, Richard E. 1985. "From Control to Commitment in the Workplace." *Harvard Business Review* 63: 76–84.

= Chapter 11 =

Intimate Transactions

VIVIANA A. ZELIZER

T RANSFERS of money, far from occurring in an impersonal world, regularly depend on and define intimate social relations. Consider the 1971 precedent-setting tax case of *Pascarelli v. Commissioner* (55 T.C. 1082). Lillian Pascarelli, the petitioner, had lived with Anthony DeAngelis for many years, but they had never married. During their time together DeAngelis transferred substantial sums of money to Pascarelli. She, meanwhile, "did his washing and cleaning, bought clothing for him, and performed wifely duties." Pascarelli's collaboration went further: she actively entertained DeAngelis's business associates at their shared home and took their wives out dining and shopping.

The Internal Revenue Service claimed that the money received by Pascarelli during those years was compensation for services, therefore taxable income. The Tax Court, however, noted that "the petitioner and Mr. DeAngelis had a very close personal relationship, and the services that she performed with respect to entertainment of his business associates were done in a spirit of cooperation similar to that which might prompt a wife to perform such duties to aid her husband in his business pursuits, and not for the purpose of obtaining compensation." "Mr. DeAngelis's dominant reasons for transferring the funds to the petitioner," the court concluded, "were love and affection and disinterested generosity." The court also noted special features of Pascarelli and DeAngelis's cohabitation. Because of her teenage children, they slept in separate bedrooms in the house, but when traveling together, "they stayed as man and wife."

The Tax Court finally ruled that the monetary transfers were gifts, not compensation for services.

A contrasting 1977 case, *Jones v. Commissioner* (T.C. memo, 329), considered the monies transferred by "James," a married grandfather, to the petitioner, Lyna Kathryn Jones, a bartender and cocktail waitress. Jones met James at Fan and Bill's Restaurant in Atlanta. They had sex in his hotel room, and he gave her cash. For the next year, each time James visited Atlanta they got together, and he gave Jones not only money and also gifts of clothing but even a $450 ring as a Christmas present. Claiming that the money she received from James was a gift, Jones did not report it as taxable income. To claims that she was a prostitute and that James was simply one of her many clients, Jones countered at trial that "after she established her relationship with James, she was a 'kept woman' and did not practice prostitution."

The Tax Court dismissed as irrelevant the accusations of prostitution, noting that regardless of her occupation, the monies she received from James could not be considered gifts: "James gave this cash to petitioner because petitioner had sexual relations with him when he was in Atlanta. . . . James did not give money to petitioner from feelings of 'affection, respect, admiration charity or like impulses.'" "Indeed," the court noted, "petitioner herself testified that James 'was getting his money's worth.'" The Tax Court found therefore that James's payments were compensation for services, not gifts.

The courts ruled that these two cases were different. But why? In both episodes, unmarried persons maintained intimate relations over a long period of time, and the man gave the woman money. Yet the courts found that in the first case the monetary transfers qualified as gifts, while in the second they qualified as compensation for services.

Look closely. Despite the common supposition that the law judges individual action and intent, and despite the courts' concessions to the language of intention, decisions in these precedent-setting cases did not turn on what actions the principals actually performed, with what conscious intentions they performed them, or even whether the law condoned such actions. Judges and lawyers appear to have agreed on those matters. The decisions hinged instead on characterizations of relationships between the principals: husband-wife, client-prostitute, employer-employee, master-servant, paramour-mistress, or something else. Just as an observer who watches a woman pass a twenty-dollar bill to a man cannot tell whether the monetary transfer is a tip, a bribe, wages, an allowance, a routine purchase, or some other sort of payment without first ascertaining the pair's relationship, courts cannot decide whether the transfers in these cases constituted gifts, entitlements, or compensation until they determined the prevailing relationship between the principals. The ruling in *Commissioner v. Duberstein* (363 U.S. 278, 285, 1960) had long since made the donor's intent crucial to acceptance of a transfer as a gift. Hence, the courts found themselves translating from observations on relationships into the language of individual intent. Courts make similar determinations all the time when sorting out transactions between public officials, contractors, and members of firms.

Yet in these cases the combination of intimacy and monetary transfers makes that very determination perplexing for the law. The cases were perplexing because of the deep, if often implicit, presumption that money and intimacy belong in separate spheres. The courts divide relationships according to some very powerful principles. Some intimate relations are "meretricious": they consist essentially of exchanging sensual satisfaction for money. Other intimate transactions belong to the quite separate world of legitimate affection. Here monetary transfers qualify as proper gifts. The distinction rests on a sharp boundary between two different worlds.

The law courts are simply borrowing from a much larger set of dichotomies. Like giraffes returning to the same old water hole, since the nineteenth century social analysts have repeatedly assumed that the social world organizes around competing, incompatible principles: Gemeinschaft and Gesellschaft, ascription and achievement, sentiment and rationality, solidarity and self-interest. Their mixing, goes the theory, contaminates both; invasion of the sentimental world by instrumental rationality desiccates that world, while introduction of sentiment into rational transactions produces inefficiency, favoritism, cronyism, and other forms of corruption. The water of that particular hole often causes intellectual indigestion—for example, indefensible assumptions that unregulated labor markets generate optimal outcomes for all their participants. Nevertheless, social analysts—including economic sociologists—recurrently stick out their necks and drink tainted water.

Nowhere has the assumption of incompatible principles done more damage than in the analysis of intimate social relations. Explicitly or implicitly, most analysts of intimate social relations join ordinary people in assuming that the entry of instrumental means such as monetization and cost accounting into the worlds of caring, friendship, sexuality, parent-child relations, and personal information depletes them of their richness—hence that zones of intimacy only thrive if people erect effective barriers around them. Thus emerges a view of "Hostile Worlds": of properly segregated domains whose sanitary management requires well-maintained boundaries.

Uncomfortable with such dualisms and eager to forward single-principle accounts of social life, opponents of Hostile-Worlds views have now and then countered with reductionist "Nothing-But" arguments: the ostensibly separate world of intimate social relations is nothing but a special case of some general principle. Nothing-But advocates divide among three principles: nothing but economic rationality, nothing but culture, and nothing but politics. Thus, for economic reductionists, caring, friendship, sexuality, and parent-child relations become special cases of rationalizing individual choice under conditions of constraint—in short, of economic rationality. For cultural reductionists, such phenomena become expressions of distinct beliefs. Others insist on the political, coercive, and exploitative bases of the same phenomena.

Neither Hostile-Worlds formulations nor Nothing-But reductionisms deal adequately with the intersection of intimate social ties and ordering institutions such as money, markets, bureaucracies, and specialized associations. Careful observers of such institutions always report the presence, and often the wild profusion, of intimate ties in their midst. To describe and explain what actually goes on in these regards, we must move beyond Hostile-Worlds and Nothing-But ideas to the analysis of "Differentiated Ties": recognition that in all sorts of social settings people differentiate strongly between different kinds of interpersonal relations, marking them with distinctive names, symbols, practices, and media of exchange. Such differentiated ties compound into distinctive circuits, each incorporating somewhat different understandings, practices, information, obligations, rights, symbols, and media of exchange.

Differentiated ties form in all arenas of social life, including schools, armies, churches, corporations, and voluntary associations. Since Hostile-Worlds and Nothing-But formulations have most often caused confusion in the analysis of intimate transactions, let me concentrate here on issues raised by caring, friendship, sexuality, and parent-child relations. For intimate transactions, here is my overall argument:

- Neither Hostile-Worlds nor Nothing-But accounts adequately describe, much less explain, the actual working of intimate transactions.

- Intimate transactions work through Differentiated Ties, which participants mark off from each other through well-established practices, understandings, and representations.

- Such differentiated ties compound into distinctive circuits, each incorporating somewhat different understandings, practices, information, obligations, rights, symbols, idioms, and media of exchange.

- Far from determining the nature of interpersonal relationships, the media of exchange (including legal tenders) incorporated into such circuits take on particular connections with the understandings, practices, information, obligations, rights, symbols, and idioms embedded in those circuits.

- Indeed, participants in such circuits characteristically reshape exchange media to mark distinctions between different kinds of social relations.

- Each circuit maintains a distinctive network pattern and set of enforcement practices—hence a characteristic form of trust.

- Movement from one relation or circuit to another—for example, in the passage from relations within households to transactions in courts of law—therefore poses a serious problem of translation for all participants.

- In the course of such translations, participants actually construct and deploy Hostile-Worlds and Nothing-But theories concerning the relations in question.

- Hence, analysts should not simply dismiss Hostile-Worlds and Nothing-But theories; they should make the creation and deployment of such theories objects of systematic explanation.

This chapter concentrates on documenting only the first two parts of this argument: the limitations of Hostile-Worlds and Nothing-But arguments, and the desirability of developing a third Differentiated-Ties approach. To do so, it identifies parallel difficulties in these regards within three apparently distinct literatures: economic sociology, legal philosophy, and feminist arguments. It argues that the normative theses of legal philosophy and feminism depend in part on descriptive and explanatory theses they often share with economic sociology. Improvement of economic sociology's descriptive and explanatory accounts of intimate social ties can therefore advance the normative work of legal theory and feminism.

Money and Intimacy

By now the idea that money acts as a universalizing, standardizing medium has taken hard blows. Social scientists, social critics, and ordinary economic actors all recognize as a practical matter—if not necessarily as a matter of principle—that food stamps, subway tokens, local currencies, and commercial paper all qualify somehow as varieties of money but circulate within restricted circuits rather than merging into a single, homogeneous medium. Nevertheless, a closely related idea dies hard: that money and intimacy represent contradictory principles whose intersection generates conflict, confusion, and corruption. Thus, people debate passionately the propriety of paid surrogate motherhood, the sale of blood, the purchase of child care or elderly care, and wages for housewives.

What is surprising about such debates is their usual failure to recognize how regularly intimate social transactions coexist with monetary transactions: parents pay nannies or child care workers to attend to their children; adoptive parents pay money to obtain babies; divorced spouses pay or receive alimony and child support; parents give their children allowances, subsidize their college educations, help them with their first mortgage, and offer them substantial bequests in their wills. Friends and relatives send gifts of money as wedding presents, and friends loan each other money. Immigrants dispatch remittances to kinfolk back home.

Collectively, such intimate transactions are not trivial. They have large macroeconomic consequences, for example, in generating large flows of remittances from rich countries to poor countries, and in transmitting wealth from one generation to the next. As the intergenerational transmission of wealth illustrates, furthermore, intimate transactions also create or sustain large-scale inequalities by class, race, ethnicity, and even gender.

The secret is to match the right sort of payment with the social transaction at hand. That matching depends strongly on the definition of more general ties among the parties. Indeed, the meanings and consequences of ostensibly similar monetary transfers such as allowances, remittances, fees, bribes, tips, repayments, charity, and occasional gifts emerge only from identification of the social ties in question. All these payments, and more, commonly occur in the company of intimate transactions, take their meanings from the longer-term social ties within which those transactions occur, and vary in consequences as a function of those longer-term ties—the limiting and exceptional case being the tie defined as no more than momentary.

In this chapter, intimate transactions include all those social interchanges that depend on extensive trust. Negatively, trust gives one person knowledge or attention of the other that, if made widely available, would damage the second person's social standing. Positively, trust entails deep, immediate influence of one person's injunctions over a second person's actions and emotions in the face of risk, but without the exercise of threat. Trust in either sense is often asymmetrical—for example, a young child trusts its parent more than the parent trusts the child—but fully intimate relations involve mutual trust. (For a survey and synthesis of trust's place in social structure, see Barber 1983.)

The range of intimate transactions includes bodily care, sexual relations, emotional management, the sharing of knowledge about malfeasance, and personal protection. Relations commonly hosting intimate transactions obviously include parent-child, siblings, spouses, lovers, and friends, but also include prostitute-client, spy–object of espionage, psychiatrist-patient, and child care worker–client. Each of these relations, and each major type of transaction within each relation, generates its own forms of monetary transfers and creates its own circuits within which certain meaningfully different forms of money circulate. (For a clear statement of the assertion that such circuits emerge from small-scale social interactions, see Collins 2000.) Those circumstances create formidable problems of description and explanation for economic sociologists, legal scholars, feminist critics, and other observers of social processes. So long as observers imagine that money is unitary, homogenizing, and perfectly transparent, those problems remain intractable.

Echoing the great dichotomies, analysts of money and intimacy have recurrently formulated the idea of "Hostile Worlds." In this view, a sharp divide exists between personal ties and monetary transfers, making any contact between the two spheres morally contaminating. Consider as just one instance of this perspective Robert Kuttner's (1997) provocative analysis of contemporary markets. "As the market vogue has gained force," worries Kuttner in *Everything for Sale*, "realms that used to be tempered by extra-market norms and institutions are being marketized with accelerating force" (55). This "relentless encroachment of the market and its values," Kuttner claims, "turns the shallow picture of economic man into a self-fulfilling prophecy" (57).

As if to bid up Kuttner's already extreme position, activist-critic Jeremy Rifkin (2000) argues that the world of "hypercapitalism," with its instantaneous transfers of money and information, is accelerating and aggravating the substitution of market transactions for genuine human relationships. "If there is an Achilles' heel to the new age," he declares,

> it probably lies in the misguided belief that commercially directed relationships and electronically mediated relationships can substitute for traditional relationships and communities. The premise itself is deeply flawed. The two ways of organizing human activity flow from very different sets of assumptions and values, making them irreconcilable

rather than analogous. Traditional relationships are born of such things as kinship, ethnicity, geography, and shared spiritual visions. They are glued together by notions of reciprocal obligations and visions of common destinies. They are sustained by communities whose mission it is to reproduce and continually secure the shared meanings that make up the common culture. Both the relationships and the communities are regarded as ends.

Commodified relationships, on the other hand, are instrumental in nature. The only glue that holds them together is the agreed-upon transaction price. The relationships are contractual rather than reciprocal in nature. They are sustained by networks of shared interests for as long as the parties involved continue to honor their contractual obligations (241).

Hostile-Worlds doctrines are alive and well in the twenty-first century. Some scholars, however, are impatient with such ominous Hostile-Worlds dichotomies. They have often turned instead to Nothing-But analyses of three sorts: one arguing that intimate relations are nothing but exchange relations of a special sort; another arguing that intimate relations are nothing but straightforward expressions of general values or ideological scripts, regardless of what economic connection they may entail; and a third arguing that intimate relations are nothing but the outcome of political processes.

In social science as a whole, economic reductionism has provided the most coherent and powerful challenge to Hostile-Worlds views. Let me therefore concentrate on the economic alternative (for cultural and political approaches, see, for example, Barry 1995; Butler 1990, 1993; Chapkis 1997; Hartman 1981; Hochschild 1983; Laqueur 1990; Rubin 1975). In that category we have the example of Richard Posner (1992), who in the tradition of Gary Becker claims the equivalence of all transfers as rational quid-pro-quo exchanges. Take away any cultural camouflage, such Nothing-But theorists maintain, and we will find that intimate transfers—be they of sex, babies, or blood—operate according to principles identical to those that govern transfers of stock shares or used cars. Consider how Posner, champion of the influential "law-and-economics" paradigm and a pioneer in its extension to the analysis of sexuality, justifies the "feasibility and fruitfulness" of an economic approach to sexuality:

The effort may seem quixotic, for it is a commonplace that sexual passion belongs to the domain of the irrational; but it is a false commonplace. One does not will sexual appetite—but one does not will hunger either. The former fact no more excludes the possibility of an economics of sexuality than the latter excludes the possibility of an economics of agriculture. (4–5)

Similarly, David Friedman (2000, 172) another law-and-economics enthusiast, explains why long-term contracts work as efficiently for marriage as for business:

> Once a couple has been married for a while, they have made a lot of relationship-specific investments, borne costs that will produce a return only if they remain together. Each has become, at considerable cost, an expert on how to get along with the other. Both have invested, materially and emotionally, in their joint children. Although they started out on a competitive market, they are now locked into a bilateral monopoly with associated bargaining costs.

Thus, law-and-economics analysts argue that markets provide efficient solutions, and efficient solutions exhaust the legal problems posed by intimacy. Intimate relations, in this view, pose the same problems of choice within constraints as ordinary market transactions.

Not only economic but also cultural and political Nothing-But counters to Hostile-Worlds views, however, have increasingly come under attack. For the past twenty years or so, social scientists, legal scholars, and feminist advocates—from very different perspectives and in deplorable isolation from each other—have been seeking more persuasive accounts of economic processes that avoid both Hostile-Worlds and Nothing-But explanations. Within each of these fields— economic sociology, legal theory focused on economic process, and feminist analysis concerned with gender inequality—Hostile-Worlds views once prevailed, Nothing-But arguments arose to counter them, but more recently alternative accounts of Differentiated Ties have begun to emerge. Let us turn first to economic sociology.

Sociological Uncertainties

Sociologists have long wavered between Hostile-Worlds and Nothing-But accounts of economic processes. The Hostile-Worlds view rested on a sharp division between economy and society, with the one embodying impersonal rationality and the other intimate sentimentality. Such theorists as Talcott Parsons saw sociology as providing the normative and social context for markets but assumed economic and personal spheres were highly differentiated from each other and operated on the basis of contradictory principles. Writing in 1978, while attempting to articulate the relationship between family and market,

Parsons drew on familiar polarities: "The prototypical institution of the modern economy is the market, but inside the family anything too much like market relationships, especially competitive ones, are, if not totally excluded, very significantly limited" (1978, 15).

As economic sociology grew into a self-defined specialty, it implicitly accepted such divisions between a market sphere and a non-economic sphere. However, economic sociologists began to consider the social structure that underlay what they continued to regard as a semi-autonomous economic sphere. This led people into a variety of Nothing-But explanations. Although, as in studies of consumption and household economies, both cultural and political reductionism have abounded, within self-defined economic sociology economic reductionism has been most common. Nothing-But economic arguments appear in the assimilation of a wide variety of social processes into something resembling the neoclassical paradigm of individual choice within constraints.

More recently, economic sociologists have worked hard to move beyond Hostile-Worlds and Nothing-But economic reductionism. They do so by treating economic processes and behavioral assumptions—such as markets, rationality, or self-interest—as products of underlying social processes. As Harrison White (1988, 232) puts it, market activity is "intensely social—as social as kinship networks or feudal armies." Other contributions to this book demonstrate that tendency abundantly. Yet, as my own other contribution (chapter 5) says at greater length, current economic sociology has not yet fully relinquished its Hostile-Worlds tradition. The field, as we have seen, repeatedly focuses on firms and corporations, allegedly "true" markets, while relegating other forms of economic activity—such as gift transfers, informal economies, households, and consumption—to a non-market world.

Scholars who are developing alternative views have nevertheless provided more radical departures from standard treatments of intimate economies, in several ways: first, by expanding the definition of work; second, by shifting the emphasis to recognition of differentiated social ties; third, by looking at the actual content of transactions among economic actors; and fourth, by locating cultural content within those very transactions instead of treating them as external constraints.

Chris Tilly and Charles Tilly (1998, 22), for instance, define work in ways that directly challenge the Hostile-Worlds split vision: "Work," the Tillys declare emphatically, "includes any human effort adding use value to goods and services." "Only a prejudice bred by Western capitalism and its industrial labor markets," they tell us, "fixes on strenuous effort expended for money payment outside the home as 'real work,' relegating other efforts to amusement, crime, and mere housekeeping." "Work's many worlds," therefore, include employment for wages but also unpaid domestic labor, barter, petty commodity production, and volunteer work.

Paul DiMaggio and Hugh Louch's (1998) analysis of consumer behavior illustrates the second shift toward recognizing differentiated social ties. As they survey preexisting noncommercial ties between buyers and sellers in consumer transactions involving the purchase of cars, homes, and legal and home repair services, DiMaggio and Louch find a remarkably high incidence of what they call "within-network" exchanges. A substantial number of such transactions take place not through impersonal markets but among kin, friends, or acquaintants. Noting that this pattern applies primarily to risky one-shot transactions involving high uncertainty about quality and performance, DiMaggio and Louch conclude that consumers are more likely to rely on such noncommercial ties when they are unsure about the outcome.

Looking at the actual content of transactions among economic actors, Nicole Woolsey Biggart (1989) observes the operation of intimate ties within direct selling organizations. Companies such as Amway, Tupperware, or Mary Kay Cosmetics, far from introducing narrow, professionalized relations, rely on intimate social networks for merchandising their products. Close relatives—spouses, mothers, daughters, sisters, brothers, cousins, or nephews—sponsor each other into the organization. Moreover, direct selling is perceived as strengthening marriage and family bonds. Blue-collar women, Biggart observed, often define direct selling "as a sideline and not a 'real job.' They can have the happy combination of making money and being an 'at home' mother." Biggart reports a revealing statement by a Tupperware dealer:

> I was driving my son and four friends to a birthday party, and I heard them talking in the back about their moms working. And one of the kids says, "Say, does your mommy work?" And he goes, "No." That's what I want. I don't want them to think I work. They don't even think that I have a job because I'm not gone from eight to five. (82)

Ironically, as they break down the reality, participants themselves recreate the mythology of hostile worlds.

What about cultural content? My own analysis of monetary transfers locates cultural content within social ties rather than seeing them as external. For example, the crucial distinctions between gifts, compensation, and entitlements show how people differentiate forms of payments in correspondence with their definitions of the sort of relationship that exists between the parties. They adopt symbols, rituals, practices, and physically distinguishable forms of money to mark distinct social relations and forms of monetary transfers (see Zelizer 1994).

Economic sociologists studying intersections of monetary transfers and intimate ties, in short, long hesitated between Hostile-Worlds and Nothing-But formulations. They never arrived at a satisfactory adjudication between such views because the social reality in question requires not a choice between the two but their transcendence. Recognition of differentiated ties, each involving distinctive forms of payment, offers an exit from the impasse.

Legal Debates

Legal scholars share some of the concerns and difficulties of economic sociologists. Reacting against a long-standing Hostile-Worlds tradition, a number of critics and theorists have challenged the two-spheres model. With Posner, we already saw one attempt to get rid of a Hostile-Worlds view by replacing it with a Nothing-But economic alternative. The law-and-economics approach, as Dan Kahan (1999, 1) describes it,

> presents a comprehensive theory of legal rules founded on the rational actor model. Descriptively, it posits individuals who react to legal incentives in a manner rationally calculated to maximize their material well-being. Normatively, it appraises legal rules according to their contribution to social wealth. And prescriptively, it presents a programmatic collection of maxims and algorithms deigned to make the law efficient.

In recent years a number of legal scholars have reacted against this extraordinarily influential economistic paradigm. In some cases, scholars have returned to a Hostile-Worlds argument, insisting that there are some ranges of social behavior that commodification does corrupt after all. Others have moved toward cultural reductionism by emphasizing social norms, meanings, and values as an alternative to economic rationality. Still others have begun to formulate more substantial institutional and relational accounts as competitors of the economic narrowness of the law-and-economics paradigm.

Legal scholars can hardly avoid a fact that challenges extreme versions of both Hostile-Worlds and Nothing-But arguments: for all their

Hostile-Worlds rhetoric, in practice courts frequently engage in monetary evaluation of intimate ties. They do so in divorce settlements, premarital agreements, breach-of-promise suits, and compensation for death or disability of close kin. In none of these cases do courts actually adopt a strict market criterion of value. (For fuller discussion of this issue, see Zelizer 2000; for legal practice, see also Estin 1995; Horsburgh 1992; Silbaugh 1996.)

For instance, in their analysis of tort compensation for pain and suffering, Steven Crowley and Jon Hanson (1995) contest the dominant view put forth by legal economists that such awards should be eliminated since no consumer demand exists for nonpecuniary losses. Using an array of empirical evidence—including parents' insurance of their children—Crowley and Hanson argue that consumers are in fact prepared to quantify personal losses even when not incurring financial injury. To explain the relatively thin market for insurance against pain and suffering despite such consumer demand, Crowley and Hanson rely on the effect of social norms discouraging such transactions. Even more significantly, they show how contextual variation redefines the meaning and legitimacy of contested economic transfers. Children's insurance, for instance, sold more successfully as investment than death insurance. Tort compensation, despite drawing explicit monetary equivalences for nonpecuniary losses, is legitimized, possibly because the monetary award is seen not as replacing but as assuaging a sentimental loss.

Instead of surveying the entire tumultuous debate, let us concentrate on how these legal analysts handle the economic valuation of intimate social relations, a problem that has preoccupied them far more than it has economic sociologists.

Consider legal philosopher Margaret Jane Radin's (1996) widely known arguments. Beginning with a critique of both Posner-like "universal commodification" theories and Hostile-Worlds accounts, Radin in the last instance returns to a modified version of the latter view. In her *Contested Commodities,* Radin proposes a body of law that would regulate and distinguish the zone she calls incomplete commodification—where "the values of personhood and community pervasively interact with the market and alter many things from their pure free-market form" (114). As Radin states clearly, this zone includes instances of commodified sexual relations and parent-child ties. In her model, "payment in exchange for sexual intercourse," along with "payment in exchange for relinquishing a child for adoption," are "nodal cases of contested commodification" (131).

Sexual relations, she argues, "may have both market and non-market aspects: relationships may be entered into and sustained partly for economic reasons and partly for the interpersonal sharing that is part of our ideal of human flourishing" (134). However, despite her insistence on the interaction of culture and law as well as her well-taken objections to what she calls the "domino" theory of commodification, Radin implies that "complete commodification" would occur with monetization in the absence of institutional—especially legal—protections. In the case of prostitution, for instance, while she advocates the decriminalization of the sale of sexual services, she also insists that "in order to check the domino effect," the law should prohibit "the free-market entrepreneurship" that would tag along with decriminalization and "could operate to create an organized market in sexual services." Different forms of regulation—including a ban on advertising—are necessary, she concludes, "if we accept that extensive permeation of our discourse by commodification-talk would alter sexuality in a way that we are unwilling to countenance" (135–36).

When it comes to baby markets, ranging from what she calls "commissioned adoptions" and surrogacy to "paid adoption of 'unwanted' children," Radin wavers even more visibly. Although baby giving may in fact constitute an act of "admirable altruism," both toward the baby's and the adoptive parents' welfare, baby selling would put that altruism in question. Radin concedes that in principle babies could belong to a zone of "incomplete commodification," with "coexistent commodified and noncommodified internal rhetorical structures," allowing altruism along with sales (139). But once again, as with prostitution, she fears the ultimate dominance of market discourse. "If a free-market baby industry were to come into being," Radin predicts,

> how could any of us, even those who did not produce infants for sale, avoid measuring the dollar value of our children? How could our children avoid being preoccupied with measuring their own dollar value? This measurement makes our discourse about ourselves (when we are children) and about our children (when we are parents) like our discourse about cars. (138)

While Radin comes close to rejecting the Hostile-Worlds dichotomy, in the last instance she hesitates.

Similarly, Margaret Brinig (2000) recognizes the weaknesses of both Hostile-Worlds and Nothing-But formulations, yet hesitates to specify what lies beyond them. She directly confronts the standard legal treatment of intimate family relations. We cannot, she argues, make wholesale transfers of commercially rooted concepts of market, firm, and contract to the sphere of family interactions. While conceding that a contract or market model might be usefully applied to the formative stage of family relationships, as in courtship and adoption, Brinig contends that the model fails to accommodate ongoing family ties. Most notably, contract law "does not have the right concepts or language to treat love, trust, faithfulness, and sympathy, which more than any other terms describe the essentials of family" (3). Struggling to move beyond an orthodox Nothing-But economism, Brinig often veers toward traditional Hostile-Worlds polarities, declaring:

> Marriages, or at least most marriages, are not like these contracts or Chicago School law and economics efficiency-seeking venturers. When marriages are good, they involve self-sacrifice, sharing, and other-regarding behavior, perhaps a more "feminine" view of the universe. They are relationships, not just relational contracts. . . . As a society we have tremendous incentives to promote the noncontractual, non-market view of marriage. (18)

Brinig moves cautiously, however, toward less dualistic or reductionist paradigms. To replace the monistic contract model, she distinguishes between contracts and covenants: the first are restricted to "legally enforceable agreements," and the latter to "agreements enforced not by law so much as by individuals and their social organizations" (1). Covenant, Brinig further specifies, "is a compact or promise that cannot easily be broken even if one side does not perform fully or satisfactorily. It thus has durability beyond that of many firms and far beyond the time horizon of the market, where a transaction may be entirely episodic or discrete" (6). Such covenants—especially applicable to husband and wife and to parent and child relations—imply not only "unconditional love and permanence" but third-party involvement, such as God, the community, or both.

Brinig never quite specifies the differences in relations or transactions that characterize what she calls contracts and covenants. She declares:

> Although the classical theory of the firm gives us some valuable insights into marriage, it falls short in part because of the special characteristics of marriages, primarily intimacy and privacy. It may tell us why a continual stream of contracts will not work in the context of marriage, and even why people marry, but not why in the most successful of marriages each spouse will gladly contribute without "counting the cost." Here the new institutional economics does far better. Through stressing transaction costs, the new institutional economics approaches the idea of covenant and the broader community concerns about marriage. (109)

Extended only slightly, however, Brinig's covenant and contract distinction conveys not just polarities but appropriate ways of representing social relations.

Like Radin and Brinig, legal theorist Cass Sunstein (1997) is trying
to find a superior analytic position somewhere between Hostile-
Worlds and Nothing-But economic reductionism. Sunstein and other
proponents of what Lawrence Lessig (1998) calls the "New Chicago
School" of law, are paying close attention to social meanings and
norms (in addition to Kahan 1999, see Lessig 1995,1996, 1998).

More specifically, in his *Free Markets and Social Justice*, Sunstein
(1997, 36) insists "we should agree that social norms play a part in
determining choices; that people's choices are a function of their particular social role; and that the social or expressive meaning of acts is
an ingredient in choice." Noting that economics "at least as it is used
in the conventional economic analysis of law often works with tools
that, while illuminating, may be crude or lead to important errors"
(4), Sunstein challenges economistic accounts of human motivation
and valuation. Sharply critical of "monistic" legal theories of value,
Sunstein makes a compelling argument for the multiplicity and incommensurability of human values, such as the distinction between
instrumental and intrinsic values attached to goods or activities (on
issues of commensurability, see Espeland and Stevens 1998).

When it comes to the economic valuation of intimacy, Sunstein's
notion of norm-determined incommensurability marks a sharp cultural divide between financial and intimate exchanges. He notes that,
"if someone asks an attractive person (or a spouse) for sexual relations in return for cash," the offer would be insulting, as it reflects "an
improper conception of what the relationship is" (75). As Sunstein
explains:

> The objection to commodification should be seen as a special case of the
> general problem of diverse kinds of valuation. The claim is that we
> ought not to trade . . . sexuality or reproductive capacities on markets
> because economic valuation of these "things" is inconsistent with and
> may even undermine their appropriate kind (not level) of valuation.
> (76)

Yet Sunstein opens a significant wedge in his analysis. While on
the one hand, he endorses the view that some kinds of transactions,
including intimate ones, are utterly incompatible with the market—
hence incompatible with monetary transfers—he also acknowledges
that markets and monetary transfers can accommodate multiple systems of valuation. Markets, Sunstein points out, "are filled with

agreements to transfer goods that are not valued simply for use. People . . . buy human care for their children. . . . They purchase pets for whom they feel affection or even love." Therefore:

> The objection to the use of markets in certain areas must depend on the view that markets will have adverse effects on existing kinds of valuation, and it is not a simple matter to show when and why this will be the case. For all these reasons, opposition to commensurability, and insistence on diverse kinds of valuation, do not by themselves amount to opposition to market exchange, which is pervaded by choice among goods that participants value in diverse ways. (98)

In the same way, he agrees that money, rather than necessarily flattening goods and relations, is itself socially differentiated: "Social norms make for qualitative differences among human goods, and these qualitative differences are matched by ingenious mental operations involving qualitative differences among different 'kinds' of money" (41). Although at first Sunstein seems to have responded to Nothing-But "law and economics" with a Nothing-But cultural alternative, he moves on to a much more sophisticated analysis of social relations.

As in economic sociology, legal scholars who long struggled unsuccessfully to adjudicate between Hostile-Worlds and Nothing-But doctrines are moving toward an examination of differentiation in connections between intimate ties and monetary transfers. More clearly than in economic sociology, however, legal scholarship brings out the dependence of consequential and hard-fought normative positions on descriptive and explanatory accounts. Hence the desirability of knowing collaboration between sociologists and legal scholars. The same sorts of controversies and opportunities appear in recent feminist discussions of intimate relations.

Feminist Alternatives

The feminist literature raises many issues similar to those considered in the literatures of economic sociology, the law of economic relations, and legal philosophy. It is likewise subject to division between Hostile-Worlds and Nothing-But analyses, and therefore susceptible to clarification through examination of Differentiated Ties. Let us concentrate on two overlapping themes in this literature: first, the issue of just compensation, and second, the economics of care.

Feminist legal scholars have taken the lead in challenging and subverting long-standing Hostile-Worlds legal principles, claiming that separation of spheres fundamentally undermines women's interests. Turning traditional women's work exclusively into a matter of sentiment dangerously obscures its economic value. American courts, these scholars argue, have long collaborated in such disentitlement.

Carol Rose (1994), for instance, has offered a powerful critique of Hostile-Worlds reasoning in the legal sphere. Pointing out that property transfers occur extensively within households and that property relations outside of households rest on elaborate social connections, Rose rejects conventional boundaries: "There is no 'In-Here' of family and 'Out-There' of work. . . . These spheres interact incessantly" (2417). The traditional "rhetoric of sharing and nurturance," she warns, builds the illusion that "property questions stop at the homestead door. They don't" (2414). Only by addressing such questions will we achieve gender equality both during marriage and after divorce: "When we see the unspoken property within arrangements that masquerade as 'sharing,' we can also see their injustice and hypocrisy. It is only when we neglect the property aspects of marriage that we dub as 'equal' relationships that may be profoundly hierarchical" (2415). Courts, however, strongly resist treating family disputes as matters of property, as Rose points out, and typically ignore, for instance, the economic contributions of women's household labor.

Indeed, as Reva Siegel (1994) amply documents, splitting the family and market spheres took painstaking legal effort. Focusing on nineteenth-century debates over the valuation of household labor, Siegel shows how courts carefully kept that labor as nonmarket exchange. As earning statutes increasingly gave wives a right to income from their "personal labor" for third parties, they consistently excluded the household labor performed for her husband or family. Courts, Siegel tells us, "refused to enforce interspousal contracts for household labor, reasoning that such contracts would transform the marriage relationship into a market relationship" (2139–40). Thus, courts assumed and defended Hostile Worlds. Their strategy worked. More than a century later, as Siegel notes,

> we live in a world in which unwaged labor in the home stands as an anomaly lacking explanation but not requiring one either. In this world it takes an act of critical scrutiny to discern that market relations have been systematically delimited—and that labor vital to their support is, with equal systematicity, expropriated from women on an ongoing basis. (2210)

Similarly unmasking what she calls "commodification anxiety," Joan Williams (2000, 118) argues that "the fear of a world sullied by commodification of intimate relationships feeds opposition to granting wives' entitlements based on household work." More radically departing from Hostile-Worlds views than Margaret Jane Radin, Williams notes that, along with other legal experts in commodification, Radin ignores that "women's key problem has been too little commodification, not too much."

Williams calls attention to the arbitrary gendering of commodification that goes on in divorce settlements. As a result of what she calls the "he-who-earns-it-owns-it" rule, husbands typically are awarded a greater share of marital property. The prevailing Hostile-Worlds assumption that "family work is an expression of love" (120), Williams remarks, disregards that family work is also labor. Williams gives the crucial example of "degree cases" where wives at divorce claim compensation for having financed their husband's professional degree. She reports courts' hostility to such requests, in ways that directly parallel the nineteenth-century decisions cited by Siegel. In one 1988 West Virginia case, for instance, the court declared that "characterizing spousal contributions as an investment in each other as human assets, demeans the concept of marriage" (117).

Determined to undo such prejudicial sentimentality, Williams puts forth remedial policies to achieve just compensation for women. For instance, her joint property proposal would recognize family work as economically valuable, justifying income sharing by spouses after divorce. It would thereby undermine courts' and legislatures' assumption that "men's claims give rise to entitlements while women's claims are treated as charity" (131).

At times Williams's hard-nosed critique of "Hostile Worlds," like Brinig's, edges toward Nothing-But economistic reductionism. Nevertheless, she is careful to distinguish her income-sharing proposals from others that rely on what she sees as "strained analogies to commercial partnership law" (126). In so doing, she begins to recognize differentiation of social ties among such settings as families, firms, markets, and organizations. At the same time, however, she wants a reading of the law in which such relations cast legal shadows that are financially equivalent.

The economics of intimacy is being similarly revisited by a number of other feminist critics concerned with American devaluation of care. (For an introduction to selected social science approaches to caring, see Cancian and Oliker 2000; for related views on regard as an incentive for reciprocity, see Offer 1997.) The parallels with feminist legal scholars are striking and not coincidental. Hostile-Worlds assumptions that see love and care as demeaned by monetization, analysts of personal care contend, may in fact lead to economic discrimination against those allegedly intangible caring activities. As sociologist Paula England and economist Nancy Folbre (1999, 46) point out: "The principle that money cannot buy love may have the unintended and perverse consequence of perpetuating low pay for face-to-face service work." Noting that typically it is women who are expected to provide caring labor, we should suspect, they warn, "any argument that decent pay demeans a noble calling" (48).

With the aging of the baby boom generation, and as most mothers in the United States participate in paid work, the care of children, the elderly, and the sick is being thrust onto the national political agenda. In a *Nation* editorial, Deborah Stone (2000, 13) declares: "We have the Bill of Rights and we have civil rights. Now we need a Right to Care, and it's going to take a movement to get it." Noting both the emotional strains and professional constraints of informal caregivers, as well as the systematic economic exploitation of underpaid formal caregivers, Stone insists: "We need a movement to demonstrate that caring is not a free resource, that caring is hard and skilled work, that it takes time and devotion, and that people who do it are making sacrifices."

As they struggle for practical solutions, feminist analysts are directly confronting the constraints imposed by Hostile-Worlds ideologies. If payment corrupts intimacy, how should care be compensated? Should the state subsidize women, the traditional caregivers, to return home? What happens when care is purchased from non-kin? Does caring turn into nothing but impersonal transactions? Increasingly, feminist critics are breaking away from traditional answers to such questions and constructing, along the way, a new ethics of care. Questioning the idealization of unpaid caring, these analysts ponder possibilities and explore actual practices in which payments and care fruitfully coexist. They shift away from rigid certainties about money's corruption to a clear-eyed investigation of both paid and unpaid caring.

As a case in point, consider British feminist economist Susan Himmelweit's (1999, 36) contention that "in practice, it seems that the relationships developed through paid and unpaid care differ less than talk in terms of the rigid dichotomies of 'public and private,' 'paid and unpaid,' and 'market and nonmarket' suggest." Noting that paid caregivers in continuing relationships with recipients of their care often go beyond the call of duty in tending to clients, Himmelweit rejects the assumption that "personal attachments cannot develop in market relationships." "It is not so much," she asserts, "that we are adding an element of the unpaid to the paid but that paid relationships themselves can include strong feelings and personal attachments" (32).

Take, for instance, Deborah Stone's (1999) study of home-care workers in New England. Despite Stone's own ambivalence about her findings, she documents two points of great importance for my argument:

1. A highly bureaucratized monetary payment system for intimate personal care does not by any means produce a cold, dehumanized relationship between caregiver and recipient.

2. Caregivers actually manipulate the payment system to make sure they can provide care appropriate to the relationship.

Deeply concerned with the effects of turning care into a profit-making business, Stone investigated how changes in Medicare and managed care financing restructured caring practices. Interviewing home-care workers, she discovered a payment system that compensates caregivers exclusively for patients' bodily care, not for conversation or other forms of personal attention or assistance. She also discovered, however, that home-care workers do not transform themselves into unfeeling bureaucratic agents, but remain, Stone reports, "keenly aware that home health care is very intimate and very personal" (64).

Almost without exception, for example, the care providers she interviewed—who included nurses, physical and occupational therapists, and home-care aides—reported visiting clients on their days off, often bringing some groceries or helping out in other ways. The agency's warnings against becoming emotionally attached to their clients, aides and nurses told Stone, are unrealistic: "If you're human" or "if you have any human compassion, you just do" (66). To circumvent an inadequate payment system, home-care workers define their additional assistance as friendship or neighborliness. Or they simply manipulate the rules, for instance, by treating other than the officially approved problems and sometimes even attending to the health of a patient's spouse. (For examples of European variation in types of paid care and similar manipulation of payment systems to fit relations, see Ungerson 1995, 2000.) To be sure, as Stone remarks, inadequate payment structures exploit paid caregivers' concern for patients. Her interviews conclusively demonstrate, however, that payment systems do not rule out caring relations.

Economist Julie Nelson forcefully articulates the new skepticism concerning traditional Hostile-World accounts. She locates her critique within a broader revision of mainstream economics. As long as the subject of economics remains "the study of processes by which things—goods, services, financial assets—are exchanged," Nelson (1998a, 44) argues, "most of the traditional non-market activities of women—care of the home, children, sick and elderly relatives, and so on—[will be] considered 'non-economic,' and therefore inappropriate subjects for economic research." The political implications of "backgrounding" care activities (Nelson 1999, 56) are substantial. "In budget discussions," Nelson (1998a, 33) points out, "this means that programs to address problems in these [social] areas tend to be considered secondary—luxuries—and are therefore often postponed and first to be eliminated or scaled back in any time of budget tightening."

The economic-social divide brings with it the further assumption that caring labor should be unpaid or only meagerly rewarded, thus protecting such tasks against the corruption of market exchanges. Nelson (1999, 56) unequivocally rejects such distinctions, insisting that markets and money are profoundly social arrangements, operating "*within* networks of social relationships." Paid care, therefore, is not, as Nelson puts it, "relationally second rate" (1998b, 1470).

Pointing to the child care market as thickly social and relational, Nelson (1998b, 1470) notes that parents or caregivers seldom define that market "as purely an impersonal exchange of money for services. . . . The parties involved engage in extensive personal contact, trust, and interpersonal interaction." "The specter of the all-corrupting market," she argues, "denies that people—such as many child-care providers—can do work they love, among people they love, and get paid at the same time."

Allowing for the social and moral legitimacy of paid care, the feminist agenda stops fretting over whether or not to pay for caring labor, turning its attention instead to the amount and form of payment and to the investigation of actual caring relationships. The problem is not, they discover, whether money is involved, but whether the type of payment system matches the caring relationship. As Nancy Folbre and Julie Nelson (2000, 123–4; see also Folbre 2001) convincingly argue:

An a priori judgment that markets must improve caregiving by increasing efficiency puts the brakes on intelligent research, rather than encourages it. Likewise, an a priori judgment that markets must severely degrade caring work by replacing motivations of altruism with self-interest is also a research stopper. Instead, the increasing intertwining of "love" and "money" brings us the necessity—and the opportunity—for innovative research and action.

To be sure, recent feminist critics were not the first to identify these challenges. Historians have long since documented the nineteenth-century ideology of separate spheres segregating domestic from market worlds (see, for example, Cott 1977; Boydston 1990). Nineteenth-century movements advocating wages for housework moved the issue into practical politics, while developmental psychologists (see, for example, Chodorow 1978; Gilligan 1982) have debated extensively the cognitive gendering of such worlds. Whether stressing just compensation or the economics of care, however, feminist critics of Hostile-Worlds ideology bring out even more clearly than their predecessors both the social construction and the specific political and moral consequences of separate spheres.

Conclusions

Venerable, deeply entrenched dichotomies hinder the analysis of the intersections between economic transactions and intimate personal relations. So long as analysts presume a sharp, consequential distinction between one world of instrumental rationality and another of sentimental solidarity, they will never adequately describe, explain, prescribe, or intervene in sites where intimate ties and economic transactions coincide. A view of all economic transactions as conforming to differentiated ties that vary in degrees and kinds of intimacy points toward an escape from the Hostile-Worlds antinomy as well as the Nothing-But impasse.

In order to examine differentiated ties effectively, economic analysts must rethink the impact of exchange media. Analysts must avoid two pitfalls: first, surreptitiously returning to Hostile-Worlds or Nothing-But formulations by postulating a fundamental distinction between legal tender and all other exchange media; or second, at the other extreme, arguing that all media ultimately resolve into more or less efficient representations of some universal, abstract, perfectly liquid money. Instead, they must recognize that every single medium attaches to some organized circuit of exchange, that each circuit incorporates some institutional structure, shared understandings, practices, and interpersonal relations that set it off from other such circuits. Thus, to choose a medium is not primarily to undergo the influence of the medium as such, but to involve oneself in a particular set of institutional structures, shared understandings, practices, and interpersonal relations. To choose legal tender is not to plunge into the acid bath of instrumental rationality but to involve oneself in a particular circuit that happens to privilege legal tender as its medium.

Economic sociologists, legal theorists, and feminist critics approach intimate transactions from somewhat different angles. Economic sociologists, for the most part, seek to extend, complement, or challenge the account of production, consumption, and exchange already proposed by economists. They therefore divide on whether to exclude intimate transactions as non-economic, reduce them to strictly means-ends calculations, or construct full-fledged alternatives to standard economic accounts. True, Mark Granovetter (this volume) identifies "spheres of exchange" and their breaking as promising subjects for further analysis. Nevertheless, he and other economic sociologists generally concentrate on description and explanation, as compared with the more explicitly normative concerns of legal theorists and feminists.

Legal theorists appropriately seek to fashion legal remedies for what they regard as inefficiencies, inequities, or inaccuracies in current legal assumptions, prescriptions, and practices. Like economic sociologists, they frequently oscillate between Hostile-Worlds and Nothing-But doctrines, both now including prominent prescriptive as well as descriptive and explanatory components. They too have searched in vain for a middle ground between strict dichotomies and strong reductionisms. They too have begun to explore the possibility of formulating a fuller view of Differentiated Ties, and thus of escaping from a theoretical impasse.

A similar sequence has appeared among feminist critics. Although an earlier generation of feminist critics sometimes forwarded their own special version of sharply dichotomized female and male worlds, the critics reviewed here have generally rejected that view as perpetuating gender inequality. They have experimented with various Nothing-But ideas—cultural and political as well as economic. Yet recently they have moved toward more direct consideration of differentiated ties as an alternative to straightforward reductionism. Thus, in all three of these otherwise distinct fields we see similar stirring of relational, deeply sociological ideas.

It may be premature to speak of convergence, much less of synthesis. Yet it is encouraging to see the possibility of a fruitful division of labor. Although effective sociological analysis of intimate ties always raises normative questions, by and large sociologists properly concentrate their efforts on description and explanation. Legal theorists and feminist critics, in contrast, frequently start with normative questions, then work their way into description and explanation. We can easily turn that opposition into collaboration. Every valid normative position rests, however implicitly, on assertions about what exists, why it exists, and what would change it. Every valid description and explanation of social interaction carries some implications for possible normative positions. The study of intimate transactions offers a splendid invitation for confrontation and synthesis.

I have adapted a number of ideas and a few paragraphs from my article "The Purchase of Intimacy," *Law and Social Inquiry* (2000). A French version of this paper appeared as "Transactions intimes" in *Genèses* 42(March 2001): 121–44. For help, advice, and criticism, I am grateful to Paula England, Alexandra Kalev, Julie Nelson, and Charles Tilly.

References

Barber, Bernard. 1983. *The Logic and Limits of Trust*. New Brunswick, N.J.: Rutgers University Press.

Barry, Kathleen. 1995. *The Prostitution of Sexuality*. New York: New York University Press.

Biggart, Nicole Woolsey. 1989. *Charismatic Capitalism*. Chicago: University of Chicago Press.

Boydston, Jeanne. 1990. *Home and Work*. New York: Oxford University Press.

Brinig, Margaret F. 2000. *From Contract to Covenant: Beyond the Law and Economics of the Family*. Cambridge, Mass.: Harvard University Press.

Butler, Judith. 1990. *Gender Trouble*. New York: Routledge.

———. 1993. *Bodies That Matter*. New York: Routledge.

Cancian, Francesca M., and Stacey J. Oliker. 2000. *Caring and Gender*. Thousand Oaks, Calif.: Pine Forge Press.

Chapkis, Wendy. 1997. *Live Sex Acts*. New York: Routledge.

Chodorow, Nancy. 1978. *The Reproduction of Mothering: Psychoanalysis and the Sociology of Gender*. Berkeley: University of California Press.

Collins, Randall. 2000. "Situational Stratification: A Micro-Macro Theory of Inequality." *Sociological Theory* 18: 17–43.

Cott, Nancy. 1977. *The Bonds of Womanhood*. New Haven, Conn.: Yale University Press.

Crowley, Steven P., and Jon D. Hanson. 1995. "The Nonpecuniary Costs of Accidents: Pain-and-Suffering Damages in Tort Law." *Harvard Law Review* 108: 1785–1917.

DiMaggio, Paul, and Hugh Louch. 1998 "Socially Embedded Consumer Transactions: For What Kinds of Purchases Do People Most Often Use Networks?" *American Sociological Review* 63: 19–37.

England, Paula, and Nancy Folbre. 1999. "The Cost of Caring." In "Emotional Labor in the Service Economy," *Annals of the American Academy of Political and Social Science* (special issue edited by Ronnie J. Steinberg and Deborah M. Figart) 561(January): 39–51.

Espeland, Wendy Nelson, and Mitchell L. Stevens. 1998. "Commensuration as a Social Process." *Annual Review of Sociology* 24: 313–43.

Estin, Ann Laquer. 1995. "Love and Obligation: Family Law and the Romance of Economics." *William and Mary Law Review* 36: 989–1087.

Folbre, Nancy. 2001. *The Invisible Heart*. New York: New Press.

Folbre, Nancy, and Julie A. Nelson. 2000 "For Love or Money—Or Both?" *Journal of Economic Perspectives* 14: 123–40.

Friedman, David D. 2000. *Law's Order*. Princeton, N.J.: Princeton University Press.

Gilligan, Carol. 1982. *In a Different Voice: Psychological Theory and Women's Development*. Cambridge, Mass.: Harvard University Press.

Hartman, Heidi. 1981. "The Family as the Locus of Gender, Class, and Political Struggle: The Example of Housework." *Signs: Journal of Women in Culture and Society* 6: 366–94.

Himmelweit, Susan. 1999. "Caring Labor." In "Emotional Labor in the Service Economy," *Annals of the American Academy of Political and Social Science* (special issue edited by Ronnie J. Steinberg and Deborah M. Figart) 561(January): 27–38.

Hochschild, Arlie. 1983. *The Managed Heart*. Berkeley: University of California Press.

Horsburgh, Beverly. 1992. "Redefining the Family: Recognizing the Altruistic Caretaker and the Importance of Relational Needs." *University of Michigan Journal of Law Review* 25: 423–504.

Kahan, Dan M. 1999. "Memo of October 1, 1999." Yale Law School. Unpublished memo.

Kuttner, Robert. 1997. *Everything for Sale: The Virtues and Limits of Markets*. New York: Knopf.

Laqueur, Thomas. 1990. *Making Sex: Body and Gender from the Greeks to Freud*. Cambridge, Mass.: Harvard University Press.

Lessig, Lawrence. 1995. "The Regulation of Social Meaning." *University of Chicago Law Review* 62: 943–1045.

———. 1996. "Social Meaning and Social Norms." *University of Pennsylvania Law Review* 144: 2181–89.

———. 1998. "The New Chicago School." *Journal of Legal Studies* 27, pt. 2: 661–91.

Nelson, Julie A. 1998a. "Labor, Gender, and the Economic/Social Divide." *International Labor Review* 137: 33–46.

———. 1998b. "One Sphere or Two?" In "Changing Forms of Payment," *American Behavioral Scientist* (special issue edited by Viviana A. Zelizer) 41: 1467–71.

———. 1999. "Of Markets and Martyrs: Is It Okay to Pay Well for Care?" *Feminist Economics* 5: 43–59.

Offer, Avner. 1997. "Between the Gift and the Market: The Economy of Regard." *Economic History Review,* 50, 2d series: 450–76.

Parsons, Talcott. 1978. "The Changing Economy of the Family." In *The Changing Economy of the Family: Report of an Interdisciplinary Seminar*. Washington, D.C.: American Council of Life Insurance.

Posner, Richard A. 1992. *Sex and Reason.* Cambridge, Mass.: Harvard University Press.

Radin, Margaret Jane. 1996. *Contested Commodities.* Cambridge, Mass.: Harvard University Press.

Rifkin, Jeremy. 2000. *The Age of Access.* New York: Jeremy P. Tarcher/Putnam.

Rose, Carol. 1994. "Rhetoric and Romance: A Comment on Spouses and Strangers." *Georgetown Law Journal* 82(September): 2409–21.

Rubin, Gayle. 1975. "The Traffic in Women: Notes on the 'Political Economy' of Sex." In *Toward an Anthropology of Women,* edited by Rayna Rapp. New York: Monthly Review Press.

Siegel, Reva B. 1994. "The Modernization of Marital Status Law: Adjudicating Wives' Rights to Earnings, 1860–1930." *Georgetown Law Journal* 82(September): 2127–2211.

Silbaugh, Katharine. 1996. "Turning Labor into Love: Housework and the Law." *Northwestern University Law Review* 91(Fall): 1–85.

Stone, Deborah. 1999. "Care and Trembling." *The American Prospect* 43: 61–67.

———. 2000. "Why We Need a Care Movement." *The Nation,* March 13(270): 13–15.

Sunstein, Cass. 1997. *Free Markets and Social Justice.* New York: Oxford University Press.

Tilly, Chris, and Charles Tilly. 1998. *Work Under Capitalism.* Boulder, Colo.: Westview Press.

Ungerson, Clare. 1995. "Gender, Cash, and Informal Care: European Perspectives and Dilemmas." *Journal of Social Policy* 21: 31–52.

———. 2000. "Cash in Care." In *Care Work: Gender Labor and the Welfare State,* edited by Madonna Harrington Meyer. New York: Routledge.

White, Harrison C. 1988. "Varieties of Markets." In *Social Structure: A Network Approach,* edited by Barry Wellman and S. D. Berkowitz. New York: Cambridge University Press.

Williams, Joan. 2000. *Unbending Gender: Why Family and Work Conflict and What to Do About It.* New York: Oxford University Press.

Zelizer, Viviana A. 1994. *The Social Meaning of Money.* New York: Basic Books.

———. 2000. "The Purchase of Intimacy." *Law and Social Inquiry* 25: 817–48.

= Part IV =

The Economic Sociology of Development

= Chapter 12 =

Social Capital and Community Development

ALEJANDRO PORTES AND MARGARITA MOONEY

T

HE PURPOSE of this chapter is threefold: to review the origins and definitions of the concept of social capital as it has developed in the recent literature; to examine the limitations of the concept as a causal force able to transform communities and nations; and to present several relevant examples from the empirical literature on regional and community development. These examples point to the significance of social networks and community solidarity in the viability of grassroots economic initiatives and the simultaneous difficulty of institutionalizing such forces.

Current interest in the concept of social capital in the field of development stems from the limitations of an exclusively economic approach in the achievement of the basic developmental goals: sustained growth, social equity, and citizenship. The record of application of neoliberal adjustment policies in less developed nations is decidedly mixed, even when evaluated by strict economic criteria. Orthodox adjustment policies have led to low inflation and sustained growth in some countries, while in others they have failed spectacularly, leading to currency crises, devaluations, and political instability (Portes 1997a; Centeno 1994). The one-size-fits-all package of economic policies foisted by the International Monetary Fund and the U.S. Treasury on countries at very different levels of development has led to a series of contradictory outcomes that orthodox economic theory is itself incapable of explaining (Filgueira 1996; Diaz 1996; Castells and Laserna 1989).

In the social terrain, the record is even more problematic: giving way to unrestrained market forces by removing state protections has produced growing income disparities and an atomized social fabric marked by the erosion of normative controls. Rising crime and widespread corruption of public institutions, including those charged with maintaining public order, have been associated with this normative decline. In the new "everyone for himself" environment promoted by the free reign of the market, there is little incentive for public officials to adhere to standards of probity or for the poor to respect the social order that has abandoned them. Instead of promoting growth with justice, current market liberalization policies may be leading to a Hobbesian problem of public order as individuals fight for survival under the harsh conditions in which they find themselves (Diaz 1996; Castells and Portes 1989).

Although the situation in most Third World countries has not yet reached this crisis level, the trend is visible enough to inspire policymakers to seek ways to reinstitute or create anew community bonds and social institutions. It is in this context that we have seen the appearance of the notion of social capital, which holds out the promise of a popular, grassroots-initiated alternative to the top-down policies promoted by international financial organizations in the recent past. In the more optimistic versions, the rise of social capital performs double duty as a counterweight to the unfettered individualism of the market and, simultaneously, as a means to gain advantages in it (Putnam 1993, 1995). Such rosy views have not gone unchallenged and in fact have been subjected to extensive criticism.

In the next sections, we review the origins of the concept of social capital, its evolution from an individual trait to a feature of communities and nations, and its limitations as a potential new model of development.

Social Capital: Origins and Definitions

Much of the controversy surrounding the concept of social capital has to do with its application to problems at different levels of abstraction and its use in theories involving different units of analysis. Its original systematic development by the French sociologist Pierre Bourdieu (1979, 1980) and the American sociologist James Coleman (1988, 1990) centered on individuals or small groups as the units of analysis. With some significant variations, both scholars focused on the potential benefits accruing to individuals or families by virtue of their ties with others. Bourdieu's treatment of the concept, in particular, was instrumental, going as far as noting that people intentionally build their relations for the benefits that they will bring later on. In a few brilliant pages (Bourdieu 1979, 3–6; 1980, 2–3), the French sociologist deals with the interaction between money capital, social capital, and cultural capital, the latter being defined as an individual's formal educational credentials and the more intangible complex of values and style in demeanor. Bourdieu's key insight was that these three forms of capital are interchangeable, that is, they can be traded for each other and actually require such trades for their development. Thus, social capital of any significance can seldom be acquired without the investment of some material resources and the possession of some cultural knowledge, enabling the individual to establish relations with valued others.

The subsequent literature followed, for the most part, these guidelines by focusing on the ability of individuals to gain access to resources by virtue of their social connections and the types of resources that become available through them. In sociology a tripartite family of effects developed as researchers explored the implications of the concept. Social capital became defined as a source of social control, a source of family-mediated benefits, and a source of resources mediated by nonfamily networks. The last usage of social capital, exemplified by the personal connections that facilitate access to jobs, market tips, or loans, comes closest to Bourdieu's original definition of the concept.

On his part, Coleman paid particular attention to the first usage of social capital, that is, as a source of control. In the waning years of his life he became preoccupied with the disintegration of what he called the "primordial" social ties that guarantee the observance of norms. A whole gamut of pathologies follows from this state of affairs, he warned, from crime and insecurity in the streets to freeloading by teachers and students in American public schools. In seeking remedies to these social ills, Coleman pursued a double path. First, he wrote in defense and celebration of the community ties that remain in place. Second, he advocated the replacement of the primordial social structures that have disappeared with "purposively constructed" organizations in which schedules of incentives will take the place of vanishing social capital (Coleman 1993).

Sources of Social Capital

The definition of social capital as the ability to secure resources by virtue of membership in social networks or larger social structures is the most widely accepted definition of the term in sociology at present. This definition is not without problems. First, there is a common tendency to confuse the *ability* to secure resources through networks with the resources themselves. This can easily lead to tautological statements in which a positive outcome necessarily indicates the presence of social capital, and a negative one its absence. In fact, an actor's ability to obtain resources through connections does not guarantee a positive outcome. Given the unequal distribution of wealth and resources in society, actors may have trustworthy and sound social ties and still have access to limited or poor-quality resources. Saying that only those who secure desirable goods from their associates have social capital is tantamount to saying that only the successful succeed. (This point has been developed in greater detail in Portes 1998; and Portes and Landolt 1996.)

Second, the literature on this topic tends to emphasize the positive consequences of social ties, to the exclusion of their less desirable consequences. Yet the same mechanisms that are appropriable by individuals as social capital can lead to a set of negative outcomes for others. Recent studies have identified at least four such negative consequences of social capital: exclusion of outsiders, excess claims on group members, restrictions on individual freedoms, and downward leveling norms (Portes and Sensenbrenner 1993). For instance, the same strong ties that enable group members to obtain privileged access to resources bar others from securing the same assets. The particularistic preferences granted to members of a clan or circle of friends is commonly done at the expense of the universalistic rights of others. For the latter, the situation is tantamount to *negative* social capital, and they often resort to legal means to break down the barriers created by cozy social ties (Waldinger 1995).

Similarly, under certain conditions, community closure may prevent the success of business initiatives by enforcing excessive claims on entrepreneurs. In Bali, for example, Clifford Geertz (1963) observed that successful businessmen were constantly assaulted by job- and loan-seeking kinsmen on the strength of the community norms enjoining mutual assistance. As a result, the growth of their business initiatives was stunted and they were eventually bankrupted (see also Granovetter 1995). In the Ecuadoran highlands many successful cloth and leather artisans have converted to Protestantism. The reason has little to do with their religious convictions or affinity for the Protestant "ethic," but with the need to escape the host of obligations enforced by the Catholic cofradías (parish-based guilds). For these hardworking artisans, negative social capital comes in the form of repeated requests to finance religious festivities and bear the cost of food and drink for the rest of the community (Portes and Landolt 1996).

From the point of view of recipients, the resources made available through social ties have the character of a gift. More problematic, however, are the motivations of donors. This points to a third problem with our definition of social capital: it leaves untheorized the motivations of donors in these transactions. Drawing from the observations of Durkheim, Marx, Weber, and Simmel on the dynamics of groups (see Portes and Sensenbrenner 1993), we have identified four sources of social capital distinguished by the presence or absence of overarching structures that define the character of the transaction. There are two primary sources of altruistic social capital: granting resources to others out of moral obligation (parents' gifts to their children, alms to the poor), in gestures that are undergirded by values that were introjected by individuals during the process of socialization; and granting resources to other members of one's territorial, ethnic, or religious community ("bounded solidarity"). Acts arising from this latter source are not based on general values but on particularistic loyalties to a relevant ingroup (for example, endowing a scholarship for young co-ethnics, or donating time to a union of fellow workers).

There are also two sources of instrumental social capital: face-to-face reciprocal transactions, which carry the full expectation of commensurate return by the benefited party ("simple reciprocity"), and the resource transactions embedded in larger social structures that act as guarantors of full returns to donors, either from the benefited party or from the community at large ("enforceable trust"). The latter source is exemplified by the granting of loans without collateral to members of the same community on the expectation that community controls will guarantee repayment and, in addition, generate status and approval for the donor.

Trust exists in these situations precisely because it is *enforceable* through the power of the community. This source of social capital is closely associated with the emphasis placed by Coleman on community structures as a mechanism of social control. This was actually the theme that caught the eye of scholars in other disciplines as they proceeded to transform social capital into a remedy for social ills, oblivious to its negative consequences and the distinction between its causes and effects. This distinction and the preceding discussion are summarized in figure 12.1.

Social Capital as a Feature of Communities and Nations

For Bourdieu, Coleman, and other sociologists, social ties were important for the benefits that they yielded to individuals or small groups

Figure 12.1   Individual Social Capital: Sources and Effects

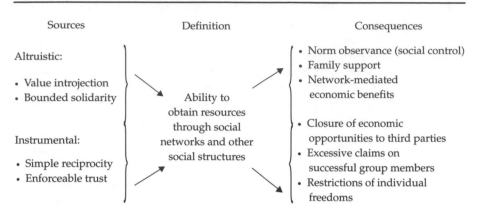

Source: Adapted from Portes 1998a.

in the form of reliable expectations. A subtle transition took place as the concept was exported to other disciplines where social capital became an attribute of large political structures. In this new garb, its benefits accrued not so much to individuals as to the collectivity in the form of reduced crime rates, lower official corruption, and better governance.

This conceptual stretch, led by the political scientist Robert Putnam, produced the metaphor of a "stock" of social capital possessed by cities and even nations. Social capital as a property of nations is not the same as its individual version, a fact that explains why the research literatures based on Bourdieu's and Putnam's definitions have diverged. There are several differences between the two that deserve careful attention. First, the transition of the concept from an individual asset to a national characteristic was never theorized explicitly, giving rise to the present state of confusion about the meaning of the term. In one sentence social capital is an asset of intact families; in the next it is an attribute of networks of traders; and in the following it becomes the explanation of why entire cities are well governed and economically flourishing. The heuristic value of the concept suffers accordingly as it risks becoming synonymous with all things that are positive or desirable in social life.

This confusion becomes evident when we realize that the individual and collective definitions of the concept, though compatible in some instances, are at odds in others. For instance, the right "connections" allow certain persons to gain access to profitable public contracts and bypass regulations that are binding on others. Individual social capital in such instances consists precisely in the ability to undermine collective social capital, defined as "civic spirit" and grounded on impartial application of the laws. To cite another instance, the strong bonds in Mafia families and inner-city gangs confer benefits on their individual members at the expense of public order and peace (Gambetta 1993).

Second, the causes and effects of social capital as a feature of collectivities have not been disentangled, giving rise to much circular reasoning. The theoretical spadework done by Bourdieu and his successors prevented this from happening to social capital as an individual trait. At this level, the sources of social capital are clearly associated with a person's networks, including those that he or she explicitly constructs for that purpose, while effects are linked to an array of material and informational resources.

Collective social capital, or "civicness," lacks this distinct separation. As a property of cities and nations, measurable in stocks, social capital is said to lead to better governance, and its existence is simultaneously inferred from this outcome. When not tautological, the argument takes the form of a truism:

> For every political system,
> If authorities and the population are imbued with a sense of collective responsibility and altruism,
> Then the system will be better governed and its policies will be more effective.

It is difficult to see how it could be otherwise. Yet, paradoxically, the self-evident character of the argument made it popular in policy circles: the "truth" that such a statement conveys is immediately graspable without need for complex explanation. Thus, if some cities are better governed and richer than others, it is because they are "blessed" with substantial stocks of social capital. The intuitive appeal of such an argument conceals but does not remove its basic flaw, namely, that the actual factors leading to social capital are left untheorized. Without a clearer understanding of its sources, arguments involving collective social capital inevitably become circular.

A third and related issue is the possibility that the causal role attributed to "civicness" is spurious. In other words, the celebrated traits of the population, such as greater membership in associations and greater political participation, and their alleged effects in terms of better governance may both be consequences of other exogenous factors. Once these are controlled, all or most of the assumed effect of

Figure 12.2   Alternative Causal Patterns of Collective Social Capital

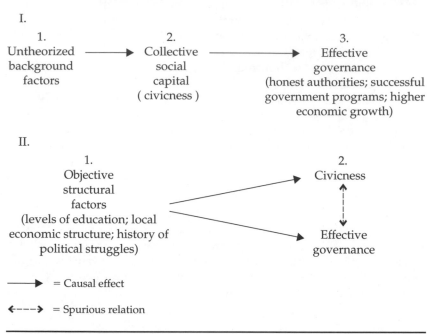

I.

| 1. | | 2. | | 3. |
| Untheorized background factors | → | Collective social capital (civicness) | → | Effective governance (honest authorities; successful government programs; higher economic growth) |

II.

1.
Objective
structural
factors
(levels of education; local
economic structure; history of
political struggles)

2.
Civicness

Effective
governance

———▶   = Causal effect

◀---▶   = Spurious relation

Source: Adapted from Portes 2000.

civicness may disappear. Likely candidates for such a causal role include the literacy and education of the population, the structure of the local economy, and the history of past struggles for equality and incorporation. Figure 12.2 illustrates these alternative interpretations.

These limitations must be kept in mind when attempting to apply the concept of social capital to problems of development. It is possible to find instances in which high levels of collective solidarity have accompanied sustained economic growth or other positive developmental outcomes. The all-too-common logical fallacy is to conclude that one causes the other without consideration of the possibility that both are determined by common external causes. It can be those external factors, not social capital, that play the key role in the process. Even when strong collective solidarity plays an unambiguous causal role, the question remains as to how it came about. Without this understanding, it is impossible to determine whether such bonds and their alleged effects can be re-created elsewhere.

Lastly, as with the individual version of the concept, it is possible that strong community bonds do not always have positive effects but sometimes yield unanticipated and negative consequences. These may take the form of restrictions on individual freedoms and enterprise or arbitrary exclusion of nonmembers. Searching for positive developmental outcomes to which a social capital story can be attached is a particularly pernicious form of sampling on the dependent variable.

In the following sections, we review several instances of the relationship between social capital and community development that highlight both its potential contributions and its limitations. It is necessary, however, to begin by clarifying what is meant by "development" in different contexts. Like the concept of social capital itself, "development" also has different meanings at various levels of generality that must be disentangled.

Development: Nation and Community

The concept of development refers to a set of positive outcomes that benefit certain collectivities and the processes leading to them. The most common of these collectivities is the nation-state, especially the nation-state in the Third World or on the periphery of the world economy. At this level the outcomes of interest include sustained economic growth, the fair distribution of economic resources leading to greater equality, and the consolidation of democratic political institutions (Hirschman 1963; Cardoso and Faletto 1979; Portes and Kincaid 1989). "Community development" refers to similar positive outcomes at a subnational level involving smaller collectivities—towns, neighborhoods, or rural communities, or a set of such contiguous communities within the same region. The most common developmental goals at this level are physical infrastructure, entrepreneurship and investment, wealth distribution, and the quality and effectiveness of local political institutions (Bunker 1989; Massey et al. 1998, ch. 9).

Though "development" has been applied to even smaller units, the most common usages of the concept are at the national and community levels. The two are not synonymous. It is possible for poor and backward communities to exist within an advanced nation-state, and for prosperous regions to emerge in otherwise stagnant countries. It is even possible for a nation to be fractured into regions that are at very different levels of political and economic development; Italy is a poignant example (Brusco 1982; Piore and Sabel 1984). At the national level, arguments for the positive effects of social capital are commonly made in terms of civicness, as indexed by survey items indicating participation in associations, exposure to the media, and generalized expressions of trust (Putnam 1993).

Arguments about the role of social capital in national development are invariably ex post facto: causes are inferred from events that have already occurred, leading to circular reasoning. These interpretations are also widely open to the problem of spuriousness noted previously. In the 1980s, for example, efforts to attach a social capital story to the economic success of Japan and other Asian nations became something of a cottage industry. According to these accounts, it was the strong networks of solidarity within and between Japanese firms and the "embeddedness" of Japanese state agencies in these networks that provided the basis for rapid economic development (Chalmers 1982; Arrighi 1994; Evans 1995). By the same token, the lack of such embeddedness in agencies of the U.S. federal government and the more competitive, less solidaristic orientation of American firms condemned the American economy to stagnation and decay. With the reversal of the economic fortunes of the two countries during the 1990s, these post hoc arguments quickly disappeared from view. They even gave way in some quarters to the opposite interpretation, one based on a triumphalist celebration of free markets and unrestrained competition.

The difficulty of disentangling cause from effect and of ruling out possible sources of spuriousness makes the proposition that collective social capital leads to national development very dubious. No persuasive empirical proof has yet been offered that national participatory behavior, in its various guises, produces its alleged economic and social effects, controlling for other factors. By contrast, the relationship between social capital and *local* community development is easier to establish and to study, for two reasons. First, at this level, the definition and sources of social capital are the same as those theorized for individuals. In other words, rather than generalized "civicness," measured by survey questions, we return here to the social structure of the community and the character of its networks. It is thus possible to speak of bounded solidarity and enforceable trust at this level, focusing on its effects for the *entire community* rather than for its individual members.

Second, it is easier to trace the historical development of specific community structures and to observe their operations in daily life. At this closer range, it is feasible to establish causal direction unambiguously and to rule out sources of spuriousness because of the visible and recurrent presence of networks and the evident character of their effects. Thus, Jeremy Boissevain (1974) had little difficulty establishing the historical roots of the tightly knit social structures in the Maltese villages that he studied and to show their effects in terms of effective social control and the suffocation of personal initiative. Similarly, Min Zhou and Carl Bankston (1998) persuasively traced the history of the Vietnamese community of New Orleans and showed how, despite its poverty, its strong networks and bounded solidarity had decisive effects on the educational and occupational achievements of its children.

We follow these leads and leave national civicness behind, focusing instead on the relationship between social capital and development at the level of particular communities. The following cases illustrate some of the disparate manifestations of this relationship.

First, we examine the phenomenal post–World War II industrial growth in Emilia-Romagna, a region of Italy. We analyze how particular historical circumstances led to instrumental and altruistic sources of social capital that propelled the region's development. Second, we present the case of Ecuadoran indigenous entrepreneurs from Otavalo, who have built transnational businesses of crafts and music based on trust enforced through community bonds. The case of Otavalo also demonstrates how the ability of one group to produce "closure" through tight social bonds can have negative consequences for other groups excluded from such networks. In the third case, bounded solidarity, an altruistic source of social capital, led Salvadoran migrants to the United States to donate resources for community development in their places of origin. Despite the initial success of these projects, trust between U.S.-based migrants and local political leaders has not been strong enough to guarantee the continued success of migrant-led development efforts. These three cases show different sources and consequences of social capital, as represented in figure 12.1.

Flexible Specialization and Industrial Growth in Emilia-Romagna

The phenomenal post–World War II economic growth of Emilia-Romagna, one of Italy's twenty-two political-administrative regions, led to a proliferation of studies seeking to uncover the key to its success. During its high-growth period, Emilia-Romagna developed an agglomeration of industrial districts whose production accounted for an increasing share of Italian exports. Because of these industries, Emilia-Romagna had greater labor force participation, lower rates of unemployment, greater household incomes, and higher wages than other regions of Italy (Brusco 1982; Capecchi 1989; Harrison 1994). The success story of Emilia-Romagna intrigued economists and sociologists because this growth took place under a model of flexible specialization. This mode of production differed greatly from the vertically integrated mass production that dominated industrial production at the time. In this section, we analyze the origins of the ties between government officials, entrepreneurs, and workers and the effects of these ties on the development process in this particular region and time.

Social Capital in a Flexible System of Production

In the 1970s the region of Emilia-Romagna had several industrial districts comprising numerous small and medium-sized firms, the largest of which had about three hundred employees (Brusco 1982). Each of these firms specialized in making a component of a certain product that was later assembled under another roof. A significant amount of the production also came from the informal economy, through homework or the "putting out" system (Capecchi 1989). Emilian firms used machinery and techniques that allowed them to produce in short series and thus they could shift quickly from one product to another, providing great flexibility in output. These networks of small and medium-sized firms produced diverse goods such as knitwear, motorcycles, tomato canning, and various kinds of machinery (Brusco 1982).

The decentralization of production in Emilia-Romagna required cooperation between firms to maximize the efficiency of flexible short runs. Sebastiano Brusco (1982, 173) describes the regionwide associations created by the small entrepreneurs of Emilia-Romagna: they "prepare the pay slips, keep the books, and pay the taxes of the small firms, giving to the latter the expertise of a large office in administration and accountancy at a minimal price." These associations also provide consulting services for firms on technical matters, promote cooperation in the acquisition of raw materials, coordinate marketing strategies, and form cooperatives to offer loans at low interest rates.

In addition to high levels of interfirm cooperation, the specialization of production has encouraged individual entrepreneurship and innovation in Emilia-Romagna. Workers often learn a trade in a large factory and then start their own business to complement already-existing production (Brusco 1982; Capecchi 1989). The potentially negative effects of the extensive use of informal labor and industrial housework are mitigated by social welfare programs and high levels of solidarity between workers and employers. The resulting flexibility is a key component of the success of Emilia-Romagna's industrial system: it allowed the region to absorb external shocks without suffering a recession in the twenty-year period from 1960 to 1980.

The type of interfirm cooperation that fueled the development of

Emilia-Romagna cannot be explained by individual interests alone. As Mark Granovetter (this volume) points out, such cooperation can be explained only by social relationships based on trust. The firms in Emilia-Romagna rely on two instrumental sources of social capital, simple reciprocity and enforceable trust, to provide services for each other. Entrepreneurs obtain a reliable flow of resources from these social ties, resulting in network-mediated economic benefits (see figure 12.1).

Historical Antecedents of Community Social Capital

It is worthwhile at this point to examine the historical process leading to the notable sources of social capital in this region. Vittorio Capecchi (1989) notes that agricultural production in Emilia-Romagna at the turn of the century was characterized by a higher degree of entrepreneurship than existed in other regions of Italy. In addition, before the beginning of the twentieth century, intellectuals had founded several technical schools in the region that helped train workers and entrepreneurs. A couple of small industries using flexible specialization methods were started in the 1920s. These seed conditions allowed entrepreneurs to take advantage of a series of political and economic changes that occurred after World War II.

Since the beginning of the twentieth century, the people of Emilia-Romagna have strongly supported the Socialist and Communist parties. In response to threats from fascism during World War II, agricultural workers and other working-class groups overcame previous conflicts and united under the Communist banner. After the war ended, numerous Communist Party officials were elected to office in Emilia-Romagna. These regional government officials provided strong support for both entrepreneurs and workers. For example, the regional government encouraged the development of small industries by providing credit to entrepreneurs (Capecchi 1989). Other social services, such as day care and affordable housing, promoted labor force participation and social welfare for workers. Finally, the regional government also organized cultural events and tried to revive old urban centers, further strengthening Emilian identity among entrepreneurs (Brusco 1982).

Another intriguing aspect of this case is that the growth in Emilia-Romagna took place without the support of the national government. In fact, the regional government clashed on numerous occasions with the national government, which was controlled by the center-right Christian Democratic Party. Because of the hostility between regional and national politicians, the Italian government built few public or semipublic firms in Emilia-Romagna, which at the time would have represented a significant form of government investment. Furthermore, compared to other regions of Italy, the national government invested less in public infrastructure and gave fewer credit concessions in Emilia-Romagna (Brusco 1982).

The central government's neglect of, even hostility toward, Emilia-Romagna had several unanticipated but positive effects. First, tax collection was weak, allowing Emilian firms to keep and reinvest a greater share of their profits. Second, the clash between local authorities and the central state reinforced solidarity between workers, entrepreneurs, and regional officials. For example, the people of Emilia-Romagna responded to the government's decision to close munitions factories by helping displaced workers start their own businesses, an altruistic action based on bounded solidarity. In summary, key historical antecedents to community solidarity in this instance are found in past struggles against fascism. These struggles, and a continuing struggle with the political party in national power, created a strong class ideology among the local population, which strengthened the preexisting bonds underlying entrepreneurial development.

The Emilian experience is a justly celebrated instance of the role played in community development by the sources of social capital examined previously—bounded solidarity and enforceable trust. In this instance, the process was not limited to a single village or town but encompassed an entire region. Ironically, successful capitalist entrepreneurship in Emilia-Romagna was cemented by a solidaristic class ideology that was opposed to large capitalist firms and the state. This shows how good proletarians can make effective small entrepreneurs by drawing on the community bonds created by past class struggles. In addition, however, the Emilian industrial districts drew on a set of unique historical resources, including entrepreneurial traditions dating back to the medieval period and the strong influence of an artisanal-technical culture promoted by specialized trade schools (Capecchi 1989).[1]

This successful experience has inspired a number of scholars who have seen Emilian flexible specialization as a blueprint for economic growth with greater social equality (Piore and Sabel 1984). The truth, however, is that the conditions giving rise to bonds of solidarity and trust among small producers travel poorly. The normal pattern revealed by studies of small firms in other national contexts is one of competition and mutual distrust, with only sporadic instances of cooperation. In Spain, high-tech electronic firms in the suburbs of Madrid never developed the requisite social networks to give rise to industrial districts (Benton 1989), and informal producers of garments, toys, and furniture in Alicante never coalesced into anything resembling solidaristic communities but reverted instead to atomized production and exploitative labor practices (Ybarra 1989).

A deliberate search for instances of solidaristic entrepreneurial communities resembling the Emilian model in five Caribbean Basin countries yielded consistently negative results (Portes, Dore-Cabral, and Landolt 1997). In those countries market behavior and individualistic competition were usually the norm. In the single instance of bounded solidarity found by the study—an indigenous Mayan community in Guatemala—the absence of support from the authorities and lack of technical know-how confined entrepreneurs to the role of producing low-value-added garments at the bottom of a subcontracting chain (Pérez-Sáinz 1997).

The Transnational Migrant Entrepreneurs of Otavalo

Our next example of social capital and community development examines how a particular indigenous community in South America, the Otavalans, have used social capital based on bonds of solidarity and trust to create and maintain a market niche for their crafts and music. Using the framework laid out earlier, we argue that Otavalan transnational businesses have succeeded because of their ability to recognize their advantageous position vis-à-vis other indigenous groups. The case of Otavalo is in line with Ronald Burt's point (this volume) that dense networks do not always guarantee positive outcomes. Individuals must be able to connect members of their network to outside opportunities, as seen in this example.

The region of Otavalo, Ecuador, is inhabited by an indigenous people who live in several contiguous communities and speak the same language, share a common dress, and have a common identity. Otavalans have combined international migration and entrepreneurship to create a market for their cultural identity through handicrafts and music. In his fieldwork in Otavalo, David Kyle (1999) found that Otavalans travel back and forth to at least twenty-three different countries to sell locally produced handicrafts. In addition, hundreds of groups of Otavalan musicians travel through North America and Europe and enjoy notable success. Otavalan artisans represent the single documented experience of something resembling an "industrial district" in Latin America. The social resources behind the success of this indigenous community offer additional lessons on the distinct origins of this resource and its bearing on local economic development.

A Privileged Colonial Relationship

As in the case of Emilia-Romagna, the roots of Otavalan entrepreneurship lie in the region's unique historical development. Early on during the colonial period, Spaniards singled out Otavalans from other indigenous groups in Ecuador for being "cleaner" and "more businesslike." Noticing that Otavalans were highly skilled in weaving, Spanish colonials hired them to make specialty fabrics, such as "English" tweed, because they could produce it at a much lower price than was obtained for European imports (Kyle 1999). The proximity of Otavalo to the colonial administrative capital of Quito also facilitated the transportation and sale of these goods.

This special relationship between Otavalan weavers and the white and mestizo elite had several effects. First, as the work of Otavalans came to be known throughout colonial Spanish America, the market for Otavalan products expanded and their positive ethnic identity was strengthened. Second, Otavalan weavers worked as independent entrepreneurs. This independence was not granted by a benevolent colonial authority but rather resulted from the failure of local elites to industrialize cloth production to compete with cheap imports from Europe. Had these industrialization efforts been successful, Otavalan weavers probably would have been proletarianized as wage workers in textile factories. However, because they worked as independent producers, Otavalans developed a privileged position in the colonial system and gained a direct link to the cash economy (Kyle 1999). The positive external and ingroup identification created durable bonds of solidarity and trust among Otavalan artisans. The opportunity for entrepreneurship and direct interaction with consumers allowed Otavalans to develop external ties and to gain skills in dealing with outsiders.

In the twentieth century another set of factors came together to transform Otavalans from a locally privileged indigenous group into a transnational entrepreneurial community. In the 1940s a few Otavalan communities began to industrialize their production. Their resulting prosperity allowed them to purchase even more advanced technology, further increasing production. In the 1960s international development agencies, including the Peace Corps, recognized the potential of Otavalan trade and offered technical and financial assistance. At this time Otavalans began to develop products that marketed their own cultural identity, such as woolen ponchos and indigenous hats and scarves. They even incorporated the designs of nearby native communities. The number of Otavalan handicraft producers grew as community members supported each other's efforts to gain access to the credit and raw materials needed to start a business. These instrumental sources of social capital allowed Otavalans to obtain valuable resources through their network memberships.

The shift to the production of indigenous textiles and styles made Otavalo a "poster city" for Ecuador's growing tourist business, and a tourist market was built in the center of town. In the 1970s the ability to commercialize goods outside of Otavalo was increased by the construction of the Pan-American Highway, which reduced the trip from Otavalo to Quito and its international airport to about two hours. Otavalans used connections they had been cultivating for centuries to establish markets for their garments in the rest of the country and then made their move abroad. Some permanent Otavalan settlements were established in large American and European cities, but most producers and merchants continued to travel to and from these overseas "colonies," staying in them for periods of less than one year. Hence, unlike other Ecuadoran and Latin American immigrants, Otavalans do not settle permanently in their places of destination but use them instead as outposts of a dynamic international trade. The boom in production and sales created significant prosperity in Otavalo, one of the few places in Latin America where an indigenous people actually enjoys a higher standard of living than the otherwise dominant whites and mestizos.

Not all Otavalans are able to participate in the handicraft trade. Indeed, by the 1980s greater competition and higher capitalization costs had made it difficult for young Otavalans to start new handicraft businesses. Around this time Otavalan folk music groups began to enjoy success abroad. As with the handicraft business decades before, Otavalans recognized that their cultural identity provided them with an advantageous position, and they used their position to create a new niche—music—in which young Otavalans could participate. By the late 1990s, Kyle (1999) estimates, hundreds of such groups of Otavalan musicians were traveling through Europe and North America. Because these groups are so successful, local travel agents are willing to issue international plane tickets on credit. Thus, to get a start in this new occupation, potential touring musicians need little more than their cultural identity to get access to the resources they need, such as credit, to start their business.

Ethnic Identity as Economic and Social Capital

Among Otavalans, group identity has become a resource that opens a door to a productive activity (handicrafts and folk music) and the financial resources to initiate it (loans for production, credit for plane tickets). According to Kyle (1999), the key to Otavalans' success has not been their weaving or music in and of themselves, but rather their ability to *market* their cultural identity and to establish and maintain political and economic ties abroad without losing their distinctness. Despite numerous changes that have taken place in Otavalo during the last forty years, such as urbanization, new industrial technologies, and greater contact between Otavalans and outsiders through trade and tourism, Otavalans maintain a strong group identification. Even those who drive luxury cars maintain their distinctive traditional dress. Their success at weaving and trade since the colonial era and today's successful marketing of their handicrafts have heightened a sense of cultural distinctness that forms the basis for bounded solidarity. Nearby villages that are not Otavalan but have a similar lifestyle and history have not been able to enter the profitable handicraft market.

The early success of Otavalan weavers has become a source of social capital that is available to group members but not to others. As described by Kyle (1995, 330):

> Far from being atomized actors, the actions of an Otavalan weaver, merchant or musician depend very much on what other Otavalans have done before them and are currently doing. Group membership carries with it . . . the possibility for social capital, though not necessarily in the form of direct aid, and also sets parameters on what is acceptable and what is not.

A common ethnic identity implies norms and values that set limits on entrepreneurial competition and individual aggrandizement. This normative structure is not kept in place by legal contract but rather by enforceable trust—the capacity of the community to monitor and regulate its members. The proven success of economic strategies grounded on such bonds reinforces them and guides the course of future entrepreneurial activities.

Burt's concept of "structural holes" (this volume) is helpful in understanding how Otavalans created a niche for their products. However, as the editors point out in chapter 1, Burt does not theorize precisely how individuals and groups discover such opportunities. It is clear that the privileged social location of Otavalans vis-à-vis other indigenous groups dating back to the colonial era provided them with expertise in a particular craft, knowledge of external markets, and the capability to capitalize on the advantages they held. For Otavalans, their privileged social location was a necessary condition to perceiving a sequence of external opportunities that passed other groups by.

Internal Competition and Social Capital

The existence of social capital does not imply the absence of social hierarchies. Indeed, the growth of transnational migration in Otavalo reinforced preexisting social inequalities. At the individual and family levels, financial resources and technical expertise differ greatly among entrepreneurs. Successful Otavalan weaving families have their own networks of social ties linking them to external markets, and they closely guard information about markets and clients abroad. There is indeed a clear status hierarchy differentiating the more successful, internationally oriented artisan families from those producing for the local market with more primitive methods.

Social differentiation and internal competition may seem to run contrary to the ideal of an entrepreneurial community driven by social capital. This is a mistake. As illustrated in the case of Emilia-Romagna, there is room for competition and differentiated success among entrepreneurs. The significance of social capital in these settings is manifested in the *normative limits* imposed on competition and the *elective affinity* that leads entrepreneurs to seek loans and market advice within their community and hire their members in preference to outsiders.

Looking for vocal expressions of solidarity as evidence of social capital overlooks the fact that the sources and effects of this mechanism can be measured only over extended periods of time. In addition, they can be assessed only through the aggregate effect of numerous individual transactions (Portes 1997b). Thus, we must examine not just what groups of people *say* about each other, but how they treat each other *in practice,* such as through hiring and marketing norms and the prevalence of informal business transactions that require enforceable trust.

In Otavalo, as in Emilia-Romagna, the existence of social capital does not eliminate all forms of competition between producers or cause all financial resources and information, such as contacts, to be shared equally. Nonetheless, competition can coexist within a normative system grounded on enforceable trust. In both cases, however, the origins of social capital must be traced to unique historical processes that culminated in distinct cultural patterns and community networks. Evidence that such outcomes are exceptional and not easily reproducible is found by looking no further than nearby indigenous communities whose socioeconomic condition is quite different. Despite the consistent success of Otavalans, other Andean peoples have been unable to reproduce their entrepreneurial performance and indeed have fallen into a relationship of dependency, as Otavalans acquire other groups' handicrafts to market them abroad as their own.

Committees of Salvadoran Migrants and Community Development

We turn now to a case that manifests primarily altruistic sources of social capital—Salvadoran migrants in the United States and their organization of civic hometown committees. From 1980 to 1992, El Salvador suffered a civil war during which one in every five Salvadorans left the country. By the end of the 1990s an estimated 1.2 million Salvadorans were living in the United States (Landolt et al. 1999). Throughout the 1980s remittances sent by these migrants to their families in El Salvador consistently reached a total of $600 million annually. By 1996, four years after the end of the civil war, this amount had doubled to $1.26 billion (Landolt et al. 1999). Remittances sent directly to family members constitute crucial sources of support and thus are spent on subsistence needs, including food and health. Sometimes remittances are invested in a business or land. In a certain number of cases, however, groups of migrants have pooled their resources to contribute to community development projects in their hometowns. This last phenomenon has attracted the attention of scholars and politicians alike, because it represents an instance of spontaneous collective altruism outside established institutional structures.

With the end of the Salvadoran civil war in 1992, civic associations of immigrants began to appear. These associations were often led by former members of the solidarity network that had supported the insurgent guerrilla force, the Frente Farabundo Martí para la Liberación Nacional (FMLN). Rather than being organized around party lines, however, these groups used community of origin as their basis for solidarity. The groups are called comités del pueblo (hometown associations). Their objective is to support the reconstruction process in El Salvador, in particular by contributing to public works in their communities.

The primary motivation for the founding of these associations was solidarity based on a sense of bounded moral obligation to family and friends who remained in El Salvador after the civil war. The emergence of the comités was also influenced by Salvadoran migrants' reception in the United States. Despite the fact that they were fleeing political violence, Salvadorans did not receive official recognition as refugees. As a result, most of them entered the United States as illegal migrants at a time when the U.S. economy was in a recession and the backlash against immigration was increasing. This precarious legal situation, their social marginalization, and fear of deportation further encouraged Salvadorans both to bond together in the United States and to remain closely linked to their places of origin. At the same time their past history of political struggle, both in the Salvadoran war and in support of migrants' rights in the United States, provided the leadership experience necessary to found the new civic committees.

Although their initial poverty prevented Salvadoran immigrants from making significant contributions to their hometowns, the subsequent improvement of their economic situation led to both the proliferation of the committees and more significant civic projects financed by them. Thus, while solidarity grew among Salvadoran migrants as they settled in the United States, they could use it to pursue development in their hometowns only after their economic situation in the United States had improved. This observation accords with Burt's point that the quality of social capital varies with changes in social location and supports our earlier argument that one must pay attention to the quality of resources to which social capital provides access.

Patricia Landolt and her colleagues (1999) report that more than seventy hometown organizations exist in two of the most concentrated settlements of Salvadorans in the United States, Los Angeles and Washington, D.C. These associations vary in size from just a few paisanos (people from the same town) up to twenty-five core members. Leaders of these groups have forged extensive ties among Salvadorans residing in different U.S. cities who share a common origin. Ingroup solidarity is further strengthened by committee sponsorship of social and cultural events in the community. These efforts both reinforce Salvadoran identity in the United States and generate significant contributions for public works at home.

Civic committees have collected up to $50,000 for community development projects in their towns. Projects financed by these funds— roads, parks, schools, and hospitals—have the character of public goods, that is, they are equally available to all community members. To be successful, such projects depend on local cooperation with municipal and provincial authorities or with counterpart comités in El Salvador. In the absence of any supervisory authority, the success of such projects depends on the norm observance guaranteed through enforceable trust. It is here that problems have emerged, given the uncertain contours of the transnational community underlying these initiatives.

Despite the committees' initial success in raising funds, the fact that many Salvadoran migrants still live in precarious economic and legal conditions decreases their ability to continue contributing to these organizations. In addition, migrants have competing sets of relations and obligations that weaken their ties to hometown associations over time. Most important, the operation and success of community projects depend on personal ties between migrants and hometown leaders without any supervising institutional structure. Conflicts have sometimes developed because the migrant associations and local leaders do not necessarily share the same vision of development. Because they are populated largely by new residents who settled there during or after the civil war, some communities find it more difficult to establish trust and common goals with the expatriates.

Despite the hometown committees' humanitarian goals and their leaders' efforts to promote cooperation, the context of reconstruction in El Salvador has given their work an unintended political dimension. For example, to carry out a project a local counterpart in El Salvador must be chosen. Inevitably this choice becomes a political statement. Furthermore, the substantial remittances sent by Salvadoran migrants to their families and often to their hometown as well for civic projects have sparked reactions from the local and national governments. The government of El Salvador has become aware of this economic potential and has encouraged its consulates to create organizations that essentially compete with the hometown associations by raising funds for local investment. Thus, although the comités arose as a series of grassroots efforts, the transnational fields of actions that they have created have evolved into a contested terrain (Landolt et al. 1999). Unlike the case of Emilia-Romagna, government action does not support popular initiatives but competes with them.

The Salvadoran experience highlights the fragility and unexpected effects of community development projects based solely on social capital. Despite the strong commitments of many expatriates to their home communities, their efforts are hampered by the absence of institutional enforcement mechanisms to guarantee appropriate behavior by all parties involved. The tenuous nature of ties across national borders weakens enforceable trust, while the legal system of the home country is seen as illegitimate. A great deal of suspicion arises concerning the real motivations of immigrant and local leaders, the destination of funds, and the viability of projects. Finally, those instances of successful completion of local works give rise to unintended consequences, including the reactions of nearby communities that lack a comité abroad and vigorous efforts by national authorities to co-opt and redirect this flow of resources.

Conclusion: Theoretical and Practical Lessons

The three cases we have examined are illustrative, but not exhaustive, of all the variations that the relationship between social ties and community development can take. As mentioned at the start, other cases include those studied by Geertz (1963, 1965) in Bali and by Boissevain (1974) in Malta, places where dense social ties ended up suffocating individual initiative and entrepreneurial ventures. Taken together, these various instances indicate that bounded solidarity has a positive impact on local development when found in conjunction with well-established entrepreneurial traditions, artisanal or technical skills of some sort, and a favorable external environment. The successful local economies of Emilia-Romagna and Otavalo possess these elements in various measures. The development potential of Salvadoran transnationalism is stunted, on the other hand, by an adverse environment in which powerful political actors seek to co-opt rather than support these ventures.

Granovetter (this volume) argues that a key goal of economic sociology is to demonstrate under what circumstances trust can be used for development. We contribute to this agenda by exploring three distinct network structures that have propelled local initiatives. One could correctly describe the cases of Emilia-Romagna, Otavalo, and Salvadoran migrants as groups of entrepreneurs who learned how to access external opportunities and implement grassroots initiatives. The history of how social capital emerged in each case and was sustained (or not) over time, however, is sui generis and not easily subject to reproduction. In each instance, changes in external conditions also affected the continuation of particular developmental experiences. For example, the success of industrial districts in Emilia-Romagna sparked interest and successful takeover bids by large corporations (Harrison 1994), and the amount of resources channeled by Salvadoran hometown committees to their communities led to political competition in the effort to control this economic flow and its allocation. Hence, the very success of grassroots initiatives can draw into the picture external actors who change the nature of the interactions.

In summary, these examples illustrate three key aspects of social capital as bonds of solidarity and trust within a community: first, in conjunction with other factors, this economic and political mechanism can lead to successful, grassroots-led outcomes; second, it is quite difficult to bring it about; and third, unexpected consequences often emerge in the process of building the required preconditions. For the most part, the research literature has not found successful attempts at "social engineering" that seek to build solidaristic networks when few or none exist. More often than not, such attempts end in failure, either because of free-riding by some participants or because the communitarian structures quickly weaken after outside supports are removed (Portes and Itzigsohn 1994). Rather, successful developmental experiences build on what already exists, reinforcing existing social ties and working alongside definitions of the situation that are the product of specific historical trajectories. Colonialism in Ecuador, fascism in Italy, and a civil war in El Salvador are the direct historical antecedents for the surge of bounded solidarity in these particular settings.

There is no generalized formula to put such social ties to use in development. Instead, future successful experiences of community development will be achieved one at a time by combining existing community networks with careful nurturing of local skills and the provision of strategic external support. Bureaucratic top-down formulas that posit social capital as a magic wand for local ills will consistently fail. The best chance of positive developmental outcomes is offered by a more modest approach that departs from the need to adapt any external intervention to local traditions and forms of solidarity and to support popular initiatives with appropriate material resources.

A revised version of this chapter was originally presented at the Second Annual Conference on Economic and Organizational Sociology, University of Pennsylvania, March 4, 2000. Sections are drawn from Portes (2000), Portes and Landolt (1996), and Portes and Sensenbrenner (1993).

Note

1. This heritage is not social capital, as defined previously, but is akin to Bourdieu's (1980) definition of cultural capital as the skills and traditions common to members of a particular collectivity.

References

Arrighi, Giovanni. 1994. *The Long Twentieth Century: Money, Power, and the Origins of Our Times.* London: Verso Books.
Benton, Lauren A. 1989. "Industrial Subcontracting and the Informal Sector: The Politics of Restructuring in the Madrid Electronics Industry." In *The*

Informal Economy: Studies in Advanced and Less Developed Countries, edited by Alejandro Portes, Manuel Castells, and Lauren A. Benton. Baltimore: Johns Hopkins University Press.

Boissevain, Jeremy. 1974. *Friends of Friends, Networks, Manipulators, and Coalitions.* New York: St. Martin's.

Bourdieu, Pierre. 1979. "Les trois états du capital culturel." *Actes de la recherche en sciences sociales* 31: 3–6.

———. 1980. "Le capital social: Notes provisoires." *Actes de la recherche en sciences sociales* 31: 2–3.

Brusco, Sebastiano. 1982. "The Emilian Model: Productive Decentralization and Social Integration." *Cambridge Journal of Economics* 6: 167–84.

Bunker, Stephen. 1989. "Staples, Links, and Poles in the Construction of Regional Development Theories." *Sociological Forum* 4: 589–610.

Capecchi, Vittorio. 1989. "The Informal Economy and the Development of Flexible Specialization." In *The Informal Economy: Studies in Advanced and Less Developed Countries*, edited by Alejandro Portes, Manuel Castells, and Lauren A. Benton. Baltimore: Johns Hopkins University Press.

Cardoso, Fernando H., and Enzo Faletto. 1979. *Dependency and Development in Latin America.* Berkeley: University of California Press.

Castells, Manuel, and Roberto Laserna. 1989. "The New Dependency: Technological Change and Socioeconomic Restructuring in Latin America." *Sociological Forum* 4: 535–60.

Castells, Manuel, and Alejandro Portes. 1989. "World Underneath: The Origins, Dynamics, and Effects of the Informal Economy." In *The Informal Economy: Studies in Advanced and Less Developed Countries*, edited by Alejandro Portes, Manuel Castells, and Lauren A. Benton. Baltimore: Johns Hopkins University Press.

Centeno, Miguel Angel. 1994. *Democracy Within Reason: Technocratic Revolution in Mexico.* University Park: Pennsylvania State University Press.

Chalmers, Johnson. 1982. *MITI and the Japanese Miracle: The Growth of Industrial Policy, 1925–1975.* Stanford, Calif.: Stanford University Press.

Coleman, James S. 1988. "Social Capital in the Creation of Human Capital." *American Journal of Sociology* 94: S95–121.

———. 1990. *Foundations of Social Theory.* Cambridge, Mass.: Belknap Press of Harvard University Press.

———. 1993. "The Rational Reconstruction of Society" (1992 presidential address). *American Sociological Review* 58: 1–15.

Diaz, Alvaro. 1996. "Chile: ¿Hacia el pos-neoliberalismo?" Paper presented to the Conference on Responses of Civil Society to Neoliberal Adjustment, University of Texas at Austin (April).

Evans, Peter. 1995. *Embedded Autonomy: States and Industrial Transformation.* Princeton, N.J.: Princeton University Press.

Filgueira, Carlos. 1996. "Estado y sociedad civil: Políticas de ajuste estructural y estabilización en América Latina." Paper presented to the Conference on Responses of Civil Society to Neoliberal Adjustment, University of Texas at Austin (April).

Gambetta, Diego. 1993. *The Sicilian Mafia: The Business of Private Protection.* Cambridge, Mass.: Harvard University Press.

Geertz, Clifford. 1963. *Peddlers and Princes.* Chicago: University of Chicago Press.

———. 1965. *The Social History of an Indonesian Town.* Cambridge, Mass.: MIT Press.

Granovetter, Mark. 1995. "The Economic Sociology of Firms and Entrepreneurs." In *The Economic Sociology of Immigration,* edited by Alejandro Portes. New York: Russell Sage Foundation.

Harrison, Bennett. 1994. *Lean and Mean: The Changing Landscape of Corporate Power in the Age of Flexibility.* New York: Basic Books.

Hirschman, Albert O. 1963. *Journeys Toward Progress.* New York: Twentieth Century Fund.

Kyle, David. 1995. "The Transnational Peasant: The Social Construction of International Economic Migration and Transcommunities from the Ecuadoran Andes." Ph.D. diss., Johns Hopkins University, Department of Sociology.

———. 1999. "The Otavalo Trade Diaspora: Social Capital and Transnational Entrepreneurship." *Ethnic and Racial Studies* 22: 422–46.

Landolt, Patricia, Lilian Autler, and Sonia Baires. 1999. "From Hermano Lejano to Hermano Mayor: The Dialectics of Salvadoran Transnationalism." *Ethnic and Racial Studies* 22: 290–315.

Massey, Douglas S., Joaquin Arango, Graeme Hugo, Ali Kouaouci, Adela Pellegrino, and J. Edward Taylor. 1998. *Worlds in Motion: Understanding International Migration at the End of the Millennium.* Oxford: Clarendon Press.

Pérez-Sáinz, Juan Pablo. 1997. "Guatemala: Two Faces of the Metropolitan Area." In *The Urban Caribbean: Transition to the New Global Economy,* edited by Alejandro Portes, Carlos Dore-Cabral, and Patricia Landolt. Baltimore: Johns Hopkins University Press.

Piore, Michael J., and Charles F. Sabel. 1984. *The Second Industrial Divide.* New York: Basic Books.

Portes, Alejandro. 1997a. "Neoliberalism and the Sociology of Development: Emerging Trends and Unanticipated Facts." *Population and Development Review* 23: 229–59.

———. 1997b. "Immigration Theory for a New Century: Some Problems and Opportunities." *International Migration Review* 31(Winter): 799–825.

———. 1998. "Social Capital: Its Origins and Applications in Modern Sociology." *Annual Review of Sociology* 24: 1–24.

———. 2000. "The Two Meanings of Social Capital." *Sociological Forum* 15: 1–12.

Portes, Alejandro, Carlos Dore-Cabral, and Patricia Landolt. 1997. *The Urban Caribbean: Transition to the New Global Economy.* Baltimore: Johns Hopkins University Press.

Portes, Alejandro, and José Itzigsohn. 1994. "The Party or the Grass Roots: A Comparative Analysis of Urban Political Participation in the Caribbean Basin." *International Journal of Urban and Regional Research* 18: 491–508.

Portes, Alejandro, and Douglas Kincaid. 1989. "Sociology and Development in the 1990s: Critical Challenges and Empirical Trends." *Sociological Forum* 4: 479–503.

Portes, Alejandro, and Patricia Landolt. 1996. "The Downside of Social Capital." *The American Prospect* 26: 18–22.

Portes, Alejandro, and Julia Sensenbrenner. 1993. "Embeddedness and Immigration: Notes on the Social Determinants of Economic Action." *American Journal of Sociology* 98: 1320–50.

Putnam, Robert D. 1993. "The Prosperous Community: Social Capital and Public Life." *The American Prospect* 13: 35–42.

———. 1995. "Bowling Alone: America's Declining Social Capital." *Journal of Democracy* 6: 65–78.

Waldinger, Roger. 1995. "The 'Other Side' of Embeddedness: A Case Study of the Interplay Between Economy and Ethnicity." *Ethnic and Racial Studies* 18: 555–80.

Ybarra, Josep-Antoni. 1989. "Informalization in the Valencian Economy: A Model for Underdevelopment." In *The Informal Economy: Studies in Advanced and Less Developed Countries,* edited by Alejandro Portes, Manuel Castells, and Lauren A. Benton. Baltimore: Johns Hopkins University Press.

Zhou, Min, and Carl L. Bankston. 1998. *Growing up American: How Vietnamese Immigrants Adapt to Life in the United States.* New York: Russell Sage Foundation.

= Chapter 13 =

Globalization and Mobilization: Resistance to Neoliberalism in Latin America

Susan Eckstein

Neoliberal restructuring, designed to privilege market forces and diminish the state's economic role, has taken the Third World by storm since the mid-1980s. Third World governments have had little choice in the matter. The new economic model has been imposed by multilateral lending institutions and by the U.S. government, which are committed to restructuring the world in their image. Packaged as a model that maximizes efficiency, the discourse conceals measures designed to benefit capital over labor—and big multinational capital above all—through the removal of fetters that previously obstructed the global mobility of capital.

Third World countries differ, however, in how deeply they have transformed their political economies, owing to differences both in government commitment to the reform process and in civil society resistance. How have ordinary people experienced the reforms, and how have they reacted to those reforms not to their liking? In this chapter, I explore the propositions that many in the lower, working, and even the middle class have suffered as a result of the restructuring, and that victims have resisted the reforms in a variety of ways. They typically have not attacked neoliberalism directly or in the abstract. Rather, they have responded to the effects of restructuring in their everyday lives. The range of resistance reveals that ordinary people are not mystified by the rhetoric of reform.

Strategies of resistance range from overtly coordinated protest to covert individual and collective noncompliance with demands made from "above" and abroad to "exit"—that is, to depart for more promising prospects elsewhere. A combination of new deprivations and newly felt injustices, new frames for interpreting them, and new perceptions of how they can be corrected have stirred diverse efforts to contain neoliberal globalization. Mobilizations draw on postmodern and antimodern as well as modernist claims and strategies. Responses to market reforms are shaped by the social context in which economic life is embedded. That context includes institutional life and the cultural beliefs embedded in institutional life.

The relationship between neoliberalism and resistance is rarely direct. People's reactions are tempered by mediating factors such as state structures and strength, relations between state and society, conceptions of rights, the vibrancy of civil society and society in its less organized form, and underlying identities. Mediating factors may change over time, sometimes as a result of earlier mobilizations for change, and they shape how people perceive objective conditions, options, and the risks of rebellion. They also shape the strategies and cultural expressions that movements take on. While resistance can thus best be understood from a contextualized institutional perspective, responses are socially patterned but not predetermined.

Because responses to reforms are contextually contingent, they are best understood from a comparative and historical vantage point. For this reason, the chapter focuses on resistance to neoliberalism in a single region, Latin America. I begin by briefly describing macro political, social, cultural, and economic changes since the mid-1980s. That description is followed by an analysis of two key exit strategies through which people have sought greener pastures elsewhere, migration and immigration. The remainder of the chapter focuses on the social mobilizations that have been stirred by specific neoliberal reforms and that involve people who have opted not to exit.

Contrasting with this contextualized institutional approach, at one extreme, are neoliberal economists and others who attach primacy to global modernization dynamics and transnational homogenizing tendencies, as well as international policymakers and political analysts who point to a correlation and natural affinity between democratization and market reforms. They perceive the homogenization to be good and believe that political institutions provide appropriate venues for channeling concerns. Their frame of analysis does not point them to social movements, which they would see as obstructions both to the full play of market forces and to democratic institutional practices.

Postmodernists, at the other extreme, focus on local resistance and local variability, which they attribute to disparately held beliefs and norms. From their perspective, Third World people do not automatically accept the views and practices imposed from above and abroad, and there is no unilinear path of development. In place of global universal structures, processes, and values, postmodernists highlight what they call "decentered" particularities, which are rooted not merely or mainly in institutional relations but in individual and group perceptions and beliefs. Paradoxically, these two extreme perspectives gained currency in the 1990s.

Meanwhile, Marxian analyses continue to attribute primacy to class dynamics on the national and international levels, and they see social change as driven first and foremost by class interests. To the extent that they focus on resistance to change, they highlight economically rooted social movements—above all movements rooted in production or market relations.

State-centric analysts, in turn, highlight how the state, institutionally and ideologically, mediates between globalization tendencies, on the one hand, and civil society, on the other. Social movements are thus seen as responses not merely to globally grounded tendencies, class dynamics, or decentered local beliefs, customs, and norms, as neoliberal-modernization, Marxist, and postmodern analysts emphasize, but to state institutional structures, practices, and discourse.

Finally, "moral economists" argue that people's understandings of life, including of what is just and unjust, are grounded in institutional arrangements filtered through distinctive cultural views of the world. Ordinary people are especially likely, from this perspective, to envision any economic situation that threatens their subsistence as morally unacceptable (see Thompson 1971; Scott 1976). But moral economists recognize that views toward injustices are not necessarily overtly transparent. Hegemonic groups typically propagate ideology and discourse in a manner that presents their own views as the generalized views of society, and people in subordinate positions may feel the risks are too great to challenge publicly conditions they consider unjust (see Scott 1985, 1990). Under the circumstances, they are likely to turn to "everyday forms of resistance," to borrow Scott's now-famous terminology, such as foot-dragging, deceit, and pilfering, and to cultural repertoires of resistance. Over time such disobedience may do more to bring about change than overt challenges to authority. Publicly concealed noncompliance may undermine productivity and legitimacy to the point that elites feel the need to institute significant reforms.

Each perspective focuses on distinctive features of a world that in the concrete is complex. Each frame of analysis highlights certain ten-

dencies while leaving others unnoticed, undocumented, and un-
analyzed. Although a specific frame of analysis may reveal more and
may account more accurately for what indeed transpires, precisely
because different frames privilege different information, each is more
illuminating in certain contexts than others. In the following sections,
I explore the ways in which the features identified with the different
perspectives highlight and explain resistance to neoliberal reforms insofar as these features take meaning through historically grounded
institutional life.

Global Restructuring

With the collapse of the Soviet Union and the Soviet bloc, capitalism
emerged indisputably victorious. In the new world order a new economic model emerged, one that the United States and the multilateral
institutions with which it associates used their power to impose: neoliberalism. Neoliberalism privileges market forces. It calls for efficient
land use and for the removal of obstacles that prevent the free mobility of capital and product markets, globally and not merely within
the confines of nation-states. Although neoliberalism calls for the removal of institutional labor market protections within individual
economies, it does not extol the free mobility of labor across national
borders. Neoliberalism thus expands the rights of capital, not labor,
on a global scale.[1]

Neoliberalism is premised on the rejection of import substitution
industrialization (ISI), the development strategy of choice in Latin
America and other parts of the Third World after World War II. Conceived in Latin America, it was premised on antiforeign sentiments
and designed to carve out space for national capital. While granting
labor certain rights, with import substitution governments promoted
industrial production for the domestic market. In so doing, they neglected exports that would offset import costs, and they installed tariffs that shielded inefficient enterprises from foreign competition. The
debt crises of the 1980s, rooted in good part in the weak export sectors, proved the coup de grâce to import substitution. The development model was discredited, and the crises created the conditions
under which the International Monetary Fund (IMF), together with
U.S. and foreign banks, pressed for neoliberal restructuring.

In contrast to import substitution, neoliberalism was imported
from the north and is foreign-friendly. It is premised on a modernization conceptual frame that envisions poor countries as potentially and
ideally replicating the experience of the industrial world, above all

the United States. What is perceived as good for the United States is presumed to be good, in turn, for the less developed world.

In joining the neoliberal bandwagon, Latin American governments lowered barriers to trade, eliminated or reduced price subsidies, privatized their economies, encouraged exports and policies to make their export sectors more competitive, and reduced state social expenditures. The changes facilitated a restructuring of production, consumption, and capital accumulation globally.

By the 1990s democracy as well as neoliberal capitalism appeared victorious. The world experienced a so-called third democratic wave, and Latin America joined the bandwagon. The repressive military regimes that had ruled in most countries in the region since the 1960s and early 1970s were relegated to the dustbins of history, though not before hundreds of thousands of Latin Americans were murdered, millions internally dislocated, and others forced into exile. Both domestic changes and changes abroad contributed to the political transformations. Abroad, Washington retracted military aid after the cold war ended, except to drug economies in the region. Latin America became, from Washington's vantage point, safe for democracy. U.S. authorities began to believe there was a natural affinity between market economies and competitive party electoral regimes.[2] Meanwhile, on the domestic front, broad-based cross-class movements in a number of countries helped delegitimate the military governments (see Eckstein 2001 [1989]). The interests of most Latin Americans and Washington here converged.

At the same time new global social and cultural trends made their way to Latin America. New nongovernmental organizations (NGOs) and networks brought new material resources and, more important, new ideas and social capital to the region. Church-linked groups, their work based on new biblical interpretations, became especially influential, initially when repressive regimes closed down formal political channels and when governments implemented neoliberal austerity policies that caused subsistence crises among the poor. The NGOs brought new conceptions of rights, and they sparked new identities, including among indigenous peoples, women, and social minorities. Reflecting the new views, the constitutions of the new democracies addressed for the first time the rights of minorities, not merely as individuals but as collectivities.

Turning now to my analysis of the combination of macro changes that influenced first the proclivity to exit and then to rebel, I focus on arenas of neoliberal reforms: trade liberalization and export promotion, state-sector downsizing, and price liberalization. Although analytically distinguishable, movements often are grounded in a combination of neoliberal changes, and they often are fused with grievances that have other social roots.

The examples of protest, which should be viewed as illustrative, are based on information combed from newspaper accounts, summary sources of Latin American weekly news events, statistical compilations, and secondary sources.[3] I focus on economically grounded protests but include movements centering on new socially constructed identities that combine non-economic with economic demands. Under the conditions of the 1990s, for example, ethnicity and gender, not merely class, became important sources of identity and bases through which the new economic order was experienced and challenged.

Exit Versus Voice

People unhappy with their plight can make individual efforts to improve their situation. One form of such individual effort, exit, has been more common in twentieth-century Latin America than collective resistance.[4] Exit poses fewer risks, and the potential gain is often better. However, such individuated responses are not risk-free and not without personal costs. And because individuated responses are embedded in family and community, they need to be understood in the context of collective traditions and practices.

In the post–World War II period, mounting impoverishment in the Latin American countryside contributed to rural-to-urban migration, especially to the key cities in the region. This trend originated during the era of import substitution. In 1980, before neoliberalism took Latin America by storm, the region already had an urbanization rate at least twice as great as that of other Third World regions—a rate not much lower than the rate in wealthy countries, which had more developed industrial and post-industrial infrastructures (see World Bank 1999). The pressure to leave the provinces was rooted first and foremost in the highly inegalitarian distribution of land and rural income traceable to colonialism. Additional factors were the virtual absence of twentieth-century state supports for making productive use of land, abysmal rural wages, and the urban bias of import substitution governments.

With the deepening of neoliberalism in the 1990s, Latin America became as urban as industrial countries, but without comparable urban opportunities (World Bank 1999). Three-fourths of Latin Americans came to live in cities (see table 13.1). Latin Americans migrating to the cities at this time built on long-standing rural-urban networks.

The rates of urbanization were so high by the 1990s that the rural-

Table 13.1   Latin American Population Living in Cities

Year	Percentage
1960	49
1970	57
1980	65
1990	71
1994	73
1997	74

Source: Author's calculations for World Bank 1999.

to-urban migration option for all intents and purposes closed down. On a reduced scale, some city-dwellers engaged in "reverse migration." More significantly, urban and rural dwellers alike turned increasingly to emigration, primarily but not exclusively to the United States. The migration across borders reflects a growing disparity in opportunities between the weakest and strongest economies in the region, and most of all between all Latin American countries and the United States, the core economy in the hemisphere. It is noteworthy that neoliberalism in the Western Hemisphere does not allow for the free legal international mobility of labor along with the free mobility of capital.

Latin America came to account for 43 to 54 percent of all legal immigrants to the United States between the mid-1980s and the century's end (see table 13.2)—close to the percentage of legal immigrants who were European in the midtwentieth century (see Borjas 1999, 10). Immigration from the region picked up following state implementation of austerity and other IMF-backed reforms designed to reduce fiscal expenditures and increase export earnings. In some countries, especially El Salvador, Guatemala, Nicaragua, Peru, and Colombia, political violence that was only partially explained by neoliberal-linked economic dislocations and impoverization also contributed to emigration.

But U.S. law restricted the exit option. Washington privileged the entry of skilled workers and professionals and foreigners seeking family reunification. For this reason, some Latin Americans who could not enter legally came illegally. Of the estimated 5 million undocumented immigrants in 1996, 80 percent came from Latin America (U.S. Immigration and Naturalization Service 1999, 199–200). Mexico, which shares a two-thousand-mile border with the United States, accounted for the largest number of illegal U.S. entrants. The North American Free Trade Agreement (NAFTA) allowed for the free mo-

Table 13.2   Latin American and Caribbean Immigration to the United
             States (Legal Immigrants)

Year	Number of Immigrants
1961 to 1970	1,303,064
1971 to 1980	1,812,796
1981 to 1990	3,458,287
1995	218,650
1997	295,918

	Percentage of Total U.S. Immigration
1955 to 1964	41
1965 to 1974	46
1975 to 1984	40
1985 to 1994	54
1995 to 1997	43
1998	45

Source: U.S. Immigration and Naturalization Service 1999, 20, 25–31.

bility of investment and goods between Mexico, the United States, and Canada, but, once again, not for the free mobility of labor.

Domestic Resistance to Changes Grounded in Trade and Foreign Investment Liberalization and Promotion

Pressed to generate hard currency, to pay for imports, and to repay foreign debts, Latin American governments since the mid-1980s have used their powers to promote exports, both traditional and nontraditional. Given the close ties between authorities and economic elites and typically biased especially toward big business, governments favored large-scale commercial farm exporters over domestically oriented peasant producers. (The large farmers are more efficient in terms of output per unit of labor input, but often not in terms of acreage yields.) And within the industrial sector, governments promoted low-wage, labor-intensive, subcontracting, maquila-type firms that produced for overseas sales. In this sector Latin America (and other Third World) countries had a competitive advantage, based on cheap labor.

To favor exports, the governments adjusted their exchange rates.[5] These adjustments may have been economically sound at the macro level, but many peasants and workers, as well as the credit-dependent middle class, experienced dislocations, deprivations, and new insecurities as a result. Had exit not been an option, tensions undoubtedly would have fueled more protests. Even resistance movements that were grounded in dislocations brought about by trade and investment liberalization, however, reflected an interplay of cultural, social, political, with economic forces. Because of such interplay, the key agrarian, industrial, and urban movements described here took different forms in different countries.

Agrarian Resistance

The removal of trade barriers and the new export emphasis subjected peasant producers to new and fierce competition from domestic and foreign agribusiness and to world market vicissitudes, more than during the import substitution era. And in countries where neoliberal governments retracted agrarian reforms that had protected peasant land rights, such as Mexico and Chile, small-scale producers were made especially vulnerable to market forces. Large farmers, with their access to more capital, technology, and land and their better marketing networks, were much better placed to compete in the new economic order.

The renowned Zapatista movement in Chiapas, Mexico's poorest region, was explicitly framed in terms of neoliberalism. The Zapatistas timed their appearance in the public arena with the 1994 inauguration of NAFTA. They challenged the neoliberal economic model underlying that agreement as no other group had, and in so doing inspired a range of social movements elsewhere in the country (and abroad).

NAFTA formalized free trade, a key feature, as noted, of neoliberalism. Although the accord was not the cause per se of the new movement, it provided a frame for channeling grievances, including those having to do with conditions that antedated neoliberalism and were unrelated to it. And in strategically timing their emergence from the jungle, where they had trained, with the initiation of the historic agreement, the Zapatistas immediately brought their cause to the attention of the world. As the Zapatistas well knew, the international media had gathered in Mexico to cover the event.

From the onset Zapatistas combined a variety of strategies and a variety of demands. They combined guerrilla with populist and electoral tactics, indigenous rights claims with neoliberal-linked grievances, a shared sense of socioeconomic deprivation with political and cultural demands, pressure for national change with pressure for local change, and usage of historical symbolism, including the very naming of the movement, with state-of-the-art cyberspace strategies.[6] Meanwhile, human rights groups, other NGOs, and a new center-left political party, the Revolutionary Democratic Party (PRD), helped champion their cause.

To the extent that Zapatistas constructed their movement around the new economic order, they attacked not merely free trade but other measures as well. Along with calling for the repeal of NAFTA, they demanded protection of the communal lands threatened by President Carlos Salinas de Gortari's market-oriented agrarian reform as well as the restoration of the farm price subsidies retracted by Salinas and his predecessor.

From a neoliberal vantage point, the Zapatista movement reflects an effort to contain market permeation. But Zapatistas simultaneously pressed for respect for cultural and political autonomy and for community and collective along with individual rights. The latter demands were grounded in local ethnic identities that were long-standing but had not previously served as the basis for claims. Although the Zapatistas did not stop neoliberal restructuring, either nationally or locally, they did temper state market interventions. Authorities pumped record funds into the state of Chiapas for infrastructure and other projects, and they tolerated semisubsistence cultivation.

Officials gave a higher priority to maintaining political order and political loyalty than to deepening the market. Brutality on a large scale would have fueled support for nascent opposition parties. Meanwhile, the involvement of new internationally linked NGO human rights groups compelled the government to be more accountable for its actions than in years past.

The Zapatistas, though the most famous, were not the only agriculturalists in Mexico to protest the deepening of neoliberal restructuring. Dairy farmers, as well as grain, bean, and corn farmers, became defiant when the government lowered or ended tariffs that had shielded local producers from cheaper goods from abroad. In the sixth year of NAFTA, dairy farmers, for example, demonstrated in Mexico City against new powdered milk imports, with which they could not compete. As they paraded through the streets, they dumped rancid milk they could not sell.

Concomitantly, in Ecuador neoliberal trade-linked reforms, in the context of a slimmed-down state, also fueled an indigenous movement (see Zamosc 1994; Yashar 1998; Peeler 2002). In response to liberalization of the foreign investment regulations designed to encourage hard-currency-generating exports, Amazonian Indians there pressed for territorial autonomy and a say in the terms of oil exploration in their region. The indigenous movement came to include Indians in the more populated highlands as well, Indians affected less by trade liberalization as by other neoliberal reforms. As in Chiapas, in Ecuador the indigenous movement combined market-linked grievances with collectivistic and antimodern claims, and restorative pressures with demands for new rights. The movement sought a redefinition of citizenship that recognized indigenous rights to cultural distinctiveness, including a right to bilingual education and the legalization of Indian medicine (Zamosc 1994).

By the turn of the century the previously marginal and powerless indigenous population had gone so far as to seek inclusion in the ruling Ecuadorian political coalition (though without success). Leadership crafted a new trans-ethnic village social formation. As the movement gained momentum, the indigenistas allied with organized urban groups, especially labor, and they combined their economic and cultural demands with broader political demands.

That trade liberalization is not the only base of new indigenous movements is demonstrated by trends in the three other Latin American countries with substantial Indian populations: Guatemala, Bolivia, and Peru. (For a comparative analysis of indigenous movements in the 1990s, see Yashar 1998.) In Guatemala, neoliberal pressures and the human rights language that accompanied transitions to democracy left many Mayans aware of growing economic disparities and their exclusion from new institutional arrangements. Building on frustrations rooted in the civil war of the 1980s, a multi-class, pan-Mayan, rural-urban movement arose. New Mayan organizations criticized the Western development model and its assimilation emphasis and, as in Ecuador, promoted a new social formation that transcended local ethnic differences (Warren 1998). Yet the movement to date has not been framed around any specific neoliberal critique.

Meanwhile, in Bolivia, indigenous activism, which began in the 1970s, by the 1990s had been co-opted by the neoliberal government. President Gonzalo Sánchez de Lozada (1993 to 1997), a prerevolutionary latifundista (large landowner who utilized servile labor), selected an indigenous vice president, introduced bilingual education, and paved the way for the incorporation of Indian customary law into the country's legal system. Although the state's ethnic-inclusionary approach was designed to preempt ethnicity from becoming a basis for resistance to market reforms, under Sánchez de Lozada's successor it failed to contain protests by indigenous peoples.

Peru is the one country with a sizable Indian population that experienced no indigenous movement of significance, around neoliberalism or any other issues. There, in response to a partially Maoist-inspired guerrilla movement, Sendero Luminoso (Shining Path), the government promoted anti-Sendero community groups (rondas) and the militarization of the countryside. These initiatives served to divide the countryside in a manner that submerged ethnic identities and ethnically grounded resistance, even when neoliberal reforms exacerbated poverty (McClintock 1997).[7] The election of Toledo as president in 2001 kindled Indian politicization but not around indigenous issues. Toledo was Peru's first top official with Indian features and heritage.

The agrarian social structure in Brazil was not grounded in comparable Indian roots. But neoliberal deepening there fueled support for a non-indigenous agrarian movement. In a country that already had one of the world's most unequal distributions of land, export-oriented commercial farmers aggressively expanded their holdings and capitalized their operations in the 1990s. As a result, the number of small farms in Brazil dropped from over 3 million to under 1 million in a ten-year period (Langevin and Rosset 1997, 2).

With small farmer marginalization and growing landlessness, the ranks of the Landless Workers Movement (MST) swelled. The MST appealed to rural laborers' desire for both land and social welfare. Between the mid-1980s, when it was first formed, and the mid-1990s, the MST successfully helped negotiate land claims for 146,000 families involving nearly 5 million hectares (Langevin and Rosset 1997; Hammond 1999). For the first time landless peasants pressed not merely for land but for other entitlements. Emphasizing community building within and solidarity among encampments, the MST also successfully pressed for health care, education, and agricultural extension services. To advance its cause it organized invasions of idle land, blocked highways, and organized a two-month one-thousand-kilometer march to the country's capital in 1997.

The most dynamic and influential Brazilian social movement of the 1990s, the MST built on earlier pro-democracy movements and on the work of trade unions and church groups. The MST also benefited from a government—under Fernando Henrique Cardoso—that was publicly committed to reform, not repression. But the movement experienced losses as well as gains. Some one thousand activists and landless MST sympathizers reportedly were assassinated or injured during the first ten years of the movement's existence. Military police troops, who sided with landowners, were responsible for most of the fatalities, and they operated in the main with impunity (Hammond 1999; Langevin and Rosset 1997). The government intervened only minimally in landowner-labor conflicts, which on balance worked to the advantage of large farmers.

In the Brazilian Amazon, indigenous movements simultaneously gained a footing, but of a different sort from the main movements in Mexico, Ecuador, and Guatemala. Accounting for a smaller portion of the national population and reflecting a different ethnic-social organization, Brazilian Amazonian groups focused initially on rights to their traditional means of livelihood. Large farmers encroached on their lands to take advantage of expanding export market opportunities. With their own hired militia, the large farmers murdered some one thousand indigenous peoples, the famed leader of the rubber-tappers, Francisco "Chico" Mendes, among them (see Keck 1995). The assassins here too operated with impunity, reflecting close ties between large landowners and juridical and other authorities.

To strengthen their cause under these circumstances, Amazonian groups allied with national and international NGOs and other sympathetic groups. The explosion of social movements in the final years of military rule (which ended in the mid-1980s) included environmental and "new unionism" groups. Brazil came to have the leading environmental movement in Latin America, a movement that included a Green Party and diverse territorially dispersed ecological groups. In this context, and with the help of NGOs, rubber-tappers and other Amazon indigenous peoples brought their concerns to the attention of the world. But the support came with a reframing of their movement as an effort to save the rain forest (Keck 1995).

As dependence on international markets picked up with trade liberalization, peasants turned, where ecological conditions were suited, to production of the one crop in Latin America that proved increasingly profitable, owing to growing foreign demand: coca (cocaine). Here, Latin American governments, under U.S. pressure, sought to *restrict* free trade and market-driven production, while peasants favored liberalization. Defending their economic interests, peasants protested U.S.-backed government crop eradication efforts and sided with guerrillas who protected their crops.

Cocaine fueled Latin America's largest and most violent guerrilla movement of the 1990s, in Colombia. By the century's end paramilitary forces and local private armies had entered the war previously fought between guerrillas and the military. Under a veneer of democracy the rule of law disintegrated. Colombia in the 1990s had one of the highest homicide rates in the world, and the highest rate identified as politically motivated. There were an estimated 35,000 murders in a ten-year period, more than under any of the notoriously repressive South American military regimes of the 1960s through 1980s. Some 62, 27, and 11 percent of the Colombian deaths in the mid-1990s were attributed, respectively, to paramilitaries, guerrillas, and the military (Chernick 1997). The struggle also left more than 1 million Colombians refugees in their own country. As the decades-old Colombian Revolutionary Armed Forces (FARC), the main guerrilla group, came to control 40 percent of the countryside, the conflict increasingly centered on cocaine, not ideology. While stepping up kidnappings, murders, and extortions, they defended coca producers, processors, and distributors—in return for a "cocaine tax." In the late 1990s the guerrillas were believed to collect $60 million a month.

The strife was exacerbated by neoliberalism, but not primarily grounded in it. Colombia's neoliberal restructuring became tied to the worst economic downturn since the Depression. The new economic model contributed to a contraction of economic opportunities, which made stakes in the drug economy all the greater. Colombia, the world's largest cocaine paste producer, has a comparative advantage in production of the commodity. No other economic activity in the country is as lucrative. At the same time the strife built on a culture of violence dating back at least to the 1930s. The economic crisis then fueled a civil war, known as La Violencia. Although it is not the principal cause of the 1990s breakdown of law and order, violence is part of the Colombian repertoire of resistance.

Washington, anxious to stop the drug problem "at its source," even if such efforts were inconsistent with its neoliberal commitment, became part of the problem in the very process of attempting to be its solution. U.S. intervention had the effect of exacerbating violence and the breakdown of the rule of law. Not only did military aid contribute to military (and paramilitary) brutality, but U.S.-backed coca crop eradication projects angered coca farmers to the point that they mobilized in protest and increasingly sided with the guerrillas. With their means of livelihood threatened, some 241,000 coca-growing campesinos, for example, staged a protest march in 1996. Threatened with massive unrest, the Colombian government cut back the eradication program. Forced to choose between termination of coca production and threats to its claims to rule, it opted for its immediate institutional political interests. More significantly, state authority withered as the illegal drug economy became entrenched.

On a more reduced and less violent scale, and without ties to a guerrilla movement, Bolivia also experienced tumult associated with the world demand for coca. Under U.S. pressure and with U.S. assistance, the Bolivian government also sought to eradicate export-oriented coca production. And there too coca growers did not acquiesce, at least not initially. In the Chapare, where one-quarter of the world's cocaine supply originates, crop eradication projects stirred coca growers to organize, blockade crucial roads, and fight security forces (*New York Times*, February 22, 1998, 4). Only when fear of losing U.S.

certification and U.S. aid induced President Hugo Banzer at the turn of the century to move massive military forces into the region and to pay peasants thousands of dollars to destroy their bushes did peasants cut back their yields. Nonetheless, with coca generating up to four times as much income as other crops, production moved to other locations where it was not policed (and to Colombia). In essence, peasants resisted state (and U.S.) intrusion into their export-based, market-driven production. Yet, Bolivia only produced the coca; it did not engage in the more profitable industrial processing of cocaine. With lower stakes, Bolivia avoided civil disorder and violence on the Colombian scale.

Urban and Industrial-Based Movements

Although export promotion and trade liberalization in Latin America mainly stirred collective resistance in the countryside, these practices also stirred some urban movements and some movements that straddled the rural-urban divide. In particular, neoliberal-linked currency devaluations designed in part to strengthen export competitiveness hurt those who relied on bank loans to finance their economic activity. Devaluations drove up the cost of hard currency loan repayments and business-related imports. Devaluations are not unique to neoliberalism, but their effect is felt more deeply in an open market economy. Meanwhile, within the growing export-oriented industrial sector, labor showed incipient signs of trying to organize for improved conditions—with the support of transnational solidarity groups.

In the 1990s debtors banded together for the first time to protest conditions that had caused their debts to spiral. One of the most interesting of such movements was El Barzón in Mexico. Starting in 1993 with a few thousand farmers angered about state termination of production and consumption supports, the movement spread to urban settings, where it came to include tens of thousands of the under- and unemployed, as well as housewives, retailers, taxi drivers, workers, and businessmen. What unified El Barzón supporters was a tripling of bank interest rates, combined with a precipitous plunge in living standards, after the 1994 devaluation.

The Mexican debtors' alliance combined new strategies of defiance and new postmodernist cultural expressions with old ones. Supporters staged raucous street theater and parades and sometimes featured effigies of corrupt judges. They demonstrated in public places, sometimes with their machinery, their means of production, in hand. And in August 1996 they all but halted trading on the Mexican stock exchange. Concomitantly, they collectively organized defenses against moneylenders and police who confiscated their properties when they were forced to default on loans. Barzonistas sometimes successfully reclaimed their tractors, cars, and farms and convinced bank officials both to restructure outstanding loans and extend new credit lines. They also convinced the government to initiate debt relief programs. The multi-class base of the movement, combined with multiple strategies of resistance, induced banks and authorities to be responsive. And in selectively responding to El Barzón demands, the government defused movement support.

Possibly inspired by El Barzón, a debtors' movement arose in Brazil. There too the movement was a response to macro economic policies that had caused interest rates to soar and the value of the national currency to plunge. Formed in 1997, the debtors' rights movement claimed ten thousand members in two dozen Brazilian cities by early 1999 (*Wall Street Journal,* January 6, 1999, 1). The Brazilians deployed a different strategy than their Mexican counterparts. They deliberately clogged the courts with lawsuits. Debtors thereby had leverage. Since legal cases can drag on for years, creditors would settle for debt rescheduling or partial debt forgiveness.

Both trade and foreign investment liberalization contributed to the expansion of maquila, subcontracting firms that have become especially common in the apparel and assembly-line electronic field. Set up to produce for consumer markets in the United States (and other wealthy countries), they located in the region (especially in Central America, Mexico, and the Caribbean) to take advantage of cheap labor. Global competition in this export-oriented sector contributes to a so-called race to the bottom. Foreign-financed, these export-oriented industries reflect the neoliberal-linked globalization of product markets. Workers in the sector, unlike in the industries of the import substitution era, typically had limited work benefits, if any. But several factors made unionization and protest difficult. For one, with the world open to such firms, business could easily relocate if labor became demanding. Second, local officials, anxious to attract business, typically sided with management in disputes. Third, there was a seemingly unlimited supply of unskilled laborers in each country who were willing to work in the factories, undermining maquiladora worker bargaining power.

Not surprisingly, nascent strike activity was concentrated in the more skilled sector. Skilled labor, in scarce supply, had bargaining power that unskilled labor lacked. By the turn of the century the main maquila factory to experience protest was the Han Young plant in Tijuana, which produces car chassis for the Korean Hyundai Corporation. Workers had tried to form a union independent of government control beginning in 1997. But management, in its effort to quell the labor strife, had the backing of the state government and local police. (For reports on the labor strife in the maquila sector, see the International Confederation of Free Trade Unions' "ICFTU OnLine.")

Privatizations and Public-Sector Retrenchment

Under import substitution, the public sector grew in economic importance, including through the proliferation of state-owned enterprises. And the public sector became the strongest unionized sector, involving salaried professionals and other middle-class employees, along with industrial workers.

Unions, however, were not sufficiently forceful to shield members from some of the most far-reaching privatization programs in the world. In the process, middle- and working-class employees lost some of the economic and social rights they had enjoyed, including rights to jobs, a minimum wage, and health and other benefits, as well as the right to unionize. Even though democratization in principle restored such labor prerogatives, such as the right to strike (which the military governments in the region had retracted between the 1960s and 1980s), the neoliberal-committed regimes in practice contained those rights.

The neoliberal attack on the public sector was multi-pronged. First, governments sold off state-owned enterprises. Second, in attempting to make state-owned enterprises more attractive to potential private investors, governments sought to bring public-sector unions to heel. This happened, for example, in El Salvador and Nicaragua. Third, governments slashed employment and wages in the remaining public sector to reduce fiscal expenditures and maximize efficiency. And in the private as well as the public sector, governments sought to reform labor codes to weaken worker rights.

But governments encountered resistance. Although globalization had weakened labor's bargaining power with capital, governments were less immune to protest. For one, government activity was somewhat shielded from global market pressures. This gave labor a certain leverage. Second, by their very nature states are politically vulnerable, especially democracies, which depend on electoral backing. This vulnerability works to the advantage of public-sector employees as well. Third, as large employers, governments hurt many workers simultaneously when they downsized. Aggrieved workers accordingly realized that their personal deprivations were collectively shared. For this combination of reasons, virtually all countries experienced pub-

Table 13.3   Shifts in Strike Activity in Latin America, by Country, 1990 to 1999 (Percentage)

Country	Change in Number of Strikes	Change in Number of Strikers	Change in Workdays Not Worked
Bolivia	+480	—	—
Brazil	−69	−73[a]	−91
Chile	−39	−57	−96
Colombia	−39[a]	−96[d]	—
Costa Rica[b]	−79	−35	+61
Dominican Republic	−71	+262[c]	—
Ecuador	−90[a]	−92[a]	−83
El Salvador	+80	+1660	+308
Guatemala	−5	—	—
Honduras[e]	−14	—	—
Mexico	−69	−11	−70
Nicaragua	−96	−97	−99
Panama[f]	—	—	—
Peru	−88	−94	−77

Source: International Labor Office 1998, 1205, 1230; 2000, 1336–40, 1358–61, 1380–83.
[a]1990 to 1994 change.
[b]1990 to 1997 change.
[c]1995 to 1998 change.
[d]1990 to 1993 change.
[e]1990 to 1998 change.
[f]1990 to 1998 change. In 1990 Panama had no strikes. In 1998, there were three strikes, carried out by 269,260 strikers, and 154,130 days were not worked.

lic-sector strikes in the 1990s, and at a higher rate than in years past. State-employed police, bureaucrats, doctors, nurses, teachers, and other public-sector workers became the most defiant opponents of work-based restructuring.

With redemocratization, strike activity initially picked up in the private sector as well as the state sector. The strikes were more politically than economically inspired. They reflected the lifting of repression and labor efforts to press for pent-up demands. Protest soon tapered off, however, even as work conditions deteriorated. It waned especially in the private industrial sector, which had previously been the center of strike activity.

Table 13.3 summarizes data on Latin American strike activity in the 1990s, the period of both neoliberal and democratic consolidation. According to available information, substantially more countries experienced decreases than increases on the three standard indicators of workplace disruptions: number of strikes, number of workers in-

Table 13.4   Employment and Salaries in Latin America, 1985 to 1996

	1985	1990	1995	1996	1997[a]
Unemployment rate	8.3	5.7	7.2	7.7	7.2
Informal-sector employment[b]	47.0	51.6	56.1	57.4	n.d.
Industrial salaries[c]	89.9	84.7	98.8	102.2	102.6
Minimum wage[c]	83.5	68.5	70.8	69.9	73.7

Source: V. Tokman 1997, 152.
[a]Estimates.
[b]Non-agricultural employment.
[c]1980 = 100.

volved, and workdays not worked. Moreover, strike activity declined even though real industrial wages in the region, on average, declined at the time and did not surpass the 1980 level until 1996, and the minimum wage (in real terms) dropped with debt-crisis-linked restructuring without rebounding even by the latter 1990s (see table 13.4).[8] Not merely global competition but labor-unfriendly governments made work-based disruptions and general strikes difficult to organize and personally risky.[9]

The tempering of strike activity in Latin America takes on added significance when compared to the United States. During the same period labor in the United States also became a shadow of its former self. Strike activity declined, though by less than in most Latin American countries: from 1990 to 1999, the number of strikes in the United States decreased by 23 percent, the number of strikers decreased by 61 percent, and the number of workdays not worked decreased by 66 percent (International Labor Office 2000, 1065, 1073, 1342). In essence, the deepening of neoliberalism eroded labor's power in the stronger as well as weaker economies of the hemisphere, though more in the latter economies.

Illustrative of worker resistance to public-sector downsizing, miners in Bolivia protested the closing of mines. Having won political and economic rights through their participation in the nationalist-populist revolution of 1952, they suffered the ultimate coup de grâce in the mid-1980s. The government of Paz Estenssoro, the leader of the revolution, by then had returned to power as a born-again neoliberal. His new government, with U.S. and IMF backing, shut the tin mines that he had nationalized during his first term of rule. Labor had for a period of time even enjoyed the right to comanage the mines, in return for their support in the anti-oligarchy insurrection.

Whatever the economic logic to the mine closings, workers did not passively acquiesce to the elimination of their means of livelihood.

Miners—who live in relative geographic isolation, are fairly economically homogeneous, and experience difficult work conditions—have been militant worldwide. In Bolivia in the late 1980s, as earlier, they were no exception. In response to the mine closing, they organized a hunger strike and a march from the mines through the countryside to the nation's capital, La Paz. They were joined by some ten thousand peasants, teachers, shop-owners, students, and religious leaders who depended on the mining communities for work, who sympathized with the miners, and who opposed, for their own reasons, other neoliberal economic reforms. (For example, IMF-proposed new taxes.) Such transregional, public-private-sector, multi-class mobilizations are new to the Latin American social movement repertoire. They reflect not merely alliances built on shared and complementary grievances but also networks that have expanded through migration, coordination with union, church, and other NGO groups, and new media strategies made possible by the reduced censorship accompanying democratization.

In Bolivia, however, the protests proved to no avail. Fiscally strapped and dependent on international financial support, the government deferred to foreign financiers and their demand that the mines, which had long been globally uncompetitive, be closed. The isolation of the mines removed the government somewhat from the political pressures it would have experienced with comparable firings in the city. But the miners lost more than their jobs. Their communities were destroyed, and their families were dislocated and often torn apart. With alternative employment options in their communities close to nonexistent, many of the dismissed miners migrated. Ex-miners did best economically by going to the Chapare and joining the booming coca economy.[10]

The weak Bolivian government had difficulty containing protest. Yet victims of state-sector downsizing protested under stronger states as well. The combination of economic restructuring, redemocratization, and budgetary cutbacks, for example, stirred strike activity in Argentina. However, it shifted the loci of such activity from the private to the public and mixed-ownership sectors, from the working to the middle class, and from Buenos Aires, the nation's capital and historical epicenter of labor militancy, to the provinces. In particular, public-sector wage cutbacks and withholding of wage payments under both the Peronista President Carlos Saúl Menem (1989 to 1999) and his Radical Party predecessor, President Raúl Alfonsín (1983 to 1989), fueled protests (McGuire 1996). The two governments gave a higher priority to their own institutional concern with fiscal deficit reduction than to workers' right to a livelihood, including their right to payment for services rendered. Confrontations became especially violent when authorities withheld paychecks. Automobiles were set aflame, and buildings were sacked. Tumult was so disruptive that Menem's successor, Fernando de la Rúa (1999 to 2001), immediately upon taking office oversaw a federal takeover of the bankrupt provincial government of Corrientes. Unpaid state employees there were blocking vital foreign trade routes. The fiscal crisis in Corrientes exemplifies how neoliberal decentralization and public sector downsizing often left local governments without adequate fiscal resources to provide the goods and services for which they had become responsible. But nationwide protests led de la Rúa to resign after two years.

Strikes in Argentina, however, reveal no mechanistic relationship between economic deprivation and protest. The number of strikes, strikers, and days lost to strikes were lower under Menem, especially in the first half of the 1990s, than under Alfonsín during the preceding decade, even though Menem's aggressive restructuring involved more layoffs and greater deprivations. In Argentina, as elsewhere, democratization initially breathed new life into previously repressed labor. This explains why strike activity picked up under Alfonsín, the first democratically elected president in over a decade. The tapering off of strikes for a time under Menem, in turn, partially reflected the political popularity of the government's taming of inflation, even when associated with a decline in earnings and employment.

Strike activity in Brazil as well was a political, not merely an economic, matter. There too the number of strikes and strikers, and the duration of strikes, rose substantially immediately following the restoration of democratic rule. Strike activity picked up even as labor conditions improved. It picked up because the risks of rebellion subsided with the political transition (Noronha, Gebrin, and Elias 1998), and because the first new democratic governments remained weak, owing to difficulties consolidating power. But encouragement from a new union movement and church groups also fueled protests.

Yet in Brazil, as in Argentina, labor strife tapered off with routinized democratic rule and lowered inflation. The number of yearly strikes dropped from a peak of over two thousand to under one thousand in the course of the 1990s, even though work conditions in the interim deteriorated with a deepening of neoliberalism, a condition that included a major currency devaluation. The remains of strike activity there too centered almost entirely on the slimmed-down public sector. And as in Argentina, workers became especially defiant when fiscally strapped local governments withheld paychecks.

The experiences of Chile and Mexico further illustrate how politics mediates labor resistance. They also point to the importance of the timing of reforms. Chile, the first country to make massive downsizings in its state sector and eliminate barriers to trade, did so under the repressive military government of Augusto Pinochet (1973 to 1990). As unpopular as the measures initially were—they caused living standards to plunge and many workers to lose their jobs—protests then were few and only minimally coordinated (see Garretón 2001 [1989]). The risks were too great. By the time Chile returned to civilian rule, the economy was on an upswing, employment opportunities had expanded, and many workers experienced improvements in their earnings even as income inequality increased. Meanwhile, the formation of a new center-left political pact contributed to the depoliticization of civil society.

In Mexico, in turn, state-crafted business-labor pacts, not government repression, contained protests against reform measures and caused real wages to fall and income inequality to increase (Ros 1998). In agreeing to the pacts, the main labor confederation lent formal support to worker-unfriendly stabilization measures.

While pacts in Mexico tamed protests in the private sector, two deep recessions, in the mid-1980s and a decade later, stirred unrest in the public sector. The delegitimation of the government that resulted from the economic crisis and the revelation of major corruption scandals, combined with the gradual assertion of civil society, made aggrieved workers less submissive than in years past. For example, in the new milieu public-sector nurses, upset with shortages of medicines for state-supported hospitals, in 1997 drew blood from their own arms with syringes and squirted it at the front doors of the hospital administration (*New York Times*, January 21, 1997, 10). At issue were neoliberal cutbacks in social spending that undermined the ability of state workers to fulfill their professional duties. Low-skilled public-sector employees in the provinces also protested abuses. The same year street-sweepers in the state capital of Tabasco demanded compensation for the extra private services that politicians demanded of them, as well as job reinstatements when austerity policies had cost them their jobs. They staged a hunger strike, raided Congress, where they peeled off their clothes, and marched together to Mexico City (*New York Times*, January 21, 1997, 10). Not only had protests grounded in such abuses been anathema in the past, but public-sector workers, now with access to the media, turned to creative new postmodernist expressions of their rage, as did others in the region.

A comparative study of a few Latin American countries suggests that labor strife varies with political party and union institutional dynamics, somewhat independently of macro political and economic conditions. Labor militancy has varied sectorally within and among the countries, with union and party competition. Labor militancy has been greatest when political parties competed for the labor vote while union competition was minimal (Murillo 1995).

In sum, neoliberal structural changes, combined with institutional political and union arrangements, have weakened labor's bargaining power. As a consequence, deprivations and injustices experienced at work stir less strike activity than they did under import substitution. Marx's claim that work-based conflicts are a driving force of history no longer holds. Although income inequality has worsened and real wages have fallen, the globalized context in which work life is embedded has made mobilizations for labor rights, especially in the private sector, difficult. While declining job options and labor-unfriendly governments have made public-sector protests difficult as well, angry state employees have mobilized in self-defense more than private employees have. And they have done so in new, postmodernist ways that draw media attention. Diminished state control of mass communications with democratization makes this strategy possible.

Resistance to worsening formal-sector work conditions must be understood, in turn, in the context of alternative job options—the option to exit to other jobs, as well as to migrate and immigrate. Indeed, displaced workers and persons experiencing declining earning power increasingly turn to self-employment and other easy-entry jobs (in terms of skills, financing, and so on) on a full- or part-time basis. This refuge defuses pressure to engage in collective, work-based protests. Accordingly, broader labor market conditions also shape worker responses.

Viewed comparatively and historically, labor market informalization takes on added significance. Informal-sector work had been central to Latin American subsistence even during import substitution, when industrialization and state provisioning of goods and services expanded. Yet between 1950 and 1980 the portion of the Latin American labor force informally employed dropped somewhat, from 47 to 42 percent. During a roughly comparable period of U.S. economic development, the portion so employed dropped from 51 to 31 percent (see the sources cited in Castells and Portes 1989, 19). With the deepening of neoliberalism, however, Latin Americans became *more* dependent on informal work, which provides no income or social welfare guarantees (see table 13.4). Indeed, by 1996 more Latin Americans depended on informal- than formal-sector work: the portion of the labor force in the informal sector had risen to 57 percent (and the portion so employed would be higher if part-time informal-sector employment were taken into account).

Latin American governments, their commitment to neoliberalism notwithstanding, sought to regulate the expanding informal sector. Some of their methods were exclusionary; for example, to appease politically influential shop-owners and established market stall-holders, as well as maintain order and appeal to tourists, they officially limited street vending. Yet with their formal-sector options circumscribed, city-dwellers resisted the obstacles thrown up by governments. They aggressively fought, for example, for street vending and other informal-sector rights, especially in Mexico and Peru, countries with large impoverished populations. Would-be vendors borrowed squatter settlement tactics to lay private claims to public vending space. They collectively "invaded" sidewalks, streets, and other public spaces and then pressured authorities to honor their locational claims (see Eckstein 1988). Cognizant that vending was labor-absorbing and that widespread unemployment was politically explosive, officials often acquiesced to the pressure. Authorities were most apt to be accommodating when ambulantes, as such vendors are called, had the support of influential politicians and when they deftly manipulated the political system (Cross 1998).

Price Liberalizations and Movements to Minimize Consumption Costs

As earning power declined in both the formal and informal sectors, families turned to collective strategies to minimize their cost of living. They did so when governments in the region cut back import substitution–linked consumer subsidies. Under IMF pressure to reduce expenditures and increase revenue after they incurred severe fiscal crises in the early 1980s, Latin American governments reduced basic food and fuel subsidies (affecting the cost of public transportation) and raised charges for services that had previously been provided free. The cost of urban subsistence thereby rose substantially.

Resistance to Increased Costs of Food, Fuel, and Education

Table 13.5 gives a sense of how severe the cost-of-living increases were. Using 1990 as a price index base, by the decade's end, food prices had more than doubled in fifteen of nineteen countries, and in half of them fuel prices had more than doubled (among countries with available data).[11] By contrast, during the same period food and fuel prices barely increased in the United States: food prices increased by 25 percent, and fuel and electricity costs increased by only 9 per-

Table 13.5 Latin American Consumer Price Increases, 1990 to 1999

Country	Food			Fuel-Electricity		
	200 Percent or Less	201 to 500 Percent	501 Percent or More	200 Percent or Less	201 to 500 Percent	501 Percent or More
Argentina	—	379[b]	—	—	441	—
Bolivia	—	224[c,i]	—	166[h]	—	—
Brazil	180[a]	—	—	—	—	—
Chile	—	231	—	—	—	—
Colombia	—	491	—	—	—	—
Costa Rica	171[d]	—	—	118[j]	—	—
Dominican Republic	—	212[f]	—	—	—	—
Ecuador	—	—	1574	—	—	962[j]
El Salvador	—	246[c]	—	176	—	—
Guatemala	—	261	—	—	—	—
Haiti	—	216[g]	—	—	—	—
Honduras	—	—	506	—	340	—
Mexico	—	474	—	177[i]	—	—
Nicaragua	164	—	—	—	—	—
Panama	111	—	—	103	—	—
Peru	—	—	1918[b]	—	—	—
Paraguay	—	275[j]	—	—	—	—
Uruguay	—	—	1496[e]	—	—	1782
Venezuela	—	—	2516	—	—	2723[f]

Source: International Labor Office 1998, 1045; 2000, 1063–73.
Note: 1990 = 100.
[a] Index base: 1992 = 100.
[b] Metropolitan area.
[c] Urban areas.
[d] Central area.
[e] Capital city.
[f] 1997
[g] 1995
[h] 1996
[i] 1993
[j] 1998

cent (International Labor Office 2000, 1065, 1073). Only Panama experienced lower price hikes than the United States.

It is noteworthy that the strike activity I have described in this chapter bears little relation to cost-of-living increases. In most countries where subsistence costs more than doubled, strike activity declined (compare tables 13.3 and 13.5). A correlation between the two factors might suggest work-based efforts to press for better wages to offset stepped-up living costs. Meanwhile, U.S.–Latin America comparisons highlight that workers in the United States, unlike those south of the border, barely faced inflationary consumer pressures as wage contestations declined.

As strike activity tapered off, however, consumer protests entered the Latin American repertoire of resistance. Consumer revolts, which at least half of all Latin American countries experienced in the 1980s (Walton 2001 [1989])—Ecuador, Bolivia, and Argentina would experience them well into the early years of the twenty-first century—were the contemporary equivalent of the sans culottes' and workers' bread riots of eighteenth- and nineteenth-century France and England (see Rudé 1981; Thompson 1971).

Yet price hikes per se do not account for the new source of unrest or determine the form it takes. Consumer subsidy cutbacks stirred different combinations of demonstrations, riots, strikes, looting, and attacks on government buildings in different countries, varying with different country repertoires of resistance, different macro political-economic conditions, different state and societal relations, different group alliances, and different group organizational involvements. They evoked street demonstrations in Chile, for example, and strikes and roadblocks in Andean nations.

The seemingly spontaneous eruptions typically involved some degree of organization and occurred especially where protesters had the backing of unions and clergy inspired by liberation theology, where political divisiveness and power struggles had prepared the ground, and where governments were weak and unpopular (see Walton 2001 [1989], 1998). By way of illustration, in 1999 Brazil's national bishops' organization sponsored, in coordination with unions, parties of the Left, and the MST, nationwide demonstrations in opposition to neoliberal policies that had caused poor people's living standards to crumble. They called their movement "The Cry of the Excluded Ones."

To assess the importance of consumer as well as other revolts, I coded incidences of protest recorded in a single year, 1995, which was at least ten years after governments in the region had initiated their first neoliberal reforms. I recorded incidences reported in the *Latin*

American Weekly Report (*LAWR*), the best single news summary source on Latin America. Because *LAWR* describes only the most important incidences and underreports ongoing unrest, it provides only a rough approximation of actual tumult. Those qualifications aside, *LAWR* reported price-based protests in six countries (over education costs as well as retail prices). During the same year *LAWR* reported protests against neoliberal-linked state-sector downsizing and privatizations in ten countries, and against wage reforms (including proposals to eliminate the indexing of wages to cost-of-living increases), elimination of the right to strike and organize, cutbacks in labor security (through new, more flexible hiring policies), and paycheck-withholding for work rendered in eleven countries.

Viewed comparatively, no other region experienced as many consumer protests as Latin America (see Walton 1998). And in Latin America, such protests were more gendered (that is, more female-based), as well as more secular in orientation, especially in comparison to North Africa and the Middle East. The greater involvement of women in Latin America reflects their greater absorption into the paid labor force and their greater involvement in the public sphere, plus the region's higher rate of urbanization. (As Walton [2001 (1989)] notes, most consumer protests are city-based.) Women's involvement in protests also built on collective efforts of the 1980s, when women formed communal soup kitchens and purchasing cooperatives (for example, in Peru and Chile), as austerity policies had left families poor and hungry. They did so with the help of community organizations linked to the Catholic Church and other NGOs (see Schneider 1995; Barrig 1989).

Not merely the incidences but also the impact of consumer revolts varied within and among countries in the region, in ways that can only be contextually understood. When unrest was broad-based, insurgents typically succeeded in persuading governments, which were anxious to reestablish order and their own claims to rule, to retract or reduce the price hikes and implement popular social programs. In Brazil, for example, the Cardoso government responded to the stepped-up nationwide protests at the turn of the century with an ambitious spending program. But even when retracting price hikes, weak governments have collapsed under the weight of consumer protests. A notable example is Ecuador, where trade union and indigenous group protests against food and fuel price increases brought down two governments, in 1997 and again in 2000. Ecuador was experiencing neither the highest food price increases nor the highest oil price increases in the region, but protester roadblocks brought the economy to a standstill and left the government between a rock and a hard place. In attempting to appease the populace by allocating resources domestically and retracting price increases, authorities defaulted on foreign loans, and then in desperation turned to hyperinflationary policies that made them yet more unpopular.

But governments on occasion have responded with repression rather than reform. Such occurred in Bolivia under Hugo Banzer in April 2000. Though democratically elected at the time, Banzer, a general, had commanded a repressive junta two decades earlier. Consistent with his past, he responded to countrywide protests against increased water and other consumer costs by suspending constitutional guarantees and calling out the troops.

In no Latin American country, however, did "IMF protests" have as great an impact as in Indonesia in 1998. Austerity measures there sparked a movement that forced the notoriously corrupt autocratic ruler Suharto from power and ushered in a democratically elected regime, and the political opening quickly fueled a successful independence movement in East Timor, which, in turn, had been colonized by Indonesia. Comparable rulers in Latin America, such as Cuba's Batista, Nicaragua's Somoza, and Paraguay's Stroesner, had already been ousted by mass movements in decades past.

Aware of the politicizing effects of austerity measures, some governments targeted antipoverty funds selectively to preempt resistance. President Salinas, for example, through his famed Solidarity Program, masterfully channeled social expenditures to those Mexican communities he considered politically problematic, in a manner that made beneficiaries directly dependent on the central government. The Fujimori government in Peru made similar allocations and in so doing undermined the grassroots community mobilizations that had mushroomed after the introduction of austerity prices in the 1980s. Fujimori's autocratic interventions, which concomitantly reined in the guerrilla group Shining Path, managed to contain consumer revolts even as the country experienced what were among the highest cost-of-living increases in the region in the 1990s.

Latin America students, meanwhile, stepped up protest not merely against the cost of subsistence but also against the cost of education, sometimes in collaboration with labor groups. Their mobilizations became less explicitly political and more economically driven than in years past. In 1997, for example, Venezuelan students rioted against cuts in school and transportation subsidies. And in nine Argentinean provinces the same year, tens of thousands of students joined angry street vendors, current and dismissed public-sector workers, and sugar workers in blocking roads and government buildings, hurling stones, and setting up barricades. Meanwhile, in the Dominican Republic blackouts along with price hikes sparked protests in over a dozen towns, at the instigation of student groups in collaboration with unions. Protesters burned tires and cars, threw stones and home-made bombs at the police, and staged a general strike. And in Nicaragua students protesting over university funding allied with shanty-town dwellers who had their own grievances.

Mexico experienced some of the most tumultuous student strike activity in the region, which contributed to the erosion of state legitimacy and the lengthy paralysis of university education. In 1988, when President Salinas's neoliberal government sought to impose revenue-generating fees and entrance exams, students took to the streets. University education had been entirely subsidized until then, but the government introduced fees at a time when a major peso devaluation, along with austerity measures, had driven up living costs dramatically. In capturing the imagination of the capital, the students won (Castañeda 1993, 204). The government, wanting no repeat of a politically unpopular student massacre twenty years earlier, retracted the charges.

Again in the 1990s, Mexican students closed down the main university campus, this time for the better part of a year. Stirred, like their predecessors, by newly authorized university charges, the strikers insisted that the fee be voluntary and that a council of academics, students, and employees run the university. In contrast to the past, however, strike organizers refused to back down when the government agreed to retract the charges. As university education remained paralyzed, many students turned on the strike organizers. The movement became internally divided and prey to party machinations in the context of unprecedented political competition nationally.

Mobilizations to Contain the Cost of Housing

Concerns about the cost of consumption of so-called collective goods, such as group claims to housing rights and urban services, took a somewhat different turn. By the 1990s squatter movements in the major cities of the region, which mushroomed in the post–World War II era, had declined. They tapered off partly because government tolerance of them waned. That tolerance had been grounded in macro political-economic conditions that no longer prevailed. During the era of import substitution, governments accommodated the urban land claims of poor people to keep living costs down for the massive influx of migrants in a manner that would consolidate a populist base of support. Under the circumstances, political parties both in and out of power defended illegal collective land claims in exchange for political loyalty.

For several reasons, neoliberalism ceased to favor such invasions. For one, governments became less populist and more austere in their outlays. Squatter settlements on previously unsettled land had required state provisioning of schools, markets, medical facilities, public transportation, electricity, street pavement, and the like. Under fiscal pressure, the less populist governments cut back on such services. Even in Argentina, where the government initiated Plan de Arraigo in 1990 to regularize squatter settlements for the first time, social provisioning received little attention. The program concentrated merely on regularizing property transfers, consistent with neoliberalism, and on providing housing on government-owned lands (Martinez Nogueira 1995, 61–66). Second, the neoliberal governments were biased toward market, not political, processes. Consistent with their bias, they favored informal commercial dealings over land invasions to address pent-up demand for affordable housing (Durand-Lasserve 1998, 236). By the 1990s real estate developers who previously backed irregular settlements had acquired access to more profitable alternatives. Third, the neoliberal emphasis on decentralization placed a greater onus on local governments to reduce pressures on the central government, including for urban services.

Venezuela briefly was an exception, owing to a populist resurgence. President Hugo Chávez, whose term spanned the turn of the century, consolidated support among the urban poor by overseeing a boom in land invasions. Crowds waving Venezuelan flags and placards with the effigy of the president would march on vacant land and erect rudimentary ranchos, as shantytowns were called. However, after floods in December 1999 left thousands of residents of hillside squatter settlements in Caracas homeless, Chávez felt compelled to abandon his strategy in the capital and instead evacuate and resettle low-income storm survivors.

Conditions in Brazil gave rise to an alternative type of housing movement. "The Movement of Roofless People," made up of very poor people who lived in slums or in the streets, organized seizures of unoccupied urban buildings. By the turn of the century theirs was one of the most forceful movements in urban Brazil, especially in Rio de Janeiro and São Paulo but also in Bahia and Rio Grande do Sul. Though protective of their independence, they had the support of the Workers Party, the left labor confederation, and the progressive wing of the Catholic Church. In São Paulo, where they worked closely with the mayor, Luiza Erundina, they succeeded not only in obtaining housing but in getting land tenure and housing legislation changed. But with a limited number of unoccupied buildings to seize, the movement cannot be expected to become a twenty-first-century alternative to the squatter mobilizations that made claims to vacant land in the past.

Antisocial Defiance

By the 1990s anger and disillusion were contributing, in turn, to stepped-up antisocial defiance. Leaner and meaner than governments under import substitution, neoliberal regimes experienced breakdowns of law and order in the context of declining economic opportunities, cutbacks in official social expenditures, increased income inequality (often accompanied by increased poverty rates), and increased living costs.

Crime, including violent crime, became pervasive in cities throughout the region. Rates of theft, pilfering, looting, illicit dealings, kidnapping, and homicide rose to unprecedented levels. People broke the law not only individually but collectively through gangs, crime rings, and coordinated corrupt dealings. The region became the most violent in the world.

Crime generated more crime as a culture of illegality became entrenched and lawbreaking went unpunished. The spread of drug use and mounting police corruption exacerbated the problem. Law enforcement agents became part of the problem, not its solution. They joined the ranks of the criminals and operated with impunity.

The breakdown of safety sparked movements to restore public order. In Rio de Janeiro, for example, the civic group Viva Rio oversaw a massive demonstration in 1995 for a cleanup in the police department and improved urban services. Hundreds of thousands of rich and poor and old and young, cloaked in white, joined the demonstration, which was named "React Rio." The demonstration combined elements of a political rally, religious revival, and carnival. Similarly, in Mexico City two years later tens of thousands of frustrated and frightened residents of all social classes, but especially the middle class, paraded, with white ribbons and blue flags, in outrage over a mounting wave of violent crime. Like the Brazilians, the Mexican protesters demanded an end to police corruption and violence as well as common crime. These movements exemplify new ways in which civil society came together, not against neoliberal reforms per se but against the effects of the new economic (dis)order.

Had city-dwellers not increasingly turned to immigration and, to a lesser extent, reverse migration as urban subsistence became more problematic, Latin American cities undoubtedly would have experienced even greater disarray. And the economic relief provided by emigrants' remittances to the family members they left behind defused urban social pressures all the more. Transnational networks increasingly are called upon to mitigate the economic conditions exacerbated, if not caused by, neoliberalism.

Conclusion

Whatever the logic to Latin American economic restructuring, especially from a First World business vantage point, the deepening of the reform process carried seeds of obstruction to its unfettered permeation, though not, to date, seeds of its own destruction. State-sector downsizing and trade and price liberalizations addressed state fiscal exigencies, but they also generated unemployment, new economic vulnerabilities, and cost-of-living increases for people who could ill afford them. Accordingly, the removal of market encumbrances generated new grievances, new coping strategies, and new social movements for change, which included groups and people with newly framed identities. The movements countered the free play of market forces, except in the countries producing and processing drugs, where Latin Americans saw market dynamics as personally and collectively advantageous.

The Latin American economic restructuring experience suggests the following empirically grounded propositions:

Although neoliberal changes may correct macro import-substitution-linked problems, many in the lower and working classes, and even the salaried and credit-dependent middle classes, have suffered with the restructuring. When they resist aspects of the new model that they find especially egregious, they rarely protest neoliberalism in the abstract. Rather, they rebel against neoliberalism as they experience it in their everyday lives. They do not necessarily even understand that the new economic model is the source of their discontent.

There is no mechanistic relationship between neoliberal-based material deprivations and defiance. State structures, resources, policies, and discourse, state-society relations, the vibrancy and politicization of civil society, conceptions of individual and collective rights, and underlying identities are all mediating factors that influence how victims of reform respond to macro economic changes. Also, the aggrieved may opt to exit, in the form of migration, emigration, or employment shifting, rather than make the riskier choice to join attempts at coordinated collective redress. The weaker the state, the more politicized the society, and the less institutionalized state-society relations are; and the fewer perceived exit options, the more probable collective resistance is. Different mixes of these contextually important institutional dynamics help explain why the same reforms have generated differently configured movements (or no movements at all) in different countries and at different points in time.

The new economic order has modified the Latin American social movement repertoire. Most significantly, global competition has made strikes too risky and ineffective a weapon for private sector workers to use routinely to counter falling wages. This is so even where workers formally regained rights to organize with redemocratization. And the new regime commitment to market solutions has eroded the political-economic base of the squatter movements that were so pervasive under import substitution. Meanwhile, neoliberalism has had the unintentional effect of directly and indirectly stirring new types of movements and new movement demands, and fostering movements based on new socially constructed identities. For example, trade liberalization, together with other state policies, marginalized the peasantry to the point that those who did not opt for exit mobilized in new types of rural movements for land and other claims; price liberalizations prompted consumer revolts; privatizations prompted public-sector protests; and devaluations designed to stimulate exports stirred debtors' movements. Many of these movements appealed to multiple classes and groups, owing to shared grievances and leadership that coordinated common concerns.

As neoliberalism shifted the focus of movements from tensions rooted in class dynamics to tensions rooted in state and market relations, states became more vulnerable politically. Leaner and meaner, the state became less able to assert itself over society than during import substitution, and state-induced deprivations led victims of reforms to direct their grievances more at the government and less at capital than during the preceding economic period.

Democratization, which accompanied neoliberalism in Latin America, in principle opened formal channels of making demands and articulating interests. However, while partially opening up institutional opportunities for previously excluded groups, *democratization* on a number of occasions had the unintended effect, for a combination of reasons, of stirring defiance. It did so by reducing the risks of rebellion, by allowing for new individual and collective rights, by inadequately containing or countering market-rooted injustices, and by extending formal more than substantive political rights. And whatever the natural affinity between democracy and market capitalism, individually and in combination the two sets of reforms generated new ideas and new tensions, and thus new extra-institutional movements for change.

Although premised on a globalized market economy and universalistic modern values, neoliberalism evoked movements with antimodern and premodern claims. Newly experienced and newly perceived injustices led new socially constructed indigenous movements in particular to press for rights rooted in community customs that antedated modernity, as well as to movements to counter market efficiency.

As bases of movements for change broadened, so too did mobilization strategies. Groups turned to new mechanisms of communication, such as the Internet, and to the media once state censorship softened with democratization. Indigenous movements in particular made use of cyberspace information-sharing, thereby learning from one another as well as from support groups. They no longer depended exclusively on domestic political alliances.

As postmodernist as movements on occasion appeared, in their symbolism and public displays, and as localized as some movements were, their patterning often reflected translocal processes. Movements in diverse countries shared common economic roots, and groups worked with common international NGOS and movement organizers. NGOs provided moral, material, and human capital support that was new to the region.

Historical institutional dynamics help account for the generalizable as well as the particularistic features of the movements grounded, directly and indirectly, in neoliberalism. Accordingly, an institutional analysis highlights localized responses that neoclassical economics and modernization-based societal analyses overlook, both analytically and empirically, and translocal features about which local-centric postmodern analyses do not theorize. Like "moral economy" and "subaltern" analyses, the institutional approach points to the importance of culture, including the importance of group-based beliefs, in patterning resistance to neoliberal reforms. But it grounds the study analytically in global institutional dynamics and mediating structures as well as local group life.

A class-based analysis as conventionally conceived would miss much of the resistance to the new world order. Strike activity, organized around relations of production, has declined. Global economic pressures led Latin American workers to turn instead to alternative ways to improve their lot, through exit and mobilizations to lower living costs. A class-based analysis would also miss and provide no bases for explaining the new non-class-based movements that have proliferated since the 1980s. Nonetheless, a class analysis helps pinpoint the continued significance of work- and market-based tensions even when not transparent through overtly coordinated defiance.

Similarly, a state-centric analysis points to the role of national political institutions, policies, and discourse in mediating both globalization trends and resistance to them. Yet, state features and state interventions need to be explained, including their variations over time.

The patterning of mobilizations traced to the permeation of global economic processes speaks to issues raised by other contributors to this volume. For one, it speaks implicitly to the role of social capital. Alejandro Portes and Margarita Mooney describe how the informal ties that bind kin and non-kin, under certain conditions, can be an economic development resource. In this chapter, we have seen that such networks, grounded in community, ethnicity, class, and gender, independently and in combination, influence whether neoliberal-induced changes cause emigration or collective resistance.

Second, differences both in implementation of market measures and in resistance to them across countries point to the importance of sociological analyses of markets, as highlighted in Neil Fligstein's essay. The institutional dynamics associated with state structures, state exigencies, and state-society relations, as well as civil society organizational life and society in its more informally organized forms, influenced the nature and depth of market reforms and the grassroots reactions to the changes. Meanwhile, the range of resistance implicitly also points to the disjunction between the values embedded in neoliberal economic policies initiated from above and abroad and the values rooted in local group and community relations. While states, under foreign pressure, initiated reforms to maximize global market efficiency, peasants, workers, and segments of the middle class demonstrated that they assessed efficiency from a localized vantage point, distinct from the perspective of international business and international institutions, and that they did not always value efficiency over other concerns. What is good for a peasant or market vendor in Latin America, for example, often differs from what is good for a large foreign producer or retailer. In taking advantage of new markets opened up by the removal of import substitution tariffs, large foreign producers and multinational businesses, through their Latin American subsidiaries, benefiting from economies of scale and better technology, may squeeze out domestic small businessmen. Whose "efficiency" is at stake here?

Third, the mobilizations stirred by neoliberal reforms confirm Viviana Zelizer's claim (in chapter 5) that culture—namely, meanings and beliefs—needs to be incorporated into the study of markets. Different groups of Latin Americans framed their resistance to similar market reforms in distinctive ways. They drew on different symbols of resistance, on different cultural traditions, on different ways of absorption of new ideas, including foreign ideas, and on distinctive identities. The repertoire of resistance is inexplicable solely in terms of objective economic conditions.

Scholarly efforts at explanation aside, neoliberal-linked injustices that persist in the twenty-first century and changing conceptions of injustice are likely to continue to stir resistance to reforms. Latin Americans can be expected to keep on pressing the limits of the art of the possible, as they have to date. They are their own best hope for a more humane and just future. Their views should be taken into account by policymakers as well as by social analysts so that fair and effective economic policies can be implemented.

My thanks to Mauro Guillén and Marshall Meyer for comments on an earlier version of this essay and to Emily Chang for her superb editing of the essay.

Notes

1. In contrast, in the prior neoliberal period (before World War I), there was substantial mobility of labor as well as capital and product markets. Accordingly, more in the current period than in the past, markets have been constructed to strengthen capital over labor on a global scale.

2. The "natural affinity" came with collective amnesia about recent political-economic history. Some of the repressive military governments were the first to embrace neoliberalism. Indeed, General Pinochet's Chile, transformed with the advice of the so-called Chicago Boys, became the economic model for the region.

3. Information in the text draws on a synthesis of material from my principal primary sources, the *New York Times* and *Latin American Weekly Report*. My statistical information is drawn from data compiled by the World Bank (1999), the International Labor Office (1990, 1998, 2000), and the U.S. Immigration and Naturalization Service (1999). For a more detailed discussion of Latin American social movements in the 1990s, including sources, see my epilogue in Eckstein (2001 [1989]).

4. For a discussion of the conditions that give rise to "exit" rather than "voice," on the one hand, and to "loyalty," on the other, see Hirschman (1970). My analysis of the range of responses to unfavorable conditions is consistent with James Scott's (1985, 1990) seminal work on "everyday forms of resistance."

5. Currency reforms are not distinctive to neoliberalism, but they took on special significance with the economic restructuring.

6. The Zapatistas, for instance, made use of the Internet to publicize and coordinate their campaigns (see Womack 1999; Collier and Quaratiello 1994). Although they never pressed for revolution, they took their name from the peasant hero of the country's early-twentieth-century social transformation and wore masks resembling those used by the earlier Zapatistas.

7. Isolation from the international banking community and Washington when President Alan García in the mid-1980s tried to resist foreign debt payments and neoliberal restructuring exacerbated the country's economic crisis and served to strengthen sympathy for Shining Path. Be-

tween the mid-1980s and the mid-1990s, when García's successors succumbed to neoliberalism, conditions went from bad to worse. The proportion of the population living in poverty rose from 38 percent in 1985 to 50 percent a decade later (McClintock 1997).

8. Only workers in the so-called formal sector, those covered by labor laws, qualify officially for the minimum wage. By the 1990s most of the Latin American labor force was employed in the informal sector, with no wage or other guarantees, and most new jobs offered no guarantees. These trends reflect the breakdown of the institutional protections instituted under import substitution, protections that had segmented the labor force to the advantage of those covered by labor laws.

9. In Colombia, for example, labor unions in 1999 called off an indefinite general strike after more than seventy people died in armed clashes in the first two days of the work stoppage. Right-wing paramilitary forces and the army were responsible for the killings (New York Times, September 3, 1999).

10. I am indebted to June Nash for information on the impact of the mine closings. For more detail on the mine closings, see Eckstein (2001 [1989], epilogue).

11. It should be remembered that the first major price hikes had occurred already in the 1980s.

References

Barrig, Maruja. 1989. "The Difficult Equilibrium Between Bread and Roses: Women's Organizations and the Transition from Dictatorship to Democracy in Peru." In The Women's Movement in Latin America: Feminism and the Transition to Democracy, edited by Jane Jaquette. Boston: Unwin Human.

Borjas, George. 1999. Heaven's Door: Immigration Policy and the American Economy. Princeton, N.J.: Princeton University Press.

Castañeda, Jorge. 1993. Utopia Unarmed: The Latin American Left After the Cold War. New York: Knopf.

Castells, Manuel, and Alejandro Portes. 1989. "World Underneath: The Origins, Dynamics, and Effects of the Informal Economy." In The Informal Economy, edited by Alejandro Portes, Manuel Castells, and Lauren Benton. Baltimore: Johns Hopkins University Press.

Chernick, Marc. 1997. "The Crisis of Human Rights in Colombia." Latin American Studies Association Forum (Fall): 20–22.

Collier, George, and Elizabeth Lowery Quaratiello. 1994. Basta!: Land and the Zapatista Rebellion in Chiapas. Monroe, Oreg.: Institute for Food and Development Policy.

Cross, John C. 1998. Informal Politics: Street Vendors and the State in Mexico City. Stanford, Calif.: Stanford University Press.

Durand-Lasserve, Alain. 1998. "Law and Urban Change in Developing Countries: Trends and Issues." In Illegal Cities: Law and Urban Change in Develop-

ing Countries, edited by Edesio Fernandes and Ann Varley. London: Zed Books.

Eckstein, Susan. 1988. *The Poverty of Revolution: The State and Urban Poor in Mexico.* Princeton, N.J.: Princeton University Press.

————. 2001 [1989]. *Power and Popular Protest: Latin American Social Movements,* updated ed. Berkeley: University of California Press.

Garretón, Manuel Antonio. 2001 [1989]. "Popular Mobilization and the Military Regime in Chile: The Complexities of the Invisible Transition." In *Power and Popular Protest: Latin American Social Movements,* updated ed., edited by Susan Eckstein. Berkeley: University of California Press.

Hammond, Jack. 1999. "Law and Disorder: The Brazilian Landless Farmworkers' Movement." *Bulletin of Latin American Research* 18(4): 469–89.

Hirschman, Albert. 1970. *Exit, Voice, and Loyalty.* Cambridge, Mass.: Harvard University Press.

International Labor Office (ILO). 1990, 1998, 2000. *Yearbook of Labour Statistics.* Geneva: ILO.

Keck, Margaret. 1995. "Social Equity and Environmental Politics in Brazil: Lessons from the Rubber Tappers of Acre." *Comparative Politics* (July): 409–24.

Langevin, Mark, and Peter Rosset. 1997. "Land Reform from Below: The Landless Workers Movement in Brazil." *Backgrounder* (Institute for Food and Development Policy) 4(3): 1–3.

Martinez Nogueira, Roberto. 1995. "Devising New Approaches to Poverty in Argentina." In *Strategies to Combat Poverty in Latin America,* edited by Dagmar Raczynski. Washington, D.C.: Inter-American Development Bank.

McClintock, Cynthia. 1997. "The Decimation of Peru's Sendero Luminoso." Paper presented at the Conference on Comparative Peace Processes in Latin America, Woodrow Wilson Center, Washington, D.C. (March).

McGuire, James. 1996. "Strikes in Argentina." *Latin American Research Review* 31(3): 127–50.

Murillo, Maria Victoria. 1995. "From Populism to Neoliberalism: Labor Unions and Market-Oriented Reforms in Argentina, Mexico, and Venezuela." Ph.D. diss., Harvard University.

Noronha, Eduardo Garuti, Vera Gebrin, and Jorge Elias. 1998. "Explicacoes para un Ciclo Excepcional de Greves: O Caso Brasileiro." Paper presented at the Congress of the Latin American Studies Association, Chicago (September).

Peeler, John. 2002. "Social Justice and the New Indigenous Politics: An Analysis of Guatemala, the Central Andes, and Chiapas." In *The Politics of Injustice in Latin America,* edited by Susan Eckstein and Timothy Wickham-Crowley. Berkeley: University of California Press.

Ros, Jaime. 1998. "Employment, Structural Adjustment, and Sustainable Growth in Mexico." Paper presented at the Congress of the Latin American Studies Association, Chicago (September).

Rudé, George. 1981. *The Crowd in History, 1730–1848.* London: Lawrence and Wishart.

Schneider, Cathy. 1995. *Shantytown Protest in Pinochet's Chile.* Philadelphia: Temple University Press.

Scott, James C. 1976. *The Moral Economy of the Peasant: Rebellion and Subsistence in Southeast Asia.* New Haven: Yale University Press.

————. 1985. *Weapons of the Weak: Everyday Forms of Peasant Resistance.* New Haven, Conn.: Yale University Press.

————. 1990. *Domination and the Arts of Resistance: Hidden Transcripts.* New Haven, Conn.: Yale University Press.

Thompson, E. P. 1971. "The Moral Economy of the English Crowd in the Eighteenth Century." *Past and Present* 50(February): 76–136.

Tokman, Victor. 1997. "Generación de Empleo y Reformas Laborales." *Anuario Social y Político de America Latina y El Caribe* (Facultad Latinoamericana de Ciencias Sociales [FLACSO]) 1: 151–58.

U.S. Immigration and Naturalization Service (INS). 1999. *Statistical Yearbook of the Immigration and Naturalization Service 1997.* Washington: U.S. INS.

Walton, John. 2001 [1989]. "Debt, Protest, and the State in Latin America." In *Power and Popular Protest: Latin American Social Movements,* updated ed., edited by Susan Eckstein. Berkeley: University of California Press.

————. 1998. "Urban Conflict and Social Movements in Poor Countries: Theory and Evidence of Collective Action." *International Journal of Urban and Regional Research* 22(3): 460–81.

Warren, Kay. 1998. "Indigenous Movements as a Challenge to the Unified Social Movement Paradigm for Guatemala." In *Cultures of Politics/Politics of Cultures,* edited by Sonia Alvarez, Evelina Dagnino, and Arturo Escobar. Boulder, Colo.: Westview Press.

Womack, John. 1999. *Rebellion in Chiapas: An Historical Reader.* New York: New Press.

World Bank. 1999. *1999 World Development Indicators.* Washington, D.C.: World Bank.

Yashar, Deborah. 1998. "Contesting Citizenship: Indigenous Movements and Democracy in Latin America." *Comparative Politics* (October): 23–42.

Zamosc, Leon. 1994. "Agrarian Protest and the Indian Movement in the Ecuadorian Highlands." *Latin American Research Review* 29(3): 37–68.

= Index =